Recent Social Trends in Russia 1960–1995

The newest volume in the Comparative Charting of Social Change Series, which documents patterns of social change in modernized societies, *Recent Social Trends in Russia* is a collection of statistical and sociological data on trends in Russian society that have never before been assembled in a comprehensive and systematic manner. It presents an extensive analysis of the major social transformations that took place in Russia both before and after the fall of the Communist system and dispels many illusions about Russian society in the twentieth century.

Recent Social Trends in Russia reveals remarkable similarities between emerging trends in Russia and in Western countries during the last thirty-five years. Russian society shows a strong tendency toward modernization, although the speed of change is sometimes slower than in Western industrialized countries. Similar to Western societies, Russia's population is aging, unemployment is prevalent among the young, and a new class of young professionals is emerging. The institution of marriage is losing its significance, emotional disorders and consumption of mood-altering substances are increasing, and religious beliefs and habits are becoming more diversified. Political upheavals over the last ten or twelve years and the collapse of Communism have not had much effect on the social landscape in Russia. There has, however, been an increase in the influence of Western culture and a violent backlash in fields that underwent forceful modernization.

The findings suggest that Russian and Western societies are more similar than one would imagine and contradict the popular conception that Communist Russia fell out of world history for seventy years.

IRENE A. BOUTENKO (fortuna@glasnet.ru) is a sociologist and director of the Research Department of the Russian Institute for Cultural Research. KIRILL E. RAZLOGOV (razlog@riku.msk.su) is head of the Russian Institute for Cultural Research.

Series: Comparative Charting of Social Change
Series Editor: Simon Langlois
Volume Editors: Irene A. Boutenko and Kirill E. Razlogov

Recent Social Trends
in Russia 1960–1995

Edited by
IRENE A. BOUTENKO AND
KIRILL E. RAZLOGOV

McGill-Queen's University Press
Montreal & Kingston · London · Buffalo

© McGill-Queen's University Press 1997
ISBN 0-7735-1610-7

Legal deposit second quarter 1997
Bibliothèque nationale du Québec

Printed in the United States on acid-free paper

Canadian Cataloguing in Publication Data

Main entry under title:
  Recent social trends in Russia, 1960–1995
  (Comparative charting of social change)
  Translation of: Tendentsii sotsiokul'turnogo razvitiya
  Rossii, 1960–1990
  Includes ibliographical references.
  ISBN 0-7735-1610-7

  1. Soviet Union – Social conditions – 1945–1991.
  2. Russia (Federation) – Social conditions – 1991–
  I. Boutenko, Irene A., 1955– II. Razlogov, Kirill E.
  (Kirill Émil'evich), 1946– III. Series.

  HN523.5.R43 1997   947.085   C97-900414-4

306.0947   BoU

Contents

Series Editor's Introduction / xi

Acknowledgments / xiii

Preface / xv

Introduction / 1

0 Context / 5

    0.1 Demographic Trends / 5

    0.2 Macro-economic Trends / 11

    0.3 Macro-technological Trends / 16

1 Age Groups / 20

    1.1 Youth / 20

    1.2 Elders / 24

2 Microsocial / 29

    2.1 Self-identification / 29

    2.2 Kinship Networks / 32

    2.3 Community and Neighbourhood Types / 35

    2.4 Decentralization / 40

    2.5 Voluntary Associations / 43

    2.6 Social-Interaction Networks / 47

3   Women / 51

  3.1   Female Roles / 51

  3.2   Childbearing / 55

  3.3   Matrimonial Models / 58

  3.4   Women's Employment / 64

  3.5   Reproductive Technologies / 68

4   Labour Market / 70

  4.1   Unemployment / 70

  4.2   Skills and Occupational Levels / 73

  4.3   Types of Employment / 76

  4.4   Sectors of Employment / 78

  4.5   Computerization of Work / 81

5   Labour and Management / 85

  5.1   Work Organization / 85

  5.2   Personnel Administration / 90

  5.3   Size and Types of Enterprises / 94

6   Social Stratification / 98

  6.1   Occupational Status / 98

  6.2   Social Mobility / 102

  6.3   Economic Inequality / 108

  6.4   Social Inequality / 112

7   Social Relations / 117

  7.1   Conflicts / 117

  7.2   Negotiation / 122

7.3 Norms of Conduct / 124

7.4 Authority / 129

7.5 Public Opinion / 132

8 State Institutions / 137

8.1 Educational System / 137

8.2 Health System / 141

8.3 Social Welfare / 145

8.4 The State / 149

9 Mobilizing Institutions / 156

9.1 Labour Unions / 156

9.2 Religious Institutions / 159

9.3 Armed Forces / 164

9.4 Public Associations and Political Parties / 167

9.5 Mass Media / 171

10 Institutionalization of Social Forces / 177

10.1 Dispute Settlement / 177

10.2 Trade Unions / 180

10.3 Social Movements / 184

10.4 Interest Groups / 188

11 Ideologies / 192

11.1 Political Differentiation / 192

11.2 Confidence in Institutions / 196

11.3 Economic Orientations / 201

11.4 Radicalism / 207

11.5 Religious Beliefs / 211

12   Household Resources / 216

   12.1 Personal and Family Income / 216

   12.2 Informal Economy / 219

   12.3 Wealth / 223

13   Lifestyle / 232

   13.1 Consumer Market / 232

   13.2 Consumption of Mass Information / 236

   13.3 Health and Beauty Care / 243

   13.4 Time Use / 245

   13.5 Daily Mobility / 251

   13.6 Housework / 256

   13.7 Forms of Erotic Expression / 260

   13.8 Consumption of Psychotropic Substances / 266

14   Leisure / 272

   14.1 Amount and Use of Free Time / 272

   14.2 Vacations / 275

   14.3 Athletics and Sports / 281

   14.4 Cultural Activities / 284

15   Educational Attainment / 290

   15.1 Basic Education / 290

   15.2 Vocational Training / 296

   15.3 Continuing Education / 298

16   Integration and Marginalization / 304

   16.1 Immigrants and Ethnic Minorities / 304

   16.2 Crime / 310

   16.3 Emotional Disorders / 315

   16.4 Poverty / 323

17   Attitudes and Values / 329

   17.1 Satisfaction / 329

   17.2 Perception of Social Problems / 335

   17.3 Attitudes Toward the Future / 341

   17.4 Values / 344

   17.5 National Identification / 348

References / 353

COMPARATIVE CHARTING OF SOCIAL CHANGE

Theodore Caplow, Howard Bahr, Bruce Chadwick, and John Modell
Recent Social Trends in the United States 1960–1990, 1991.

Simon Langlois, Jean-Paul Baillargeon, Guy Fréchet, Madeleine Gauthier, and Jean-Pierre Simard
Recent Social Trends in Québec 1960–1990, 1991.

Wolfgang Glatzer, Karl Otto Hondrich, Heinz Herbert Noll, Karen Stiehr, and Barbara Wörndl
Recent Social Trends in West Germany 1960–1990, 1991.

Michel Forsé, Jean Huges Deschaux, Jean-Pierre Joslin, Henri Mendras, and Denis Stocklet (eds.)
Recent Social Trends in France 1960–1990, 1991

Simon Langlois, with Theodore Caplow, Henri Mendras, and Wolfgang Glatzer (eds.)
Convergence or Divergence? Comparing Recent Social Trends in Industrial Societies, 1995

Irene Boutenko and Kirill Razlogov (eds)
Recent Social Trends in Russia 1960–1995, 1997.

Books in preparation

Salustiano del Campo (ed.)
Recent Social Trends in Spain 1960–1995.

Alberto Martinelli, Antonio Chiesi, and Sonia Stefanizzi
Recent Social Trends in Italy 1960–1995.

Dimitris Charalambis, Laura Alipranti, and Andromaque Hadjiyannis
Recent Social Trends in Greece 1960–1995.

Yannick Lemel and Heinz Herbert Noll (ed.)
New Structures of Inequality

Series Editor's Introduction

In keeping with the title of the series – *Comparative Charting of Social Change* – this volume on Russia offers an empirical description and analysis of radical changes occurring in the formerly communist country and is also closely linked to the previous works already published by the members of the International Research for Comparative Charting of Social Change – the CCSC Group. This is the fifth volume to present a profile of recent social trends – the previous ones having dealt with the United States, Quebec, West Germany, and France. Three additional volumes, *Recent Social Trends in Spain 1960–1995*, *Recent Social Trends in Greece 1960–1995*, and *Recent Social Trends in Italy 1960–1995*, are expected to appear in 1997 or early 1998.

    The series also includes comparative works on social change based on these profiles and written by the members of the CCSC Group. *Convergence or Divergence? Comparing Recent Social Trends in Industrial Societies* appeared in 1994 and *New Structure of Inequality* is in preparation. A complete list of titles and authors in this series appears at the end of this volume.

Simon Langlois
Series Editor

Acknowledgments

The authors are greatly indebted to the Russian Institute for Cultural Research and the Ministry of Culture of the Russian Federation for financial support for the present study; to the Russian Foundation of Fundamental Research, which made possible a discussion of many Russian reports at a conference in Moscow in July, 1994; to the Kultur-Kontakt Foundation (Austria), for the opportunity to publish a preliminary form of the reports; to the Russian Foundation for Research in Humanities (grant 1995-6-18668) and the Research Support Scheme of the Higher Education Support Programme, grant no. 641/1995, which made preparation for publication of the Russian version of the book possible; and to Andrey J. Elez, L. Petrunina, and M. Hevesi for their contribution at the discussion and translation stages.

The Russian Institute for Cultural Research also wishes to express its gratitude to Gary Caldwell for his help with editing the volume in English, and to Simon Langlois for his support and his co-ordination of the publication of the book in English.

Finally, we are grateful to Käthe Roth for her stylistic revision of the book.

Preface

Recent Social Trends in Russia 1960–1995 is part of a series which in past few years has included similar works on recent social trends in the United States, Quebec, West Germany, and France. The collective author of this series is the International Group for the Comparative Charting of Social Change – a voluntary organization established in 1987 that grew out of several years of informal collaboration between those involved in a large multidisciplinary study of social change in French communities (Project OSC) and those working on a similar study in North America (the Middletown III Project). The roster of the Comparative Charting Group includes historians, political scientists, demographers, and economists, as well as a large number of sociologists, all of whose participation in the national teams is entirely voluntary. The Quebec team has provided the project with an efficient secretariat since the beginning, but the Group has no executive except a coordinator. Each national team is responsible for its own organization and its own funding; common tasks are allocated by mutual agreement at the semi-annual meetings. This flexible pattern of organization has worked so well for us that we are tempted to offer it as a model for other projects of international social research.

The general purposes of this collective effort are (1) to prepare a comprehensive, numerically grounded description of recent social trends in industrial societies; (2) to identify similarities and differences among these societies with respect to ongoing social trends; (3) to subject the similarities and differences to comparative analysis; (4) to develop a non-traditional model of social change to accomodate these data; (5) to establish benchmarks for future tracking of social trends.

When some of us met in Paris in 1987 to establish permanent connections between the ongoing investigations of social change that had occupied us in our respective countries during the previous decade, we were aware that, although our separate studies had attracted a fair amount of scholarly and popular attention, lack of a comparative perspective had prevented them from advancing our understanding of contemporary industrial societies as they should have. Without systematic international comparisons it was impossible to determine whether the trends we had discovered in a particular national society were local accidents or features of a larger system.

We were specifically interested in the major industrial countries in the late twentieth century, and the social structures and institutional patterns that characterize the behavior of large populations, especially those structures and patterns associated with the family, work, leisure, religion, education, government, politics, and voluntary associations. As we compared our separate bodies of work, we had the impression that we were surrounded by the bits and pieces of a new theoretical model that was waiting to be assembled – a model that does not require social change to resemble scientific-technical progress, that takes the future to be open rather than ordained, and that acknowledges the mixture of objective and subjective elements in social reality.

The construction of national profiles in comparable form was a preliminary task that had to be done in order to prepare for the construction of such a model. Each national profile is constructed on the same pattern, which consists of 78 trend reports grouped under 18 major headings in an identical sequence that includes most of the salient features of modern industrialized societies, from 0.1, Demographic Trends, to 17.5, Trends in National Identity.

Most trend reports present and interpret multiple trends related to the designated topic. A trend report has four sections: an abstract of findings, an explanatory text, a collection of statistical tables or charts, and a bibliography of the sources drawn upon. The trends described in these reports are empirical and quantitative. They are based on good quality time-series which, to be used in a trend report, must consist of empirical enumerations or measurements, must refer to an entire national society or a representative sample of it, must cover a period of at least ten years and end to the present, must include data for three or more points or intervals of time recorded contemporaneously, must be amenable to independent verification, and must be replicable both in the same national society and in other national societies.

The factual emphasis is fundamental. No trend is included that is not known with practical certainty, and no directionality is asserted without empirical data. Where possible, studies of these tendancies by scholars outside the team are used to challenge or buttress a team's interpretations. These empirical predilections keep alive the happy possibility that the end result of the research may be surprising, and indeed it often is.

It should be emphasized that the tendencies documented in these national profiles are not merely interpretations of the quantitative series. They reflect an underlying sense of social theory and of social reality that goes far beyond the raw data. The themes we have chosen, our methods of examining the available indicators, our decisions about selective emphasis among the evidence at hand, and our estimation of the significance or insignificance of observed trend provide an intellectual structure derived from diverse national and disciplinary perspectives.

The fundamental purpose of this exercise is to provide comparable, reliable data that permit international comparison of recent social trends. Solid results along those lines have already been demonstrated in *Convergence or Divergence? Comparing Recent Trends in Industrial Societies* (1994), a volume in this series that presents systematic comparisons of demographic and family trends, changes in the division of labor and social movements, and trends in conflict resolution, personal relationships, and value systems in the first group of countries for which these profiles were prepared.

In preparing the trend report presented here, the members of the Russian team, like their predecessors, have also uncovered a great deal that was not previously known about the condition of their society. The Russian team faced unprecedented difficulties in preparing their national profile. One obvious problem was the shift in national identity that occurred with the dissolution of the Soviet Union. Another was the questionable reliability and validity of many official statistics from the Soviet era. But perhaps the greatest obstacle was the sheer velocity of change in the past few years and the need, in many cases, to interpret trends that have barely begun to present an intelligible pattern but are too important to disregard. That they have succeeded so well is a tribute to the competence and dedication of Irene Boutenko, Kirill Razlogov, and their colleagues.

The publication of this volume marks a significant milestone in the intellectual enterprise for which the CCSC Group was formed.

Theodore Caplow
University of Virginia
Henri Mendras
CNRS, Paris
December 1996

Introduction

This volume merits attentive study. It can be seen as either a proof of things long known or a revolution in beliefs concerning how society is developing in a country that comprises one sixth (and since 1991, one seventh) of the world's surface.

No consensus has emerged among the authors concerning the results of this unique study, and this is no accident. Our task was analytically descriptive. Like the authors of the books *Recent Social Trends in the United States: 1960–1990* and *Recent Social Trends in West Germany: 1960–1990,* we refused to accept any preconceptions (even if some of us considered them quite well founded).

The results are available to be tested against past and present dominant conceptions of social change in Russia in the twentieth century (as well as those of the more distant past and those projected for the future). There is no dearth of such conceptions – theories of convergence and post-industrial societies; construction of a communist paradise (or hell); vanguard of world development; even the premise that Russia stood outside of history for as long as seventy years – usually elaborated in the complete absence of reliable sociological and statistical data.

Though the historical development of Russia from 1960 to the mid-1990s has been evaluated in various ways by both apologists for and detractors of "real socialism," it has generally been divided into several commonly accepted periods corresponding to journalists' labels rather than scientific definitions. The period of the rule of N.S. Khrushchev (1956–64), who unmasked the "cult of Stalin's personality, was connected with some liberalization in social life and dubbed "the thaw" (perhaps optimistically forecasting the end of the cold war, which, as it turned out, was far from over). The subsequent period was called "stagnation." In 1985, Gorbachev's "perestroika" started. This started as an attempt to provide "socialism with a human face," give some freedom to economic enterprises, and limit the power of the Communist Party. At the end of the 1980s, however, these changes led to a disintegration of the entire socialist system and further growth in decentralization and liberalization. An attempt to stop the reforms resulted in a failed coup in 1991, after which the USSR broke up.

The Russian Federation became a sovereign republic within the Commonwealth of Independent States, which comprised most of the ex-USSR republics (but the meaning of the CIS is different for some member states and continues to evolve for all member states). After that, labels such as "radical reform," "economic crisis," "radical change," "transition to market," and "transitional period" – though the transition from what to what was not clear – became common, reaching an apex in 1991, the last year of fixed prices.

Soviet socialism itself has been and remains a puzzle for sociologists. What sort of society was it? Did it react to changing political orientations, and if so, how? In what respects were the trends in this society different from those prevailing in other societies? What was the scale of changes taking place?

Answers to these (and other) questions can be found in these pages, where we have tried to collect and systematize factual material that, in its entirety, had never been assembled in a systematic manner anywhere in the world. Many of the trends we discovered will dispel illusions and force people trying to write about Russia to take the facts into consideration. Following the methodology used in the Comparative Charting of Social Change project, we refrained from generalizing or making direct comparisons with data on other countries, including those presented in already published volumes. At the future stage of comparative studies, we may be able to determine whether Russia succeeded in defying history or not.

The common scheme of the study, accepted in different countries, assumes that all will use the same measurements, but it is absolutely natural that the indicators cannot be identical. Owing to national features, sociological tradition, and the personal interests of the social scientists involved, some spheres of society are studied in more or less detail and from different viewpoints. While this difficulty had been overcome by the authors of the German, Canadian, French, and American volumes, who were able to use a common terminology, the Russian scientists were faced with particularly acute problems in this respect.

In the USSR, Marxist-Leninist sociology imposed itself as the only scientific paradigm for social sciences. Soviet socialist society was considered to be the closest step to true communism, the "bright future of all humankind." The theoretical paradigm of Soviet sociology was constructed on the postulate that socialist societies were organized substantively differently, and most of their features were predicted and prescribed. There were no (and in theory there could not be) strikes, nationalism, poverty, unemployment, or homelessness. Labour productivity and the satisfaction level of the population were to grow together. Because of this peculiarity of the USSR's socialist society, its analysis required special terms and a simultaneous constant critique of the inadequacy of foreign (bourgeois) theories and their methodologies. On the one hand, Soviet sociology used such terms as "socialist competition," "socialist consciousness," "social funds of consumption," "branches of the economy" (each administered by a corresponding ministry), "moral stimuli to work," and "obligatory streaming of high-school graduates," which are not really comprehensible to the Western reader without special comments. On the other hand, notions such as private property, injustice, the middle class, the élite, and many other widely used sociological terms were not applied to socialist society. In addition, Soviet society included such units and elements as the *kolchoz, the subbotnik,* and communal flats (apartments). Thus, many terms in Soviet and Western sociologies had unequal content.

Taking this into account, the authors of this volume had to manoeuvre between the Scylla of comparability of measurements with those of other countries and the Charybis of describing a very different type of nation.

Sociological studies faced additional complications. In Russia, sociology as a science was constituted only in the mid-1970s, and even then it was endowed with the reduced status of empirical knowledge, the goal of which was to prove Marxist-Leninist teachings about the advantages of socialism over capitalism. A sociologist was, above all, an ideological worker, and empirical studies (in which sociologists worked under supervision of the communist authority) were extremely limited in terms of subject of inquiry and depth of interpretation of results. This is why there is a certain lack of representative empirical sociological data providing a detailed description of social trends in the 1970s and 1980s. As well, since Russian society developed according to five-year plans until the late 1980s, many official statistics are given on a five-year, rather than an annual, basis.

Statistical and sociological data were often regarded as a channel of information susceptible to discrediting official activity. All of the above has led to the authors of the present volume taking an extremely critical stance toward the data they have managed to find and sifting them grain by grain, as it were.

In the late 1980s, sociological information began to be collected extensivly. This was not merely a nod to fashion, but arose from a perceived societal need for more knowledge.

Since the tradition of presenting all methodologically justified results is just now being formed, the authors limited themselves mainly to data in the 1990s, produced by the best-known research centres: All-Union (since 1991, All-Russian) Centre for Public Opinion Studies (VCIOM), and Vox Populi (VP), a public-opinion polling service. Since these services began to publish bulletins only recently, the authors had to use the results of their research, published in the newspapers: the daily *Izvestia* and the weekly *Arguments and Facts*. Also taken into consideration were data published by prominent economists, political scientists, and sociologists in newspaper articles.

The authors concentrated on casting a light on the situation and avoiding, as far as possible, any evaluations. Thus, literature in the references by no means always reflects the most important publications on a given topic, but simply represents a list of sources from which quantitative data were taken. When such data were unavailable, the authors had to use experts' evaluations, as was done in the descriptions of social trends in Quebec and France.

A note on citations and the reference list: all sources are listed by the original Russian-language titles (accompanied by an English-language description) at the end of the volume. Each reference is numbered, and the reference's respective number appears in the text in square brackets where appropriate.

I.A. Boutenko and K.E. Razlogov

0 Context

0.1 Demographic Trends

The population of Russia has been decreasing and growing older: the proportion of persons living apart from their family has remained considerable, and families have been getting smaller.

The population had been increasing at a slower rate and began to decrease in 1990. Of the former population of the USSR, 51% live in Russia; 78% of these Russians live in the European part of the country.

Population growth was high until the mid-1960s; after that, the average annual increase was cut by nearly half. Since the end of the 1980s, the rate of growth has slowed noticeably. In 1992, the population of Russia decreased by 31,000; in 1993, by 30,800 (see table 1).

Until the mid-1980s, the increase in the overall population was due to natural growth, whereas the influence of migration remained insignificant for a long period of time. In the 1990s, both factors – intensification of the migration stream to Russia and a significant drop in natural increase – began to play an important role (see table 2).

Before the 1990s, the proportional relationship between urban and rural populations varied under the influence of cross-migration, with urban populations being predominant. However, the growth rate of urban populations gradually diminished as the migration potential in the countryside dropped; in the 1990s, a potential increase in the proportion of the rural population was noted, as the migratory stream reversed its trend (see table 3).

There was a stable prevalence of women in the population (see table 4). In the postwar years, this was connected with war losses. In subsequent years, the trend continued due to a higher mortality rate, especially during their working years, and a shorter life span among men. On average, the proportion of men living in cities and towns was somewhat higher than that in the overall population, since clearly larger numbers of men migrated from rural localities to cities.

Table 1
Population of Russia, 1951–93

	Population at end of period (000)	Increase over period (000)	Mean annual increase (%)
1951–55	112,266	9,321	17.5
1956–60	120,766	8,500	14.7
1961–65	127,189	6,423	10.4
1966–70	130,704	3,515	5.5
1971–75	134,690	3,986	6.0
1976–80	139,165	4,475	6.6
1981–85	144,080	4,915	7.0
1986–90	148,543	4,463	6.1
1991	148,704	162	1.1
1992	148,673	(31)	(0.2)
1993	148,365	(308)	(5.1)

Sources: [183], p. 8; [195], p. 33; [329], p. 19.

Table 2
Population growth, Russia, 1960–93 (000)

	Natural increase	Net immigration	Total
1960	1,896	(176)	1,720
1965	1,032	(152)	880
1970	773	(148)	625
1975	796	119	915
1980	677	60	737
1985	750	262	1,012
1986	988	292	1,280
1987	968	260	1,228
1988	779	256	1,035
1989	577	86	663
1990	333	169	502
1991	104	57	161
1992	(207)	176	(31)
1993	(738)	430	(308)

Sources: [183], p. 10; [195], p. 35; [329], p. 12.

Table 3
The proportion of urban and rural populations, Russia, 1959–93

	Urban (%)	Rural (%)	Total (million)
1959	52	48	117.5
1960	54	46	199.0
1965	58	42	126.3
1970	62	38	130.1
1975	67	33	133.8
1979	69	31	137.6
1980	70	30	148.3
1985	72	28	142.8
1989	74	26	147.4
1990	74	26	148.0
1991	74	26	148.7
1992	74	26	148.7
1993	73	27	148.4

Sources: [171], p. 52; [242], p. 86.

Table 4
Ratio of men to women, selected age groups, Russia, 1959–92

	Total female population	0–14 years (men per 100 women)	60 years and over (men per 100 women)
1959	80.5	103.4	44.3
1979	85.7	103.1	40.3
1989	87.7	103.3	44.6
1992	85.2	103.6	45.5

Source: [241], p. 88.

Until the mid-1960s, the mortality rate decreased rapidly as a result of the introduction of new medicines, particularly antibiotics, into the health-care system. By the mid-1960s, the infant-mortality rate had dropped sharply (to 26 per 1,000 births; see table 5), while average life expectancy rose to 64 years for men and 73 years for women (see table 6). The trend toward longer life expectancy after 1964–65 later reversed itself, especially among men, although their previous gain was sustained up to the early 1990s. By 1995, mean life expectancy had decreased to 57.3 years among men because of the increased number of deaths in young and middle age.

Table 5
Infant death rate, Russia, 1960–93 (per 1,000 live births)

	City	Village	Total
1960	34.9	38.1	36.6
1965	26.4	26.7	26.6
1970	22.1	24.5	23.0
1975	22.5	26.2	23.7
1980	21.2	24.0	22.1
1981	20.3	24.3	21.5
1982	19.5	22.4	20.4
1983	19.2	22.4	20.1
1984	19.9	23.4	20.9
1985	19.8	22.8	20.7
1986	18.8	20.8	19.3
1987	18.8	21.0	19.4
1988	18.2	20.4	18.9
1989	17.3	18.9	17.8
1990	16.7	17.7	17.4
1991	17.3	19.1	17.8
1992	–	–	18.0
1993	–	–	20.0

Sources: [183], p. 41; [195], p. 23; [329], p. 42.

The difference in mean life expectancy between men and women is 10 years. In rural localities, this gap is more apparent. Approximately 75% of the difference in life span between urban- and rural-dwelling males is due to a very high death rate resulting from accidents, poisoning, and trauma, the last of which is closely connected with alcohol consumption.

There have been no substantial changes in the infant-mortality rate since the 1970s. This indicator varies widely over the territory, from 12 to 14 per 1,000 in central Russia up to 40 per 1,000 among the rural populations in Tuva, Chechnya, and Ingushetiya, with a Russian mean of 18 per 1,000 for 1992 ([84]).

The drop in the birth rate that continued over several decades resulted in a constant growth in the proportion of older groups in the population. The proportion of persons over 60 years old was 16.5% (1992), twice as high as in 1959 (see table 7). This indicator is especially high in rural localities because of the migration of young people to cities.

There is a trend toward an increase in the proportion of families comprising two to four persons, and a decrease in the proportion of large families of seven and

Table 6
Life expectancy of urban and rural residents, Russia 1961–93 (years)

	Men			Women		
	City	Village	Total	City	Village	Total
1961–62	63.9	63.4	63.8	72.4	72.3	72.4
1965–66	64.6	63.3	64.3	73.1	73.5	73.4
1970–71	63.8	61.8	63.2	73.5	73.4	73.6
1975–76	63.4	58.9	62.3	73.2	72.4	73.0
1979–80	62.3	59.3	61.5	73.1	72.4	73.0
1980–81	62.4	59.3	61.5	73.2	72.5	73.1
1981–82	62.8	59.7	62.0	79.8	72.8	73.5
1982–83	63.1	59.8	62.3	73.7	73.0	73.6
1983–84	62.9	59.4	62.0	73.4	72.7	73.3
1984–85	63.1	59.8	62.3	73.4	72.6	73.3
1985–86	64.5	61.8	63.8	74.0	73.6	74.0
1986–87	65.4	63.2	64.9	74.4	74.4	74.6
1987	65.3	63.2	65.0	74.4	74.6	74.5
1988	65.4	62.7	64.8	74.2	74.4	74.4
1989	64.8	62.6	64.2	74.5	74.2	74.5
1990	64.4	62.0	63.9	74.5	74.2	74.4
1991	64.1	61.8	63.5	74.4	73.9	74.3
1992	–	–	62.0	–	–	73.8
1993	–	–	58.9	–	–	71.9

Sources: [171], p,120; [195], p. 23.

Table 7
Average age of the population and proportion of selected age groups, Russia, 1959–92

	Average age	0–14 years old (%)	60 years and over (%)
1959	29.5	29.2	8.9
1970	33.5	26.5	11.9
1979	33.9	21.6	13.7
1989	34.6	23.1	15.4
1992	35.2	22.6	16.5

Sources: [171], p. 99; [314], p. 27.

more. The average number of family members is decreasing more substantially in rural areas. Thus, the number of families is growing, whereas the families themselves are getting smaller (see table 8), due in part to a decrease in the average age at which people marry. There has also been a generalized change in the age and sex structure of the population, resulting from marriage break-ups among young families; a trend toward having fewer children; and an increase in one-parent families.

The proportion of persons living apart from their family is increasing. According to the 1989 census, there were 17 million single persons and people living apart from their family, or over 12% of the population. Single persons make up nearly one third of the total number of households (see table 8); most of them reside in cities, especially large ones.

The predominant household form (82%) is a couple with or without children. The proportion of households including only one parent with children was comparatively large and continued to grow in the mid-1980s. These households were the result of divorce, death of a spouse, or births out of wedlock ([183]).

Forced migration has grown in importance. A refugee phenomenon that had not existed in the country since the early 1920s re-emerged in the 1990s. In 1990–91, the process of migrating to Russia from other CIS countries became generalized, with the exception of the Ukraine and Belorussia. At that time, there were 279,500 registered refugees in Russia, only 73,500, or slightly more than 25%, of whom were Russians. In 1994, there were 552,000 refugees, 70% of them Russian ([195]).

Table 8
Household size, Russia, 1959–89

	Total households (000)	One-person households (000)	One-person households (%)	Average size of households (persons)	Average size of multiple-person households (persons)
1959	41,663	13,134	31.5	2.62	3.6
1970	47,021	14,403	30.6	2.61	3.5
1979	54,077	17,353	32.1	2.54	3.3
1989	57,297	17,051	29.8	2.56	3.2

Sources: [114], p. 7; [330], p. 254.

L.M. Prokofieva

0.2 Macro-economic Trends

Macro-economic indexes characterizing the development of Russia from the 1960s to the 1980s showed a trend to constant growth. The economic reforms at the end of the 1980s changed this situation. Conversion toward a market economy was painful and halting. Russia is now in a period of deep economic crisis.

Gross domestic product constantly increased till the end of 1980s. Total volume of gross social output (production of material goods) and national revenue in constant prices tripled between 1960 and 1992. Over the period, however, the rates of growth of these indexes gradually slowed (see table 1). This was connected to lower production in the main economic sectors, while the rise in material consumption was cutting into Russia's balance of foreign trade. The increase in these indexes in actual prices in the 1990s was the result of inflation. Prices were 18 times higher in 1992 than in 1991 due to inflation ([241]).

The volume of capital investments increased until 1990 and then decreased sharply (see table 2). The structure of distribution of capital investments in different economic sectors did not change considerably over the 30 years from 1960 to 1990: most capital investments continued to be directed to the production sector. The proportion of capital investment in this sector increased from 53% in 1985 to 60% in 1993, while investment in other sectors (education, culture, science, health) ' dropped from 47% to 40% over the same period.

Most capital investment in the production sector has been directed to industry – in 1960, 42%; in 1993, 36% – and a considerable proportion is involved in the fuel-energy complex. This sector's share of all capital investment was in 11% in 1971–75; 14% in 1981–85; 16% in 1986–90; and 21% in 1992 ([171]). Beginning in 1989, investment began to slow, particularly in sectors that had formerly benefited from the political determination of the economic structure. The reasons for this situation were increases in prices for all types of construction resources and a reduction in state-financed construction and in funds available from personal savings.

A characteristic feature of industrial development during the last three decades has been the priority placed on development of production of the means of production, as opposed to production of consumer goods. By the late 1980s, the growth rate of production of the means of production was somewhat higher than was production of consumer goods; in 1991, two thirds of all industrial production

Table 1
Gross social product (production of material goods) and national income, Russia, 1960–93 (rate of growth, %)

Year	Gross social product	National income	Consumption of material goods and services
1960	100	100	–
1970	191	198˘	–
1980	317	325	100
1985	374	385	114
1986	387	394	120
1987	397	397	123
1988	411	415	128
1989	417	423	132
1990	411	406	134
1991	365	348	124
1992	291	271	–
1993	235	–	–

Sources: [171], p. 14; [177], p. 46; [242], p,12.

Table 2
Indexes of growth in total capital investment and in industrial and agricultural products, Russia, 1960–94 (%)

Year	Capital investments	Industry	Agriculture
1960	100	100	100
1970	185	215	135
1980	318	374	146
1985	375	442	155
1986	409	462	165
1987	434	478	163
1988	467	486	169
1989	486	503	171
1990	487	503	165
1991	411	463	158
1992	226	376	145
1993	192	315	139
1994	142	249	126

Sources: [171], p. 14; [177], p. 46; [277], p. 62; [305], p. 5.

was devoted to the former. In total, industrial output tripled between 1960 and 1993. The production slowdown that began in 1990 was not structural, but general (see table 2); its significance appeared to go beyond the contraction of the gross social product (the sum of gross production of material goods). In large measure, it was a result of the fact that about 75% of the military-industrial complex of the CIS and most production of capital goods was concentrated in Russia ([285]).

The recent liberalization of prices did not produce a stimulating effect on industry, due to a high level of concentration and monopolization of production.

For many years, Russia had a problem with structural economic distortion caused by a very high proportion of heavy industry and military-industrial production in the economic structure. The share of agriculture in gross social product was always rather small: in 1980 it was 11%; in 1992, 8% ([241]). Growth of agricultural production was assured for a long time by the ability of the socialist economy to mobilize financial resources on a large scale and direct them through state channels to economic development. On this basis, a large and ineffective agricultural complex was built. Production increases were constrained by a low level of mechanization in agriculture and a weak forage reserve. In the 1990s, there was a trend toward a reduction in the number of species of cattle. Major production losses were tolerated at the stages of production, purchasing, transportation, storage, processing, and selling. Furthermore, the social infrastructure in villages was rudimentary, and in many regions the demographic situation has worsened.

Agrarian reform in the late 1980s did not improve the difficult situation in this economic sector. Growth in agricultural production from 1960 to 1989 was suddenly reversed in 1990 (see table 2). The considerable decrease in production took place at the expense of the state sector. On private farms, the production volume increased; by 1992 it made up one third of agricultural production in Russia ([241]).

Up to the end of the 1980s, inflationary pressures developed in a hidden form, as the deficit grew ever larger alongside relatively stable prices. After that, inflation, connected with the structural disproportions of state production, began to be reflected in prices as shortages increased. This change in form of inflationary processes was caused both by the crisis of the economic system and by the absence of control over the amount of currency in circulation, which increased by a factor of 37 from 1961 to 1991. In 1992, the monthly increase in currency in circulation was approximately 20% [171]. The growth in the credit infusion into the economy, increases in budgetary expenditures, and the forcing up of prices stimulated inflation. When inflation hit 50%, in January of 1993, the Russian economy entered a state of hyper-inflation ([242]). The early 1990s were characterized by decreases in the rouble's purchasing power and a rapid increase in prices in all the sectors of the economy.

Table 3
Household income and expenditures, Russia, 1985–93

	1985	1990	1991	1992	1993
Income:					
- billions of roubles	245	383	830	6,263	78,252
- compared to previous year, %	104	118	217	750	1,100
Expenditures on goods and services, personal finance charges:					
- billions of roubles	232	335	586	3,867*	5,374
- compared to previous year, %	103	115	175	750	1,000

Sources: [171], p. 205; [244], p. 86.
* Expenditures on consumer goods and services.

For many years, the growth in nominal incomes offset increases in expenses (see table 3). From the 1960s to the 1980s, under conditions of total shortage of supply in the market, a considerable proportion of income was set aside to accumulate, mainly in saving banks. One third of these savings represented unsatisfied demand for goods and services. In recent years, the gap between incomes and expenditures increased considerably. Much of the population preferred not to spend a good part of their income. By 1992, this situation had changed as a result of the dramatic rise in prices for goods and services, leading to a reduction by half in personal savings from 1991 to the end of 1992 ([171]).

Price increases introduced considerable changes into the consumer-price structure; between December 1992 and December 1993, consumer prices for goods and services rose by a factor of nine (see table 4), whereas from 1960 to the end of the 1980s, prices increased insignificantly. One important index of living standard, share of expenditures on food, has decreased. Over a long period, these expenditures decreased in comparison with incomes and total household expenses. In 1980, the share of expenditures for food in total family income of workers and employees was 35%; in 1985, 33%; in 1990, 28%. In 1992, this share increased to 40%, indicating a decrease in real household incomes ([171]).

Labour reserves in Russia gradually decreased, reaching 86.2 million people in 1992, or nearly 60% of the total population (see table 5). In 1960, 82% of the population active in the national economy worked in the material-goods production sectors; 37% of these worked in industry and construction, 32% in agriculture and forestry. In 1992, the proportion working in industry and construction was 42%; in agriculture and forestry, 13%.

The development of private joint ventures and other non-state enterprises (see section 5.3) led to a redistribution of labour reserves according to type of occupa-

Table 4
Aggregate consumer-price index, Russia, 1991–94 (change, December to previous December, multiple)

	1991	1992	1993	1994
Foodstuffs				
(not including alcoholic beverages)	2.7	26.7	9.4	3.2
Alcoholic beverages	1.5	24.7	7.5	2.3
Services	1.8	22.2	24.1	6.2
Other goods	3.1	26.7	7.4	2.8
Total goods and services	2.6	26.1	9.6	3.2

Sources: [171], p. 165; [305], p. 35.

Table 5
Labour reserves, average annual rate of growth, Russia, 1961–92, percentages

1961–65	3.80
1966–70	2.80
1971–75	2.20
1976–80	1.60
1981–85	0.10
1986–90	0.10
1991	(0.05)
1992	(0.10)

Calculated from [171], p. 152; [177], p. 46.

tion. Starting in 1987, the number of people working in the public sector of the economy began to drop, while the total number of people working in the private sector increased from 1.6% in 1990 to 14% in 1993 ([242]). A slowdown in production in all economic sectors resulted in layoffs and thus an increase in the numbers of unemployed.

Starting in the late 1980s, foreign trade gradually decreased (see table 6). Total volume in 1993 was 70 billion dollars, 12% less than in 1992 and half the 1990 figure. The export structure remains unbalanced. As in the 1970s and 1980s, the main source of currency earnings was energy resources, the proportion of which in exports increased to 48% in 1992. A reduction in export volume – and, as a result, a drop in currency receipts – led to decreases in imports. The value of imports in 1993 was $27 billion, 27% lower than the 1992 level ([277]).

The commodity structure of Russian foreign trade varied greatly, depending on the country with which it was trading, until the end of the 1980s. In exports to industrially developed countries, energy resources and certain heavy-industry

Table 6
Foreign trade, Russia, 1988–93 ($ billion)

Year	Export	Import	Foreign trade balance
1988	74	72	2
1989	75	78	(3)
1990	71	82	(11)
1991	50	44	6
1992	38	35	3
1993	43	27	16

Source: [193], p.46.

products dominated. In exports to COMECON countries, heavy machinery and metal products also played an important role. Imports from these countries included heavy machinery, foodstuffs, and medical supplies.

Russia's traditional trading partners for many years were the former COMECON countries. The disintegration of COMECON resulted in the rupture of many contacts with countries in Eastern Europe. The share of these countries in trade with Russia dropped considerably: in 1990, it comprised 40%; in 1992, only 18%. The shift of priorities in foreign trade in favour of non-socialist countries in general (commodity circulation increased from 37% in 1990 to 61% in 1992) gave rise to a situation in which unfixed prices for Russia's main exports were lower than those in effect in the world market, and prices for imported goods were higher ([171]).

L.N. Sivashenkova

0.3 Macro-technological trends

Russia went from moderate prosperity, in the 1960s, to deep crisis, at the beginning of the 1990s; this was a result both of the unreceptivity of its economy to technological progress and of resource concentration in the military industry. Slow rates of scientific-technological progress were a result of the inefficiency of the Russian economy. The centrally planned system did not encourage innovation, thus discouraging competition and private initiative, without which innovations could not be disseminated effectively.

From the 1960s to the 1990s, the productivity of the technology and energy used in production increased by 1% a year, but Russia's technological lag became more and more obvious.

Throughout the period, demand for new technology was lower than supply. The introduction of new technology had an imposed and arbitrary character. Unrealized technological progress was compensated for by a disproportionate growth in investment in and wasteful consumption of natural resources.

Over the period, superfluous investment activity was typical, as was accumulation, primarily in the production sector. Most investment was directed toward industry. Starting in the mid-1970s, investment in transportation and communications began to increase, mainly in the form of construction of oil and gas mains, accompanied by a gradual decrease in investment in housing construction, trade, medicine, science, and culture. The investment rate in 1985 was 118% in comparison to that in 1980; 153% in 1990; and 60% in 1993. Over the same period, the rate of growth of the productive plant was 177% in 1985; 182% in 1990; and 191% in 1992 ([171], [277]). This rate exceeded the growth rate of investment, which was, of course, an anomaly; growth in productive capacity was, in fact, increasing more rapidly than was the renewal of the technological productive plant. In other words, the existing productive plant was expanding faster than it was being amortized by the introduction of more technologically advanced equipment (see table 1). Ageing of the productive plant was an important reason for low labour productivity and superfluous consumption of raw materials and energy.

From 1960 to the 1990s, energy consumption grew, though the rate of growth slowed somewhat before the end of the 1970s, mainly due to the stabilization and successive decrease in the use of oil and coal and an increase in the use of natural gas. At the end of the 1980s, energy consumption per unit of gross national product was about twice as high as the average in the OECD countries. Throughout the period, a low level of installed power capacity per production unit and of energy consumption was noted in the social, cultural, and domestic sectors in comparison with the industrial and agricultural sectors (see table 2). A considerable proportion of energy consumption in industry was the result of industrial policy considerations, which gave a high priority to development of heavy industry. The share of energy consumed by the military-industrial complex was considerable. The officially admitted share of military expenditures in the gross national product – about 30% – suggests that the military's share of energy consumption could not be reduced ([77]).

A gradual decrease in labour productivity over the period led to a decrease in national income and gross domestic product in 1990–92. A high rate of increase in the national income in the 1960s (by 6.2% in 1961–65; by 7.9% in 1966–

70) and 1970s (by 5.9% in 1971–75; by 4.4% in 1976–80) ([177]) was accompanied by an increase in expenditures on science. Low levels of investment in science appeared to be less advantageous than those in other economic sectors. In 1991, the share, in gross national product and in gross domestic product, of expenditures on science began to decrease (see table 3). The military-industrial complex received about three quarters of expenditures on science ([307]). Though half of these expenditures were used for civil projects, decreased military expenditures was one more factor in the relative contraction of science funding.

There was a sharp growth in the number of scientists in the 1960s (see table 4). At the end of the 1980s, a general deterioration in Russia's scientific potential became evident; this trend became stronger from 1991 to 1995 as the economic crisis deepened. There was an absolute reduction in the number of scientists, ageing of existing personnel, and a decrease in their real wages and in the general volume of science funding; consequently, there was a decrease in efficiency (see table 5).

Table 1
Growth in investment and productive plant, Russia, 1985–93 (%)

	1985	1990	1993
Growth in capital investment	18	53	(40)
Growth in productive plant	77	82	91

Sources: [171], p. 4; [277], p. 6.

Table 2
Consumption of electrical energy, Russia, 1960–92 (billions of kwh)

	1960	1970	1980	1985	1990	1991	1992	1993
Industry and construction	146	331	520	597	645	622	571	513*
Agriculture	6	19	56	74	96	103	103	104
Transportation	14	41	77	91	104	97	87	77
Other sectors	20	5	99	122	145	150	147	–
Loss in thee systems	12	35	64	81	84	84	84	–
Total	198	479	816	965	1,074	1,056	992	938

Sources: [171], p. 323; [177], p. 84; [242], p. 318.

* In industry only.

Table 3
State expenditures and investments in scientific development, Russia, 1985–92

	1985	1990	1991	1992
Expenditures on science from state budget and other sources (in current prices, billion roubles)	17.3	22.6	25.1	185.0
Investments in science (billion roubles)	3.5	4.2	1.8	18.0
Share of expenditures on science in the national revenue (%)	4.9	5.1	3.1	3.1
Share of expenditures on science in the gross national product (%)	3.4	3.6	2.4	0.9
Share of investments in science in general volume of investments (%)	2.2	2.1	0.9	0.4

Source: [186], p. 33.

Table 4
Number of scientists, all disciplines, in Russia, 1960–91 (000)

	1960	1970	1980	1985	1990	1991
Doctor	8	16	26	30	33	32
Candidate*	67	145	257	299	316	306
Total (including scientific and pedagogical staff at institutions of higher education)	243	631	938	1,019	1,031	947

Sources: [171], pp. 323, 335; [177], p. 55.

* The candidate level represents persons who have written and presented a first thesis. Of these, one eighth normally accede to the doctoral level by writing and presenting a second thesis.

Table 5
New technological devices produced, Russia, 1971–92 (000 units)

	New models of machines, equipment, instruments and means of automation
1971–75	12.4
1976–80	11.4
1981–85	10.0
1986–90	6.5
1991	0.9
1992	1.0

Sources: [177], p. 69; [241], p. 342.

L.N. Sivashenkova

1 Age Groups

1.1 Youth

During the period under study, the proportion of young people in the general population varied between one quarter and one fifth. The period from 1960 to the 1980s was characterized both by a relatively stable proportion of youths among working people and by a considerable rise in educational level among young people and in the number of young specialists.* The trend toward marrying and having children at a young age persisted, accompanied by an increase in the number of young people cohabiting. The social and economic changes of the 1990s were manifested in a transformation in the young people's value system, expectations, and life-goal strategies.

The proportion of young people 16–19 years old among the population changed in waves over the period under study. During the 1960s, this proportion decreased, a consequence of the demographic "echo" of the war. During the following decade, the proportion of young people increased, reflecting the postwar "baby boom" and a certain stabilization of living conditions. Later on, there was a gradual decrease in the proportion of young people, which reached its lowest level for the period in 1993 (see table 1). From 1990 to 1992, the number of children and teenagers below age 15 dropped by 2.5%, largely due to a decrease in the fertility rate ([242]).

There was a considerable change in the childbearing-age profile. Before the mid-1980s, the fertility of women over 30 years of age was dropping (see table 2), and the number of children per family was decreasing. This was associated with a new wave of women entering the job market and with the spread of the concomitant life style. This trend persisted and grew stronger over the following decade.

Early marriages (before age 25) and a high level of divorces among young families were prevailing trends. From the 1950s to the 1970s, the age of men and

---

* Until the 1990s, graduates from professional schools were obligatorily streamed to certain offices and/or enterprises. For the first two years of their employment, they could neither change their place of work without special permission nor be dismissed from their position.

Table 1
Proportion of young people aged 16–29 in the population, Russia, 1970–93 (%)

1959	1970	1979	1989	1993
25.7	20.5	25.5	20.5	20.4

Sources: [157], p. 5; [242], p. 66; [329], p. 59.

Table 2
Children born in Russia according to mother's age, 1980–91 (% of total number of births)

Mother's age	1980	1985	1986	1989	1990	1991
Under 20	11.2	9.1	8.7	11.8	13.9	15.4
20–24	45.4	39.9	37.2	35.9	36.6	37.7
25–29	27.6	30.4	31.3	29.0	27.0	25.2
30–34	11.8	15.1	16.4	16.2	15.6	14.9

Source: [329], p. 132.

women at first marriage dropped. At the same time, marriages that took place from 1970 to 1975 were dissolved during the first three years of married life three times more often than marriages that took place in the 1960s ([56]). During the 1980s and 1990s, the average age at marriage for men (24) and women (21–22) was quite low, and a high rate of divorce among young families persisted. For example, in the 1990s, an average of 40% of registered marriages were dissolved and more than 30% of young couples divorced after less than five years of married life ([175], [242]).

Informal (unregistered) marriages became typical matrimonial behaviour among young people. In 1958–59, of those eligible to marry, only 22.4% were married; in 1969–70, this figure dropped to 19.2%; in 1988–89, it dropped further, to 14.3%. In the 1950s and 1960s, most children born out of wedlock were born to women above 35, who for various reasons could not get married; in the 1990s, however, the constantly growing number of children born out of wedlock were born into informal families ([98]).

A trend toward receiving a general secondary education and toward higher education prevailed from the 1960s to the 1980s. Officially, general secondary education for all young people was proclaimed by the government as a goal to be achieved by the end of the 1970s. Before the mid-1980s, about 80–85% of young people received a secondary education (eleven-year secondary schools, vocational secondary schools, vocational technical schools, and evening schools) ([250]). Most young people who finished secondary school preferred to continue their education. Analysts even noted that during the 1980s a stereotype developed in which graduates from general secondary studies would go on to higher education. In spite of the fact that not everyone who planned to enter an institution of higher education was able to realize his or her plans, the number of graduates from colleges and universities constantly increased up to the beginning of the 1980s (see table 3).

Beginning in the 1960s, a discrepancy developed between the professional education of young graduates and their actual professions. By the end of the 1980s, every third young graduate from university or college was not working at his or her specialty ([157]).

In the 1990s, when the radical changes in Russia began, young people's attitudes toward higher education evolved, with a "work" orientation becoming more important. This change was reflected, for example, in a survey comparing aspirations and achievements of primary-school graduates in 1965 and 1993. In 1965, 37% of these graduates wanted to graduate from general secondary school, while 52% actually did so; in 1993, 91% expressed the wish to finish secondary school, but only 76% did so. However, by 1993 there had been a radical – sixfold – drop in the number of those who planned to go to college and a fifteenfold drop in the number of those who wanted to attend vocational technical schools ([250]). The number of students in institutions of higher education and in colleges dropped radically at the beginning of the 1990s (see table 4), but grew in the mid-1990s.

Beginning in the 1960s, a life pattern that presumed a later entry into the labour force and a more prolonged period of education was formed. Though the minimum age to start work was officially 16 years, in practice a very small proportion of young people began to work at this age. According to the 1970 census, fewer than one half of young people aged 16 to 20 were employed. During the 1970s and 1980s, as a result of general secondary education and an increase in the role of vocational technical schools in preparing new workers, more young people started to work when they were 18 or 19 years old. A rise in the number of young people with a higher education contributed to the fact that still more of them began to work when they were 20 ([325]).

At the beginning of the 1990s, a new orientation toward work and commercial activities, along with a drop in the prestige of education and an increase in youth unemployment, resulted in a greater proportion of young people beginning to work earlier. On evidence derived from selective polls in 1993, the average age of the unemployed was 33.9 years old, while people under the age of 30 made up about 42.2% of the total unemployed ([242]). One of the new problems that young people faced at the beginning of the 1990s was the need to migrate to foreign countries to find jobs. The data before the end of 1991 showed that among those who wanted to emigrate, 27% were aged from 18 to 33 years ([233]).

Table 3
Graduates from institutions of higher education, Russian Federation, 1970–88 (per 10,000 population)

1970	1975	1980	1985	1988
28	30	33	33	30

Source: [157], p. 111.

Table 4
Number of high-school and other students, Russia, 1980–94 (per 10,000 population)

	1980/1981	1985/1986	1992/1993	1993/1994
High-school students	219	206	178	171
Other students	190	172	141	134

Source: [242], p. 294.

One of the most vivid phenomena accompanying the present social transformations is a high level of criminality among young people: beginning in 1987, young people (14–29 years old) accounted for about 55% of convicts ([152], [242]).

Beginning in the 1970s, analysts recorded a radical change in the value system of the young generation, which essentially differed from that of their parents. The post-Stalin generation (born between 1940 and 1956) were more oriented toward the values of private life and individualism than were their parents. During the 1970s, nonconformity with the norms of the regime and the social processes that were taking place at the time reached the highest level yet among the younger generation.

Analyses of the 1980s showed that young people were less oriented toward such traditional values as order, career, and active participation in social life, and were becoming more and more hedonistic.

At the beginning of the 1990s, young people displayed aspirations and strategies for their realization that essentially differed from those of young people in the 1980s. A comparison of poll results among graduates in 1985 and 1990–91 revealed a radical growth in aspirations, a decrease in readiness to work hard, and an increase in hopes for assistance from associates (family, friends and acquaintances). One result of the destruction of the former social values was the transformation of where recognition was sought, from the social sphere to the private sphere (a radical decrease in the desire for social recognition) and a considerable growth in expectations and aspirations connected with living standards ([149]).

O.M. Zdravomyslova

1.2 Elders

An increase in the proportion of elderly people was observed over the period under study. This process commenced much later than in the majority of Western European countries, but proceeded more intensively.

The trend toward an increase in the proportion of old people remained stable. In 1959, there were 10.6 million people aged over 60 years, or 9% of the population in the USSR; in 1987, this age group numbered 21.3 million, or 14.7% of the population ([114]). From 1987 to 1992, the number of elderly people rose by 14.7%, while their proportion in the population during this period increased to 16.5%. Their proportion had more than doubled between 1959 and 1987, while the overall population grew by 23.7% [171].

The proportion of the population not of working age increased, and the proportion of elderly persons increased more quickly than did that of the 0–15 age group.

The proportion of older women was higher and tended to grow faster. In 1959, the proportion of elderly women exceeded that of elderly men by 5%, and this gap grew to 10.4% by 1987 (see table 1). The ageing of the female population was more intensive throughout the period. From 1959 to 1987, the number of women over 60 years of age rose by 207%, while that of men rose by 189.7% (see table 2).

There is consequently a disproportionately large number of females in older age groups (see table 3). In 1979, for example, the proportion of women in the age cohort of 60–64-year-olds was twice that of men; in the 65–69 age cohort, there were 2.2 times as many women; in the 70-and-over cohort, 3.1 times as many women. In both of these cohorts, this trend persisted until 1992, while the disproportion in the "youngest" group of 60–64-year-olds began declining in 1989, when there were 1.6 times as many females; there were 1.4 times as many women in 1992. This is caused, among other factors, by a difference in average life expectancies of males and females, which manifests itself more sharply in rural populations. The gap between life expectancies for women and for men was 12.5 years in the overall population: 10.8 years among urban populations and 13.1 years among rural populations. This gap, however, gradually diminished; in 1989, these figures were 9.8, 9.7, and 11.6 years, respectively (see table 4).

Most elderly people are not in good health. With ageing come diseases of the cardiovascular system, including arteriosclerosis, and malignant tumours. These

Table 1
Proportion of the population aged 60 and over by sex and urban or rural residency, Russia, 1959–92 (%)

	1959	1970	1979	1987	1992
Urban population, total	7.6	10.6	12.2	13.2	
men	5.0	6.9	7.9	8.4	
women	9.6	13.8	15.9	17.3	
Rural population, total	10.6	14.2	17.0	18.9	
men	7.5	9.0	10.1	11.1	
women	13.0	18.4	22.9	25.4	
Overall population, total	9.0	12.0	13.7	14.7	17.5
men	6.2	7.8	8.6	9.1	
women	11.2	15.6	18.1	19.5	

Calculated from [171], p. 82; [184], pp. 50–53.

Table 2
Growth rate of the population aged 60 and over by sex and urban or rural residency, Russia, 1959–87 (%)

	1959	1970	1979	1987
Urban population, total	100.0	183.6	248.2	300.4
men	100.0	182.0	247.1	299.6
women	100.0	184.5	148.7	300.8
Rural population, total	100.0	118.5	122.6	124.0
men	100.0	108.2	106.1	107.1
women	100.0	123.2	130.1	131.7
Overall population, total	100.0	147.3	178.0	201.8
men	100.0	139.9	166.6	189.7
women	100.0	150.6	183.1	207.2

Calculated from [184], pp. 50– 53.

diseases are considered age-specific pathologies, and they progress rapidly in the second half of life ([315]). Thus, in the cohort of sick people who need medical help in connection with treatment of cardiovascular disease, this disease occupies third place in the 40–49 age group, second place in the 50–59 age group, and first place among those aged 60 and over ([269]). However, regular statistics do not cover the disease-incidence rate of the retirement-age population as a specific group.

In the late 1970s, about 50% of aged people reported that they were in an "unsatisfactory" state of health; 10% fewer felt this way in 1992. A 1990 survey by the State Statistics Committee of Russia revealed that 67% of respondents who

Table 3
Ratio of women to men by age group and by urban or rural residency, Russia, 1979–92

	Number of women per 1,000 men of the corresponding age group		
	1979	1989	1992
Urban population, total	1,170	1,145	1,139
60–64	1,896	1,559	1,406
65–69	2,100	2,278	2,053
70 and over	3,047	2,971	2,974
Rural population, total	1,183	1,125	1,117
60–64	2,241	1,630	1,341
65–69	2,457	2,344	2,150
70 and over	3,167	3,466	3,472
Overall population, total	1,174	1,140	1,133
60–64	2,010	1,581	1,385
65–69	2,226	2,298	2,081
70 and over	3,095	3,125	3,125

Source: [171], pp. 92-94.

Table 4
Life expectancy by birth and urban or rural residency, Russia, 1979–89 (years)

	1979–1980	1987	1988	1989
Urban population. total	68.0	70.4	70.1	69.9
men	62.3	65.4	65.4	64.8
women	73.1	74.5	74.2	74.5
Rural population. total	66.0	69.1	68.7	68.5
men	59.3	63.2	62.7	62.6
women	72.4	74.5	74.4	74.2
Overall population. total	67.5	70.2	69.9	69.6
men	61.5	65.0	64.3	64.2
women	73.0	74.6	74.4	74.0

Sources: [84], p. 390; [184], pp. 494–6.

were retired persons were worried about the state of their health. In the republic of Mordoviya, 57% of respondents reported that they suffered from chronic disease; one third of them reported that they "constantly did not feel quite well." Four out of ten respondents reported negative statements regarding their health; every second respondent was satisfied with his or her health, and 2% reported a "good" state of health ([261]).

Between 1965 and 1988, age-specific death rates in people aged 60 to 84 declined. However, the situation deteriorated for males relative to females. Specifically, a definite rise in the death rate of 60–64-year-old males occurred in the mid-1980s. This was also true for the 65–69 age group (see table 5). Diseases related to circulatory malfunction were the leading cause of death. The incidence of death due to cancer was the highest in the 75–79 age groups among both men and women, after which it subsided somewhat. The incidence of death from respiratory disease grew higher with advancement of years, especially among men. An analogous trend was discerned in deaths resulting from accidents, poisoning, and trauma, but the death-rate coefficient was significantly lower compared to the causes of death discussed above (see table 6).

N.N. Simonova

Table 5
Age-specific death rates by sex, Russia, 1975–91 (average number of people who died in one year per 1,000 persons of corresponding sex and age group)

	1975–76	1978–79	1980–81	1982–83	1984–85	1986–87	1987–88	1988–89	1990	1991
Total men at age										
60–64	32.5	34.3	35.5	43.3	35.3	31.1	31.1	31.7	34.2	34.6
65–69	47.4	48.2	48.8	50.7	50.7	45.9	45.5	45.4	46.6	47.3
70–74	71.2	71.8	71.5	68.3	70.7	67.7	69.1	67.8	103.6*	104.0*
75–79	106.0	104.3	104.9	100.3	105.0	96.5	95.1	96.4		
80–84	156.8	156.1	154.0	143.1	149.1	137.0	140.0	139.8		
85 and over	223.8	231.2	237.2	229.7	241.2	225.5	218.4	207.8		
Total women at age										
60–64	13.4	14.0	14.4	13.9	14.5	13.2	13.3	13.5	13.5	13.6
65–69	21.8	22.0	22.1	22.0	23.5	22.2	21.9	21.7	22.0	22.0
70–74	37.5	37.6	37.6	36.3	38.1	37.2	38.3	37.4	77.9	78.1
75–79	69.2	64.3	62.4	61.0	64.7	61.7	61.4	61.2		
80–84	113.5	113.0	115.1	104.1	104.8	97.3	99.2	100.1		
85 and over	184.7	188.4	195.9	184.2	209.3	181.6	177.0	174.0		
Total population	10.6	11.5	11.9	11.7	12.0	10.4	10.5	10.7	–	–

Sources: [171], p. 115; [184], p. 420.
* These figures reflect the age group 75–85 and over.

Table 6
Age-specific death rates by major class of cause of death, Russia, 1987–88 (per 1,000 and %)

	Men		Women	
	1987	1988	1987	1988
Circulatory disease				
per 1,000	479.4	482.8	717.1	724.5
%	45.7	44.9	68.1	67.9
Cancer				
per 1,000	214.1	219.7	157.6	158.7
%	20.4	20.4	14.9	14.8
Respiratory diseases				
per 1,000	75.2	76.1	48.5	50.1
%	7.1	7.1	4.6	4.7
Accidents. poisoning, and trauma				
per 1,000	162.2	179.2	48.4	51.3
%	15.5	16.7	4.6	4.8
All causes				
per 1,000	1,048.7	1,072.2	1,052.5	1,065.8
%	100.0	100.0	100.0	100.0

Source: [184], pp. 588–92.

2 Microsocial

2.1 Self-identification

The official "co-ordinates" of personal self-identification, strictly regulated until the 1980s, were eroded by the socio-economic transformations of the mid-1980s. The palette of self-identification possibilities became substantially broader, its emphases moving from politico-ideological positions to economic, ethno-cultural, and religious ones.

The rule of official Soviet ideology led to fairly strict regulation of the process of personal self-identification, at least in its externally manifested forms. The number of social self-definitions around which self-identification could take place was quite limited by the ideological principles of merging, unification, and erasure of borders between strata and groups for the sake of achieving social homogeneity, the most important characteristic of a communist society under construction.

The set of self-identification definitions was not only limited in ideological scope, but also set out in various forms in which people were to supply personal information; throughout their lives, people had to fill out a variety of different official forms, answer questionnaires, and deal with other documents all of which bore the same "ideologically consistent" set of self-identification definitions (such as whether they were "worker," "collective farmer," or "intelligentsia").

The destruction of the official communist ideology and the disintegration of official social coherence in the late 1980s led to a breakdown of the established system of social self-determination of personality. The search for a new identity became one of the central issues in Russian social development in the late 1980s and early 1990s. Within this context, the acute problem arose of personal self-determination under new economic, social, and ideological circumstances, which prescribed new vectors (beyond those of prescribed political, ideological grounds) and new phases and thresholds of the process.

Establishing one's ethnic identity became a prevailing orientation in the process of personal self-determination after the mid-1980s. During the period when the idea of the "united Soviet people" ruled, belonging to a certain national group was officially reduced to a symbolic gesture such as filling out the "national-ity" line in passports, since equality of all nations and peoples was an ideological dogma. Putting this ideology into practice had very different effects on different nationalities. For instance, equality was rather doubtful for peoples who suffered repression in the 1940s and 1950s and for Jews, who were secretly but effectively limited in career movement, certain kinds of professional activity, and so on, all of which could not fail to leave its mark upon the issue of national self-identification.

The gap between ideology and practice often gave rise to an "adoptive-identification" model of behaviour among people of non-Russian nationalities, who tried to identify themselves, on the level of formal attributes (above all, in the line on the passport), with the Russian nation. This took place when children born of nationally mixed marriages (with one parent being Russian) took out passports, and in the process gave preference to the Russian ethnic lineage. At the same time, the social double standard gave birth to a double standard on the level of individual self-awareness and behaviour among people of non-Russian nationalities, whereby "playing according to the rules" of the officially declared identification was often combined with real, "internal" personal self-identification through awareness of one's ethnic roots and seeking out close interaction with others of the same nationality, through conserving ethnically coloured lifestyle elements (national cuisine, socialization traditions, etc.), private cultural studies, practising the religious rituals of one's ethnic group, and so on.

The problem of national self-identification during the social transformations of the 1980s and 1990s also arose among the Russian population, which comprised 82.6% of the total population of Russia in 1979, 81.5% in 1989, and 83% in 1993. In spite of the absolute prevalence of Russians in the national structure, the idea of "unity of nations," the historically formed multi-ethnic basis of Russian culture, and some other factors eroded, to a considerable degree, Russian-centred tendencies in the ethnic self-identification of the population. The idea of Russia as a multinational state, still alive in Russians' consciousness, is interconnected, for a relatively high percentage, with a sense that national identity (that of their own and that of others) is not important. According to the results of a 1993 survey, 62% of respondents held this opinion, while 38% answered that they "had never forgotten about their national identity" ([320]; see table 1).

After the mid-1980s, economic self-determination increasingly meant quick wealth, with a simultaneously decreasing interest in socio-professional status. Until the mid-1980s, the emphasis was not on economic success as such, but on self-determination of professional status, since economic inequality was not a legitimized fact of social life under the primacy of "collective ownership." According to the

Table 1
Significance of ethnic identity among respondents in Moscow, 1993

	Ethnic identity – my own or others' – is unimportant (%)	I have never forgotten that I am a Russian (%)
Unskilled labourers	52.7	47.3
Office workers	64.0	36.0
Graduates from specialized secondary schools	61.7	38.3
High-school graduates	67.8	32.2
Mid-level managers	57.8	42.2
Businesspeople, farmers	42.8	57.2

Source: [320], p. 112.

official ideology, all people were equal – but some of them, public opinion revealed, were "more equal than others."

The process of intensive socio-economic differentiation of the late 1980s and early 1990s stimulated individuals to comprehend their own economic status, their real position within the economic structure of society, and gave rise to processes of self-determination involving notions unknown to the socialist vocabulary, such as "poor" and "rich." Income became the most meaningful criterion for dividing people into groups and for a corresponding identification with these groups, as opposed to professional or political identification.

A survey of the adult urban Russian population in 1993 found that 5% regarded themselves as very poor, 18% as poor, and 42% as "poorly provided for." No one considered himself or herself wealthy; 2% regarded themselves as well-to-do ([342]).

A growing number of people openly define themselves as religious. Official statistics from the 1960s to the early 1980s stated that almost all of the population were atheists, with only a small percentage regarding themselves as religious. In the late 1980s, about 10% of the adult population considered themselves religious; according to a 1993 survey, this proportion was 40%. The greatest increase took place among those 16–17 years of age, where the proportion of respondents considering themselves religious was 64%, 1.5 times higher than the average in other age groups ([163]). Eleven per cent called themselves nonreligious, and a little more than 3% professed to be atheists, the latter category being almost completely absent in the youth group. Identification of oneself as religious was much higher in large cities. In Moscow, for example, 64% regarded themselves as religious, while 34% were undecided ([19]).

Religiosity bears the same correlation with education level as that found in previous periods. Among people with primary education, 89% are religious; among those with eight years of education, 66%; among those with secondary and higher education, 47% and 38%, respectively. Among those who claimed to be nonreligious, military personnel comprised 21%, teachers 11%, and workers in the cultural sector 9%. Turning to nontraditional religions became a fairly characteristic phenomenon of religious self-identification in the 1980s, when, on average, 10% of respondents adhered to such religions. Of those who professed to adhere to a nontraditional religion, 10% were intellectuals, 21% were health workers, and 18% were students ([163]).

I.M. Bykhovskaya and T.V. Kudryavtseva

2.2 Kinship Networks

From the 1960s to the 1980s, a steady value emphasis on family life was accompanied by a strengthening trend toward nuclear families. Nevertheless, it was common for two or three generations of a single family to live together because of a lack of housing. Socio-economic changes in the 1980s and 1990s brought the problems of intergenerational aid, family survival, and "social orphanage" to the fore.

Family has retained its significance as an element of the microsocial environment. Nearly 90% of the population belong to a family, and this rate is rather stable: in 1959, the proportion of family members was 89.8%; in 1970, 90.1%; in 1979, 89.8% ([341]; see table 1). The increase in absolute numbers of families from the 1960s to the 1980s was greater than was the growth of the population. The proportion of never-married people dropped.

After the 1980s, the number of marriages dropped. In 1987, over 1.4 million marriages were contracted; in 1990, 1.3 million; in 1991, almost 1.3 million; in 1992, a further reduction in the number of marriages and the marriage rate was recorded. The incidence of marriage gradually decreased. In the early 1980s, 10.6 marriages were contracted per 1,000 people, but in 1990 this figure had dropped to 8.9, and in 1991 to 8.6 ([157]). In the European part of Russia, where the number of marriages in previous years had been below average, in 1991 it decreased sharply. In the southern regions, where the number of marriages was traditionally higher, there was

Table 1
Urban household composition, Russia, 1989

	(millions of persons)
Total urban population	107.96
living in a family	95.06
living apart from a family	5.56
singles	7.34

Source: [73], pp. 146–7.

either a slower reduction or a slight increase. This trend reflected the greater significance of and higher social status accorded to family in these regions.

In the 1980s, the typical urban three-person family lost its predominance. In the 1970s, this type of family accounted for about one third of all urban families in Russia. By the end of 1980s, two-person families became more numerous, while three-person families accounted for 28% of all families, dropping closer to the proportion of four-person families (see table 2). The proportion of families with five persons or more remained stable during the 1970 and 1980s. In other words, some recent notions about family planning did not change the priority accorded to a small family.

The number of family members diminished until the 1970s and grew somewhat in the 1990s; the former was associated with fewer children being born. Families in big towns had fewer children, and the trend toward nuclear families became more evident. Increasingly, young couples wanted to live separately from their parents. More than one third of those who lived with their parents before marriage left home after marrying. In the first 10 years of married life, 58% of young couples began to live separately from their parents ([56]).

Throughout the period under study, families consisting of parents and their married children showed a tendency to cohabit, with a three-generation family as a result. Most often, adult children were living with a divorced or widowed parent or parent-in-law who needed care and support that was not available in the network of state institutions, which was underdeveloped and had a low level of service. The other reason for family cohabitation was to have grandparents help with raising small children, though the proportion of this type of cohabitation was comparatively low and failed to withstand the increasing trend toward nuclear families ([341]).

A large proportion of family members arranged to live in proximity to each other in towns in the 1980s and 1990s. In such families, elders and grown-up married children maintained separate households but lived as near as possible to each other, sometimes in neighbouring buildings or even in neighbouring apartments that

Table 2
Number of families by size in cities and towns, Russia, 1979, 1989 (millions)

| | Total | Number of persons in family | | | | | | Average family size (persons) |
		2	3	4	5	6	10+	
1979	25.5	7.8	8.6	6.3	2.0	0.57	0.018	3.2
1989	29.7	9.8	8.8	7.7	2.3	0.69	0.022	3.2

Source: [73], pp. 60–1.

they managed to obtain, from the 1960s to the 1980s, through exchanging dwellings, and in the 1990s through exchanging or purchasing. As in the case of cohabiting families, this arrangement made it easier to care for babies and small children, and for ageing grandparents, and provided for other aspects of kinship support and co-operation.

The importance of married children living with their parents in their town of origin for maintaining a community of extended families can hardly be overestimated. In 1979, 52.9% of the population was living where they had been born and had never moved away. Those born in their community of residence and those living for more than 10 years in one place accounted for about 78% of the population, with rural inhabitants prevailing ([184]).

Elders' financial support of their children, and less often vice-versa, within the framework of a cohabiting family increased. According to recent research, parents' contribution to their married children's finances has increased substantially from generation to generation. Surveys in 1991 showed that 58% of families consider their parents' support to be their only or main source of income. Only 6% of young families earn their own living, usually because of the lack of one or both parents ([157]). Without this parental support, 18% of respondents said that they would not be able to survive; 32%, that they would have to spend less money on food and clothing; 10%, that they would have to quit high school ([230]).

The dependence of young and adult children on their parents has given rise to a special kind of black humour involving ghastly portrayals of "children's liberation," with senseless cruelty and murders in which parents or grandparents and children are, in turn, their victims and executioners ([44]).

The 1980s and 1990s have given rise to a period of crisis in kinship networks, including family quarrels. In 1991, more than 37,000 children left their families, preferring to be homeless ([130b]). More than 160,000 children were being raised in state institutions (orphanages, boarding schools, foster homes), 10% of whom were so-called social orphans: each year in the 1990s there was an increase of 50,000 children whose parents either deserted them, were imprisoned, or were deprived of their parental rights ([57]).

I.M. Byhovskaya

2.3 Community and Neighbourhood Types

The growth of urban communities was stable from 1960 to the 1980s, but slowed in the early 1990s, when there was an increase in rural populations. As living conditions improved, a disaffiliation with immediate neighbourhood occurred and new types of communities arose.

From the 1960s to the 1980s, urban populations grew. The proportion of the population dwelling in large and small urban communities grew constantly up to 1991, while the proportion of the rural population decreased constantly (see table 1) because of migrations from the countryside to towns.

Young people were more likely to move from rural to urban communities. From 1959 to 1989, the number of rural dwellers aged 20 to 24 years dropped by more than half. A natural decrease was observed in a number of regions (mostly the central ones), in some of which migration losses of rural populations were combined with a fall in total population ([157]).

The mass movement from rural to urban communities gave rise to a stratum of "new urban dwellers," who retained (or tried to) many features of the rural way of life. They maintained active contacts with their relatives in the countryside, which limited the degree of their contacts with members of urban communities. Urban living standards affected a larger and larger proportion of the rural population (including those who remained in the countryside).

Deliberate importation of labour to large industrial centres – especially to Moscow and Leningrad – from other parts of the country gave rise to a special social stratum with little education, who were housed in company hostels and whose rights were limited (e.g., exile for repeated misbehaviour) and new social aspirations often went unfulfilled. This stratum aroused antipathy among a considerable part of the permanent population in large cities.

After 1991, urban populations began to decrease and those of rural regions to increase, although urban populations remained much larger in absolute numbers. In the early 1990s, the outflow of rural populations was, on the whole,

Table 1
Number and proportion of urban and rural populations, Russia, 1959–93

	1959	1970	1979	1989	1991	1993
Urban population (million)	61.1	80.9	95.3	108.4	109.8	108.9
Proportion of urban population (%)	52.4	62.3	69.3	73.6	74.0	73.0
Rural population (million)	55.9	49.1	42.2	39.0	38.7	39.8
Proportion of rural population (%)	47.6	37.7	30.7	26.4	26.0	27.0

Sources: [73], p. 9; [242], p. 52.

compensated for by immigration from other republics of the CIS, especially by young people. Simultaneously, the scale and intensity of the population influx to urban communities decreased. Thus, migration to cities among those aged 15–19 decreased from 166,800 in 1989 to 74,200 in 1991. Among people 20–30 years of age, net migration to cities became negative.

These changes were caused by decentralization of production, a rise in the threat of unemployment in industrial centres, a sharp increase in the cost of living in cities and towns, a fall in the prestige of education, and formation of a new type of economy involving farming.

Migrants to rural communities mentioned family situations (98.8%), changing work-place (20.0%), and poor living conditions (18.1%) as the main causes for their move. Of particular note was the group of those aged 24–25 moving back to the country who had not lost, in their years of living in the city, their love of the land and rural life, and gave this reason as the most important factor in their return to the country. On the whole, in the 1990s fewer young people living in rural regions were planning to move to a town. About 70% of representatives of the agricultural class were going to live in the country and only 10% of respondents expressed a firm intention to move to town ([157]).

From 1970 to the 1980s, most cities in outlying areas grew. Before the 1960s, a considerable proportion of the urban population was concentrated in industrially developed regions. In the 1960s, a "centrifugal" force developed, linked to the formation of a great number of large and small urban communities in resource-extraction sites, resulting in the creation of new urban infrastructures in previously unpopulated regions. Thus, in a number of regions of northern Russia, from the 1960s to the 1980s, urban populations grew by a factor of 3 (Yakutia), 12 (Yamal), and even 25 (Khanty-Mansi) ([184]).

New urban communities formed in the 1960s and 1970s were remarkable for rather high social (particularly professional) homogeneity, connected with their creation on the basis of large-scale industrial production (for instance, the Togliatti city motor factory) or research activities (Dubna, Pushchino, Akademgorodok near Novosibirsk, etc.). These communities also include numerous closed (secret) scientific centres in the military-industrial complex, connected with the development of advanced technologies. In new industrial cities, the absence of historical and cultural traditions meant underdevelopment of the cultural sphere and high criminality. In new and isolated scientific and scientific-technological communities, the high educational level of the population provided certain privileges and led to the formation of a special atmosphere of culturally concentrated life and intensive social interaction.

Male populations were prevalent in the new urban communities formed during the 1960s and 1970s. In the northern, Ural, and far-eastern regions and in Siberia, a considerable proportion of the migrants were people who had signed term contracts for seasonal work, most of them men. On the contrary, in many central regions, especially in cities with established "women's" production sectors and in the countryside, a substantial prevalence of female populations (in rural areas, by up to 20–30%) developed ([157]).

From 1960 to 1985, levels of urbanization in different regions of Russia were converging. A stable trend toward urbanization became evident (see table 2). Cities with a population of over one million grew most intensively between the 1960s and the late 1980s (the number of these cities in the USSR increased from 3 to 23), as well as cities with populations of between 100,000 and 1 million (see table 3).

Several large urban centres predominated in increases in population (see table 4), Moscow foremost among them; this city maintained a constant lead over the other large cities both in population size and in indexes of quality of life. Moscow alone represented 23% of the increase in urban population in the Central economic from 1960 to 1969; this proportion rose to 40% between 1979 and 1985. Moscow, which maintained a special status up to the end of the 1980s (best supply of goods and services, limitations on registration of new residents, provision of infrastructure, etc.), acted as a kind of showcase; not only for Russia, but for the entire USSR, it was regarded by the authorities as a sort of advanced model and a pattern to be followed. This resulted in animosity and envy among residents of other cities and towns, who saw Muscovites as a privileged population. It was in the large cities that the tendency to distinguish between "us" (permanent inhabitants) and "them" (free or forced migrants) was most obvious.

The increase in national self-awareness in the mid-1980s was expressed, among other ways, in the desire of many national communities to consolidate settlement areas. In 1994, Russia contained 23 national-territorial units (regions, *okrugs*, autonomous regions), historically settled and juridically established. The

Table 2
Number of urban communities, Russia, 1959–92

	1959	1970	1979	1989	1992
Cities and towns	877	969	999	1,037	1,057
small urban communities	1,495	1,869	2,046	2,193	2,164
Total urban communities	2,372	2,838	3,045	3,230	3,221

SOURCES: [73], p 5; [171], p. 87.

Table 3
Urban centres by population size, Russia, 1979–92

Communities with population of (000)	Number of urban communities			Population (million)		
	1979	1989	1992	1979	1989	1992
up to 3	537	602	613	1,0	1,1	1,1
10–20	504	564	567	6,9	7,9	7,9
20–50	379	398	396	11,8	12,5	12,5
100–300	86	87	90	13,0	13,1	13,4
500–1 million	18	22	21	12,7	14,0	13,3
over 1 million	8	12	13	18,9	25,1	26,2

Source: [171], p. 91.

Table 4
Population changes in the largest cities, Russia, 1959–89

	1959 (000)	1970 (000)	1979 (000)	1989 (000)	1992 (000)	1989 (% change since 1979)
Moscow	5,847	7,154	8,111	8,966	8,957	110.5
Leningrad	3,367	4,027	4,588	5,023	5,004	109.5
Gorki	941	1,170	1,373	1,438	1,441	107.0
Novosibirsk	885	1,161	1,343	1,423	1,442	109.5

Sources: [73], pp. 181, 193, 223; [171], p. 95; [184], pp. 38–9.

resolution of questions connected with creation of new (or sometime restoring existent) national-territorial communities (such as the German republic in the Volga region, the Cossack autonomous settlements, etc.) is, in many cases, rather difficult for various reasons (juridical, socio-historical, etc.). At the same time, there was *de facto* recognition of these settlements, where national minorities (the Koreans, the Veps, the Kazakhs, various smaller groups in the north, etc.) lived and shared cultural traditions, languages, and so on.

From 1960 to the 1970s, there was a change in the structure and type of available housing. Mass construction of apartment buildings during this period was aimed at solving the problem of resettling much of the population from ramshackle houses to simple separate apartments in hastily built modular five-storey buildings, leaving the questions of comfort and aesthetics for the future. There were still a large number of communal flats, where from 2 to 10 (and sometimes more) families lived, using a common kitchen and other auxiliary facilities. The breaking up of communal (multi-family) flats constituted a non-negligible factor of change in character of communities in large cities, which had hitherto been structured around proximity of residence. Permanent populations who had traditionally lived in the central part of a city had to move to districts with new buildings, losing not only a location they had got used to, but also their connections (formed over a long period, often generations) with neighbours. By 1989, more than 70% of the Russian population had separate flats (see table 5), which led to dislocation of neighbourhoods, the rupture of regular interaction networks, and sometimes, as a consequence, to loss of social well-being.

The development of a system of country houses and gardening co-operatives and associations led to the formation of new types of communities – neighbourhood groups at summer dwellings, which are often 150–200 km away from the main residence. This combination of vacation homes and permanent rural settlements encouraged a specific type of seasonal community.

Table 5
Distribution of urban population by type of dwelling, Russia, 1989

	(million people)	(%)
Indicated type of dwelling	102.11	100.0
individual house (or a part of it)	14.95	15.1
separate flat	72.00	73.4
communal (multi-family) flat	7.89	8.0
hostel	7.22	7.3
other type of dwelling	0.59	0.6
renting dwelling belonging to someone else	0.93	0.9
Total urban population	107.96	

Source: [73], pp. 148–9.

I.M. Bykhovskaya

2.4 Decentralization

Throughout the period studied, autonomy was conditional: at all levels of the state structure, top priority was believed to belong to the interests of the whole, but not the parts. Attempts at increasing autonomy that took place in the 1990s caused numerous conflicts.

Administrative-territorial divisions were designed to account for any expression of local autonomy. Moreover, changes in these divisions that took place in the 1990s were only partly explained by an accommodation of local concerns. Socialism was designed to be a society of centralized planning, and there was no opportunity to develop a self-governing free environment on a local level. Soviet federalism had a utilitarian character, largely determined by the necessity of preserving the multi-national state.

Until the USSR fell apart in 1991, Russia was the "first among equals" in the federation of 15 Soviet socialist republics. In 1991, as the USSR disintegrated, Russia became an independent state, its administrative-territorial divisions changed, and new entities within the federation arose (see table 1). The state structure was asymmetrical; the entities within the federation were based on different principles and enjoyed unequal powers. Thus, presidents and heads of governments were elected in the republics, while heads of regional administrations were appointed by the president, the apparatus of the federation and of its entities as a whole appeared to be intact, with the result that there was no plurality of power sources or division of power.

In available statistics, no differentiation is made between personnel in state and municipal governments. The overall decrease in staff numbers was in fact artificial: many municipal employees were camouflaged as employees of other institutions.

In 1991, after the attempted coup d'état, the question of prohibiting former workers in the Communist Party apparatus from occupying positions (except elective ones) in state structures was discussed, but public opinion did not support this idea. In 1993, a law was adopted which prohibited state officials from combining their activities with working in commercial or other private organizations.

After 1990, a trend toward regionalization became evident. In the 1990s, the central government expressed its desire for using a federal form of government as a means of limiting centrifugal tendencies, thus impeding regional aspirations for greater autonomy. The regions, for their part, tried to use the federal principle to limit the powers of the central authorities and to increase the share of the budget going

Table 1
Administrative-territorial division of Russia, 1986, 1993

	1986	1993
Autonomous republics	16	21
Autonomous regions	5	1
Districts	6	6
Regions	49	49
Autonomous *okrugs*	10	11
Moscow and St. Petersburg	–	2
Cities and towns	1,030	1,057
Small urban communities	2,178	2,164

Sources: [111c], p. 2; [171], p. 91; [177], p. 265.

to regional institutions (see table 2). In addition, a movement toward national separatism developed. Attempts by Chechnya to leave the federation in 1994–95, for instance, led to outright armed conflict.

The situation was reflected in public opinion. Even after the USSR broke up in 1991, a VP poll of public-opinion makers showed that 39% of them believed that Russian leaders should acknowledge that regions demanding separation from the Russian Federation had the right to leave; 26% believed that their leaders should act as circumstances dictated; 12% believed the regions should be kept within the federation by any means; and 9% felt that the regions should be kept within the federation by means of negotiations. Among those advocating the unity of Russia "by any means," most were representatives of executive power at various levels; those who gave this answer most often gave the following reasons: that "Russia must be united and indivisible" (47%) and that it was "necessary to protect the rights of Russians in autonomous republics" (7%) ([91g]).

In 1992, the prospect of Russia breaking into several independent states and territories was thought to be probable by 8% of respondents representing the general population; in 1993, this proportion had risen to 33.8%. Among these respondents, 19% felt that republics and territories attempting to escape subordination to the central government were acting correctly and 58% felt that they were acting incorrectly; measures taken by the government and the parliament to preserve Russian unity were considered insufficient by 66.2% and sufficient by 8.8% ([219a]).

Independence of local powers remained largely formal until the mid-1990s. Throughout the socialist period, local authorities were, to all intents and purposes, completely dependent upon Party organs and higher-level Soviet institutions and had very limited powers. Consistently, fewer people voted in local elections than in

Table 2
Share of local budget expenditures in GNP, 1992–94 (%)

1992	1993	1994
12.5	15.2	11.1

Source: [313c], p. 1.

elections to the Supreme Soviet. An indirect indicator of the low prestige of local authorities was also found in the fact that the lower the level of Soviet the higher the share of women among its deputies: in 1985, women comprised 35.3% of members of the Supreme Soviet and 49.7% of *okrugs* and regional and village soviets ([177]).

During the period of reforms, public opinion saw local authorities as bastions of conservatism. In a 1992 survey by VP, 33% of respondents felt that local authorities were most reluctant to adopt agricultural reforms (connected with the development of farming); 12% attributed this to heads of state and collective farms (*kolkhozes* and *sovkhozes*); 15%, to the central government; and 9%, to the Supreme Soviet of the Russian Federation ([91r]).

The structural reforms of local authorities were practically incomprehensible to the population. In 1991, 33% of Muscovites surveyed said that the establishment of the new Moscow government (mayoralty, prefects, etc.) was justified, while 33% said that it was not; in 1992, these figures were 50% and 39%, respectively. The influence of the new municipal institutions on individuals' lives was evaluated most negatively by persons aged 40–59 and by managers and workers in state enterprises. The highest number of positive evaluations was recorded among younger and better educated respondents and among persons involved in the new private economy ([91b]). As for the activities of the city government structures created a year and a half before the survey, 84% of Muscovites were either poorly nor not at all informed about it ([91f]).

The population began manifesting some interest in self-government only in the mid-1990s. Many investigators feel that free discussion of social themes is not well developed among Russians because of long-standing traditions, and that there is little inclination to self-government. Indeed, veterans' and pensioners' councils created in residential communities did not enjoy any authority. Local self-government councils, which were created in the late 1980s in the wake of a general politicization, almost disappeared by the beginning of the 1990s, to be resurrected in the mid-1990s.

I.A. Boutenko

2.5 Voluntary Associations

A long period of existence of pseudo-voluntary associations initiated and regulated by party and state structures, was, in the mid-1980s, supplanted by a vigorous process of formation of a large number of truly voluntary associations covering the whole spectrum of social life and built on a heterogeneous social base.

Throughout the existence of the totalitarian Soviet state, many so-called voluntary associations (trade and artistic unions, co-operative associations, etc.) were formal and occupied solely with state-regulated activities. The possibility of creating an association was determined by the similarity of its orientations to the official ideology, and the character of its activities was to be regulated strictly by the state as well as by the organs of the "state within the state" – the Communist Party.

The fact that an association was "voluntary," under these circumstances, often meant simply its formal independence from state structures, and membership in such associations as the Voluntary Society of Assistance to the Army, Air Force, and Navy was, in essence and in form, automatic, or "voluntary-compulsory," as it was unofficially called in the 1960s and 1970s.

The constant increase in membership in the Communist Party and the Komsomol, in trade unions, and in various educational associations and unions in the 1970s and 1980s was, to a large degree, an ideologically determined feature and an obligatory objective to be achieved by any means. Though perhaps a certain part of the population was motivated by real voluntarism and a real desire to enter this or that association, the overwhelming majority of citizens simply acted according to the rules of the game for the sake of preservation, enhancing their official position, or receiving a larger share of distributed goods. Thus, there were certain privileges for members of some voluntary associations (e.g., associations of artistic workers) and limitations for non-members (e.g., exclusion of a social-sciences teacher in a university for a non-Party member).

Alongside ideological or political associations from the 1960s to the 1980s were many associations with productive or commercial purposes (*kolkhozes*, producers' and consumers' co-operatives, housing and country-house co-operatives, etc.). These helped citizens satisfy specific needs (housing, organizing some forms of professional activities, etc.) within the limits of the strictly regulated system that governed even these formally non-state associations.

In addition to "legitimate" associations created by official structures, in the late 1960s and mid-1980s, associations of like-minded people oriented toward activities not corresponding with the ideology and organizational structures of the Soviet system were formed. Groups of dissidents, mostly among creative intellectuals in big cities, were the most outstanding example of such genuinely voluntary associations.

Opposition to the official orientation was characteristic not only of many unofficial political associations but also of those of other types, among them cultural, educational, and health-improvement groups. In the 1960s and 1970s, rock-music and disco fan clubs, amateur song clubs, and Yoga, Zen Buddhism, karate, and other groups were multiplying with improbable rapidity, becoming stronger and finding a base of solidarity mostly in their common opposition to the official ideology and culture. Economic, culture-protection, pedagogical, artistic and aesthetic, physical culture and health-improvement, socio-political, and other initiatives were usually seen, by both the authorities and the public, either as something exotic and unnecessary with no correspondence to the vital needs of the society, or, more often, as a political or ideological threat to the social system.

The official ideological system tried to show some flexibility toward heterogeneous informal associations, combining the "shooting down" of those seen as especially dangerous with attempts to adapt and transform the others (attempting to open a dialogue with amateur song clubs, to "tame" ecological associations, etc.). Such a policy of threats and bribery both resulted in institutionalization of some voluntary associations and their acquisition of an official status, and stimulated many associations, clubs, circles to "go underground" (in private homes, basements, etc.). Characteristic of this period of latent existence of voluntary associations was the samizdat phenomenon (home-made copies of books and articles and secret exchanges of these materials between readers).

The long period of underground existence became a kind of incubation period, during which many voluntary associations formed their "ideologies," power structures, communication systems, information channels, and so on. This is why, when political changes and the process of mass cultural pluralization started in the mid-1980s, they were, to a certain degree, accompanied by an unexpected appearance of hundreds of quite well organized socio-initiative groups.

In the mid-1980s, against the background of the weakening communist organizational and ideological system, the field of social life was being actively occupied by so-called informal associations, regarded as groups completely different in character, goals, activities, social nature, and organization from counter-cultural groups, which were emerging to become politicized associations with global ideas and intentions. The only common denominator among such diverse structures was an orientation toward independence from official power structures. Some 600 associations of this kind existed in Russia in 1990, including 230 citizens' initiatives and socio-political associations, more than 60 associations dealing with ecological problems, and about 50 national-cultural movements (see table 1). According to a 1994 survey, almost 70% of the population felt that the potential for citizens to form voluntary associations had changed fundamentally since 1985 (see table 2).

From the mid-1980s to the early 1990s, informal associations changed substantially the orientation and direction of their activities: opposition ideas lost their dominant position, as distinct from the case for dissidents' and related associations of the pre-perestroika period (1970s and early 1980s). While the latter had been characterized by their oppositionist, negative orientation, one feature of many informal associations in the late 1980s and 1990s was their positive, constructive orientation; furthermore, they defined their activities not on the basis of protest, but in accordance with their own truly voluntary and freely chosen goals.

Many associations that arose on the wave of euphoria that accompanied the downfall of the totalitarian system had politically positive programmes dealing with support of the new regime, consolidation of advocates of democratic reforms, and so on, thus reflecting a new basis for voluntary associations.

A broader spectrum of voluntary associations, determined both by the processes of social differentiation and by the rise of quite new, formerly unknown phenomena in the structure of social life, was an obvious trend of the mid-1980s to the early 1990s. Among voluntary associations, along with traditional artistic, women's, veterans', and other associations emerged such formerly unimaginable (for different reasons) associations as the Beer-lovers' Party, the Union of Advocates of Sexual Minorities, the Union of Social Protection of Military Men and Members of Their Families, and the Society of Tolkienists. New phenomena of economic life gave rise to such voluntary associations as the Association of Depositors Having Lost Their Savings and the Association of Shareholders Having Sustained Losses or Lost Their Deposits. A meaningful place in the spectrum of voluntary associations was occupied by religious associations.

The political stratum of "informal movement" was partly legitimized through the creation of parties, movements, and youth organizations and ceased to exist as a mass movement.

Most youth associations have low membership, and polls carried out in the late 1980s and the early 1990s found a substantial drop in interest among young people in joining any association, especially those with political programmes and orientations (see table 3). Only 15% of urban dwellers and 13% of

Table 1
Types of informal organizations, Russia, 1990

Group type	Number
People's fronts	32
Citizens' initiatives, socio-political associations	231
Associations of clubs	33
Rights-protecting associations	13
Memorial, voluntary historico-educational societies	4
Ecological associations	62
Religious-philosophical associations, health movements, groups of mutual social assistance and charity	8
Alternative-cultural associations	50
National-cultural movements	47
Associations of Afghanistan war veterans	20
Unofficial political associations and parties	13
Youth centres	85
Total	619

Source: [234], pp. 6–112.

Table 2
Perceived opportunity to join associations, compared with the pre-Perestroika period, Russia, 1994

Response	%
Better	67.2
Unchanged	16.0
Worse	3.9
Found it difficult to answer	12.9

Source: [111k].

Table 3
Proportion of young people involved in political activities, Russia, 1989, 1991 (%)

1989	1990	1981
6.5	4.7	1.7

Source: [157], p. 130.

rural dwellers admitted to being members of informal associations. According to polls carried out in 1993, 84.7% of respondents (young people under 30) had not heard of and did not know anything about the activities of new youth associations; no more than 7–10% expressed their intention to become active in an association ([157]).

Most associations were musical, sports, or sports-related groups; becoming more and more significant were associations of businesspeople and other representatives of the new Russian business sector.

By 1992, the Ministry of Justice of Russia had registered 54 youth and children's associations of an all-Russian or interregional scale; more than 150 associations had been created on the regional level. In 1994, there were 92 associations, including all-Russian and interregional associations and youth subdivisions of "adult" associations (e.g., the youth division of the Union of Esperantists or the Youth Section of Russian Noble Assembly). Fewer than 10 of these organizations had existed before 1990 (86).

Table 4
Structure of youth organizations, Russia, 1993 (%)

International	13.0
Interrepublican	3.7
Interregional	44.4
All-Russian	38.9

Source: [157], p. 131.

I.M. Bykhovskaya

2.6 Social-Interaction Networks

Interaction with neighbours was constant and broad in scope in the 1960s and 1970s. In the 1990s, as a result of urbanization and the breaking up of communal flats, this was accompanied by a growth in and increased significance of interactions with relatives and with a narrow circle of family and friends at a time when there was increased social instability and socio-psychological discomfort, accompanying the social transformations in the 1990s.

A significant part of the interaction structure characteristic of the 1960s to 1980s was communicating with work colleagues; although this type of network

persisted, it lost some of its significance in the structure of the 1990s. Since communication networks were ignored as a form of social practice in state statistics and were measured under the rubric of other activities, it is very difficult to analyze the structure and prevailing orientations of different population groups regarding its character, forms, and the social circles within which it took place. Studies of the 1960s and 1970s showed that time spent communicating with work colleagues in large cities was comparable to that spent communicating within the family circle and was many times important more than communication with friends and neighbours (see table 1). This was linked not only with the ample opportunities for conversations at the work place (due to inefficiency), but also with the high significance of socio-professional status and professional contacts. However, it is difficult to say whether professional topics predominated in these conversations.

In the late 1980s and early 1990s, there was an obvious drop in interest in socio-professional status, and hence in work-related networks, among many social groups. Emphasis moved to networks comprising primarily friends and relatives with similar lifestyles and outlooks. The trend was manifested most clearly among young people, among whom the right of choice, including the choice of one's circle of friends, was highly appreciated, and among whom the notions of in-group and out-group, formed on the basis of informal signs, were important.

The formation of new types of professional communities during the economic reforms of the 1980s and 1990s gave rise to new forms of professional networks based on contacts that had originated among friends. Liberalization of economic activity changed the professional networks of many people, since it created conditions and possibilities for professional consolidation beyond a given workplace. The creation of private firms by previously formed groups of like-minded persons became quite widespread in commercial activity; this, in turn, resulted in new forms of professional interaction.

Given the socio-economic instability of the late 1980s and mid-1990s, the value of interaction among relatives and of circles of friends and like-minded persons increased. The increase in the number of stressful situations and in general uncertainty was detrimental to interpersonal relations. Under these circumstances, there was an obvious trend toward an increase in the supporting role of family relations as of a sort of a "life preserver" helping to preserve stability in the dynamic stream of rapid social change.

A significant part of leisure time was given over to interaction within networks of friends, more frequently among workers than among intellectuals, though this sort of activity was quite characteristic of the latter as well (see table 2).

Table 1
Distribution of time for married people, Russia, 1969 (hours per day)

	Man	Woman
Alone (sleeping included)	10.7	10.3
With family members	6.3	4.9
With friends. neighbours	0.3	0.3
With work colleagues	6.2	5.4
With strangers (in public places)	1.0	1.2

Source: [336], p. 161.

Table 2
Leisure activities, Russia, 1980s (%)*

	Intellectuals	Office workers	Industrial workers
Studying, self-education	49.5	26.0	21.7
Attending theatres. concerts. exhibitions	25.6	18.9	17.6
Reading fiction	48.1	54.7	57.2
In artistic activities	9.4	8.5	7.9
Hobbies	10.1	4.71	5.8
Excursions, travel	15.6	11.0	16.1
Meeting friends. hosting guests	46.1	47.0	58.0
Attending restaurants. caf_s	4.9	47.8	7.2
Professional development	50.6	16.4	19.3
Attending lectures and debates	17.0	7.1	7.8

Source: [267], p. 120.
* More than one answer was possible.

According to surveys, interaction with relatives and acquaintances served as an unplanned but highly valued activity. Thus, spending one's vacation with relatives and acquaintances was seen as being as desirable as a "sanatorium" or "health resort" vacation, surpassed only by the possibility of spending a vacation at a family holiday home ([175]).

Making social contacts while involved in joint voluntary activity (social, cultural, creative, entertainment, etc.), which became widespread from the late 1970s to the mid-1980s, subsequently decreased substantially. The share of those taking part in different club activities (choral singing, amateur theatre, etc.), which was about 5% of the total population in 1980–85, decreased to 3% by the early 1990s

([346]). Considerably less important was attendance at evening social events, which were attended regularly by 30–36% of the population of different age groups in the 1970s and 1980s, while by late 1980s and early 1990s this form of leisure (discotheques, etc.) involved mostly teenagers.

The intensity of interaction with neighbours decreased substantially because of urbanization in the 1960s and 1970s, as a result of the breakup of communal flats and the formation of new housing communities in apartment complexes in towns and cities. Anonymity and impersonality of interaction in urban communities, as distinct from rural ones, was remarked upon by migrants from the countryside to towns. A decrease in the level of interaction with neighbours was one of the characteristics of urban life. ([267]).

I.M. Bykhovskaya

3 Women

3.1 Female Roles

Family structures were modernized and the female role within the family changed. Two trends clashed: the general trend toward professionalization and education of women and the trend for women to "return" to the family.

A deep transformation of the family as a social institution took place in Russia throughout the twentieth century. Over the period under study, there was an intensification of trends dating back to the 1920s and, especially, the 1930s. Most important among these trends are:

- The dismantling of peasant families and an increase in the proportion of urban families: in 1959, the proportion of urban families was 53.0%; in 1970, 63.3%; in 1979, 69.9%; in 1989, 77% ([341]).
- A reduction in the average size of families: in 1959, the proportion of large families (with five or more members) was 26%; in 1979, this proportion was only 18%. Changes in family structure ensued, due mainly to an increase in the number of nuclear families and, consequently, a reduction in that of compound families.
- Changes in intra-family relations, the most important trends of which were: a) increased probability of the family splitting up because of divorce rather than death of a spouse; b) more unmarried couples; c) an increase in subsequent marriages; d) marriages of longer duration; e) a reduction in the number of births and an earlier end of women's reproductive life.

Overall, these processes characterized the transition from a traditional family to a modern one, a main feature of which was a transformation of the principle of family power and an intensification of egalitarian tendencies. The typical urban family became a nuclear one, the spouses being occupied with their professional work, with a small and, in principle, planned number of children brought up by the family as well as by society; characterized by more regular, and more utilitarian, contacts with relatives, accompanied by an indispensable orientation of family members toward other social institutions and regular intercourse with friends ([67]).

In modern Russian families, egalitarian features combined with traditional ones in a most fascinating way. This is most obvious in how spouses share everyday roles. According to this indicator, families may be classified as follows: pure "traditional," in which husbands do not participate in household tasks or in raising the children; "egalitarian," in which husbands are involved in housekeeping duties and the children's care and education; and "transitional," in which husbands in principle do help their wives, but their efforts cannot be qualified as anything approaching equal. The greatest proportion of families, roughly one half of them, are of the transitional type ([15]).

There is still inequality in the distribution of housework. Research conducted at the beginning of the 1970s indicated that if the wife was not employed outside the home, the husband's contribution to housekeeping was only 8.3% of the wife's work; if the wife was employed, the husband's contribution was 24%. The latter figure shows that in families with both spouses employed, the share of housework was quite far from equal, a feature that persists through time. According to a poll taken in 1991 by the author of this section, in families with a working wife and at least one small child at home, the husband's participation in housework and in the children's upbringing is on average 30% of the wife's. Thus, the transformation of family relations toward egalitarianism has been extremely slow and intermittent.

Women played a leading role in making the most important family decisions, including determination of the children's future and dealing with financial problems. A 1970 poll included the question, "Who is the head of your family?" Responses showed that 50% of families are headed by women. In a 1991 survey, evaluations of the degree of the woman's influence in the family ranged, in different groups, from 50% to 100%, with most responses in the 70–80% range ([16]).

Research in the 1980s showed that though respondents supported egalitarian norms of family relations, the traditional sharing of roles remained the ideal pattern. In fact, this was one of the main reasons for the predominance of women's influence in all realms of family life, to the extent that the husband was almost completely excluded from the children's upbringing and the male role in the family shrank greatly.

In the USSR in the 1960s, the proportion of women among those with secondary or higher education exceeded that of men and remained constantly higher (see table 1). In 1960, this proportion was 59%, and it remained around 60% right up to 1985. From 1985 to 1992, the proportion of women in secondary schools was about 60%, but among students in higher-education institutes it dropped from

Table 1
Educational level of employed men and women, Russia, 1979, 1989 (per 1,000 persons)

	Total population		Higher education		Secondary specialized		General (secondary)	
	Men	*Women*	*Men*	*Women*	*Men*	*Women*	*Men*	*Women*
1979	810	801	102	98	425	463	283	240
1989	914	927	138	148	602	633	174	146

Source: [175], p. 188.

56% in 1985 to 50% in 1992 (see table 2). Apart from the demographic factors that affected this situation, there were social factors connected with the worsening prospect of post-education unemployment and the increasing threat of general unemployment. Thus, in 1990, 9% of those who graduated from colleges or universities did not receive an appointment to a job, as they would have in previous times (see section 1.1); instead, they had to depend upon their own or their parents' initiative in order to find a job. In 1991, this proportion rose to 16%; in 1994, it was 100% ([171]).

From the 1960s to the 1980s, the proportion of women at different levels of authority – from the Supreme Soviet of the USSR to local Soviets – rose, reaching 50% in local Soviets toward the end of the 1980s (see table 3). At the beginning of the 1990s, it fell abruptly and then rose a little. About one third of deputies in the Supreme Soviet of the USSR were women. Nevertheless, from 1960 to 1990, only a few women played an appreciable role in the political life of the country. Women's real status was revealed during the first democratic elections in 1989, when 352 women were elected to the First Congress of People's Deputies (15.6% of the total). In the Supreme Soviet of Russia, 5% of deputies were women at the beginning of the 1990s. In the State Duma (elected in 1993), women constituted 13.5% of all deputies.

Conflicts between family and work – home and professional duties – was an unavoidable feature of Soviet women's lives for decades. The entire period under study was marked by this conflict and the resulting problem of women's "two careers." Spot investigations in the 1970s showed that about 95% of women, including those employed in physical labour, preferred to work even if they were living comfortably, giving the reason that their work benefited the general public. Respondents felt that a working wife had a higher status in her husband's and children's eyes. About 80% of women ranked employment as on a par with or more important than family. Up to 90% of women considered work and home to

Table 2
Percentage of women enrolled in colleges and universities, USSR and Russia, 1958–92

1958	1962	1970	1973–74	1980–81	1985–86	1990–91	1991–92
47	42	49	50	53	56	51	50

Sources: [90], p. 15; [242], p. 188.

Table 3
Proportion of women among deputies in soviets, Russia, 1959–88

Levels of Soviets	1959	1967	1970	1973	1975	1985–88
Supreme Soviet of the USSR	27.0	28.0	30.5	31.4	31.4	33.0
Supreme Soviets of republics	32.0	34.0	34.8	–	35.4	36.0
Supreme Soviets of federated republics	32.0	35.0	38.0	45.4	39.1	40.0
Regional soviets	40.0	–	44.5	44.9	–	–
Local soviets	41.0	43.0	45.8	47.4	48.1	50.0

Source: [91], p. 111.

be complementary spheres, although more that half of them noted that it was difficult to combine family and professional duties ([351]).

Starting in the mid-1970s, there was a "rehabilitation" of the "natural female role," connected with home, family, and children. The last wave of intensive female involvement in professional occupations, which coincided with the late 1950s and early 1960s, provoked a revival of the terms "Family, without daily routine" and "woman-worker" (actually the ideology of the 1930s) into new and quite different social and economic conditions. In the mid-1970s, two trends clashed: the trend toward general female professional employment and a concomitant stronger value accorded to education and professionalization, and the contrary trend of women "returning" to the family. The gradual strengthening of the latter – in fact, a patriarchal trend – was affected by the fact that as civil society became more dynamic, private life, with its focus on the family, became more important. Social anxiety became increasingly acute due, among other reasons, to the drop in fertility and the rise of youth crime. Correspondingly, the attitude toward women's role in the family changed – its importance and immutable value were increasingly stressed.

At the beginning of the 1990s, the model of "a professionally oriented woman" and the accompanying model of girls' and women's socialization were revised radically. This revision was promoted in particular by the new social and economic situation, in which many women were running up against the cruel necessity of surviving under conditions of economic crisis and the prospect of unemployment and had to "return to the family." The main change was the availability of a variety of female life strategies to be chosen in accordance with personal preferences and material conditions.

O.M. Zdravomyslova

3.2 Childbearing

Insofar as fertility is concerned, there were at least two poles in the European and Asian parts of the former USSR over the period studied: low and high birth rates, respectively. Modern Russia is comparable to Western European countries in terms of an overall trend toward a drop in the birth rate, though over the last 10 to 15 years it has remained higher in Russia than in Europe.

Beginning in the 1960s in Russia (and in the USSR), a trend toward a decrease in the birth rate is easily discerned. Nevertheless, there were clearly distinguished low- and high-birth-rate areas (see tables 1 to 3).

In spite of a birth-rate increase after the Second World War – the so-called baby boom of 1958–59 – the average number of children in Soviet families was already below three. There were two reasons for this: widespread family planning and the fact that by the 1960s few of the women who were born during the Second World War had reached childbearing age.

Between 1965 and 1978, the deceleration in the birth rate slowed: total fertility fell by half between 1926 and 1959, but between 1965 and 1978 it fell only by 6%, and during the second part of the 1970s the average figures remained at the 1969–70 level. It is thus feasible to conclude that there was stabilization in the average number of children in a family, as borne out in polls of the time. Results showed that the average number of desired children was 2.42 between 1964 and 1973. The number of children considered ideal, as opposed to desired, was 2.89, varying from 2.6 in Latvia to 4.55 in Uzbekistan. Thus, the average number of desired children in the USSR over the period was enough for to assure population replacement. The data about ideal number of children in a family suggested that fertility could increase if circumstances were favourable (a "fertility reserve") (92).

In the Russian Federation, the first period of transition to the new fertility behaviour was completed by the middle of the 1960s (see table 4). Beginning in that time, it could be distinctly observed that the trends characterizing fertility in

Table 1
Total fertility rate, selected republics of the USSR, 1958–90

	Russia	Latvia	Tadjikistan	USSR
1958–59	2.6	1.9	3.8	2.7
1965–66	2.1	1.7	5.4	2.4
1969–70	1.9	1.9	5.9	2.4
1975–76	1.9	1.9	6.3	2.3
1978–79	1.8	1.8	5.9	2.2
1980–81	1.8	1.8	5.6	2.2
1982–83	2.0	2.0	5.4	2.3
1986–87	2.1	2.1	5.6	2.5
1987	2.2	2.1	5.6	2.5
1988	–	2.1	5.3	2.4
1989	2.1	–	–	2.3
1990	1.9	–	–	–

Sources: [171], p. 102; [184], pp. 326, 331, 332.

Table 2
Birth rate and total fertility rate, Russia, 1958–93

	Number of births per 1,000 women aged 15–49	Total fertility rate
1958–59	82.9	2.6
1965–66	59.0	2.1
1969–70	53.4	1.9
1975–76	57.4	1.9
1978–79	59.0	1.8
1980–81	60.6	1.8
1982–83	65.8	2.0
1986–87	67.8	2.1
1987	68.2	2.2
1988	64.5	2.1
1989	59.8	2.0
1990	55.5	1.9
1991	–	1.7
1992	–	1.6
1993	–	1.4

Sources: [176], p. 192; [184], p. 326; [195], p. 18.

Table 3
Age-specific birth rates (births per 1,000 aged
20–24 and 30–34 years), Russia, 1958–88

	Age	
	20–24	30–34
1958–59	157.9	101.9
1965	150.3	77.7
1970	146.9	69.3
1975	157.7	58.2
1978	155.0	55.6
1980	157.6	57.0
1982	163.8	59.9
1986	169.2	67.1
1988	167.9	61.8

Sources: [176], p. 39; [184], pp. 326–31.

Table 4
Features in women's life cycle, Russia, 1935–79

	1935–40	1955–59	1965–69	1970–74	1975–79
Average age at first marriage	24.0	24.4	23.4	23.0	22.9
Average age at first childbirth	25.9	25.9	24.8	24.3	24.1
Average age of last childbirth	44.6	33.1	32.7	32.0	29.5
Duration of childbearing period	18.7	8.7	9.3	9.0	6.6

Source: [56], p. 234.

Russia and Western Europe had drawn closer. For Russia, this meant stabilization of fertility at a low level, which did not provide, as a rule, for population replacement; "rejuvenation" of fertility – the lowering of the average mother's age; increasingly similar fertility indices in different social groups, and in rural and urban populations; and a reduction of the period in the family life cycle devoted childbearing.

Nevertheless, one might distinguish the following unique features in Russia over the period studied: the fertility level was higher than that in developed countries; there was a more intensive "rejuvenation" of fertility, with a higher concentration of births during the early part of the family life cycle; and there were serious fluctuations in the fertility level, probably caused by momentary influences of periodically introduced measures of demography policy measures.

Indeed, the 1980s and 1990s were characterized by considerable fluctuations in the total fertility rate in Russia (see table 2). These changes were connected not only with social and political events in the country but also with the demographic situation in Russia. Demographic policy measures also had some influence (in 1981, the government granted partly paid leave for the care of children under one year of age, and the right to prolong this leave for 6 months; in 1989 it gave partly paid leave for women with a child up to 18 months old). The recent fall in the fertility rate (down to 1.73 in 1991) ([8]) took place under conditions of social and economic crisis, a period of significant changes in the way of life of great numbers of people. At the same time, purely demographic factors were playing a role: the recent decrease was an "echo" of the drop in the 1960s, which, in turn, was created by the fertility decrease during the Second World War.

The expected or desired number of children in Russian families dropped from 1.8 in 1991 to 1.08 in 1994. The main reasons for this were uncertainty in the future and economic difficulties ([195]).

In addition, in Russia, as in any society involved in modernization, there has been a sustained process of female emancipation, which has had a distinct influence on fertility. The most important features of this process are: a tendency for more women to take part in professional and public activities, widespread use of contraceptive methods, and an affirmation of feminist ideology. The deepening economic and political crisis also had a direct influence on the fertility rate.

O.M. Zdravomyslova

3.3 Matrimonial Models

Russian society was characterized by a high marriage rate. An increasing divorce rate was paralleled by increasing tolerance of divorce in public opinion. However, this did not diminish the prestige associated with marriage, as manifested in increasing numbers of second marriages and in the continuing low average age at first marriage. The number of one-parent families (mainly female parent) was increasing. Many unmarried couples lived together.

Changes taking place over the period studied concerned both people's behaviour (increasing divorce rate, one-parent families, common-law marriages, single persons) **and their consciousness** (moral "liberalization" involving a more tolerant attitude toward divorces, extramarital sexual relations, female-parent families, and couples living together) (see table 1). Nevertheless, these changes led neither to an increase in alternative forms of marriage nor to a lowering of the value of family and traditional legal marriage.

The period studied was characterized by a high marriage rate and by a young age at marriage, which was typical for the Russian way of life before the revolution of 1917. According to the 1979 general population census in Russia, only 1.9% of men and 4% of women had never been married by the age of 45–49 years. The 1989 census figures were 3.7% and 3.5%, respectively, lower than during the years before the revolution of 1917 ([183]).

There was an almost total marriage rate in Russia until the 1980s. An analysis of generations born between 1942 and 1952 showed that an absolute majority of men and women were still in their first marriage, and 85–90% of them married before the age of 30 ([56]).

The distinctive feature of the matrimonial conduct of Russians over the period studied was a trend toward an increasing proportion of couples who married young. The relative stability of average age at first marriage in Russia (see tables 2, 3) shows that most Russians did not turn to alternatives to marriage (the manifestation of a proliferation of such alternatives would be a delay in marriage and a rise in average age at first marriage).

Table 1

Marriage and divorce rates per 1,000 persons, USSR and Russia, 1960–93

	USSR		Russia	
	Marriage	Divorce	Marriage	Divorce
1960	12.1	1.3	12.5	1.5
1970	9.7	2.6	10.1	3.0
1980	10.3	3.5	10.6	4.2
1983	10.4	3.5	10.4	4.1
1984	9.6	3.4	9.6	4.0
1985	9.8	3.4	9.7	4.0
1986	9.8	3.4	9.8	4.0
1987	9.8	3.4	9.9	4.0
1988	9.4	3.3	9.5	3.9
1989	9.4	3.4	8.9	3.8
1991			8.6	4.0
1992			7.1	4.3
1993			7.5	4.5

Sources: 175, p. 96; [184], p. 117; [195], p. 15.

Table 2
Average age at first marriage, USSR and Russia, 1968–89

	USSR		Russia	
	Males	*Females*	*Males*	*Females*
1968	25.3	22.6		
1968	25.3	22.6		
1969	24.1	22.3		
1970	23.7	22.1		
1971	23.5	22.0		
1975	23.4	21.8		
1979	24.2	21.7	24.3	21.8
1980	23.3	21.7		
1981	23.3	21.8		
1982	23.3	21.9		
1989	24.4	21.7	24.4	21.8

Sources: [56], p. 187; [195], p. 17.

Table 3
Average age at first marriage, Russia, 1977–89

	Males	*Females*
European Russia, 1977	24.2	21.4
Russian Federation, 1979	24.2	21.8
Russian Federation, 1989	24.4	21.8

Source: [183] p. 18.

There was a drop in the number of married people and in the marriage rate in the second half of the 1980s, especially after 1987. This was not only due to the economic and social crisis, but mainly because since 1987 the least numerous postwar generation began reaching marriage age (20–24 years) ([183]).

The likelihood of divorce increased greatly. Divorce, being an extremely dramatic event in private life, stopped being seen by the public as a deviation from the norm. It is significant that annual changes in divorce rates were closely related to changes in the law. Thus, 1950 was characterized by a drop in the divorce rate in comparison with the prewar level, as a consequence of the divorce procedure having been made more complicated by a decree of the Presidium of the Supreme Soviet of the USSR on 8 July 1944. In the second half of the 1960s, a sharp rise in the divorce rate was connected with simplification of the divorce procedure by a decree of the Presidium of the Supreme Soviet on 10 December 1965.

In the mid-1970s, the divorce rate was 3.4 per 1,000 persons (see table 1), a high rate that was maintained through the rest of the period under study. Throughout the period, the divorce rate in Russia exceeded that in all other Soviet republics except Latvia.

In the 1980s and 1990s, unmarried women became the most common group in society. By 1990, every fifth Soviet woman aged 25 to 49 years was unmarried, sometimes after a divorce, but more frequently never having married ([53]). In Russia, there were more unmarried women in large cities. According to representative polls taken throughout the USSR in 1987 and 1989 among unmarried women aged 25 to 49 years, there were fewer "happy" unmarried women than there were "happy" married women of the same age. One main reason for this was that unmarried women had a low social status linked to the negative attitude toward celibacy in general ([331]). In 1994, the proportion of single-parent families reached 13% ([111h]).

The increase in the divorce rate was accompanied by a rise in subsequent marriages among the divorced; recourse to second marriages to avoid loneliness was growing. In the early 1980s, it was observed that divorced women married for the second time more quickly and more frequently than did widows. The interval between divorce and subsequent marriage was, on average, 5.5 years ([25]). The proportion of marriages that ended because of the death of one of the spouses was not high in the total number of subsequent marriages (see table 4). Thus, the considerable increase in the divorce rate and in the number of single women over the period under study was not accompanied by a loss in the value and prestige of marriage. It was, rather, a time of increased opportunities in terms of choice of marriage partner, of changes in social norms, and of moral liberalization. These trends were confirmed in poll results.

The main reasons for divorce were psychological factors such as (in order of importance): 1) hard drinking, alcoholism; 2) differences in character; 3) difficult

Table 4
Proportion of divorced and widowed among total ever married, Russia, 1980–91

	Divorced		Widowed	
	Males	*Females*	*Males*	*Females*
1980	16.1	14.3	2.8	3.6
1985	20.7	20.1	3.1	4.5
1991	22.7	20.9	3.0	4.3

Source: [183] p. 18.

relations between young couples and their parents; 4) infidelity; 5) sexual dissatisfaction; 6) dissatisfaction with economic and housing conditions; 7) one of the spouses having a dangerous chronic disease ([153]).

The divorce rate increased rapidly in the 1960s and 1970s, but levelled off in the 1980s. However, this did not mean that the institution of the family was not under pressure. In fact, there were many more divorces than the statistics showed. Many families broke down long before divorce occurred. On average, there was a lapse of three years between the actual divorce and reception of the divorce certificate, and some people never received these documents at all ([214]).

From 1989 to 1993, the number of newly contracted marriages dropped by 280,000, or 25%. Over that period, the number of divorces increased by 14% ([195]). In 1988 surveys of Moscow and Lvov (Ukraine) intellectuals and skilled workers 20–40 years of age, 37% considered divorce something that could happen to anyone, and 47% linked divorce not with moral degradation, but with higher demands made on matrimonial relations that could be satisfied only with greater effort. According to 35% of respondents, if matrimonial relations were poor it was necessary to divorce with no hesitation. Only 12% felt that the family had to be conserved at all costs ([94]).

One of the most significant trends in matrimonial conduct was the spread of unmarried cohabitation. As there are no statistical data about this, it may be inferred from data regarding out-of-wedlock births (see table 5). One of the first studies of this phenomenon was carried out by M. Tolts. According to his thorough review of birth certificates in Perm in 1966, 32.1% of the children were born either out of wedlock (12.5%) or during the first months after the marriage (15.2%), while in 4.4% of cases the marriage was registered just after childbirth but before registration of the birth. Almost one third (29%) of married women gave birth to their first child during the first eight months of marriage, and this rate was 53% for married women aged 19 years and younger. As the indices of out-of-wedlock births in Perm were almost the same as those in Novosibirsk, Tolts posited that this trend was typical for other large cities in Russia ([293]).

According to a study conducted in 1979, nearly 60% of all cases of extramarital pregnancy (if they were not terminated by abortion) resulted in childbirth within marriage or with subsequent registration of marriage. Some such marriages were forced. The other 40% of cases involved mainly women older than 30 years of age (usually a planned pregnancy) and young mothers under 20 years of age (the out-of-wedlock births of their children constitute one quarter of the birth rate) whom the father of the child refused to marry ([316]).

Between 1980 and 1993, the proportion of out-of-wedlock children increased in the USSR and in Russia from 10.8% to 19.2%; in urban populations, the rise was from

Table 5
Out-of-wedlock births, USSR and Russia, 1960–93
(% of all births)

	USSR	Russia
1960–64	11.2	
1965–69	9.4	
1970–74	8.4	
1975–79	8.4	
1980–84	8.8	10.8
1985	9.1	12.0
1987	9.8	12.7
1988	10.2	13.0
1989		13.5
1992		17.2
1993		18.2

Sources: [175], p. 102; [184], p. 344; [195], p. 20.

9.6% to 15.5%; in rural populations, from 13.45% to 17.3%. In 1991, 41% of children born out of wedlock (36% in cities and 51% in the country) were registered according to the mutual written request of both parents. These figures show the spread of "common-law" marriage (although childless, unmarried couples remain hidden). In 1993, the proportion of out-of-wedlock births was 18.2% of all births ([183]).

In the 1960s and 1970s, the number of people cohabiting increased, a conclusion drawn from analysis of some data in the population censuses. These showed that women declared their status as married, while men considered themselves single. Thus in 1959, there were about 437,000 more married women than married men; by 1970, this figure was at around 1.3 million ([316]). Nonetheless, from 1960 to 1990, the attitude toward cohabitation was rather ambivalent and the prestige of traditional juridically contracted marriage was uniformly high.

The results of polls show that only 8.5% of respondents wholeheartedly accepted out-of-wedlock childbirth, while every third respondent tolerated cohabitation ([153]).

According to the poll carried out by the author of this section in 1991 in five Russian cities, 93.9% of married women and 94.3% of married men with children saw marriage as a "very positive" way of life. Only 40% of women and 40% of men had the same opinion of unmarried couples with children; 52% of women and 43% of men had a "very negative" attitude toward the latter way of living.

O.M. Zdravomyslova

3.4 Women's Employment

Rising opportunities and levels of the professional employment of women were characteristic of the entire Soviet regime. This process, however, did not proceed evenly. The last tide of intensive involvement in professional employment was in the late 1950s and early 1960s. It concerned mainly women who were about to enter their active age and women who were simultaneously occupied as homemakers.

From the 1960s to the mid-1970s, the proportion of working women steadily exceeded that of men. Between 1956 and 1960, women comprised 53% of the work force; in 1961–65, 57%; from 1966 to the 1970s, 56%; in subsequent years, it did not exceed 50%. As a result, from 1969 to the present, women prevailed in the overall number of workers and employees (in 1960, 47%; in 1965, 49%; after 1969, 51%). Thus, by the beginning of the 1970s, the USSR had one of the highest levels of working women in the world, 86%, a proportion that gradually increased in subsequent years. In 1990, nearly 90% of the total employable female population was working. Sociological polls conducted from 1985 to 1990 showed that 50–54% of women occupied as homemakers would prefer, under certain conditions, to work outside of their homes, whereas fewer than one fifth of employed women would cease working if their husbands' incomes were higher ([306]).

Different sectors of the economy and different salary ranges were associated with differing levels of female labour mobilization. In the late 1980s, nonproduction sectors had the highest proportion of women employees (women represented 83% of those employed in public health care, 75% in education, and 51% in science). In the manufacturing industries, the proportion of women employees was, as a rule, considerably lower: 48% in industry, 41% in agriculture, and 26% in construction (see table 1). The proportion of women among those employed in manufacturing dropped from the 1960s to the 1980s, while their proportion in nonproduction sectors rose. More women were employed in industrial sectors in which the average monthly wage was lower than the national average, while fewer were employed in sectors in which the wage was higher than the national average.

Women were employed in almost all existing professions except those in which they were legally prohibited from working because of especially harmful and trying conditions. However, professional structures differed fundamentally for men and for women. On the whole, the higher the social status of the job, the lower

Table 1
Proportion of female employees by industrial sector, Russia, 1940–91 (%)

	1940	1980	1985	1989	1991
Total	41	52	52	53	6.5
Industry	40	49	48	48	10.8
Agriculture	30	42	41	40	7.8
Forestry	–	20	19	18	–
Construction	25	29	28	26	1.0
Transport	23	25	25	25	0.5
Communications	52	71	71	71	10.8
Trade	47	80	79	70	–
Information services	–	71	72	80	–
Repairs and other services	43	54	54	54	–
Public health	77	85	84	83	–
Education	–	78	79	79	–
Arts	–	53	55	55	–
Culture	–	76	77	75	–
Science	43	52	52	53	–
Financial services	43	87	89	89	–
Government institutions	36	69	71	70	–
Other	–	53	51	47	–

Source: Central Statistics Committee, unpublished data.

the proportion of women employed in it. Thus, for example, in industry women were predominantly employed as unskilled labourers, while they made up 61% of the labour force, whereas they made up as little as 24% of highly skilled labour. The level of women's employment in subordinate and auxiliary work roles, in which severe physical strain is frequently involved, was very high (80%). The proportion of women among those employed in unstrenuous but low-paying jobs was also high. An analysis of the dynamics of the structure of women's employment shows that this structure was relatively stable from the 1970s to the 1980s.

One major problem involving women's employment was their low qualification status. In industry, for example, in the mid-1990s working women constituted two thirds of all workers in the bottom categories (1 and 2), and only one fifth are at category 5 or higher. The level of women's qualification constantly lagged behind that of men: in the different industrial sectors, the ratio of the mean qualification categories of women to men varied from 0.56 to 0.82. This ratio had remained unchanged from the 1960s to the 1980s. Surveys of enterprises conducted over this period also showed that women had lower qualification categories even when they performed similar kinds of work to those performed by men. A relatively low level of qualification was one of the factors limiting the possibility for women to increase their income. Thus, a considerable proportion of women ended up working under unfavourable conditions, since the existing compensation system (extra sums of money monthly, bonuses, etc.) for harmful and unhealthy working conditions was seen by them as an additional and frequently real opportunity to increase their income or to obtain a convenient work schedule. The proportion of women among administrators at all levels of management was not high. In industry, for example, women represented 11% of company directors, 8% of assistant directors, 16% of heads of design and engineering offices, 9% of chief engineers, and 12 % of shop superintendents. Even in economic sectors in which women constituted an overwhelming majority of workers, their proportion among top managers did not correspond to their proportion among workers ([258]).

By the end of the 1980s, a series of measures for the social and economic protection of mothers had been instituted in an attempt to compensate for the unfavourable demographic situation. The basic measures in this system were paid leaves of absence for expectant mothers and partly paid leaves for mothers to take care of their children until they are 1.5 years old, and unpaid leaves of absence to take care of their children until they are 3 years old (their job being guaranteed upon their return; see table 2). An overwhelming majority of women (over 90%) took advantage of some or all of these privileges. Failure to avail oneself of one's lawful rights was, as a rule, motivated by financial difficulties. In the "pre-market situation," women did not associate taking maternity leave with the possibility of losing their job. Recently, however, cases of women being dismissed because they have young children have become more frequent.

The transition to a new social and economic structure, a developing economic crisis, and dynamic changes on the labour market resulted in the emergence of female unemployment. Women as a group appeared to be the most vulnerable; in the mid-1990s, they account for around 80% of the unemployed. According to data provided by the labour exchange, a considerable proportion of these women were well educated.

In the Soviet economy, part-time work was predominantly a privileged type of employment for certain categories of workers. Until the mid-1960s, part-time employment was used only as a means to provide certain categories of the labour pool with employment at a time of job shortages. Regulations permitted granting part-time employment only to homemakers, invalids, and pensioners as long as they worked in the services sector. After 1970, this type of employment was permitted in all industrial sectors and for all categories of the population; furthermore, as of 1987, company managers were obliged to provide an opportunity for women with children

Table 2
Maternity leaves, Russia, 1960–91

	Leave of absence before childbirth (weeks)	Paid leave after after delivery (weeks)	Paid childcare leave (years)	Unpaid childcare leave (weeks)	Receiver
1960	8	8	-	-	mother
1973	8	8	-	1.0	mother
1981	8	8	1.0	0.5	mother
1990	10	8	1.5	1.5	any relative
1991	10	10	3.0	-	any relative

Source: Central Statistics Committee, unpublished data.

under 12 years old to work less than full time if they wished to do so. This decision was intended to reduce the total work load for employed women. After 1990, this privilege was extended to women with children under age 14. However, these measures were not widely invoked; in 1974, only 0.32% of all working people worked part time; in 1984, 0.65% did so; by the mid-1990s, they comprised about 1%. Nevertheless, in the 1990s, polls showed that over one half of all working women with children would have liked to work fewer hours, if only temporarily ([92]).

In the former USSR, it was illegal for women to work at night, though there were special provisions for women to work night shifts, when unavoidable, as a temporary arrangement. Subsequently, in the textile-manufacturing industries alone almost one fourth of women worked night shifts (in 1965, every third woman was employed for work in an evening or night shift). Moreover, the numbers of women working night shifts was double to triple that of men. As a rule, in the industrial sectors in which female labour was mainly employed (light industry, bread-baking industry, chemicals, and others) the coefficient of shift labour was higher than in sectors in which men's labour was chiefly employed ([92]).

M.E. Baskakova

3.5 Reproductive Technologies

The modern practice of regulating the number of children per family began in the 1960s, coinciding with generalization of contraceptive methods. Peculiar to Russia is that the spread of contraception was combined with an extremely high abortion rate.

Family planning using contraceptive methods became part of family life in the 1960s. Two periods of such planning can be marked. The first one was characterized by low awareness of contraceptive methods among the population. Family planning was accomplished mainly by pregnancy termination and late marriage. The second one began after reliable contraceptive devices were created and the population was informed about them. This period began in the 1960s. Its main feature was the opportunity to plan the number of children, the time of their birth, and the intervals between births. Sociological research on reproductive behaviour and reproductive aims that began in the 1960s revealed that families felt that there was an "ideal" number of children, which the majority of married couples tried to attain. This ideal, for the urban nuclear family, was two or three children.

In spite of widespread awareness and use of contraceptives, pregnancy termination was the most widespread method of family planning from the 1960s to the 1990s. In the USSR, abortion was first legalized in 1920, then forbidden in 1936, and legalized again in 1955. The use of abortion was especially great in Russia. The number of abortions per 1,000 women was higher than in other republics (see table 1).

Only in the 1970s did the experts begin speaking openly about the necessity of disseminating family-planning information. The widespread model of "free and irresponsible parenthood" in Russia and other republics had such dangerous consequences as a high abortion rate, a high level of sterility, a high death rate, an increase in obstetrical and gynaecological disorders, and a high level of undesired pregnancies and children.

Family planning based on the use of modern contraceptive devices is currently an urgent issue in Russia. This situation is characterized both by a drop in fertility and by its "rejuvenation," which became more evident after 1965. From 1965 to 1991, the average mother's age in Russia dropped from nearly 27.5 to 25 years. Over the same period, the average age at first childbirth dropped from 24.8 to 22.9 years;

the average age at second childbirth, from 28.5 to 27.2 years; however, average age at third childbirth changed little, from 30.7 to 30.2 years ([8]; see table 2).

The low level of use of contraceptive methods and the high level of abortions persists in Russia. In 1993, only 20% of demand for contraceptive devices was met and 3.2 million medical abortions were registered: 233 per 100 births ([195]).

Table 1
Abortion rate among women aged 15–49 years, the USSR and Russia, 1975–93 (per 1,000)

	1975	1980	1985	1989	1993
USSR	105.7	102.3	100.3	95.5	–
Russia	126.3	122.8	123.6	117.7	88

Source: [183], p. 111.

Table 2
Average mother's age at childbirth, Russia, 1956–91

	1st	2nd	3rd	4th
1956	25.1	28.4	30.5	34.1
1966	24.6	28.7	30.9	34.5
1976	23.9	28.1	30.5	33.3
1986	23.3	27.6	30.0	32.0
1991	22.9	27.2	30.2	32.4

Source: [183], p. 111.

O.M. Zdravomyslova

4 Labour Market

4.1 Unemployment

Until the 1980s, unemployment was considered to be a capitalist phenomenon. The transition to a market economy brought about changes in labour and employment relations and the emergence of unemployment, the level of which, while not high, was constantly growing. The majority of the unemployed were women, and this proportion remained constant. The educational level of the Russian unemployed was very high, though gradually declining. The problem of youth unemployment was very acute. The problem of imbalance between job vacancies and the professional and qualification structure of the unemployed did not vary over the period.

In Russia, official unemployment did not exist for 50 years: demand for labour exceeded supply. The last labour exchanges were closed in 1930–31, and it was declared that the country had got rid of unemployment, the "damned" heritage of capitalism. Under perestroika unemployment became legal. Citizens able to work, who do not have a job, are registered at the State Service of Employment in order to find a suitable position, and are ready to start working are considered unemployed.

Extensive (as opposed to intensive) economic development in the Soviet Union led to the forced creation of job vacancies, which made it possible not only entirely to absorb the natural-labour force increment and involve pensioners, housewives, students, and other groups in productive activities, but also to create a continual shortage of labour. Although individuals were allowed to change jobs independently, this was frowned upon by enterprises and the state, which saw it as causing economic losses; such actions were thus discouraged by all possible means. If a job change was not sanctioned, the person involved was denied a large portion of his or her social benefits, since granting of such benefits was associated with continuous length of service at a particular enterprise. The necessary labour turnover was effected through recruitment, by obligatory streaming of institute graduates to different enterprises (see section 1.1), or by officially unsanctioned labour mobility (so-called manpower).

The first unemployed were officially registered in mid-1991. From 1991 to 1993, many politicians and economists predicted an onset of mass unemployment,

Table 1
Unemployment and proportion of women unemployed, Russia, 1992–94

	Jan. 1992	Jan. 1993	Sept. 1993	Nov. 1994
Registered unemployed	61,876	577,725	705,818	1,475,000
women (%)	69.7	72.2	69.8	–
On unemployment allowance	11,870	165,053	449,119	–
women (%)	87.3	66.3	71.2	–

Source: [24], p. 8.

but their prognoses were not borne out. According to the State Statistics Committee, the official number of unemployed was relatively low (800,000, or around 1% of total employable people) in late 1993; at the end of November 1994, just under 1.5 million people, or 1.8% of the labour force, were unemployed. The growth of unemployment was restrained, among other things, by the government's financial and monetary credit policy and the absence, until 1995, of a real threat of bankruptcy. Inflation constantly pumped up the Russian economy, against a background of production decline and the absence of mechanisms for reducing inflation rates, as is natural in a context of growing unemployment ([24]).

Individuals who lost their jobs and were registered with the State Employment Office had very few social-security benefits. Minimum unemployment benefits were not permanent and were equal to the amount of a minimum salary, which was, in late 1993, less than one fourth of the official subsistence level for a Russian citizen.

"Latent unemployment" developed alongside registered unemployment. In this form of unemployment, workers and employees were forced to take long-term, unpaid (or partly paid) leaves of absence or work a reduced number of days (or hours), with a corresponding reduction in wages (or salaries). These practices were a direct outcome of instability at the enterprise level. In late 1993, the number of the "latent unemployed" exceeded 15 million, or 21.4% of the employed ([193]).

One of the major problems of Russian unemployment is its feminization. Throughout the period that unemployment has existed in post-socialist Russia, the proportion of women among the unemployed has ranged from 69% to 73%, and even higher in certain areas; in Moscow, for example, it was 80%. In 1993, there were 493,000 unemployed women in Russia, or 69.8% of all registered unemployed (see table 1).

A high level of education is characteristic of unemployed women in Russia. In 1993, among all unemployed, 19.5% were women and 14.4% were men with a higher education. In the case of those with specialized secondary education, 30.4% and 19.6% were women and men, respectively. Women absolutely prevailed in all educational groups of the registered unemployed, although there were fewer among those with less education.

In Russia as a whole, the proportion of women among those looking for a job for the first time is extremely high – 77.7%. The most difficult employment situation is faced by young female graduates from specialized secondary schools (the proportion of women in this group is 84%) and institutions of higher education (78.9%).

The duration of unemployment is higher among women than among men (see table 2). In 1993, it took five months on average for a woman to find a job, while it took a man an average of four months.

The most urgent problem is youth unemployment. The proportion of young people under 30 years of age among the total number of unemployed increased from 16% to 38% in 1992 ([193]), then dropped slightly, to 37%, by the end of 1993. Because of the disintegration of the system of initial employment streaming of graduates from professional and specialized schools and from higher educational institutions, young people who were not prepared to look for jobs independently found themselves on the labour market. In addition, other negative phenomena, such as a general slump in industrial production and structural changes in the economy, resulted in employers' being unwilling to offer jobs to graduates from educational institutions over a wide range of specialties.

With a gradual increase in the number of unemployed and a general slump in industrial production, the Russian Employment Agency made efforts to help the unemployed find jobs. In late 1993, the number of officially registered unemployed exceeded the number of job vacancies by a factor of only 1.4. At the same time, some positions remained unoccupied for a long period, due to a disparity between the structure of job vacancies and the qualifications of the people seeking jobs. In 1993, 89.3% of all available job vacancies were offered to industrial workers; in 1992, this figure had been 88.3% ([193]).

Table 2
Duration of unemployment, Russia, 1993 (%)

Duration of unemployment	Total	Men	Women	Youths 16–29
Around 1 month	12.04	12.34	11.91	13.64
1 to 4 months	31.64	31.60	31.66	33.88
4 to 8 months	30.20	31.60	29.60	29.38
8 months to 1 year	18.93	18.43	19.15	16.75
more than 1 year	7.19	6.03	7.69	6.34

Source: State Statistics Committee, unpublished data.

M.E. Baskakova

4.2 Skills and Occupational Levels

The effects of "extensive" economic development in Russia were manifested in the industrial sphere in the form of a low level of mechanization, wide use of manual labour, and slow replacement rate of machinery. The state system of improvement of workers' qualification was grossly inadequate, but even this system disintegrated in the 1990s, to be replaced by more ad hoc and specialized training and sometimes by recourse to skilled foreign workers.

In the USSR, **labour statistics never corresponded to the standards of the International Labour Organization** (ILO). There was a centralized system of labour certification, which produced qualification reference manuals for 5,000 occupations. Different professions had different numbers of qualification grades (ranging from three to eight).

All occupations had been divided into two groups and five subgroups according to the level of labour mechanization and worker qualification. Codification of qualifications was carried out not on the basis of the concrete activity involved, but on the basis of whether a worker belonged to a certain occupation or trade (each with fixed wages).

Theoretically, workers had to receive special training (training was provided at the workplace and at institutions for qualification upgrading) and pass a special examination to gain grades. Before the mid-1980s, when the economic reforms began, the numbers of those who received training constantly increased (see table 1). But in reality, not everyone who was trained and passed examinations necessarily increased his or her job status or qualification grade or received higher wages. For example, in 1991 only 23% of all those who received such training had their qualification grade raised ([306]).

A characteristic of economic development in Russia before the 1990s was the unusually widespread use of manual labour. The number and proportion of manual labourers decreased extremely slowly; before the 1980s almost every second industrial worker (45% of women and 49% of men) was still engaged in manual labour (see table 2). In the 1980s, some attempts were made to diminish radically the use of manual labour and to eliminate before the year 2000 hard manual labour by creating special-purpose programs. But these attempts were not successful, because the programs were not viable under the economic system that existed at the time.

The economic crisis of the 1990s caused a breakdown of the centralized system of qualification improvement. Rising unemployment and the disparity

Table 1
Numbers of labourers and employees having undergone qualification
upgrading, Russia, 1960–92 (million)

	Total labourers and employees with qualification upgrading	Labourers only
1960	4.5	3.6
1965	6.2	4.7
1970	7.5	5.7
1975	14.5	10.2
1980	19.3	13.6
1991	6.7	4.4
1992	5.2	3.2

Sources: [284], p. 18; [300], p. 163.

Table 2
Workers in mechanized and manual labour, USSR, 1972–89 (%)

	1972	1975	1979	1982	1989
Mechanized labour	44.6	45.8	46.6	48.7	52.6
Manual labour	42.8	41.6	40.2	37.6	33.8
Machinery maintenance	12.6	12.6	13.2	13.7	13.6

Source: State Statistics Committee, unpublished data.

between vocational level of the unemployed and job vacancies forced the state to create a new system for retraining the unemployed, though the number of those retrained was not large: in 1993, only 55,000 people were retrained. The number of non-state training centres and courses gradually increased, but, as a rule, they carried out training in a rather narrow range of vocations.

The ineffectiveness of the system of qualification upgrading for women was a very urgent problem, and it continued to be so in the 1990s. Throughout Russia, the qualification level of women was lower than that of men: in different industrial sectors, the ratio of women's qualification level to that of men doing the same job varied between 0.56 and 0.82. In 1979, legislation was passed to provide women with children under eight years of age extra training without giving up their job and preserving their average monthly wages, but this legislation was never implemented. In 1985, women comprised only up to one third of all workers being trained to improve their qualifications (though the proportion of women among the employed was considerably higher in industry, where it stood at 44%; [22]). Opinion polls showed that 56% of women trained to improve their qualification grade neither improved the grade nor received higher wages after training ([306]).

The process of replacing manual labour in the production process had a differential influence on the occupational status of men and of women. Studies in the 1980s and 1990s showed that the decrease in numbers of manual labourers took place mainly among men. For example, in 1962–72, the total number of manual labourers decreased by 67,000: the number of men decreased by 161,000 while the number of women increased by 94,000 ([237]). In the 1980s, Scientific Institute of Labour data indicated that as a position involving manual labour was mechanized or automated, a woman engaged at this job was replaced by a man, and this woman was transferred to a position involving manual labour.

In the 1990s, the State Statistics Committee did not carry out general studies that might allow us to evaluate the range and parameters of the use of manual labour in the Russian economy. The last studies were carried out in 1989. Selective investigations of employment used a methodology that did not allow for tracking the dynamics of manual-labour deployment.

The effectiveness of the deployment of young specialists (see section 1.1) graduating from different schools (vocational technical schools, colleges, higher schools) was always very low. Usually, young graduates with specialties began their working life at a level lower than their qualifications. Young graduates from colleges and universities were used in unskilled labour more often than were other workers. Sociological analysis of the 1980s showed that the share of unskilled labour in total work time among this group ranged from 30% to 40%. Young graduates comprised the highest proportion of those working in jobs not connected with their direct official and professional qualifications (as *subbotniks* [general maintenance and temporary or periodic upswings in production activity], temporary casual labour at vegetable storage sheds, in agriculture, etc.).

M.E. Baskakova

4.3 Types of Employment

In socialist Russia, the main form of employment was a full working day with a fixed beginning and end. Nonstandard types of employment were regarded and used mainly as favourable working conditions only for certain categories of people. During the 1980s and 1990s, economic reforms and the economic crisis led to a situation in which this type of work became a means of decreasing the number of unemployed and increasing effective organization of production.

Starting in the 1950s, full employment with a 41-hour work week was the dominant work schedule in the USSR. For decades, this type of employment was considered the only possible choice for both men and women. Extensive development of the economy and the resulting constant need for additional labour, along with the necessity to raise the birth rate and decrease work loads, gave rise to new types of employment designed to draw new groups into production and improve working conditions for mothers. Among these new types of employment were part-time and flexible schedule, work at home, and temporary work. Those involved in these types of work had the same rights and guarantees as those engaged in traditional types of employment.

In the Soviet economy, part-time work was used mainly as a privileged type of employment for certain categories of employees. Before the mid-1980s, this type of employment was used only as a method of mobilizing more people into work in a context of labour shortage. Only housewives, invalids, and pensioners, and only in the services sector, were permitted to work part time, because this sector was suffering from an acute labour shortage. Since 1970, this type of employment has been permitted in all production sectors and for all population categories; since 1987 (in order to reduce total work loads of working women) managers of enterprises were obliged to give women with children up to 12 years old the opportunity to work half-days if they wished. In 1990, women with children up to 14 also received this privilege.

But the part-time work was not widespread: in 1974, only 0.31% of working people had this type of work schedule; in 1984, 0.56% worked part time ([135]); in 1994, still fewer than 1% worked on this type of schedule. At this time, public-opinion polls showed that more than 80% of all working women wanted to work part time ([306]; see table 1).

Table 1
Proportion of women preferring part-time work or flexible work schedule, Russia, 1991 (%)

	Prefer to work	Do not prefer to work	Currently work
Part time	83.2	15.6	1.2
Flexible schedule	75.1	14.9	10.0

Source: [306], pp. 286, 294.

At the beginning of the 1980s, flexible work schedules began to be used; these schedules meant that working people themselves defined when they began and ended their work day and when they took their lunch break, within certain limits. As a rule, flexible schedules were used in scientific and engineering institutions, for managerial and service personnel, and at certain industrial enterprises.

In spite of the obvious advantage of this type of work organization, especially for women, the number of people working on a flexible schedule increased extremely slowly, and at the end of the 1980s there were only a few hundred thousand people on this type of schedule in the country as a whole, though the number of those who wanted a flexible work week was considerably larger.

From the 1950s to the 1990s, seasonal work was most popular in Russian agriculture. However, it existed mainly in the form of "voluntary" (often forced) assistance by Soviet Army soldiers, students from institutes, universities, and colleges, office workers, scientists, and industrial workers who went to work at collective farms during the summer and autumn. The "assistants" were considered to be working at their usual workplace (though they were actually working in agriculture) and received their usual wages, salaries, and stipends. In the 1990s, this type of "seasonal work" gradually began to disappear, though even in 1994 some students and soldiers continued to work in agriculture during the autumn months.

When economic reforms began, flexible employment ceased being regarded as a privilege. Unemployment and a decline in living standards diminished the attractiveness of this type of employment (as did attempts to implement as a criterion for receiving unemployment benefits the necessity to work a full 52 weeks instead of 12 weeks, as was previously the case, which meant that half-time workers, for instance, were obliged to work 2 years instead of 6 months). Moreover, part-time workers were potentially discriminated against (no vacation pay, etc.).

The economic crisis and the resulting employment instability in a considerable number of enterprises led to the creation of a new form of part-time employment: "hidden unemployment," in which workers are forced to go on long unpaid or partly paid leave or to work fewer days and hours, with a consequent decrease in wage or salary. Federation Employment Services data show that 11 million people were affected by "hidden unemployment" during the first half of 1994.

Temporary employment (contract work) was almost unheard of during the Soviet period and began to appear only in the 1990s.

In 1994, 12.6% of respondents said they had a permanent second job and 23.4% had a temporary second job ([111b]).

When economic reforms started and a nonstate sector of private enterprises appeared, nonstandard types of employment began to be more widely used (particularly in newly formed economic structures), although general data concerning their use do not exist. Previously, state statistics did not keep track of the above-mentioned types of employment, or of differentiation by sex, age, or social status. In the 1990s, labour statistics conformed to ILO standards, but a new system of data collection adequate for the new economic reality was not yet set up, and therefore more detailed information on types of employment in recent years could be gathered.

M.E. Baskakova

4.4 Sectors of Employment

The main structural changes in employment in Russia from the 1960s to the 1990s were the result of the political priority given to the relative importance, on the one hand, of material-goods production and, on the other hand, to the services sector. Within the realm of material goods, structural changes flowed from the varying importance attached to production of capital machinery, material goods, and agricultural production.

A high level of employment is characteristic of Russia. In 1993, 71 million persons, or 48% of the total population, were employed in Russia. A breakdown by sector shows a constant prevalence of production activities, with a small proportion employed in the service sector (see table 1).

A shift in employment from agriculture to industry was the most prolonged and stable trend until the 1960s and after. By the early 1970s, the proportion of employment in industry (construction included) levelled off at 42%, where it remained into the 1990s (see table 2).

Table 1
Proportion of those employed in the production sector among all employees, Russia, 1960–91 (%)

1960	1970	1980	1991
82	76	73	71

Source: [278], p. 14.

Table 2
Distribution of employees by sector, Russia, 1960–92 (%, not including students)

	1960	1970	1980	1985	1990	1991	1992
Industry and construction	37.0	42.0	42.1	41.7	42.3	41.9	41.7
Agriculture and forestry, including individual plots	32.0	19.0	15.0	14.3	13.2	13.5	13.4
Transport and communications	8.0	9.0	9.6	9.8	7.7	7.8	7.7
Trade and catering, distribution, and maintenance	6.0	8.0	8.3	8.3	7.8	7.6	7.9
Health care, physical fitness, social welfare, education, culture and art, science	12.0	16.0	17.5	18.1	19.4	19.9	19.9
Administrative and financial services	2.0	2.0	2.3	2.4	2.9	3.3	4.0
Other sectors (housing and municipal economy, nonproductive public utilities, etc.)	3.0	4.0	5.2	5.4	6.7	6.0	5.4

Sources: [177], p. 267; [241], p. 120.

Rates of employment growth differed considerably from sector to sector. Heavy industry, and especially machine manufacturing, led the way, and their development determined the increase in total number of those employed in industry. The proportion of those employed in heavy industry among total industrial employees was 77% in 1970, 80% in 1980, and 83% in 1992, and the proportions of industrial employees involved in machine manufacturing were 41%, 45%, and 44%, respectively. The trend was manifested most clearly in the late 1970s and early 1980s; the proportion of industrial workers as a whole increased by 13% from 1970 to 1980, largely because of expansion of the capital-goods plant, which grew by 24%. In light industry and the food industry, the indexes fell by 37% and 4%, respectively, from 1970 to 1992 ([171]).

Throughout the period, agriculture had many industry-specific problems linked to training and deployment of its labour force. This sector constantly lagged behind industry with regard to labour productivity, and was therefore a less gratifying occupation. In spite of enormous investments made in the 1970s and 1980s, scientific and technical progress was disseminated to the agricultural sector with great difficulty. By the mid-1980s, agriculture was characterized by poor labour conditions, low wages, and poor prospects for professional advancement. Agriculture is static compared to the industrial and service sectors.

From the 1960s to the 1990s, the reduction in number of agricultural employees was accompanied by their redeployment to activities connected with food processing and distribution. As a result, the proportion of collective or state farm labourers within the structure of the agricultural complex fell from 65% in 1990 to 63% in 1992 ([171]). The number of farm labourers is, of course, high in Russia as compared with that in other developed countries.

For many years, there was stable, though insufficient, growth in the number of employees in the services sector. However, this did not necessarily signify progress in terms of services available because the growth took place mostly in the bureaucracy and, in the 1990s, also in new financial-services institutions. For instance, in 1991, employment in the civil service grew by 47%, a continuing trend ([23]).

In the 1990s, with the transition to a market economy, changes also took place in the public and private sectors. In 1993, as compared with 1991–92, there were no abrupt changes in earlier trends. In 1993, the total number of employees in the national economy fell by 1.4% and of those in the public sector by 14%. At the same time, the number of employees in the private sector increased by 37%, and in enterprises and commercial joint ventures it grew by 13% ([277]).

A reduction in employment was typical of all production sectors (with the exception of agriculture and forestry) and in service-sector activities financed by the state. This led to a drop in the proportion of those employed in industry, transport and communications, trade, procurement, and research-and-development organizations – that is, in sectors connected with production and distribution of material goods and the development and implementation of new technology.

In 1993, the proportion of those employed in a number of service activities, in particular those connected with banking and legal and fiscal services, grew. But these upheavals should not be regarded as a result and reflection of structural reorganization of production; underlying them is a broadening gap between sectors in terms of wages and salaries, a consequence of inflation and falling production.

L. N. Sivashenkova

4.5 Computerization of Work

Computerization in the economy began in the late 1980s. Trends in this area were linked to both quantitative and qualitative changes in technologies (know-how) and in organization of labour. Gradually, information technology became a social phenomenon that had a strong impact on work and, later, on life style.

The low rate of development of computer science from 1950 to the mid-1980s is largely linked to ideology. In the USSR, the earliest certificates of authorship and patents for inventions in the computer domain appeared in 1948, almost simultaneously with those in the United States and Great Britain, and were used for similar tasks. In Russia, however, cybernetics was designated a pseudo-science at the beginning of 1950s, although during the "thaw" period computer science progressed somewhat and major computer-science centres were established. Nevertheless, by the 1970s, nearly all research and development on the new technology had been curtailed. As a consequence, Russia failed to keep pace with the West and began to lag behind seriously. The exceptions were the space and defence programmes, in which computerization was very advanced, but this technology was not available to the rest of the economy.

In the 1970s, Russia began extensive copying of Western models. The IBM 360 computer, developed in 1965, was adopted as the only hardware used by COMECON member countries. As well, a family of small-size computers was designed, based on an American minicomputer developed in the mid-1970s. Mass production of these computers began in the 1980s. The country was flooded with foreign software, while domestic developers were engaged predominantly in "adaptations." The failure to copyright computer programs before 1993, despite rapid and widespread diffusion of computers, turned out to be a serious obstacle to the development of Russian computer science. Nevertheless, much talent was mobilized by the challenge of programming and a generation of computer experts emerged who were fully conversant with the latest developments in Western computer science and quite prolific in production of software.

Computerization of labour took place gradually in a context of an abundance of manual and poorly mechanized labour. In 1965, there were 1,900 totally mechanized and automated enterprises; in 1975, there were 5,400 ([274]). Between 1985 and 1989, the drop in expenditures on manual labour in industry slowed;

between 1979 and 1985, the proportion of manual labourers decreased by 0.9% per year; from 1986 to 1989, it decreased by only 0.4% (see table 1). In 1989, over 14 million workers, or 45% of all workers, were still engaged in manual labour, and around 50,000 manual-labour jobs in industry were eliminated, 1/3 to 1/4 the number of in previous years ([175]).

Between 1970 and 1990, costs for all computers and spare parts rose by a factor of more than 11, while 20 times more personal computers were manufactured between 1985 and 1989 (see table 2).* Mechanization and automation of labour and the introduction of machines fitted with numerical control devices (see table 3) radically changed the nature of work. Work had been burdened with a large number of operations that required manual effort, but the emergence of machines fitted with numerical control devices made work easier and less strenuous.

Almost 10 million specialists with engineering and technical education were employed in 1989. Nearly 50% of them had specialties needed in industries that were essential to scientific and technical progress, such as machine manufacturing, electronics, and automation ([175]). The number of those employed to attend to machinery fitted with numerical control devices grew, and the proportion of women in these positions increased (see table 4). However, specialists insist that computerization is being used far from effectively. The main users of computers in the 1990s are banks, publishing houses, and statistical institutions. Conversion from military production and a reduction in expenditures dedicated to space research resulted in a curtailing of computer applications.

The volume and content of education in the field of information science did not meet the needs of industry. In the second half of the 1980s, a comprehensive educational program was launched. In 1986, there were 6,600 trained specialists in the fields of manufacture of electronic and electric means of automation, computers, and microelectronic devices, and maintenance and repair of computer hardware ([177]), only 1.7% of whom had graduated from secondary vocational schools. Computer science became an obligatory school subject, but because of an acute shortage of computer installations, this programme fell short of expectations. Initially, the subject was taught by persons who did not know very much about it. The course taken by secondary students was actually limited to programming using an obsolete algorithm language. Training of users and updating of software commenced in 1993.

---

* The combined means of mechanization and computerization recorded by the State Statistics Committee makes it difficult to analyze the situation properly.

Table 1
Proportion of workers engaged in mechanized work, selected sectors, Russia, 1980–89 (%)

	1980	1985	1989
Manufacturing	–	49.6	51.6
Construction	–	44.5	47.0
Trade, food catering	–	–	13.1
Work on collective and state farms	–	41.7	46.1
Total (all sectors)	8.4	13.4	22.0

Sources: [175], p. 123; [266], p. 132.

Table 2
Value of numerical control devices, automation facilities, and computers manufactured, Russia, 1970–91 (million roubles)

	1970	1980	1985	1989	1990	1991
Automation facilities and devices (components, spare parts)	867.0	2,241.0	2,390.0	3,067.0	-	-
Hardware components, spare parts	222.0	-	2,062.0	1,894.0	3,383.0	-
Personal computers	-	-	8.8	1,262.0	313.0	254.0
Numerical control installations	-	2.3	17.9	-	3.1	1.5

Sources: [171], p. 333; [175], pp. 121, 351, 408.

Table 3
Share of metal-cutting equipment in total production volume of the equipment-construction sector, Russia, 1980–91 (%)

	1980	1985	1990	1991
High- and very-high-precision machine tools (lathes)	5.9	8.2	10.4	11.1
Tools fitted with numerical control devices	5.3	13.9	22.6	18.6

Source: [171], p. 329.

Table 4
Mean annual numbers of workers and employees engaged in information and computing services, Russia, 1980–89 (000)

	1980	1985	1989
Total	119	123	176
Women	84	89	144

Source: [175], p.110.

After 1989, almost all students in secondary school studied the fundamentals of information science and computer design. The equipment provided, however, was not complete: in the 1991–92, 51% of urban schools had classrooms equipped with computers, whereas only 43% of rural schools were so equipped ([171]; see table 5). In 1993, 77% of students in Moscow attending general secondary school at the time the new course was introduced had some experience with computers; 43% of them had acquired this skill at the age of 14–15: 74% from using calculators, 40% from using personal computers, and 21% from playing electronic games ([318]).

In the public consciousness, according to a VP poll, computers were not associated with production and work tasks. In a 1990 survey, when respondents were asked why there was so much interest in buying new electronic systems, 38% felt that it was "to lead a more interesting life, to have more conveniences"; 26%, to use for work or educational purposes; and 21%, to invest money profitably. When asked whether they would like to make use of a personal computer right away, 66% answered in the affirmative, of whom 21% would prefer to use it in the office and 19% at home, while 26% would prefer to use it both in the office and at home. The youngest respondents showed the greatest willingness to use a personal computer (91%) ([91a]). From 1993 to 1994, the number of families with computers at home tripled, from 2% to 6% ([12g]).

Table 5
Schools with computer hardware facilities, Russia, 1986–92 (at start of academic year)

	1986/ 1987	1987/ 1988	1988/ 1989	1989/ 1990	1990/ 1991	1991/ 1992
% of secondary schools	11.5	15.0	13.2	21.9	37.1	51.1
Number of computers installed (000)	22.7	33.9	39.4	75.1	142.8	209.4
Total number of schools with facilities	3,341	4,456	4,035	6,921	12,155	172,564

Sources: [171], p. 251; [175], p. 257.

I.A. Boutenko

5 Labour and Management

5.1 Work Organization

An unsatisfactory structuring of the industrial process in the 1960s and 1970s led to a significant loss in work time and an increase in the number of labourers. Since the 1980s, a search for more effective ways of structuring labour has been under way; in the 1990s, contractual agreements with groups and individualization appeared to be more widespread.

Under the régime of state property, labour organization was largely of an extensive (as opposed to intensive) character, poorly structured and intense in terms of physical labour. In the 1920s, some efforts were made to introduce Taylorism to industry, but in subsequent decades much more attention was paid to equalizing the economic rewards and moral stimuli of labour, and to provision of privileges for labourers. As a result, labour productivity grew slowly (see table 1). The poor structure of the industrial process was due chiefly to hypermonopolization of the economy and forced planning of production targets without taking into account real social needs and the specificity of the product manufactured. As a result, workers were often idle. Two thirds of work time lost was due to unsatisfactory maintenance and interruptions of input supply in the workplace: time losses because of a lack of raw materials, stock, inventory, packing, transportation, and so on,

Table 1
Average annual labour productivity indexes, Russia, 1976–89 (annual increase in %)

	1976–80	*1981–85*	*1986–89*
Industry	3.3	3.1	4.1
Agriculture*	2.4	1.9	6.0
Construction	2.2	2.7	5.6
Total	3.4	2.8	2.7

Source: [175], p. 121.
* Not including kitchen gardens.

comprised between 25% and 50% of total time lost and between 14% and 30% of time loss was the result of faulty equipment ([183]). Workers left their workplace with or without their superiors' permission or were engaged in jobs not related to their vocational skills. Very often, supervisory and support staff were temporarily deployed elsewhere (see table 2). However, by the 1990s this trend had almost disappeared, with the exception of some state enterprises.

Mechanization rates remained low (see table 3) and equipment was not used effectively (see table 4). In the 1990s, there was a sharp increase in the number of those holding shares in their enterprise and hence, presumably, interested in improving efficiency, but quantitative data are not available. In spite of the lack of an adequate social infrastructure (e.g., transport, eating facilities), by the end of the 1980s factories often operated two or three shifts (see table 5) to increase output.

The last efforts to increase production output by such means were made in 1987, when facilitating regulations were adopted. As a result, the average number of shifts increased from 1.42%, in 1986, to 1.46%, in 1987 ([177]). By the mid-1990s, due to drops in production, recourse to second and third shifts was rare.

The extensive nature of labour and numerous structural constraints created a constant labour shortage, leading to a mobilization of women with children, people with disabilities, and the elderly. The structure of the work regime was similar for all labourers from the 1960s to the 1980s. The possibility of holding more than one job was regarded as a temporary measure that negatively affected the quality and productivity of labour. In 1959, this possibility was sharply restricted by law, but in 1960 many such limitations for workers, junior service personnel, and low-paid employees were cancelled. In 1988, holding more than one job was allowed once more, but only one such part-time job in addition to one's full-time job was allowed. Throughout this period, the educational level of those holding more than one job was higher than that of the labour force as a whole (the main reason for this was that the intelligentsia and pensioners, with lower salaries and allowances, respectively, were obliged to compensate for their inadequate income in this way).

Beginning in the late 1980s, flexible schedules were allowed. A selective survey showed that the percentage of loss of work time due to absenteeism in a context where flexible schedules were available dropped by 48%; job changes, by 60%; and absence due to illness, by 13.6%.

Old-age pensioners comprised 47% of part-time labourers in 1989, as compared to 33.2% in 1978 ([183]). In the 1990s, due to a drop in industrial production, many labourers worked part time at a number of enterprises and institutions.

The majority of people who worked at home in the 1980s were mothers of small or disabled children, single mothers, retired persons, disabled persons, and expectant mothers ([107]). In the 1990s, work at home became more widespread, but statistics

Table 2
Temporary redeployment of workers and employees in other than their basic occupation, selected sectors, Russia, 1986–89 (work days per year)

	1986	1987	1988	1989
Industrial enterprises	3.3	3.1	2.4	2.1
Construction	1.9	1.8	1.4	1.3
Transport	1.8	1.7	1.4	1.2
Engineering, design research offices	3.0	3.8	2.4	1.8
Offices and institutions	5.1	4.9	3.3	2.4
Total	2.2	2.1	1.6	1.4

Source: [175], p. 125.

Table 3
Mechanized and automated production departments and enterprises, Russia, 1971–85

Production departments			Enterprises		
1971	1981	1985	1971	1981	1985
26,449	53,529	60,385	2,628	3,790	4,207

Source: [177], p. 73.

Table 4
Rate of productivity of mechanized and automatic production lines at industrial enterprises, Russia, 1985 (%)

Productivity rate	% of production lines
100% or more*	53
75–99%	26
50–74%	14
Less than 50%	7

Source: [177], p. 73.
* Due to extensive exploitation (more than one shift) and rationalization (site improvements).

Table 5
Average number of work shifts per industrial sector, Russia, 1970–91

	1970	1980	1985	1990	1991
Heavy industry	1.47	1.41	1.40	1.39	1.36
Light industry	1.57	1.56	1.47	1.42	1.40
Food industry	1.36	1.38	1.37	1.37	1.36
Industry, total	1.42	1.36	1.33	1.32	1.30

Sources: [171], p. 371; [177], p. 98.

are not available. During this period, the rhythm of work was determined chiefly by the form of ownership of the enterprise: 91% of workers at co-operatives and 62% of people working at state enterprises felt that their work load had increased ([65]).

The period from 1960 to 1990 was characterized by a policy of according priority to work regimes organized on a collective basis. In the 1990s, this trend was reversed. Under the socialist system, workers were strongly discouraged from exercising individualistic initiative; this dated from the late 1920s, when the collectivization of small individual farms into large socialist ones began (see table 6); a return to individual farms started in the late 1980s (see table 7). Nevertheless, in the early 1990s one third of these private farmers were afraid of being dispossessed ([2]).

In an effort to increase interest in work and the assumption of responsibility, at the end of the 1970s it was decided to privilege "brigade" work groups as the essential basis of workplace organization at enterprises. The extent of this "brigade" reorganization was centrally planned, and by 1983 two thirds of industrial workers were in "brigades." Actual work roles differed from brigade to brigade, and a link between individual performance and income was more evident in some than in others (see tables 8 and 9). In 1984, 71.7% of all industrial workers were in brigades, and in 65.5% of cases, the remuneration of the collective labour was evaluated in terms of brigade output. However, workers also received bonuses based on job category and time worked ([129]).

In spite of all of this, brigades had little effect on the labour-force participation rate at most enterprises. In the mid-1980s, the increase in labour productivity obtained was less than 0.25% per year, and even in sectors where the introduction of brigades was most effective, it did not exceed 0.5% ([303]).

In the 1980s, owing to ambiguity of labour regulations and definitions of duties, the relationship between labour input and financial rewards became the

Table 6
Collectivization of farms, USSR, 1928–40 (%)

	Of total farms	Per sowing area
1928	1.6	2.2
1932	59.3	78.5
1937	92.6	99.4
1938	93.1	99.5
1940	96.6	99.6

Source: [177], p. 38.

Table 7
Private farms, Russia, 1990–92

	1990	1991	1992 (July 1)
Number of farms (000)	4.4	49.0	127.0
Total area of plots granted (000 hectares)	181	2,068	5,160

Source: [171], p. 73.

Table 8
Number of brigades according to type of remuneration, Russia, 1980–86 (000)

	1980	1985	1986
Brigades assuming cost of capital "rent"	–	283	287
Brigades with common targets in terms of output and quality applied to all members	369	798	760
Brigades in which bonuses for extra production are paid	–	517	541
Total brigades	743	953	937

Source: [175], p. 99.

Table 9
Industrial workers involved in brigades, Russia, 1980–96

	Total (million)			%		
	1980	1985	1986	1980	1985	1986
Workers in brigades assuming cost of capital "rent"	–	4.19	4.65	–	36	40
Workers in brigades with common targets in terms of output and quality	3.41	9.84	9.70	47	85	83
workers who receive bonuses for extra production	–	7.96	7.98	–	69	68
workers paid according to their individual input (labour participation rate)	–	7.10	7.57	–	61	64

Source: [171], p. 99.

subject of contractual negotiations. Employees in enterprises as a group ("collectives") gained more opportunities to participate in management. In the 1990s, changes in the nature of ownership of enterprises ("joint-stock" companies, co-operatives, etc.) stimulated such changes. Wages and benefits were distributed according to collective consensus, generated by more a rational use of equipment and a more effective deployment of labour.

Before the 1990s, participation by labourers in administering production was of a formal character. In the 1980s, the basis for this participation was brigade, department, and enterprise councils, which performed advisory functions under the direction of appropriate plant officials. In many respects, the councils were prototypes for the "collective" councils (see section 9.1) that were initiated in enterprises in the late 1980s with the goal of involving workers in management of the production process and, more important, to determine how enterprises would be privatized. But the functioning of the "collective" councils was compromised by passivity, lack of independence from management, and a misunderstanding of their management role.

In 1988, co-operatives were gradually developing into a fully independent collective ownership form. The next step on the way to independent management was assuming the cost of the use of already installed facilities or amortization losses (capital "rent"). A massive transition to the true cost or "rent" basis of accounting began in late 1988. In 1991, 3,947 industrial enterprises worked on the "rent" basis; of these, 392 were in factories producing transportation vehicles. Labour "collectives" at "rent" enterprises were able to accumulate assets and profit, gradually decreasing the state's interest in these enterprises. In the 1990s, joint ventures with foreign companies began to appear: in 1990, there were 252 such ventures; by the end of 1991, there were 8,092 ([171]).

I.A. Boutenko and L.N. Sivashenkova

5.2 Personnel Administration

Production and work-organization problems constantly dominated personnel training considerations. Improving training and retraining of personnel became a major problem for the state. Although workers were paid according to their qualification grade, retraining seldom influenced pay or grade.

Before the 1990s, the state monopoly governed personnel movement through pay grade scales. There were two pay scales, according to economic sector and to region. At the end of the 1980s, average incomes in non-industrial sectors were 23% to 28% lower than those in industrial sectors (which more or less coincided with the average pay in the national economy as a whole). By the end of 1992, this difference had reached a factor of between 1.6 and 2.4 ([171]). Wages rose most in regions where the primary sector predominated.

Workers were encouraged to stay at their present job without direct dependence on their work output. Wages at state enterprises were paid according to general rates for particular grades; wages and other kinds of stimulants were not directly connected to labour efficiency (see table 1) or results, but to the type of industry and seniority.

In the 1990s, the transition to a market economy led to an increase in the wage gap. Private enterprise provided higher wages than did state enterprises, and gaps also grew within state enterprises. In 1992, managerial wages were twice as high as average wages; in 1993, this difference had increased by a factor of between 5 and 15 ([29]).

Given the level of economic development in Russia, the portion of the labour force with higher education was too large. The growth in workers' qualifications outstripped the rise in the technological and organizational levels of the economy, and thus outstripped the economy's need for a qualified labour force. The number of employed persons with higher education grew (see table 2), while the number of auxiliary and support staff dropped, with the result that rudimentary kinds of work were carried out by specialists. The low efficiency of using specialists resulted in a situation in which expenditures on education became unjustified, and in a deformation of the labour-force demand and income-compensation structure.

By the end of 1970s, Russia had achieved a high level of industrial labour employment, and it prolonged the gradual increase in the level of activity by the use of extensive means. The structure of employment in the 1980s was characterized by a considerable decrease in the proportion of agricultural labour and a concomitant increase in the proportion of industrial labour. In 1990, 77% of men and 35% of women were engaged in industrial labour; 11% of men and 20% of women, in agriculture; 3% of men and 20% of women, in communications; and 9% of men and 38% of women, in services ([34]).

The higher and secondary-vocational education systems did not correspond to economic needs. All educational institutions were, to a considerable degree, oriented toward industrial vocations. The proportion of graduates from industrial and construction higher educational institutions in 1960 comprised 33% of all graduates;

Table 1
Labour productivity and average income in selected sectors, Russia, 1980–91 (% to preceding year)

	1980	1985	1990	1991
Industry:				
Labour productivity	103.0	103.0	103.0	101.0
Average wages	103.0	103.0	113.0	195.0
Agriculture:				
Labour productivity	100.3	104.0	96.0	94.0
Average wages	103.0	104.0	119.0	158.0
Construction				
Labour productivity	101.0	103.0	98.3	97.2
Average wages	103.0	103.0	113.0	185.0

Source: [171], p. 127.

Table 2
Employed specialists with higher and secondary vocational education, Russia, 1980–89 (000)

	1980	1985	1987	1989
Total specialists	16,546	19,086	20,157	10,583
women	10,139	11,849	12,577	12,857
Specialists with higher education	6,710	7,938	8,468	8,685
women	3,689	4,451	4,769	4914

Source: [177], p. 115.

in 1970, 39%; in 1980 and 1985, 41%; and in 1991, 36%. The proportion of graduates from industrial and construction secondary vocational schools was 46% in 1960; 44% in 1970; 40% in 1980; 37% in 1985; and 34% in 1991 ([171]).

A basic reorganization of the educational system would take a long time, and the effects of such a reorganization would be felt well into the future; in the meantime (the 1990s), lay-offs and staff turnover were having their effects. The system of vocational education served as a means of expanding the number of available workers on the labour market. In the 1970s, there were two kinds of training and qualification improvement: in the workplace and in the vocational education system. Up to the beginning of 1975, 70% of workers were trained in the workplace and 20% to 25% attended special courses ([32]). In 1980, 77% of all workers trained in the workplace, while 23% attended courses; in 1992, the figures were 68% and 32%, respectively ([242]).

For a long time, personnel training, retraining, and qualification upgrading were considered to be neither obligatory nor as important as the current pro-

duction exigencies. Education in the workplace and in schools was theoretical and ideological and had little connection with industrial production problems. Students did practical work at enterprises for two to six months, but this practice was simply formal, because it consisted of carrying out once-only assignments and auxiliary tasks. Despite this, from 1960 to 1980, the number of people within the training, retraining, and qualification-upgrading systems increased constantly (see table 3). This number then decreased by 70% between 1990 and 1992 ([171]). In 1986 trade (departmental) courses trained 31,000 skilled workers; this number declined to 21,000 in 1991, and to 16,000 in 1992. In 1993, 9% of workers improved their skills; in 1990, this proportion had been 26%. Between 1989 and 1993, 24% of all specialists and managers undertook upgrading that consisted of an initiation to the market economy ([242]).

Women comprised 52% of the employed for many years, but their proportion among total personnel who had upgraded their skills was always low. From 1987 to 1992, only one third of women with 10 to 20 years' employment were trained in vocational courses, and often graduation from a vocational school did not mean a change in their career. Polls carried out in 1991–92 showed that 90% of women with training had not advanced, and 89% had not achieved a higher grade; wages rose for only one fifth of them, and even then insufficiently. Nevertheless, 25% of female respondents expressed a desire to train and retrain either on the job or on their own time (among workers, 24%; among collective farmers, 25%; among employers, 26%) ([237]).

Lower qualification was one reason for women's lack of interest in their work. According to some surveys carried out in the late 1980s and early 1990s, women under 20 years old had higher qualifications than did men. A rupture in qualification level was observed in the next age group up (20–29 years), a period associated with

Table 3
Training and qualification upgrading in enterprises, institutions, organizations, and collective farms, Russia, 1960–92 (millions of persons per year)

	1960	1970	1980	1990	1992
Retrained, total employed	2.3	3.9	4.9	3.2	2.1
workers	2.2	3.8	4.6	3.1	2.1
Qualification upgrading, total					
employed	4.1	6.5	19.4	17.4	5.4
workers	3.1	4.7	12.5	12.0	3.2

Sources: [177], p. 273; [242], p. 123.

forming a family and giving birth to children. The result was a temporary halt to training among women, whereas the level of qualification and education among men was constantly rising. However, 39% of women (labourers and office workers) considered themselves to be insufficiently trained to fulfil a management role; and female labourers considered this inadequacy to be a more frequent handicap to career advancement than were family and children ([237]).

In the 1990s, massive layoffs of women also changed the gender ratio of employment.

L.N. Sivashenkova

5.3 Size and Types of Enterprises

Throughout the Soviet period, large state enterprises were the main actors in the national economy. When centralized planning was rejected at the end of the 1980s, enterprises of a new type began to form.

From the 1930s to the 1980s, the Russian economy was oriented toward unlimited concentration of production. In 1956, there was a reorganization of enterprises in Russia: nearly all small enterprises were amalgamated into large ones. Until the end of the 1980s, the policy was to centralize all enterprises by sphere of production; every sphere considered it prestigious to have large and very large enterprises and gigantic plants ("territorial and productive complexes"). In 1986, such complexes comprised 74% of the total volume of oil production, 83% of gas production, and 48% of iron production ([177]).

Throughout the period under study, a high level of concentration and specialization of production was typical in Russian industry. Most industrial output was concentrated in large enterprises. About 2% of industrial enterprises (with more than 5,000 employees) produced more than 40% of the total volume of output ([278]). In 1993, there were 547 industrial monopolies; they comprised 3% of all industrial enterprises but produced 20% of total industrial output. These monopolies were concentrated mainly in the machine-building and metal-working industries; 354 enterprises produced 30% of total output in this sector in 1993 ([242]).

The negative effects of this policy was evident even in the 1960s: many productive and personal needs, especially for products manufactured in small numbers and for services, could not be completely satisfied.

At the beginning of the 1990s, with the transition of the Russian economy to a market system, the role of new forms of management increased, with a trend toward small and medium-sized enterprises. **State enterprises retained their monopoly status in the economy as a whole, despite widespread privatization.** In the mid-1990s, every fifth industrial enterprise still belonged to the state ([242]).

Since 1993, a transitional state in limitation of state property was the recourse to the above-mentioned ownership formula. In the case of larger enterprises, the transition from total state ownership to joint-stock companies was facilitated by the capital-rent formula whereby collectives of employees operated plants while paying a "rent" on assets. By the end of 1993, half of all industrial enterprises in Russia were joint-stock companies and they produced two thirds of total output. Private and mixed forms of property comprise about three quarters of large and medium-sized industrial enterprises, producing 47% of industrial output and employing 44% of industrial workers (see table 1).

A new policy favouring development of new, smaller economic units began in 1986, when co-operative and lease types of property began to appear (see table 2). The first wave of co-operative ownership (1986–87) was aimed mainly at legalization of "underground operators," which were oriented toward instant profits and not toward the future. It was this first wave of co-operatives that set public opinion against this form of ownership. The second wave, in the fall of 1987, involved a longer-term perspective. The third wave arose after the adoption of the law on co-operatives. This wave gradually attracted masses of employees, largely because of better remuneration offered. A major shift of employees, primarily those with a high level of qualification, into this ownership type began at that time. The fourth wave took place in the summer of 1989, and since then small enterprises have been formed more readily with varying forms of property structure.

By the end of 1993, there were about 700,000 small enterprises employing 12% of the total labour force. The number of small enterprises in the trade and services sectors continued to grow, reaching 58% of all small enterprises. The proportion of industrial and construction enterprises was 10% and 12%, respectively.

From 1992 to 1993, the number of small industrial enterprises almost doubled, reaching 79,000. They produced 7% of total output and employed 10% of the total labour force ([278]).

Data from surveys of businesspeople show that so-called mediation-fund credits administered through private commercial banks (the sources of these banks were not entirely transparent, although the state was presumably the main source), and criminal activity were the main sources of the risk capital in the organization and

Table 1
Nonstate industrial enterprises, Russia, 1993 (%)

Total enterprises type of property		Production enterprises type of property		Employees type of property	
Private	Mixed	Private	Mixed	Private	Mixed
54.0	20.0	7.9	39.0	11.0	33.0

Source: [242], p. 34.

Table 2
Development of the co-operative movement, Russia, 1987–92 (000)

	1987	1988	1989	1990	1991	1992
Number of co-operatives	7.3	39.0	102.0	135.0	78.0	44.0
Number of employees (000)	69.0	708.0	2,688.0	3,512.0	2,034.0	941.0

Sources: [176], p.70; [242], p.121.

purchase of small enterprises. Other enterprises accumulated capital from state sources and were in no hurry to free themselves from the state stewardship that guarantees them a relatively stable status.

In the 1990s, family businesses began to revive and become widespread. From the 1960s to the 1980s, most family businesses consisted of small kitchen-garden farms and handicrafts. In the cities, family businesses became possible with the appearance of the first co-operatives. At first, they were a secondary activity, and only gradually did they become a primary activity. In the mid-1990s, family businesses existed in the form of small enterprises, organized mainly on the basis of family savings, equipment available to family members, and often managed by the head of the family.

In cities, most family businesses had been involved in dressmaking and alterations and in providing nursery-school services. In 1992, small family stores and repair shops appeared.

In villages, family businesses consisted of farms and the small enterprises that service them. Sample annual studies by the Institute of Sociology (Russian Academy of Sciences) show that these were mainly family farms (see table 3).

In 1991 the privatization law was adopted, and the privatization program was worked out and was to be executed on the base of this law (see table 3). The first stage limiting privatization was planned to be 80–90% complete before 1992. By 1 October 1993, more than 57,000 small enterprises had been privatized (61% of all small enterprises that intended to privatize). The tempo of privatization of small enterprises slowed at the end of 1993. The second stage – "voucher" privatization and privatization of large enterprises – was planned to be complete before mid-1994. Before the end of 1994, 89,000 enterprises were privatized ([242]). In 1993–94, privatization of small enterprises was accomplished, as a rule, by selling them with practically no limitations by the state. Privatization of large and medium-sized enterprises was accomplished mainly by issuing shares.

Table 3
Number of farms, Russia, 1991–94

	1991	1992	1993	1994
Total (000)	4	49	183	270
Family farms (%)	79	87	89	–
Nuclear family farms (%)	58	64	62	–

Source: [242], p. 40; [255], p. 65.

Table 4
Privatization of enterprises by sphere of activity, Russia, 1992–93 (% of all privatized enterprises)

	1992	1993
Construction materials	1.5	2.0
Light industry	7.5	8.2
Food industry	3.7	5.0
Agriculture	1.8	1.7
Construction	6.5	9.0
Automobile industry	1.5	3.2
Trade	40.7	34.6
Food catering	8.0	6.9
Other sectors	5.8	11.7
Services (laundry, repairs, etc.)	23.0	17.7

Source: [242], p. 33.

L.N. Sivashenkova

6 Social Stratification

6.1 Occupational Status

The labour-participation rate has always been very high in Russia. The service, or nonproductive, sector and, correspondingly, white-collar professions expanded rapidly. This fact was directly reflected in the life plans of young people. In a context of increasing stagnation, the image of professions based on higher education was tarnished and by the mid-1990s, had suffered a loss in status.

From 1959 to 1979, the proportion of people working in the USSR and the Russian Federation constantly rose. In the 1980s, as a result of increasing economic stagnation, there was a deceleration in the labour-participation rate.

From 1959 to 1979, the proportion of workers in the total population increased from 50% to 60%. From 1980 to 1990, this figure dropped slightly; in industry, it went from 69.8% to 67.3% ([176]). The percentage of unskilled workers slowly decreased from 1959 to 1969, to reach 21% of all workers. However, the proportion of skilled mechanized workers in the labour force increased ([119]). The system of specialized secondary technical education and upgrading of qualifications was not compatible with modern needs and suffered a loss of prestige: from 1985 on, the number of graduates from technical vocational schools and qualification-improvement courses declined.

The increase in the proportion of workers in the population from the 1960s to the 1980s was linked, to a great degree, with women entering the labour force. During the 1980s, this domination of women was especially great among specialists with a special secondary or higher education (see table 1). Among collective farmers, on the contrary, the proportion of women constantly decreased from 47% in 1980 to 44% in 1989 in the USSR and from 44% to 39% in Russia ([176]).

In 1990, the labour pool in Russia amounted to 86.8 million people, or 60% of the total population. From 1980 to 1990, this number increased by 0.9 million or 1% over the ten-year period. Total growth in the labour pool over this decade was equivalent to the annual growth rate in the 1970s.

Table 1
Proportion of women specialists with secondary or higher education
to all employed specialists, USSR and Russia, 1980–89 (%)

	USSR	Russia
1980	59.0	61.2
1985	60.0	62.1
1987	61.0	62.4
1989	61.0	62.5

Sources: [175], p. 58; [176], p. 114.

Most workers were employed in the state sector until the 1990s. In 1989, for instance, the drop in the proportion of those working in the state sector to 2.3% was due to the creation of nonstate co-operatives and to a decrease in the rate of female employment as a result of an increase in the length of women's leave for child-care purposes ([175]).

The service sector and white-collar professions grew rapidly (see tables 2 and 3). The proportion of salaried employees constantly increased: in 1959, they comprised 18% of the working population; in 1989, 30%. The number of specialists with secondary or higher education, who comprised the largest share of employees, increased to 24% between 1980 and 1990. Considerable growth took place from 1980 to 1985, after which it slowed to some degree ([175]). Distortion in remuneration, typical for the period of stagnation in (1970s and 1980s), resulted in an increase in the number of specialists with higher education employed as workers (see table 4).

Among specialists, the greatest increase was noted among the engineering and technical professions, and especially among graduate engineers. In 1960, they comprised 32% of specialists with higher education; in 1970, 36.2%; and in 1973, 37.6%. The proportion of engineers grew by 785% from 1950 to 1973. This was considerably higher than the increase in proportion of other specialists and was comparable only to the growth in the proportion of scientific personnel over the same period, which was 680% ([276]). Their numbers began to diminish from 1985 on, but from 1960 to the late 1980s engineers were not only the most numerous among highly educated employees, but also the most popular professional group (see table 5). The prestige of professions that required higher education and allowed for creativity increased in the 1960s and 1970s. In the 1970s and 1980s, as economic stagnation deepened, further devaluation of skilled labour and a decrease in worker motivation set in. Preferences as to what were the most desirable occupations began to change.

Table 2
Distribution of population by means of subsistence, USSR, 1959–89 (%)

	1959	1979	1989
Working in the state sector and collective farms (except these engaged in housekeeping and kitchen gardening)	47.5	51.5	49.7
On allowance (students)	0.8	2.5	2.4
Pensioners and others on state welfare	6.0	15.3	17.6
Dependents of individuals engaged only in housekeeping and kitchen gardening	45.6	30.6	30.1
With other, unrecorded sources of income	0.1	0.1	0.2

Sources: [176], p. 26; [184], p. 153.

Table 3
Distribution of workers by production sector (material goods) and service ("nonproductive") sectors, USSR, 1959–89 (%)

	*Production of goods**	*Service sector*
1959	83.9	16.1
1970	77.1	22.9
1979	74.1	25.9
1980	74.0	26.0
1985	73.2	26.8
1989	72.2	27.8

Sources: [176], p. 47; [184], p. 164.
* Including kitchen gardens.

Table 4
Number of specialists with higher education employed as workers, USSR and Russia, 1980–89 (000)

	1980	1985	1987	1989
USSR	203.3	484.2	578.8	733.6
Russia	126.4	286.4	350.0	443.5

Source: [180], p. 62.

Among professionals with higher education, employment connected with office work, work in communal enterprises, and sales had the lowest appeal. The most desirable professions were pilot and operator. Among the engineering professions, graduates most preferred those of radio operator and geologist; the least popular professions were food engineer and clothing-industry engineer. Among rural professions requiring higher education, agronomist and veterinarian received the lowest grade. The professions of teacher and doctor were more popular among girls than among boys ([340]). Among professions that did not require higher education, employment in the services sector and agriculture were the least preferred.

The results of research conducted in the first half of the 1980s revealed that young people were becoming increasingly practical: the prestige of scientific professions dropped, while those of bookkeeper, ledger clerk, and salesperson grew ([324]). This reflected one of the main features of the period of stagnation: the consolidation of a privileged position of groups that had direct access to material goods.

Both in the 1960s and in the 1980s, there was a considerable gap between young people's personal plans and the real choices they faced.

In the mid-1990s, fewer young people were entering high school. The total number of employed dropped, and there was a redistribution of jobs (see table 6). Many specialists either left their jobs to become self-employed or had a job both in the state and the private sector so as not to forgo the stability and benefits (pension, prestige, etc.) associated with the former.

Table 5
Specialists with higher education by profession, USSR, 1980–89 (%)

	1980	1985	1989
Engineers	40.7	41.8	41.5
Agronomists, livestock experts, veterinarians	5.1	4.8	4.6
Economists	9.0	9.6	10.1
Store managers	1.2	1.2	1.2
Lawyers	1.5	1.5	1.5
University professors, librarians, cultural workers, teachers	31.5	30.5	30.0

Source: Estimated from [180], p. 760.

Table 6
Distribution of employees by type of enterprise, Russia, 1990–93 (000,000)

	1990	1991	1992	1993
In state enterprises	62.2	55.7	48.2	41.5
In "mixed property" enterprises*	3.0	7.5	8.3	12.1
In public co-operatives and associations	0.6	0.7	0.6	0.5
In joint enterprises	0.1	0.1	0.2	0.3
in the private sector	9.4	9.8	14.7	16.6
Total	75.3	73.8	72.0	71.1

Source: [242], p. 82.
* State and nonstate.

O.M. Zdravomisliva

6.2 Social Mobility

During the 1960s and particularly the 1970s, social mobility decreased in comparison with the 1930s to 1950s, when there were mass repressions and swift rises and falls of representatives of different classes, mostly of managers. The main feature of social mobility from the 1960s to the 1990s was its chaotic character; in general, the social structure became extremely fluid.

Throughout Soviet rule, ascribed status prevailed over achieved status – that is, social and professional criteria were replaced by ideological ones. The social structure was presented as consisting of the working class (to whom the vanguard role in construction of a new social order was ascribed), the peasantry, and the intelligentsia, the latter including office workers. On the one hand, equality of people, irrespective of their origin, was proclaimed; as a result, not only was serious intergenerational analysis of social mobility not carried out, but existing differences were thoroughly hidden. On the other hand, until the 1990s, any contact of an individual with the state structure (getting a job or gaining access to an educational institution, getting a bank account, visiting a clinic, registering a child at school, etc.) required filling in forms in which stating one's origin was obligatory. Of course, this influenced people's lives less than when, in the 1930s, some groups were deprived of a considerable number of civil rights (the *lishentsy*, or "deprived") because their parents belonged to "bourgeois elements"; nonetheless, individuals were physically eliminated until the 1950s, and other forms of repression continued to exist in less blatant forms.

In the 1990s, there was a voluntaristic attempt to return to an "estate" type of social organization inspired by feudalism (for example, nobles' assemblies and merchants' communities were formed); however, this amounted to no more than a new form of leisure and political association.

Until the 1990s, preference in professional advancement was given to those whose parents were workers or, more rarely, peasants. While workers' dynasties were stimulated and supported, they were considered undesirable in science, and in power structures they were tolerated only by silent consent of the initiated.

Membership in the Communist Party of the Soviet Union, which provided successful professional advancement, was differentially accessible to representatives of different classes, since admission was allowed according to quotas, with workers, and later peasants, obviously preferred.

In the 1980s, 40% of Party officials were workers by birth, 12% were of peasant stock, and the rest were the children of office workers, except for 1.5% who were children of Party, Soviet, and trade-union officials ([28]).

The aspiration of the totalitarian state to homogenize the population led to the granting of privileges for workers' and peasants' children, for example, when it came time to go to high school, and a corresponding systematic bias against the children of intellectuals. A higher rate of high-school admissions for those who had previously worked in the production sector led to a temporary (before entering a higher school) phenomenon of intellectuals' children passing to the ranks of workers (see table 1).

Until the 1980s, inter-class mobility was connected mostly with urbanization and with scientific and technical progress (see table 2). A weaker correlation between status and origin, the result of large-scale structural mobility, was most obvious in the 1960s. The number of people in the working class was almost constantly increasing due to integration of peasants' children: from the 1940s to the 1980s, the number of workers tripled, and the number of rural dwellers and peasants decreased proportionately ([265]).

The mixing of the intelligentsia with those of different origins and statuses was reinforced by the inclusion of the latter (the expression "an intellectual of the first generation," arose to characterize a low-brow person), but not to moving to other strata (although many artists were employed as unskilled workers in the 1970s and 1980s). Calculations of these class movements are hampered, however, by the fact that intelligentsia and office workers were registered together. In the transition period of the 1990s, highly skilled workers and high-level managers kept their positions; middle-level managers were more mobile, and 8% of them became businesspeople. Some semi-skilled and unskilled workers upgraded their qualifications, but most members of this group became unemployed (see table 3).

Throughout the period under study, the elite was not formed of the most educated strata; by social origin, children of the intelligentsia formed a minority in the higher Party leadership, except in the 1930s (see table 4). In the 1990s, an energetic regrouping and skilful adaptation by former high-level managers to new socio-political conditions accelerated, enabling them to maintain their status, constituted a remarkable mobility phenomenon, suggesting that they comprise a caste able to maintain itself despite changing conditions.

Higher and vocational secondary education gradually made up for differences in origin. Attaining vocational education in a city appeared to be the only opportunity that peasants' children had to become equal citizens, since, until the 1980s, passports were not given to peasants. That is why, in the mid-1980s, it turned

Table 1
Admission of individuals who had worked two years or more in production to higher and vocational secondary schools, Russia, 1960–86

	1960	1970	1980	1986
Admitted to higher schools (000)	90	54	63	55
% of total admitted to regular daytime courses	57	19	17	15
Admitted to secondary vocational-technical schools (000)	66	37	32	27
% of total admitted to regular daytime courses	27	8	6	5

Source: [177], p. 378.

Table 2
Changes in social structure of the urban population, USSR (1970 in % to 1959)

Unskilled and semi-skilled workers, service workers	92.9
Skilled workers combining intellectual and physical work	141.0
Highly skilled workers combining intellectual and physical work	144.0
Clerks with no vocational education	156.0
Highly skilled intellectual employees with vocational secondary education	189.0
Highly skilled intellectual employees with university education	263.0
Highly skilled scientific and technical employees, artists, intelligentsia	204.0
Highly skilled managers	169.0

Source: [278], p. 27.

Table 3
Proportion of different groups in the professional structure, Russia, 1985, 1993 (%)

	1985	1993
Managers	9.0	9.0
Specialists	19.6	18.9
Workers in industry	27.5	26.0
Workers in services	10.4	11.0
Businesspeople	0.7	3.1
Peasants	5.9	.4
Students	15.1	6.0
Unemployed	10.9	20.5

Source: [328], p. 136.

Table 4
Social composition of the politburo of the Central Committee of the CPSU (%)

	1917–24 (Lenin)	1925–53 (Stalin)	1953–64 (Khrushchev)	1965–84 (Brezhnev)	1985–90 (Gorbachev)
Workers	25	44	43	10	15
Peasants	19	24	26	55	43
Intelligentsia	56	20	9	20	10
Information not available	–	12	22	15	33

Source: [54], p. 23

out that one fifth of urban dwellers had moved to towns and cities from the country with the express purpose of acquiring a social status different from that of their parents ([313]).

Until the late 1980s, a considerable number of families of both industrial and office workers and intelligentsia were committed to providing their children with higher education. (Since both parents worked, as a rule, social origin of their children was unequivocally defined in only two thirds of cases [(313)]). The higher the parents' education, the more probable it was that their children's life plans would be also connected with getting a specialized education ([217]). Among general secondary-school graduates (graduating presupposed entering high school), 44.6% of their fathers and 33.8% of their mothers were workers, and 43.6% and 60.6%, respectively, were of the intelligentsia. Among the parents of those studying at vocational secondary schools, 62.6% of fathers and 58.7% of mothers were workers; 14.2% and 13.2%, respectively, were of the intelligentsia. At higher and technical schools, half of the students were from intelligentsia families, while 13–14% were from peasant families ([5]) – that is, a smaller proportion than that of peasant families in the population as a whole.

The status of graduates from institutes of higher education was quite unsatisfying: inadequate salaries and bonuses and insufficient recognition of professionalism and talent led to a situation in which, despite the constant increase in the proportion of persons with higher and vocational secondary education in the in the population as a whole (see table 5), young specialists (see section 1.1) experienced very slow progress in their careers.

Until the mid-1980s, career mobility had a spontaneous character and was affected most by payment and privileges. Working at a state enterprise was not only the right but the duty of every adult citizen, and a "parasitic way of life" was punishable under the criminal code. Changing one's work-place was considered a sign of unreliability and was limited by a set of measures aimed at stabilizing

Table 5
Percentage of people with higher education per social group, Russia, 1959–77

	1959	1970	1977
Workers	39.6	58.6	73.2
Collective farmers	22.6	39.3	56.2
Specialists	90.7	95.4	97.2

Source: [274], p. 10.

production and reducing expenses resulting from personnel fluctuations. The notion of "career" had a negative connotation. Relationships and protectionism played a significant role from the mid-1970s to the 1990s, when the situation finally changed.

From the second half of the 1970s to the late 1980s, a distortion toward downward career mobility prevailed among the educated strata of the population. Status incompatibility – having high education and low salary (since 1981, skilled workers, according to the scale of wage rates, received more pay than engineering-technical personnel) – led to a situation in which a considerable part of the intelligentsia felt the need for downward mobility. This was most obvious at the end of the work career, since pension rates, from the 1960s to the 1980s, depended upon salaries received during the last pre-pension years, and industrial workers received more pay than the intelligentsia and office workers.

The data of the 1980s show that 1–2% of workers and 2–4% of specialists wanted to move upward, while 21% of the latter wanted to move downward, to workers' jobs; among heads of departments, 1–3% wanted to move upward, and 24% wanted to move downward. Among heads of enterprises, most of whom owed their positions to CP membership, no one wanted to occupy a higher position, and 21% of them wanted to move to workers' jobs. This meant that the disposition toward downward mobility was stronger than that toward upward mobility, a result of both increased demands made of managers and the disinclination to accept responsibility without being in a position to make independent decisions ([253]).

In the 1990s and in the face of rising unemployment, the number of respondents expressing their readiness, if they were dismissed, immediately to accept another job requiring lower qualifications was 1.15 times higher than those expressing their readiness to learn a new profession ([91c]).

Until the 1990s, a person excluded from the CPSU was unequivocally destined to move down. Most upward moves took place among Party officials, and these were not always connected with a person's will to succeed: according to surveys, every fourth person promoted got a managerial position simply by following Party discipline ([270]).

Career mobility is more chaotic and higher among women, many of whom gave up their opportunity to improve their status under the pressure of their families and their everyday life (see table 6).

Behaviours directed exclusively toward achieving economic advantage became widespread only in the 1980s, although they were manifested earlier in scientific circles and also in the underground economy, seasonal work, *shabashka* (informal work gangs), and other socially looked-down-upon forms of activity. With the formation of a market economy, the significance of qualifications slowly increased. In the 1990s, horizontal career mobility became more widespread and spontaneous: more people had several part-time jobs; some of these jobs were illegal because of the existence of insufficient grade system of payment in state enterprises or for other reasons; obtaining a lower-prestige job was now compensated for by a higher income. The desire to accede to a new profession, such as lawyer, dealer or economist, was fulfilled through attendance at various short-term courses.

In the 1990s, new social groups appeared – businesspeople, financiers – mostly from the educated strata; professional groups were rapidly disappearing, appearing, and changing status. For instance, professional Party and Komsomol officials, Party secretaries in enterprises, and political instructors in military units vanished; trade-union functionaries acquired a different status; the professions of private detective and broker were legalized, and so on. Political loyalty (membership in the CPSU), which was more important for managers than their professional qualification until the 1990s, lost its significance in hiring procedures.

With the formation of a market economy, mobility increased abruptly. A stratum of businesspeople arose, whose members come from different groups: the former *nomenklatura* (Party and Komsomol functionaries), heads of state enterprises who used their official position as a springboard from which to go into business; dealers in the black market and the underground economy who had managed to legalize their assets; those who work at higher-level schools, scientists, army officers,

Table 6
Coefficient of conjugation (Pierson's coefficient) of social positions at the beginning of employment activity and at time of interview, Russia

Began working	Men	Women
in the 1960s	0.560	0.470
in the 1970s	0.601	0.790
in the 1980s	0.846	0.816

Source: [313], p. 67.

Interior Ministry and Secret Service employees; emigrants and other individuals who amassed their capital abroad and are investing it at home; and new heirs and rentiers.

In 1986, 16–18% of people surveyed, depending on the region, expressed a desire to engage in business; in 1992, this figure rose to 58% ([308]).

In the 1990s, there was mass marginalization connected with pauperization of intellectuals, physicians, cultural workers, and artists, who comprise an important segment of the middle class in developed countries. This created serious obstacles to the formation of a viable civil society.

I.A. Boutenko

6.3 Economic Inequality

The 1960s, 1970s, and 1980s were characterized by a rise in the population's wealth under the official drive to social homogeneity and egalitarianism in revenue and in consumption of goods and services. Growth of incomes did not result in greater work efficiency and a better match between qualifications and wages. An inequality of economic prospects for different groups was observed during these decades. Economic inequalities became obvious in the second half of 1980s, and blatantly manifest in the 1990s.

From the late 1950s to the 1980s, state policies were directed to two interconnected goals: to reduce the numbers of low-paid workers and of low-income ("poorly provided for") families. Under socialism there could be no other legal source of income than wages (salaries, fees), allowances, pensions, and incomes from private kitchen gardens. The main means to achieve these goals was regulation of wages, which were the main source of family income (see table 1). This improvement in the relative incomes of low-paid workers turned out to be the most significant trend during the 1960s and 1970s. Real average salary was quite stable from the late 1920s to the early 1950s: about 40–50 roubles a month in 1928, 1940, and 1950. In the second half of the 1950s, this threshold rose to 80–85 roubles per month.

The social consumption fund that financed free health care, education, and so on, grew from 140.3 billion roubles, in 1965, to 266.6 billion roubles, in 1975, while the real income of the population grew by 65%, due to the fact that the average wage rose from 96.5 to 145.8 roubles over the period ([177]; see tables 2 and 3).

Table 1
Structure of per capita total income in families of industrial workers, Russia, 1940–75 (%)

	1940	1960	1965	1970	1975
Wage of family members	71.3	75.2	73.1	74.4	74.3
Social consumption funds	14.5	20.2	22.8	22.1	22.5
Income from kitchen garden	9.2	1.5	1.7	1.3	0.9
Income from other sources	5.0	3.3	2.4	2.2	2.3

Sources: [172], p. 562; [178], p. 596.

Table 2
Average monthly family income, Russia, 1980–88 (roubles)

	1980	1985	1988
Workers and employees	121	135	153
in industry	135	150	166
in state agricultural enterprises	94	109	121
collective farmers	91	110	121
Retired workers and employees	77	91	102
Retired collective farmers	81	96	112
Average	112	127	143

Source: [26], 1990, p. 143.

Table 3
Distribution of population by family income, Russia 1988

Total population (million)	Roubles per month (%)				
	Less than 75	75–100	100–150	150–200	over 200
146.8	6.3	13.1	34.0	24.6	22.0

Source: [26], 1990, p. 143.

Until 1985, the proportion of families with low incomes and of low-paid workers remained stable. "Low income" was established in 1975 as 75 roubles per family member, and the proportion of the population living below this line was 16% of workers and employees in 1975; 16.3% in 1985. Among collective farmers, the proportion of those with a low income decreased from 39% to 27.6% over the period ([176]).

The main source of poverty was employment in the service ("nonproductive") sector, where wages were the lowest and the number of family dependents often the highest. Among low-paid workers and employees, 60% were employed in the service sector (see tables 4 and 5). One quarter of service-sector employees were workers, 20% were specialists with college or university diplomas, and 90% were women. Three quarters were from middle- and high-income families. A substantial proportion (13% of families) of low-paid persons are children and grandchildren of working age who are completely or partially supported by their parents.

Families in which both breadwinners were retired accounted for 41% of all low-income families; one third had two employed members and dependents, and more than 20% were families in which mothers had experienced temporary interruptions of employment related to children (births and illnesses) and single-mother families ([176]).

A rise in low-paid workers' wages was considered to be a priority of the state's economic plan. Real differences in quality and quantity of work, productivity, and effectiveness were ignored. As a result, egalitarian trends in wages became widespread. If the average wage of unskilled workers and employees was 100%, the average wage of technicians with a special vocational education was 91% and that of specialists with a professional (university) education was 108%. There was little connection between level of education and compensation: 15% of unskilled workers received above-average wages, and half of them received average wages. At the same time, 20% of those with higher education received below-average salaries ([176]). In the 1970s, there was an inversion in payment for labour: unskilled workers and employees received average or high pay, while many highly skilled workers received low pay.

Table 4
Average monthly wage of workers and employees in selected economic sectors, Russia, 1960–91 (roubles)

	1960	1970	1980	1985	1990	1991
Industry	91.7	136.0	191.3	217.9	310.9	604.0
workers	89.9	133.0	191.0	218.9	299.5	581.0
engineers	135.3	181.5	219.7	240.9	359.4	711.0
employees	83.6	114.0	151.8	171.6	359.4	–
Agriculture	55.5	103.7	156.8	198.4	307.2	484.0
Construction	94.5	154.5	210.0	247.4	375.8	695.0
Trade	60.3	98.4	145.8	158.7	258.4	471.0
Services sector	74.0	111.0	149.0	163.0	242.0	–
Economy, total	83.1	126.1	177.7	201.4	296.8	552.0

Sources: [171], p. 142; [177], p. 76

Table 5
Average wage in the services sector, Russia, 1960–91 (roubles per month)

	Average	Municipal housing maintenance	Health care	Education	Culture	Art	Science	Finance	Management
1960	74.0	59.3	60.1	72.5	50.4	66.4	114.8	72.6	89.7
1965	94.0	74.2	80.6	96.4	68.3	80.7	123.8	89.9	110.3
1970	111.0	98.0	94.9	109.0	87.6	99.2	143.2	116.9	130.6
1975	128.0	113.4	107.4	129.0	95.7	107.4	162.1	142.8	142.0
1980	149.0	139.4	133.7	139.9	116.4	141.7	184.9	172.6	168.7
1985	163.0	154.2	141.1	154.9	132.9	153.5	209.9	192.8	178.8
1986	168.0	156.9	143.6	161.5	124.4	157.2	215.9	202.6	187.7
1987	176.0	162.8	153.1	170.2	138.3	159.9	224.9	212.7	201.1
1988	189.0	177.9	165.3	177.6	135.3	164.4	256.6	219.5	218.7
1989	208.0	191.8	177.9	183.6	144.9	176.7	314.3	255.1	252.3
1990	242.0	224.4	202.5	202.9	180.4	215.1	351.9	410.2	363.6
1991	443.0	440.8	416.4	388.8	352.9	429.1	514.5	986.1	540.4

Sources: [171], p. 111; [177], p. 112.

High incomes did not automatically provide access to goods and services – at least, in the formal economy. Until the 1980s, groups with direct access to distribution of consumer goods and services were privileged. For instance, those working in commerce and trade and food services appreciated greatly the meals available to them. In spite of their low legal incomes, which were not much higher than those of retirees, they expressed a much higher level of satisfaction about the food they obtained (4 on a scale of 1 to 5, in comparison to retirees, who rated it at 2.89) ([176]).

In the 1990s, incomes were obtained from a much wider diversity of sources, guaranteeing access to goods and services. The latter came to be distributed by channels that made them available to everyone.

O.M. Zdravomyslova

6.4 Social Inequality

The socialist principle "From each according to his ability, to each according to his need" turned out to be false on both counts. Most of the population had unsatisfied needs in everyday goods and services. Furthermore, throughout the history of the Soviet state, there were certain privileged groups; the composition and character of their privileges were essentially altered with the formation of the market economy.

By the mid-1970s, social stratification* **had resulted in a bureaucratized hierarchy;** liberalization of society after Stalin's death (in 1953) precipitated the demise of previous elites. From the 1960s to the 1980s, opportunities to satisfy needs were determined by a number of factors, among which belonging to a particular stratum (unless it was a ruling one) did not play a major role. New elite strata were composed of bureaucrats and other people participating in the redistribution of material goods (the trade and service sectors, managers of different ranks, trade-union activists). An increase in the role of skilled labour did not create effective stimuli to work, and the strengthening of egalitarian mechanisms and the fall in prestige of intellectual work lowered the living standards of intelligentsia.

In the 1960s, inequality began to develop in connection with working at a certain enterprise in a certain sector. Social consumption funds (SCFs), which were created to equalize access to everyday necessities, played an important role up to the mid-1980s. The abundance, or even the existence, of some social benefits, although playing no role in increasing labour productivity, nonetheless were a factor in attracting and keeping workers in a particular sector, at a given enterprise, and at a given working place.

Creation of SFCs and distribution of their proceeds was centralized. Different enterprises received unequal shares of the part of the state budget earmarked for such social needs. There were considerable disproportions in the distribution of such social benefits among cities, regions, sectors, and certain enterprises. For instance, eastern regions of Siberia have received lower than average benefits.

* Unlike Western sociology, which studies social inequality as a starting point for social stratification, Marxism emphasizes the dynamics of rapprochement between workers and peasants; questions of social inequality were discussed rarely and then only as a temporary economic setback.

The production sector enjoyed a substantial advantage over the services sector, receiving much higher sums from the state budget. Science, culture, education, and health care received sums left over after production had been financed (see table 1). As a result, employees in the services sector were paid less and had more limited access to goods distributed in the workplace, and their ability to purchase goods was more often delayed than was the case for workers. The average wage of collective farmers was 65% of that of workers and clerks in 1970, 70.2% in 1980, and 82% in 1989 ([183]), but their purchases were more often delayed, with the result that they accumulated more savings (see table 2).

Many social and everyday needs were satisfied only through the enterprise where a person worked. Housing (a hostel, a room, or a flat), kindergarten and nurseries, summer camps for children, holiday resorts, tourist hostels and holiday homes, medical services and convalescent establishments, shopping and food services at enterprises, bath-houses and saunas, stadiums, swimming pools, sports halls, libraries, theatre tickets, vacation trips (including abroad), some secondary and high schools, kitchen gardens, transport to work, and, later, goods in great demand (from cars and furniture sets in the 1970s to clothes, footwear, dishes, and foodstuffs in the 1980s) – most of these "goods" could not be bought on the open market and were sold, exclusively or for the most part, through enterprises.

Consequently, feudal dependence on a person's place of work and its management (and also on the Party and trade-union committee secretaries, the so-called triangle) arose. Many goods became accessible to workers depending on the length of their service, especially at a given enterprise. A set of informal norms came to influence labour behaviour and human relationships at the workplace.

Managers' opportunities grew constantly. The share received from the SCF was directly connected with the place that they occupied on the official ladder.

Inequality arose from the fact that the staff members who performed managerial functions and were, as a rule, entrusted with distribution of the SCF benefits appropriated most of them, in spite of the fact that very few of these employees were in the "poorly provided for" category. An analysis of lists of people waiting to receive housing, as the proceedings of the sessions of trade-union committees concerning distribution of flats, and the registration journals for the issuing of passes to sanitoria, vacation homes, and hotels, drawn from a number of enterprises in different sectors, showed that the waiting period for housing seldom exceeded 3–5 years for the highest-ranking managers of enterprises, while the majority of engineers, industrial workers, and office workers could wait up to 15 or 20 years. In addition, among those who were waiting, there were considerably more managers of different levels who had access to the queue than there were workers of other categories ([11]).

Table 1
Average remuneration of labourers in selected sectors, Russia, 1980–91 (million roubles)

	1980	1985	1990	1991
Industry	191.3	217.9	310.9	604.0
Agriculture	156.8	198.4	307.2	483.6
Construction	210.8	247.4	375.8	645.4
Transport	214.8	238.5	349.3	654.8
Communications	153.5	170.2	256.5	490.7
Trade, food catering	148.8	158.7	258.4	470.0
Computer operating	134.2	152.2	288.7	510.7
Municipal housing	139.4	154.2	224.4	440.8
Health care, physical fitness, welfare	133.7	141.1	202.5	416.4
Education	139.9	154.8	202.9	388.8
Culture	116.4	122.9	180.4	352.9
Art	141.7	153.5	215.1	429.7
Science	184.9	209.9	351.9	514.5
Financial services and government insurance	172.6	192.2	410.2	986.2
Institutions of the state administration	168.7	178.8	363.6	540.0
National economy, total	177.7	201.4	296.8	552.0

Source: [171] p. 142.

Table 2
Average savings, Gorky City region, selected occupations, 1970–85 (roubles)

	Region, total	Collective farmers	Industrial workers	Office workers
1970	500	678	489	510
1975	789	1,162	738	735
1980	1,036	1,525	940	915
1985	1,301	2,003	1,281	1,123

Source: [10], p. 55.

Additional sources of income for the highest stratum were available from the earliest years of Soviet power, and this remained true up to the 1990s. More than three million administrators had privileges of two types. Legal privileges were based on precedent: special food and treatment, residences, official country houses, chauffeured transport; Until the late 1960s, delivery of "envelopes" in addition to nominal payments, took place. Those goods were strictly rationed depending on one's "influence" in the *nomenklatura*. No less significant were illegal incomes in the form of bribes, gifts, and sometimes a regularly levied "tribute."

In the 1980s and 1990s, privileges were mostly connected with government of all levels and access to newly privatized state property.

Discrimination by social group ceased by the end of the 1980s. Previously, individual labour activity (ILA) had not been encouraged; the word *chastnik* (private craftsman, driver, or trader) was, in social consciousness, derogatory. Up to the end of the 1980s, very few citizens were engaged in legal forms of ILA.

The working class lost a considerable portion of its privileges not only in connection with the loss of managerial positions provided for via the CPSU, but also because of erosion of the class itself.

Belonging to certain specific groups (invalids and participants in the Great Patriotic War [World War Two], parents of large families, people receiving personal pensions, and so on) also placed a person in a special category that received additional material goods, which gave rise to considerable tension in everyday life, because such people, in particular, had the right to jump the queue in shops while others waited in lines for hours. In the 1990s, such privileges were either narrowed considerably, as was the number of people enjoying them, or were replaced by financial compensation.

Demographic inequality in a vague, veiled form existed over the last 30 years. There has been constant discrimination against women, in a hidden form; though women numbered more than half of the production work force, production equipment (machine tools, equipment, instruments) was designed for men and did not take anthropometric and dynamometric characteristics of women into account ([57]). In groups with equal education, women, on average, were paid one third less than men, and the main managerial positions were occupied by men; with the transition to a market economy, unemployment affected women first.

Discrimination in hiring practices for youths and especially high-school graduates in the 1990s was accompanied by discrimination against persons over 40, who were the first to be dismissed.

The importance of ethnic-origin considerations in social policy began to recede in the late 1980s. In the 1950s, the "struggle against cosmopolitanism" was launched, after which, in spite of the equality of nations declared on the state level, anti-Semitism began to manifest itself more overtly; by the 1970s, this led to the existence of secret limitations in admitting Jews to prestigious higher technical schools and to enterprises in the military-industrial complex. At the same time, the social place occupied by representatives of peoples of aboriginal nationalities became disproportionate: in 1988, for instance, in 10 of the 16 autonomous republics the proportion of representatives of aboriginal nationalities among managers was higher than their proportion in the population ([171]).

Horizontal inequality eased in the 1980s. Living conditions in town and in the country differed radically (see table 3). Passport and residence registration were in effect throughout the period studied, putting citizens under complete state control, limiting their freedom to choose their place of residence and socio-legal status. Up to the end of the 1980s, place of residence determined the opportunities for health care, education, improving living conditions, appealing to judicial bodies, and so on. In the mid-1980s, under the extension of the rationing system, the opportunity to obtain coupons for buying industrial and food products was also a function of registration. Rural dwellers received passports only in 1981. Young people in the army were still obliged to return their passports to the authorities until the mid-1990s, and military personnel had special identification cards until 1995.

Table 3
Infant death rate, urban and rural residents, Russia, 1980–91

	1980	1985	1990	1991
Number of infants dying below 1 year of age, per thousand born:				
urban population	21.2	19.8	17.0	17.3
rural population	24.0	22.8	18.3	19.1

Source: [171], p. 118.

I.A. Boutenko

7 Social Relations

7.1 Conflicts

Many conflicts inherent to Soviet (and, later, Russian) society became more acute. By the end of the 1980s, they had gone from latent forms, at the personal level, to overt ones, manifesting the process of disintegration of what had recently seemed to be a stable unity – "a new historical community – the Soviet people." The weakening of social control as a result of the break-up of the totalitarian state led to the revival of religion as a substitute for the communist ideology; official internationalism was being replaced by chauvinistic nationalism.

Latent labour conflicts became manifest. The process of industrialization at the beginning of the 1930s had precluded the development of workers' rights in industrial enterprises. Mass protests were decisively suppressed, as, for example, in the massacre of demonstrators in Novocherkassk in 1962. Information on such events was kept secret.

Under these conditions, labour and social conflicts manifested themselves in other ways. In the second half of the 1950s, problems related to remuneration and qualifications become urgent; in the 1970s and 1980s, problems associated with distribution of goods and services at industrial enterprises arose (see section 6.4). Year after year, confronted with successive attempts to stimulate greater effort on their part, working people responded to unsatisfactory working conditions and organization, equal payment for all, and technocratic top-down management with working below capacity, changing jobs (see table 1), absenteeism, and a general drop in morale.

Until the mid-1980s, impediments to good working relationships, from both above and below, accumulated. Searches for a means to increase labour productivity revealed the existence of a premeditated decrease in output. Faced with this reality, special "brigades" (see section 5.1) were created to simulate motivation to produce higher output. As a rule, "foot-dragging" developed in brigades as a result of poor teamwork organization. In 1986, All-Union research showed that 88% of working

Table 1
Labour turnover, Russia, 1970–91
(% of average annual number of workers)

1970	1980	1986	1989	1991
21.0	16.0	13.0	13.3	14.8

Sources: [171], p. 130; [175], p. 126.

people felt that they were not working to their full capacity; in 1988, 81% of workers felt this way; 54% were unhappy with labour conditions; 62%, with material and technical provisions; and 23%, with social and psychological conditions of labour. Poor management practices were noted by 92% of managers and specialists ([125]; see table 2).

An important barrier from above was deliberate hiring of excess workers and specialists. According to some estimates, about 16 million positions were "unnecessary" in the USSR – in other words, 16 million people were doing needless work ([244]). However, management manipulated labour reserves to neutralize social tension among employees, compensating for the negative influence of poor labour organization and frustrations.

In 1987, a fifty-year hiatus from strikes ended. At the end of the 1980s, work stoppages began to occur; however, the initial sense of political direction was soon lost. Complaints to higher authorities, letters to the ruling bodies, collective addresses to the press, spontaneous protests against concrete conditions (poor labour conditions, theft of production, the absence of some food in the shops, violations of the rules of distribution of dwellings, etc.) were no longer the favoured means of pressing demands. In 1989, the strike movement became an avalanche. Strikes began in several production sectors to protest against dangerous and difficult working conditions (in the mining, transport, and fishing industries) and to promote socio-economic aims. Politicization of labour conflicts became evident by 1992, with the opposition of workers to central authorities, on the one hand, and to the management of enterprises, which was trying to consolidate its own right to property over enterprises under privatization. In 1990, labour conflicts became generalized and assumed a political character, reaching their peak in 1992 (see tables 3–5). When problems connected with privatization were solved, the productive sector appeared to become less strike-prone; the exceptions were the public services sectors (health, science, education), where workers were still actively pressing their claims.

Economic differentiation and unequal access to material wealth were a source of conflict between different social and professional groups over the

Table 2
Losses of work time in industry, Russia, 1980–91 (days per employee/worker)

	1980	1985	1990	1991
Total days	1.72	1.06	1.47	2.32
Laziness	0.58	0.47	0.44	0.47
Time wasted	0.16	0.14	0.23	0.46
Strikes	-	-	0.01	0.16
Paid absence	0.48	0.45	0.79	1.23

Source: [171], p. 371.

Table 3
State workers' attitude toward strikes, Russia, 1991–92 (%)

	1991	1992
Think strikes are up-to-date process	58	46
Strongly opposed to strikes; this is not the way to solve problems	34	44
Difficulty answering	8	10

Source: [6], p. 25.

Table 4
Distribution of replies to the question, "Do you think strikes are possible at your enterprise?" Russia, 1991–92 (%)

	1991	1992
Yes	56	45
No	28	38
Difficulty answering	16	17

Source: [6], p. 26.

Table 5
Distribution of replies to the question, "Have you participated in a strike?," Russia, 1991–92 (%)

	1991	1992
Yes	4	6
No	96	94

Source: [6], p. 26.

period under study. This process became more obvious and significant as a result of economic reforms in the early 1990s. "Hot money" (money that a person was willing to spend but could not because of shortages in goods and services), was the main source of social tensions between 1988 and 1991, before prices were liberalized. By the mid-1990s, this source of conflict had been reduced. From the 1960s to the 1980s, it was considered good form to feign contempt for wealth, but by the end of the 1980s, affluence became something to flaunt, provoking envy and irritation among others. As a result, co-operative stalls were set on fire and expensive foreign cars were destroyed or damaged.

Tensions arose between those working at state enterprises and those engaged in private co-operatives and joint-stock enterprises. The former felt that they were being left out of the material gains of the economic reforms, which gave rise to a sense of injustice. There was a latent conflict building: in 1989, 20.8% of bureaucrats surveyed said that they felt hostility toward prosperous groups, especially those engaged in non-state sectors of the economy. The reason for this hostility was the difference in their respective material conditions.

Potential conflicts also existed within the state sector, with its groups of managers, workers, and commerce and services employees. Before the 1990s, managers had special privileges matching their official status. Commerce and services employees, thanks to their direct participation in the distribution system (before the transition to market economy) also had a great opportunity to redistribute goods in the grey market. In 1990, 9% of workers in the state sector and 18.4% from the private sector said that they felt hostility toward managers; 41.5% felt this way toward commerce employees; and 23.7% felt this way toward services employees. The reasons for this hostility were linked, first, to different cultural levels, and, second, to different material conditions ([25]).

In the mid-1980s, conflicts in the services sector became critical, decreasing thereafter. The mere existence of shortages led to conflicts because everyone, irrespective of social and professional group, was trying to increase his or her share of limited resources. Shortages stimulated panic buying, entailing tension in the stores and among those who queued. During the 1970s and 1980s, many regions had a strict rationing system. For example, in 1988, 26 districts and autonomous republics out of a total of 72 had meat for sale by coupons only; in 32, butter was sold in this manner; in 53, sugar. Shopping for food took about one hour per day; shopping for noncomestible products took from one to three hours a week ([245]).

Standing in queues in front of shops became an activity governed by specific norms and rules. Invalids and parents of large families, who had a right to jump the queue for some products and goods, provoked particular hostility. Shop counters became barricades. Analyses of criminal cases arising from violations of the "rules of trade" (norms of product weight, queueing norms, polite treatment of customers) showed that in 25% of cases, customers were provocative, demanding to purchase goods from behind the counter or from the storage area ([259]). Official complaints and speaking to shop managers were not effective, and before the 1990s panic demand and late delivery of products sometimes led to spontaneous demonstrations, breaking of shop windows, and scuffles among customers.

By the mid-1990s, the formation of a market economy had gradually reduced the acuteness of such conflicts, but hostility toward sellers persists.

Concealed before the 1980s, conflicts among different nations of the former USSR sharpened in the 1990s, resulting in large streams of refugees and emigrants. In 1991, 30% of Russians surveyed felt that there was a possibility of ethnic conflict in the cities in which they lived, including 24% of Muscovites, 45% from the Stavropol region, 18% from the Kemerovo district, 21% from the Orenburg district, and 23% from the Pskov district ([248]). Between 20% and 35% of respondents, depending on the group, answered positively to the question, "Is there any nationality toward which you feel hostility?" ([108]). The continuing commodity shortage of the late 1980s and the rationing system based on residential segregation encouraged the perpetuation of this situation .

Ethnic conflicts of the mid-1990s were characterized by a high level of violence, with people being killed and wounded. From the point of view of the nationalist movement in Russia, there was a serious problem in the form of a double standard with regard to the sovereignty of autonomous territories, regions, and federative republics. Nationalist movements, some of them obviously of a fascistic nature, were experiencing a revival. The ideology of ethnic origins as a determinant of status took hold among large segments of the population, irrespective of nationality. This spirit compounded the influence of everyday chauvinism, which, in turn, intensified inter-ethnic tensions, especially among young people. Inequality of ethnic status became a kind of catalyst that could transform conflict into a "sacred war" against the "faithless" and the "foreign." According to polls, the reasons for these conflicts were, first, difference in cultural level; second, difference in material status; third, level of aggressiveness of the population; differences of political outlook and value orientations were mentioned less frequently ([85]).

Religious conflicts also suffer from the legacy of the privatization of church property and, in fact, they are not entirely of a religious or cultural character. Practically everywhere, ethnic and religious factions promote their leaders, gradually force their conflicts into the public forum, and impose institutionalization of their particular interests. Most conflicts, including that between legislative and executive power, are connected with nationalization of state property, resulting in political murders and even war in Chechnya (1994–96).

I.A. Boutenko

7.2 Negotiation

From the 1960s to the 1980s, negotiations were conducted only in the sphere of international and inter-state relations. In the 1990s, they were becoming an obligatory mechanism for settling conflicts at the legislative level. Mediation was undertaken not only by special civil servants at state institutions but also by members of non-state organizations. A need for trained mediators has grown and is gradually being fulfilled.

From the 1960s to the mid-1980s, open conflicts and mass protests were extremely rare, and any uprisings were suppressed and covered up. The official ideology regarded any conflict as an anomaly and a social evil, and took any means necessary to combat them. All mass and individual social and political protests were declared seditious and their perpetrators were prosecuted.

Relative to the subject matter of conflicts mediated in the 1990s, a diversification of the types of individuals and parties concerned was evident. In strikes, strike committees and trade unions represent the interests of the workers; in international conflicts, the individuals in the dispute are represented by teams of mediators, which are usually headed by local political leaders and diplomats. In conflicts between organized criminal groups and the law (for example, in hijackings, hostage seizures, etc.) negotiations are conducted by the employees of the Committee for Emergency Situations or the Federal Security Service.

A tendency to institutionalize the settling of social conflicts corresponds to the increasing number of individuals involved in negotiations. The Service for Settling Collective Labour Disputes, with ten regional subdivisions, was founded in 1994. The service's trained negotiators conduct pre-court conciliation procedures and on the site of mediation functions. The subdivision of the State Committee for the Russian Federation National Affairs has emerged as the mediation institution in negotiations with international dimensions. The problem of territorial disputes has become especially urgent. For example, from 1990 to 1994, more than 30 territorial claims were pressed by ethnic neighbours in the Northern Caucasus ([272]).

In the 1990s, settling conflicts (national and ethnic conflicts, in particular) with the participation of mediators has become increasingly widespread. Mediators disperse initial tensions, reduce the field of counterclaims of the opponents, and show the possibilities for nonviolent resolution of the dispute. Independent mediators deal mainly not with definition of the extent of guilt or the responsibility of the parties for the conflict that has arisen, but with a joint search for a mutually advantageous resolution.

In the 1990s, the conviction that there is no reasonable alternative to compromise, dialogue, and negotiations has gradually taken over from fear and lack of faith in the possibility of defending legal rights and interests before the state. In 1989, a sociological survey of miners striking in Kuzbass found that 25% of the respondents wanted absolutely no concession to management and government in the labour conflict, while 64% felt that the conflict might be settled with a mutually acceptable agreement ([333]). A representative nationwide survey on the structure and dynamics of values during the sociocultural crisis of 1991 also illustrated a polarization of ideological orientations: 62% of respondents expressed a willingness to enter dialogue with political opponents, while 23% insisted on a fight to the finish ([140]).

Nevertheless, representatives of enterprises' staff and managers are usually unable to listen to each other. They are less interested in seeking common interests and mutually acceptable ways of solving problems than in expression of mutual dissatisfaction and exposition of intransigent positions.

The need for a civilized approach to solving contradictions among the various interests of the groups represented by the political parties that formed at the beginning of the 1990s was gradually recognized and was being acted upon. Economic reform forced joint-stock enterprises to negotiate with suppliers and buyers and compels business managers to arrive at compromises in settling labour disputes with personnel.

International conflicts that broke out in the aftermath of the disintegration of the USSR required negotiations, which have been steadily reducing the latent violence in such relationships.

In the 1990s, systematic and up-to-date mediation techniques were being used in Russia's universities and colleges. From the 1960s to the 1980s, the official propaganda stated that there was no reason for social clashes, so managers received no training in practical methods of dispute settlement. In the late 1980s and early 1990s, there was a rapid development in role-playing techniques to simulate problematic and conflictual situations in industry.

In the 1990s, training programs dealing with conflict resolution (commercial negotiations, diagnosis and mediation of intra-organizational conflicts, conciliation and mediation in family disputes, facilitation of negotiations in labour disputes, etc.) became available. A number of international peacemaking organizations (Search for Common Ground, Fellowship of Reconciliation [US], International Alert [UK], United Nations of Youth Foundation) have provided great assistance in educating Russians in these matters in the mid-1990s.

V.N. Shalenko

7.3 Norms of Conduct

Up to the mid-1980s, norms of conduct were officially defined by moral principles given in the Code of the Builder of Communism. *Its official slogans of unity, equality, and brotherhood were the values that were supposed to determine the behavioural patterns established by the state. But since the 1970s, the principles of communist morality, which, in fact, were often disregarded, have lost their monolithic quality. A "dual morality" arose involving different norms for private and official conduct. Due to social and economic changes in the early 1990s, alternative individualistic and ethnic patterns of conduct have become socially acceptable. The Western "business" mode of behaviour is being actively copied.*

From the 1960s to the 1990s, the daily roles of wife and husband tended to blend. The declared gender equality in labour changed the stereotypes of family relations: 80% of woman of employable age were employed by the beginning of the 1970s, as state policy prescribed ([207]). Between 57% and 67% of men, depending on the nationality, approved of this state of affairs, feeling that women should work ([17]); 80% of women felt that family and labour were of equal value ([151]). The opinion that only working women were full members of society was widely held.

Beginning in the mid-1960s, an ideal type of family (without fixed functions of partners, in which spouses could exchange roles in the household and had an equal say in decision making) emerged in public opinion. In 1962, 20–25% of working women reported that their husbands helped with housework ([262]); however, men's contribution to housework has never equalled women's (see table 1).

Subsequent to the major socio-economic transformations in the early 1990s, unemployment became a problem, and 80% of the unemployed were women ([24]).

Table 1
Men's participation in household chores, Russia, 1963–81 (%, as reported by women)

	1963–64	1972	1979–81
Equal participation	24.3	38.1	43.0
Helps a little	46.2	36.5	36.3
Doesn't help	21.6	25.2	15.6
No answer	7.0	–	5.1

Calculated from [35], p. 70; [317], p. 446; [348], p. 190.

This situation influenced the model of family relations and women's roles. Two contradictory trends were observed: a neoconservative trend encouraged women to return to the home, and a feministic trend encouraged them to enter the business world.

Due to women's past high level of employment, there was less emphasis on raising children. The passing on of cultural values and ethical norms to offspring ceased to be the prerogative of the family. In the 1960s, during the urbanization process, there was a break-up of large, multigenerational families. The rupture of cultural continuity led to intergenerational conflict, in which parents did not accept their children's life choices.

At the end of 1960s, public opinion saw the ideal family as consisting of two generations with three to four persons living in a separate municipal apartment in a new district. The daily routine in these new apartment buildings followed the rhythm of production: people left home early (7–8 a.m.) and came home late (6–7 p.m.). The rest of the day was spent in housework because there were no domestic services. In state statistics (see table 2), there was no difference between child care and communication with children, but most official attention was paid to the former. The education and raising of children in peer groups under the supervision of teachers became not only prevalent, but normative. In the 1970s and 1980s, the proportion of children spending their time after school at various state institutionalized collectives (extended school day, sports and art schools, "pioneers' houses," etc.) increased (see table 3).

Starting in the 1970s, children moved beyond the circle of family influence and joined various informal groups. Excessive ideological pressure and the spread of the "dual morality" led to teenagers and young adults developing a distaste for playing according to the rules of adult life. This forsaking of the family's influence in favour of small, noninstitutionalized groups became a form of protest. Participation in these groups was regarded by officials as deviant behaviour and caused parents much anguish.

Table 2
Relationship between parent's time spent on raising children and leisure activities, Russia, 1965–86
(person-hour per day)

	1965		1976		1986	
	Men	Women	Men	Women	Men	Women
Active leisure (cultural institutions)	0.6	0.6	5.8	4.7	0.5	0.5
Passive leisure (radio, TV, reading)	2.5	1.5	5.8	4.7	3.8	2.8
Raising and looking after children	0.3	0.3	0.8	0.6	0.3	0.3

Calculated from [299], pp. 35, 46; [304], p. 368.

Table 3
Percentage of children attending school after classes
("extended day"), grades 1–8, Russia, 1960–85

1960	1970	1980	1985
2.0	12.2	33.2	36.8

Source: [177], p 358.

By the mid-1980s, intergenerational conflict had become obvious: 30–35% of schoolchildren in Moscow ([287]) and 47–73% of teenagers living in large cities belonged to informal groups. The proportion of those aged 16–30 who consumed drugs was around 62% ([61]) and the number of teenagers involved in criminal activity increased. About 30% of young people declared themselves ready to do anything to procure a "normal" (upper-class) quality of life ([187]).

Normative conduct in sexual relations became less strict. In the 1960s, many young people saw relationships between men and women as deeply rooted in an ideal of chivalry and a patriarchal socio-economic model. During the 1970s, a distinct gap developed between the ideal and actual behaviour (see table 4). In the 1980s, 55% of urban dwellers and 35% of rural dwellers felt it was possible to have premarital sex. Young people of similar ages and cultural levels often became sexual partners: 50–60% of young men and 35–53% of young women stated that they had had sex. Because of a relaxed attitude toward sexual intercourse outside of marriage, including among some 67% of young people surveyed, who gave reasons ranging from "love" to "need for sex," a trade in underground prostitution developed.

Until the early 1980s, sexual relations were not discussed, for they were deemed to be shameful and not associated with a happy life. Up to 85% of teenagers received their first information about sex from peers or older friends ([69]).

Table 4
Approval of premarital sex, Russia, 1967–78 (%)

	1967		1972		1978	
	Men	Women	Men	Women	Men	Women
Yes	57	46	51	42	–	45
No	16	27	11	18	–	–
No opinion	28	27	38	39	–	–

Calculated from [69], p. 68; [317], p. 193.

In the early 1990s, there was a burst of religious activity, related to the crisis in official ideology and the collapse of the prevailing ethic. In the 1960s, under the total and compulsory atheism of socialism, there was no church attendance or participation in church services.

In the mid-1970s, certain ceremonies – weddings and, especially, christenings, along with others – began to be practised again. The appeal of religious sacraments testified to the dissatisfaction with the civil form of rituals and were a form of opposition to the state's intrusion into private life.

By the 1990s, some people considered atheism to be synonymous with immorality; 30% of respondents surveyed in 1990 declared that they were religious; 60% felt that the rise of religion was a good thing because people would follow religious precepts for living ([312]).

National cultural traditions and ethnic ethical norms were becoming the reference points that informed both positive and negative values. The search for such ethical references during the years of social crises led people to rehabilitate archaic behaviour patterns. In the late 1980s, ethno-cultural communities were legalized. Intellectuals in the humanities, as a rule, regarded such developments more positively than they had previously, and young people were displaying an interest in them. In the Rostov region, 77% of young people surveyed said that they felt positive about the rebirth of the Don Cossack tradition; among older age groups, the proportion who felt positive about this tradition was considerably lower ([76]).

Before the 1980s, crime statistics were not published, but the mass media claimed that crime was on the decline. Pilfering was not considered to be a crime, but evidence of one's ability to adapt to specific situations, and it was an example to be imitated. The norms and values of the underground economy became stereotypical. In the late 1980s, thefts from enterprises were widespread. Managers knew about one-half of the perpetrators of theft, and in one-third of cases they themselves organized thefts ([74]).

In the early 1990s, the number of crimes grew considerably due to the socio-economic polarization of society and the spread of the norms of the underground economy, causing social tension (see table 5).

Hostile attitudes toward migrants became more intense in the mid-1990s. Until the mid-1980s, internal migration in the USSR was organized by state institutions and determined by economic interests. Negative attitudes toward migrants were partially mitigated by state guarantees that they would not compete for the same houses and jobs as was the local population. As the USSR broke up and republics separated, non-native populations became the object of aggression in some regions. In the mid-1990s, there was much nationalistic tension throughout the country. A refugee population sprang up alongside the migrant populations; there were 422,000 in 1988–89 and 700,000 in 1991 ([159]). A survey showed that the most negative attitudes were evoked by Russian migrants to non-Russian provincial centres, whose very presence recalled the local population's dependence on Moscow.

The negative consequences of an anti-alcohol campaign in the 1980s strengthened a trend toward indulging in hard drinking (see section 6.3). Consumption of alcohol varied widely; men prided themselves on their ability to function after drinking large amounts. Intoxicated women, however, were regarded negatively. In spite of a constant growth in consumption of alcohol, 98% of adult men considered themselves not to be hard drinkers ([319]), and thus felt that they were not exceeding the bounds of accepted behaviour. Making up for a lack of entertainment, leisure opportunities, and meaningful work were the main reasons for drinking ([251]).

Beginning in the early 1990s, there was a trend toward conforming to norms of Western business conduct. This became more obvious in behaviour in public dealings. However, there are no data at the moment that allow us to comment further on this phenomenon.

Table 5
Concern about selected societal problems, Russia, 1991–93 (%)

	1991	1992	1993
Increasing crime	30	45	55
Increasing prices	72	75	81

Source: [144], p. 25.

L.Y. Petrunina

7.4 Authority

The separation of official and unofficial authority that was most obvious in the 1970s had faded by the 1990s. The authoritarian character of power remained, but it was more a function of naked force than of any respect.

Until the 1990s, there were two types of authority: official and unofficial. The state took upon itself many qualities usually associated with the private sector, such as secrecy, inviolability, and exclusiveness, and added an emotional component – adulation of the Party. In the 1970s and 1980s, the distinction between the socio-political realm of the state and the personal domain of civil society (interaction between friends or like-minded persons) became more obvious. There were two parallel domains of morality and sociability: official and unofficial. People paid lip service to authority but did not take it seriously or orient their activities as a consequence. This discrepancy has been progressively eliminated with the development of freedom of speech and relaxation of ideological pressure.

Power within families remained quite authoritarian, with the authority vested mostly in the mother. In parents' consciousness, there was an everpresent repressive element (see table 1). Treatment of children seemed to be authoritarian and cruel: tight swaddling of babies was widespread; 60% of children of various ages from 15 Russian cities and towns said that their parents made them stand in the corner as punishment; 5% said that they were struck in the head and face ([256]). Communications with parents seemed to be much more formal and regulated than those with persons of the same age; two thirds of secondary-school and vocational-technical-school students said that they noticed considerable discrepancies between what they were taught by their parents and their parents' own behaviour ([131]). Family relationships were perceived more clearly by older cohorts (see table 2).

The older cohorts said that they more readily confided in their parents; younger cohorts were more inclined to see their mothers and contemporaries as confidants (see table 3). Secondary-school students, regardless of sex, were more honest with their mothers, more often asked their advice, and felt more sympathy for them. Fathers were turned to for information. In divorced families, 70% of fathers gave their children gifts, but only 27–36% followed their progress at school and spent leisure time with them ([273]).

According to VCIOM, young people most wanted to look like, in order of preference, literary and movie characters, popular actors, and, last, their parents,

Table 1
Responses to the questions "Can it sometimes be effective to beat a child?" and "Is it justified to be rude with an older person?," Russia, 1992 (% among selected age groups)

Age of respondent	Effective to beat a child		Justified to be rude with an older person	
	Yes	No	Yes	No
Under 20 years	17	69	28	48
35–50 years	47	37	35	49
Over 65 years	44	43	12	78

Source: [268], p. 254.

Table 2
Opinions on family relations, 1992 (% among selected age groups)

	Under 20 years	30–39 years	60 years and older
Friendly	48	63	75
Not very friendly	31	23	13
Hostile	4	5	1

Source: [268], p. 253.

Table 3
Responses to the question "Who understood you best when you were 16?" 1992 (% among selected age groups; multiple responses possible)

	under 20 years	30–39 years	60 years and older
Mother	53	55	70
Father	27	34	46
Contemporary	40	22	18
Teachers	7	15	22

Source: [268], p. 249.

while older cohorts wanted to resemble their own parents and, as a rule, wanted their children to look like them. Parents' pride in their children was the greatest source of self-esteem for 43% of parents and for two thirds of all respondents. However, only 20% of children were proud of their parents; thus, parents' source of self-esteem was not reciprocated by their children's respect for them ([268]).

Up to the end of the 1980s, diarchy was the rule in the workplace: there was a nominal leader (manager) for the production process and an ideological organizer to whom that nominal leader, as a member of the Party, was actually subordinate, as were trade-union authorities. The authority of socio-political organization, except for the Komsomol and the trade unions, increased a little in the 1990s, when some of them tried to protect employees, but, in most cases, neither sincerely nor successfully, and then declined. The CPSU possessed real power until the end of the 1980s. As the official political vanguard of society, it enjoyed power but not always authority. Party workers, paid for their political activities, were notable for their arrogance, superciliousness, and haughtiness. Workers on regional CP committees were more particularly notable for their intolerance of independent actions by subordinates (29.9%), callousness and heartlessness (21.9%), and inconsiderateness (27.7%) ([21]).

In 1988, young respondents named M.S. Gorbachev as the most respected of recent CPSU Secretaries General, but nevertheless 39.2% of them felt that the Party had lost its moral authority as a result of cults of personality and general stagnation ([58]).

The authority of trade unions was quite low and had dropped further by the end of the 1980s. Since these organizations were always under the CPSU umbrella, they were not perceived as an independent force. In 1988, only 13.4% of workers in industrial enterprises felt that their trade union had great authority among workers; 54.3% felt that it had moderate authority; and 22.6% felt that it had little authority ([128]).

Managers and superiors were appreciated not so much for their competence but as channels through which additional goods could be obtained. They were identified, to a large extent, with the state, which was supposed to take care of its charges. A superior's place in the hierarchy was defined in terms of distance from responsibility connected with his or her "work" and from obligations of solidarity toward subordinates. According to VCIOM, superiors were relatively insensitive to pressure from collectives beneath them, while the pressure of their superiors on them was mentioned frequently (eight times as often). The more subordinates a superior had, the more highly this superior was evaluated by the workers under him or her ([268]). Half of those surveyed felt that wages depended not on the final result of the work force's activities but on workers' relations with their direct superiors ([27]). According to 50% of those surveyed, the share a worker received from the social consumption funds (see section 6.4) depended on his or her ability to get along with superiors, while 24% felt that the size of the worker's share depended on good work and 12%, on working conditions ([106]).

In 1989, 19% of those surveyed said that they had been pressured by their superiors to act contrary to what they considered to be right and just; most of these respondents were older people. Fifty-six percent of respondents had strict, imperious superiors; of these, 12% felt that any manager should be obeyed for the sake of production. Finally, 33% stated that they had tried to get rid of unsatisfactory superiors. Among these respondents, 54% would prefer a strict superior, 21% a permissive superior; 58% mentioned a superior with initiative, 31% an efficient superior; 48% preferred a male superior, while 9% preferred a woman in that position ([268]). Women were greater advocates of an authoritarian style of management at all levels.

From the 1960s to the 1980s, given the constant shortage of food and services, people were subject to the whims of officials, doctors, and shopkeepers. There were sometimes widespread shortages and people were forced to look for other channels through which to obtain goods and services; this situation was gradually eliminated by the mid-1990s.

Criminals, however, began to enjoy increasing authority and conflicts were solved by brute force in the 1990s. A general crisis of power was noted by scientists, journalists, and politicians. The need for a strong hand was expressed by 69% of respondents in 1990, and by 63% in 1992. Of respondents interviewed by VCIOM in 1989, only 22% stated that they were afraid of the potential despotism of the authorities ([268]).

The crisis was also evidenced by a growth in common crime and the collusion of managers of state enterprises and the criminal world against the public administration, which facilitated the spread of corruption. High authorities were implicated in crime, often violent crime. According to Internal Affairs Ministry data, in 1993–94, 16 deputies committed crimes in the Trer region; 18, in the Kyrof region; 18, in Veoronezh; 22 in the Republic of Mordovia; 28 in the Republic of Tatarstan. Thirteen percent of these deputies were convicted ([111m]). An escalation in state repression of criminality was manifested in the ideological cost of the war in Chechnya in 1994–95.

I.A. Boutenko

7.5 Public Opinion

The free expression of public opinion began to play a significant role in the late 1980s, when political activity in the population increased; thereafter, interest in expressing opinion and attention paid to polls fell abruptly. By the mid-1990s, public opinion was not a very important factor.

Formally, expression of public opinion was considered important, but until the mid-1990s it tended to be fabricated by Communist Party organs. In the context of the totalitarian state, public opinion was usually unnecessary and functioned only as an object of education. Party and all-national debate had disappeared as long ago as the 1930s; Stalin's monolithic Party unity allowed for not even the slightest allusion to a deviation from the Party line or for doubts concerning the rectitude of the chosen social path, either by Party members or by ordinary citizens. References to public opinion were made, if necessary, when the authorities wanted to make an unpopular decision. For example, such measures as moving of holidays, price increases, and the introduction of various limitations of rights and freedoms were justified as being suggestions from or the desire of the "working people." Public condemnations of scientists, writers, and artists (despite the fact that their work could not be known to the public) out of favour with the authorities were widespread.

From the 1960s to the 1980s, interest in public opinion was shown mostly by the state security organs concerned with searching for dissidents and by different educational institutions. As a result, a double standard arose in the 1930s and existed (with a gap from the late 1930s to the 1950s, when it was dangerous to speak sincerely about political topics even among relatives and friends) through the late 1980s: this led to certain opinions being expressed officially, at meetings, while other opinions were expressed by the same people among friends in informal contexts.

In the late 1980s, disregard for public opinion was replaced by the authorities' stated desire to consider it constantly; this resulted in the organization of all-national discussions on the new CPSU Rules (1989), in projects of law, and in decrees in the press.

There was no substantial change in the 1990s, when elected officials' tendency regularly to present their personal opinion to be that of the electorate became widespread. On the whole, their evaluation of advance of democratization of public life achieved was more positive than was that of population (see table 1).

Until the mid-1980s, formal channels of expression of public opinion were, to all intents and purposes, closed: the texts of speakers at meetings, sessions, and plenums were specially prepared and verified. "All-national" discussions of the Party's and the government's decisions always received unambiguous support in the press, whether these decisions dealt with mass repressions or condemnation of dissidents, with harvesting, or with the "imperialist threat." Widely advertised all-national debates on the New Constitution of the USSR (1977) at meetings and in the mass media led to almost no changes in the text.

Censorship existed until the late 1980s and was applied to all printed materials. For this reason, direct broadcasting was extremely limited, as was access to photo-

Table 1
Opinions on the democratization process in the Russia, May, 1989 (% of respondents)

	Elected representatives	Voters
The democratization process has become irreversible	21	3
Additional measures are needed to guarantee irreversibility of democratization	40	22
Half-measures only have been taken; more resolute steps are necessary	34	52
Almost nothing has been done and the democratization process has not yet begun	1	18
No answer	4	5

Source: [30], p. 29.

copying equipment. The development of *glasnost* in the late 1980s opened channels for expression of the population's demands, opinions, and moods. From 1988 to 1990, there was a resurgence of newspaper and magazine circulation due to this newly attained freedom of speech. From the 1960s to the 1980s, public opinion had found an outlet in unofficial oral expression: various political and erotic anecdotes were extremely widespread; in the 1990s, due to *glasnost*, the oral tradition suffered a setback, having been reified in the print media.

The conducting of opinion polls stopped in the 1930s; the practice began again only in the 1960s, with a certain liberalization of social life, which evaporated with the end of N.S. Khrushchev's rule. In the 1970s, opinion polls fell under the total control of the CPSU. They were carried out under the aegis and with permission of its central and local organs and dealt with specific cases, and the results usually remained unpublished. As there was no market economy, there was no need for market-research-oriented opinion surveys. In the late 1980s, a great number of market-research centres, services, and laboratories were founded, and their results were constantly being published in the mass media. Little by little, opinion polls became a normal part of life in the country. After a period of enthusiasm, people began showing some scepticism toward polls by the mid-1990s. This was connected, to a large extent, with a rather low degree of professionalism or with political involvement that led the country's major survey centres to a completely false prognosis of election results in 1993. Nonetheless, the authorities' disinterested attitude toward public opinion in the mid-1990s could be explained by the fact that no contender had yet gained a more or less solid base among the electorate.

Until the mid-1980s, demonstrations, peace marches, staged meetings with leaders of other socialist countries, and other public displays were organized solely by the CPSU. Students and employees – members of the CPSU – working at enterprises were obliged to participate. As for unsanctioned meetings that took place during those years, their organizers and participants were immediately arrested and/or sent to a psychiatric clinic; the fact that such meetings had taken place became known to the population only in the 1990s.

Until 1986, elections were single-party and intended to demonstrate "the moral and political unity of the Party and the people," through the population's unanimous choice of the "inviolable bloc of communists and non-Party men." Elected representatives voted unanimously in favour of all motions brought by the Party, and their function was limited to seeing to the everyday needs of their electors (helping them get admitted to hospital, helping obtain a place in a kindergarten for a child, and so on). The first electoral campaign that proposed alternatives was launched in 1989; widespread was the opinion, a holdover from past years, that deputies were largely preoccupied with responding to individual demands. The electorate focused first on the candidates' personality and biography; by the 1990s, it was more important to know whether the candidate had belonged to either of the two political factions that had preceded formation of true political parties; beginning in 1992, although party membership became more important, the charismatic nature of leadership remained important to the electorate.

The participation of every adult citizen in elections was obligatory and compulsory till the late 1980s; failure to vote was regarded as a manifestation of dangerous dissidence or, at the very least, a lack of responsibility. On the other hand, citizens used the threat not to vote in local municipal elections as an extreme pressure tactic. Relaxation of Party pressure in the late 1980s led to a drop in the number of electors, followed by an abrupt rise and another drop. In 1989, 70% of the active population took part in political life in different ways, one third of them actively; in 1990, 35–40% were interested in political campaigns, and this proportion dropped to 12–15% in 1992 ([127]). It is notable that the abrupt growth of interest in politics did not influence the electorate's participation rate, which was dropping by 1990, and falling even further as the elections approached ([82], table 2).

In 1989, the electorate had a choice of local Party and Soviet elites, intellectuals, independent candidates, volunteer-association leaders, workers, and peasants' representatives to vote for. Elderly men abstained from voting because they had problems getting to polling booths, young people because of their indifference toward the process or dissatisfaction with how the elections were organized locally; more than 20% of voters interviewed after the elections said that they had decided

Table 2
Percentage of Muscovites voting in elections, 1931–93

1931	1934	1939–1984	1989[a]	1990[b]	1991[c]	1992[d]	1993[e]
84	97	99.8	83.5	64.5	68	66.8	63.5

Source: [12e].
[a] Elections to Soviets of all levels.
[b] Elections of deputies of RSFSR
[c] Referendum on the USSR
[d] Elections of the President of RF
[e] Referendum on confidence in the President and in the Supreme Soviet

for whom to vote only at the voting booth ([126]); 42% declared themselves in favour of the multi-party system ([63]). However, the multi-party elections of 1993 attracted even fewer voters.

Experts link the drop in the electorate's participation to an insufficient level of political culture both among the population and in the candidates' pre-election campaigns; to an unperfected system of nominating candidates; to inadequate clarification and application of the Election Law ([81]).

In everyday life (as opposed to political circles), the opinion of others was crucial throughout the Soviet period. Opinion was formed in the workplace. Party committees were supposed to have the authority to reconcile husbands and wives, re-educate drunkards, and get rid of laziness. Intrusions into citizens' private life was constant, facilitated by the fact that flats were often shared by many families and the government encouraged citizens to keep an eye on each other. People's opinions concerning everyday problems and their neighbours' way of life and appearance were expressed openly. In the 1990s, this phenomenon disappeared quite quickly and people became more indifferent to those around them. According to some experts, since in the mid-1990s civil society in Russia remained frozen at a very embryonic stage, incapable of expressing itself on public issues ([62], [298]).

I.A. Boutenko

8 State Institutions

8.1 Education System

The education system was state-run, uniform, free, and institutionally stable up to 1991. Between 1960 and 1985, educational levels rose and the prestige of education grew. Major changes in this sector took place in the late 1980s: decentralization, privatization, introduction of different forms of tuition charges.

The structure of the education system remained relatively stable between 1960 and 1992. The government ran the system, which was financed by the state budget. This structure was under centralized administration and was accessible to all citizens of the USSR, including both sexes and all nationalities. It was intended to provide equal opportunity for all citizens to receive an education, to advance their education later in life, and to achieve their goals by raising their level of education, expanding their knowledge, and so on.

The Russian education system comprised two relatively independent subsystems: basic and complementary. The basic subsystem was oriented to involving a person in socially useful labour and different kinds of public activities. It comprised pre-school education at institutions such as kindergartens, day nurseries, and so on; general compulsory full-time education based on complete secondary schooling up to the seventh grade, in 1951, and up to eleventh grade, in 1990, including primary education (grades 1 to 4) and initial general secondary education (grade 8 in the early 1980s; grade 9 later); vocational and technical education at vocational technical schools that provide specialized secondary education; and higher education at institutes, universities, and academies, complemented by post-graduate courses (*aspirartura*, science candidate, and *doktorantura*, doctor of science; see section 0.3).

Progression to the next educational stage was ensured by unified, standard requirements, in terms of extent and content of knowledge specified for each level, and by a standard, normative curriculum that provided relatively equal opportunities for students taught at different types of educational institutions across the country. However, such an arrangement led, in the long run, to unnecessary formalism and mechanistic unification, giving rise to counterproductive phenomena throughout the educational system.

The structure of continuing education within the state system was as follows: personnel retraining, mastering new skills, and in-service training within the basic occupational profile of workers in all industries; retraining also involved intermediate and senior managers; general complementary education in the public system was based on "people's universities," which provided knowledge in the areas of general culture, law, economy, politics and other areas.

Management of the state system of continuing education was centralized up to the late 1980s. Since 1985, its functions have been fulfilled by the Russian Federation's Ministry of Education. Not only were unified qualification requirements, academic curricula, and other standards established on a centralized principle based on directives, but education planning using standard quantitative indicators was conducted in all units of the state educational system up to the end of the 1980s.

In the 1990s, various lyceums and specialized gymnasiums (some of them charging tuition) were opened and educational programmes diversified. The basic components of their programmes were supervised by the Ministry of Education, while the other disciplines (local history, art, and so on) were licensed by local education departments.

After 1985, financing of the education system changed. Educational institutions of all kinds had been state owned and financed and free to all students before the 1990s; only in pre-schools were parents asked to pay. Nevertheless, state expenditures on education rose (see table 1), although their proportion in the national budget decreased from 13.5% in 1990 to 11.4% in 1992. This is still the trend.

Competition arose among schools – and not only among private ones. At public schools, conditions and teachers' attitudes toward students were not necessarily very positive, but nor was there any guarantee that the private schools would be any better.

Since the early 1990s, certain paid forms of tuition have gradually been introduced into the network of state educational institutions. For example, tuition fees were collected for more thorough study of certain subjects, individual courses at schools and institutes, and so on. Private educational institutions also emerged, such as lyceums and mini-kindergartens in private apartments. Various private courses that provide professional training in bookkeeping, accounting, management, computer maintenance, and so on, have been set up. Moreover, commercial educational centres have been created. Over all, the proportion of the tuition-charging schools within the state educational system is comparatively small, though it has

Table 1
State expenditures on education, Russia, 1990–92 (% of national budget)

1990	1991	1992
13.5	13.5	11.4

Sources: [196], p. 22; [241], pp. 27, 28.

tended to grow since 1993. In the early 1990s, a great number of private higher-level educational institutions were founded, and students could enter them without meeting any entrance requirements. Among the students in these schools were a certain number of boys who wished to avoid military service. This exemption was available to those attending all-male high schools. But in 1994, many of these universities were no longer able to offer this exemption.

The number of students at educational institutions of different types was on the rise in 1985 (see table 2). Overall, the number of students diminished by half between 1990 and 1994. The number of those attending primary and general secondary schools remained relatively stable. Some variations – for example, a 5% increase between 1960 and 1970 – could be attributed to demographic fluctuations due to changes in birth rates: 1.5 as many children were born in 1960 as in 1970. This demographic bulge contributed to the rise in numbers of students in the 1970s. Subsequently, the number of schoolchildren dropped by 5.8% in the 1970s and 1980s and then stabilized, with a slight increase between 1985 and 1992.

The increase observed in the number of students attending specialized secondary educational institutions, and higher educational institutions during the 1980s was later superseded by a reduction. This testifies to a decline in the prestige of education, primarily in specialized, secondary, and higher education, caused by a situation in which many specialists could not find a job during the economic crisis and, in fact, were unemployed more often than were others.

Moreover, in the 1990s it was comparatively easy to earn a living without obtaining specialized training certificates. This trend manifested itself most obviously in the field of continuing professional education (trade-improvement courses, where the number of learners quadrupled between 1960 and 1985, then dropped by two-thirds between 1985 and 1993).

The proportion of students in the overall population, including those attending trade-improvement courses, reached a maximum of 39.3% in 1985 (as compared to 25.6% in 1960), and then dropped to 21.1% by 1994 ([241]).

The role of the pre-school system had diminished by the 1990s. When employment was high, the network of pre-school institutions of all kinds grew (see

Table 2
Number of students by type of education, Russia, 1960–94 (000,000)

	1960/ 1961	1970/ 1971	1980/ 1981	1985/ 1986	1990/ 1991	1991/ 1992	1992/ 1993	1993/ 1994
Total number of students	30.7	43.9	52.3	56.9	48.2	37.5	35.2	27.2
At general primary and secondary schools	20.4	25.8	20.2	20.2	20.8	20.3	21.0	21.0
At specialized secondary, vocational, and technical schools	0.7	1.4	2.1	2.1	1.9	1.9	1.9	1.7
At secondary specialized educational institutions	1.3	2.6	2.6	2.5	2.3	2.2	2.1	2.0
At higher educational institutions	1.5	2.7	3.1	3.0	2.8	2.8	2.6	2.5
In retraining and qualification improvement	6.9	11.4	24.3	29.1	20.4	9.7	7.5	–
% of students to total population	25.6	33.7	37.5	39.3	32.4	25.2	23.6	21.1

Sources: calculated from [171], p. 233; [177], p. 352; [197], p. 25.

table 3), but it still could not meet demand. The number of children attending pre-schools between 1960 and 1985 nevertheless rose by 202.2%, causing overcrowding of kindergartens, day-care centres, and other such institutions. Between 1985 and 1994, the number of children in thee institutions dropped by one fifth. Between 1990 and 1992, enrolment at pre-school institutions fell by 19.0%, a trend that continued for two reasons. First, in the late 1980s, an extension of the three years of government-supported leave of absence paid to mothers after a birth of a child made it possible to extend the period the child remained at home. Second, starting in 1989, there was a substantial rise in the fee for attending public pre-schools, a reduction in subsidies allocated to the pre-schools, and the closing of some pre-schools.

The educational level of the population of Russia remained high enough, though it dropped slightly, that it was among the top ten countries in this respect. Between 1970 and 1988 the number of people who had higher and secondary education at the age of 15 and up rose from 489 to 806 per 1,000. In addition, the number of those who had completed higher and secondary specialized education grew 2.6 times, and the number of those who completed general secondary education rose 2.5 times. The proportion of the Russians who had not completed secondary education over the same period fell from 272 to 210 per 1,000. This was accounted for by the introduction of compulsory, full-time secondary education (see table 4).

Table 3
Pre-schools, Russian Federation, 1960–93

	1960	1970	1980	1985	1990	1991	1992	1993
Pre-schools (000)	47.6	65.0	74.5	81.7	87.9	87.6	82.3	78.3
Children in pre-school (000)	3,038	5,666	8,149	9,180	9,009	8,433	7,300	6,763

Sources: [171], p. 231; [196], p. 250; [197], p. 83.

Table 4
Educational level of the population, Russian Federation, 1970–89 (per 1,000)

	1970	1979	1989
Secondary and higher education at age 15 and over, total	489	696	806
Completed higher education	44	77	113
Incomplete higher education	13	17	17
Secondary specialized education	73	127	192
General secondary education	108	205	274
Incomplete secondary education	251	272	21

Source: [196], p. 10.

E.V. Bykova

8.2 Health System

Before the 1980s, access to medical services was free, but it depended upon one's residence and, in certain cases, upon one's workplace. This steadily expanding infrastructure and subsequent medical care were dependent on available state funds, after production and investment commitments to the economy had been met. In the late 1980s, a burgeoning nongovernment health-care network spectacularly enlarged the choice of services. Indices of national health regressed from the low but stable level of the late 1980s.

Soviet health services were dispensed according to place of residence and administered by a government system up to the second half of the 1980s, based on a fundamental principle of free treatment. Fees at the few clinics in large cities that charged for their services were quite affordable for most people. Because demand was not satisfied, there were long queues and waiting lists of eligible patients. The beginning of the 1990s saw a rapidly emerging nongovernment health-care system and an expanding network of paid services within public institutions financed from various sources.

From the 1960s to the 1990s, the health-care infrastructure steadily grew, and its administration was streamlined. The size of hospitals grew, along with the number of beds and of outpatient clinics, and their absolute numbers shrank as specialized institutions were promoted. The indicators of the functioning of health-care institutions were, to a great extent, ideologically biased. Equipment was not updated to keep up with this increase. From the 1970s to the 1990s, there was a drop in average annual bed occupation and average length of hospital treatment (see table 1) due to advances in medical research and their practical implementation, which sped up treatment and rehabilitation for a number of diseases. As well, there was a trend toward the emergence and permanent expansion of the network of short-term health-care centres, which hospitalized patients for more short periods.

The number of physicians in all specialties grew steadily from the 1960s to the 1990s: from 20.8 per 10,000 total population in 1960 to 48.0 in 1990 and 45.0 in 1992 (see table 2). The number of internists, pediatricians, and psychiatrists grew the most quickly. At the same time, the number of nurses was below that of doctors; a gap between this number and the actual demands of mass health care was a permanent trend throughout the period under study, and was most acute after the 1980s.

The government financing system was gradually replaced by an insurance pattern in the latter half of the 1980s as obligatory health-care deductions from corporate and private revenues became an accepted practice. Steady government medical financing shrank in the early 1990s, from 3–4% of GNP in the late 1980s and 1990 ([53b]) to 1.8% of GNP in 1993 ([12c]).

Public demand for health-care services in the state-run system has been dropping since the end of the 1980s as certain sectors of the population turned from health as a top priority to sheer survival or short-term betterment in a new and different situation. Some patients began to prefer alternative (non-state) medical institutions that were more competitive than their established rivals in advertising, technologies, pioneering methods, and other respects. Before the 1990s, up to 20–25% of patients went to doctors not for treatment but to obtain sick leave and other official papers, which no longer mattered for many segments of the population after the transition to a market economy.

At the same time, the relative number of visits to paid establishments was rising; in Moscow, such visits accounted for 12% of total visits to health-care institutions in 1991, compared to 3% in 1988. In the 1970s and 1980s, most of these visits were made by people in low- and medium-income brackets in the 1970s and 1980s, while

Table 1
Medical establishment statistics, Russia, 1960–92

	1960	1970	1975	1985	1990	1992
Number of hospitals (000)	14.3	13.8	13.1	12.5	12.7	12.6
Number of beds (000)	991.0	1,470.0	1,650.0	1,937.0	2,048.0	1,941.0
Number of beds (per 10,000 population)	82.0	112.0	122.0	134.0	138.0	131.0
Outpatient clinics (000)	–	15.0	19.0	19.4	21.0	20.7
First-aid stations and maternity wards (000)	–	53.0	51.0	48.8	47.9	46.8
Average annual occupation per hospital bed (days per year)	–	–	341.0	322.0	315.0	–
Average length of hospital treatment (days)	–	–	19.0	17.0	16.1	–

Sources: [102], p. 52; [279], p. 189.

Table 2
Medical personnel, Russia, 1960–92 (000)

	1960	1970	1975	1985	1990	1991	1992
Physicians, total	251	378	469	646	699	858	663
Per 10,000 population	21	29	35	45	48	44	45
Dentists	26	31	51	58	66	–	25
Nurses (semi-skilled)	817	1,212	1,416	1,730	1,810	1,692	1,685
Per 10,000 population	63	84	105	120	123	114	114

Sources: [102], pp. 42-44; [279], p. 189.

a considerable number of high-income persons were added in the 1990s ([103]). Like the old elite, the "new rich" demanded top-quality health care, but they could no longer get it free in the "special" clinics that for several decades catered to Communist Party bosses, economic managers, leading artists, and other Soviet dignitaries.

Despite fairly steady general rates, morbidity has been growing for certain groups of diseases since the mid-1980s – mainly psychological, gastric, and osteomuscular. Hypertension and diabetes affect ever younger patients ([116]). The morbidity of measles, diphtheria, scabies, and some other contagious diseases rose in 1993. After 1991, tubercular morbidity by 26% in just three years, after a decrease lasting many years. The 1990s saw an upsurge of venereal diseases: 50% more cases of syphilis and 3.5% more cases of gonorrhea were reported in 1993 than in 1992 ([241]). The number of cases of mental illness rose by 20% between 1989 and 1993 ([99]). Worsening environmental pollution accounted for a growing number of patients who were children and adolescents, many of them with allergies. Between 1975 and 1990, the average number of children with asthma tripled nationally, and it increased by a factor of five to six in industrial cities. Immunity problems affect 75% of urban children ([241]). Many children are born ill (see table 3).

The number of AIDS cases is steadily increasing. The first were detected in 1987, and the total reached 563 by 1992, of whom 269 were children. Many received HIV in government medical establishments. The average man:woman ratio of people with AIDS was 1.5:1 nationally, but varied between 6:1 and 1:7 in different parts of Russia ([103]). The number of HIV-infected persons increased by 18.5 per cent in 1993 ([99]). A certain proportion of the increase in these rates is a result of changed reporting methods and the possibility of anonymity.

The number of handicapped persons has grown spectacularly since the end of the 1980s, largely due to such socio-economic factors as declining industrial safety, the mounting number of armed and other conflicts, growing migration, and declining living standards in a country undergoing changes. Labour-market crises in some regions both raised stress levels and incited people to seek official disability status in order to guarantee an income in the face of looming unemployment. This group is referred to as economically handicapped.

In the early 1990s, according to official statistics, Russia had nearly 300,000 handicapped children, while experts estimated the number at one million ([99]). This number steadily grew from the 1970s to the 1990s (see table 4).

Table 3
Proportion of children born ill and of anemic mothers, Russia, 1985–92 (%)

	1985	1988	1990	1991	1992
Children	9.0	11.5	15.0	17.5	21.5
Mothers	5.5	8.5	12.0	18.5	20.0

Source: [236], p. 278.

Table 4
Persons handicapped since childhood, Russia, 1975–92

	1975	1980	1985	1990	1992
Per 10,000 population	10.2	14.4	17.1	42.8	37.3
Increase, %	-	141.2	118.8	145.0	150.4
% of total handicapped persons	4.0	5.4	6.6	9.1	11.5

Source: [241), p. 8.

I.M. Bykhovskaya

8.3 Social Welfare

From the 1960s to the 1990s, social welfare was the state institution most subject to reform. More people were receiving social assistance, its forms became more diversified, and the number of financial sources increased, but an adequate level of services could not be maintained. In the 1990s, non-state forms of social welfare arose.

Beginning in the late 1930s, there were frequent attempts to increase the egalitarian character of the social-welfare system, of which working people were the main beneficiaries; in the 1990s various privileges were introduced to many other groups. Social welfare institutions were created in a strictly centralized economy with limited financial resources; consequently, there were excessive standardization, an extremely low quality of services, and coverage of only a small segment of the population in need.

For a long time, the most attention was paid to the pension regime, which was based on a person's labour contribution. In the 1920s, one of the lowest pensionable ages in the world (60 years for men, 55 years for women) was introduced in Russia, and this age limit still exists. The first reform of the pension system was carried out in 1918–22, the second in the early 1930s, and the third in 1956, when the law on state pensions was adopted, supplemented in 1964 by the law on pensions and benefits to collective farmers (*kolkhozes*). In 1990, another law on pensions was adopted, which was adjusted and supplemented from 1991 to 1993. Until 1990, personal pensions in individual republics and across the USSR were granted to individual citizens according to their labour contribution when they were working. However, at this time, such modulated pensions were abolished in favour of a universal standard with an overall maximum.

In the second half of the 1980s, sources of financing for social welfare were broadened; the state gradually lost its monopoly over social welfare. In addition to pensions, there were benefits and some tax privileges for those with children, for the disabled, and for single mothers. The proportion of social welfare in payments and privileges from the social consumption funds (see section 6.4) increased: from 1960 to 1980 the number of pensioners doubled, and expenditures for payment of pensions quadrupled, while expenditures for payment of benefits increased by a factor of 3.6 over the same period. In total, expenditures for social welfare increased 4.1 times (see table 1).

Table 1
Payments and privileges from social consumption funds, Russia, 1960–80 (billion roubles)

	Payments for health and social services, total	Payments for social welfare	Payments for pensions and benefits
1960	17.2	6.5	4.7
1965	25.6	9.1	6.8
1970	37.6	14.0	10.0
1975	52.6	20.5	14.8
1980	67.8	26.8	19.9

Source: [299], pp. 180–1.

In the late 1980s, the funds that provided for the social welfare of citizens were constituted, in some cases, through insurance fees levied on enterprises, individuals, and state contributions (labour pensions), and in other cases through allocations from the state budget (payments to military personnel, the disabled, parents of large families, etc.). The amount of the insurance payments was defined according to the amount of wage funds. Obligatory insurance fees were not accumulated, but were used to make current pension payments. Insurance fees were not individualized and had no influence on the amount of individual's pension. Since 1992, pension contributions, via the state budget as well as insurance fees, have accumulated in the Pension Fund of Russia and been distributed by the Ministry of Social Security. Local power organs have been granted the right to set up pension supplements for pensioners in great need, but at the expense of local budgets. In the 1990s, non-state pension funds were created to pay supplementary pensions. This kind of pension provision, unlike the state pension, which was paid out automatically by every enterprise, was based on the voluntary participation of individuals.

Unemployment benefits are paid from the employment fund, which is formed from insurance fees from employers, workers, and allocations from the federal and local budgets.

The number of people covered by social welfare grew for both social and demographic reasons. Between 1960 and the 1990s, the number of pensioners tripled (see table 2), to total more than 36 million people, or 24% of the population. There was an annual increase of about one million in the number of pensioners.

All individuals had a right to temporary disability benefits. The amount of the benefit paid depended upon the cause of the disability, how long the person had been working (from 50% to 100% of the salary), or, in cases not connected with work-related injury or illness, upon membership in a trade union (taken into consideration till the early 1990s).

Table 2
Pensioners in Russia, 1961–94 (000,000)

	Total	Old-age pensioners	Pensioners with disabilities	Survivors and dependents receiving pensions
1961	13.7	3.7	–	–
1966	19.0	9.0	–	–
1970	22.8	13.4	–	–
1980	27.4	19.0	3.5	3.9
1985	31.2	22.5	3.5	3.7
1988	32.6	24.5	3.5	2.9
1989	33.2	25.2	3.6	2.6
1990	33.8	25.7	3.5	2.8
1994	36.4	29.1	3.7	2.4

Sources: [4], p. 18; [176], p. 131; [299], p. 184.

The period spent nursing a child was regarded as work time, to be included in the period of one's employment and taken into consideration in provision of pensions. In the 1990s, mothers of large families and people with disabilities since childhood were provided with state pensions.

Since 1991, benefits for those who have lost their job have been provided. According to the Federal Employment Service, since 1992 the number of unemployed more than doubled, while the number of those receiving benefits increased by a factor of 3.5, with the share of persons receiving unemployment benefits having more than doubled among the latter.

The living conditions of people drawing social benefits and pensions were extremely low throughout the period under study, particularly among collective farmers (*kolkhoz* workers). This situation forced many pensioners to keep their jobs despite poor health; connected with this were limitations that had existed till 1990, whereby working pensioners did not receive pensions or pensioners could have their previous job for only two months a year.

The average old-age pension payment almost doubled among industrial and office workers and more than tripled among *kolkhoz* workers; thus, by 1971, the difference between maximum industrial workers' and *kolkhoz* workers' pensions, which had been at a factor of 1.8 in 1965, was eliminated; in the 1980s, the difference in minimum pensions (which was 2.5 times in 1967) was eliminated ([228]).

In the early 1990s, pensioners' incomes lagged behind consumer prices. The ratio of average old-age pensions to average wages dropped from 71% to 37% between 1991 and 1993 ([7]). The relationship between the minimum pension and the cost of living is quite unstable. As a result of the introduction of indexation of pensions and compensatory payments and benefits, which are paid to all pensioners, the gap between the maximum and minimum pensions decreased, and a trend toward equal pensions reasserted itself. The number of those receiving the minimum pension decreased by 2.3 million people ([4]). This helped to move most pensioners above the poverty line, which had an obvious influence upon the proportion of the population with income below a living wage.

State aid to families with children was provided in financial (benefits, payments) and nonfinancial (free and discounted services) forms for the entire period under study. In the 1990s, for children, passes to vacation homes and sanitoria; paid medical and educational services; after-school organized activities; imported goods; and food products were free of certain taxes. Enterprises that produced food for children and those that built or repaired facilities used by children were exempted from certain taxes. The length of leaves for pregnancy and childbirth was increased; in 1991, partly paid leave for nursing a child was extended to 1.5 years and several social benefits were replaced by a general monthly benefit for each child, depending on the child's age. Until the 1990s, parents had to pay only up to 20% for their children's attendance at a state-run pre-school. Tax deductions were given to all families with minor children (one tax-free minimum benefit per child to every parent); children under two years of age were supplied with milk products free of charge, children under three years age received free medications.

The social-aid network broadened and its services became more diversified. Formerly, those unable to work were provided with special means of transportation, with aid in getting services at home or at specialized health resorts, with discounted or free services in sanitoria and health resorts for pensioners, and with obtaining prostheses. However, given the situation of widespread shortage that prevailed from the 1960s to the 1980s and the abrupt price increases and inability of the state of finance institutions in the 1990s, this aid has been almost symbolic in nature. The network of senior citizens' residences and the number of people in them increased slowly until 1991, then began decreasing (see table 3). The waiting list for places at these institutions dropped because of their extremely unsatisfactory physical conditions. On the other hand, home assistance became more and more widespread (see table 4).

About 50 territorial centres of social aid to family and children, 26 centres of psychological and pedagogical aid and 37 telephone call-in crisis centres were created in the 1990s; such networks were developing intensively. in 1991, a new specialty was introduced within the system of higher education: social work; 52 universities currently offer bachelors' and masters' degrees. Eight thousand people obtained social-work degrees but this proved insufficient ([4]).

Table 3
Beds at homes for senior citizens and people with disabilities, Russia, 1981–93 (000)

	1981	1991	1993
Number of places at homes	236	263	259
For the aged and for disabled adults	202	225	221
For disabled children	34	38	38

Source: [241], p. 320.

Table 4
The social aid network, Russia, 1990–93

	1990	1993	1993/1990, %
Number of social-work offices	3,360.0	7,833.0	233.1
Number of social workers (000)	32.0	97.9	305.9
Number served by social aid (000)	315.0	724.2	229.0
Number served per social worker	9.9	7.4	74.7

Source: [231], pp. 17-18.

G.N. Grigoryantz

8.4 The State

The totalitarian state of the 1920s to the 1950s was replaced by an authoritarian state in the late 1960s, after a brief interlude of liberalization. The 1990s were marked by the loss of the state's power monopoly, the restriction of its functions, and the diminution of its territory; privatization or decentralization of "the people's" – that is, the state's – property began.

From the very beginning of its existence, the Soviet state was associated with the Communist Party. Monopolism was the main principle of social organization till the 1990s: one chief for one party, one ideology for the entire people, with a single goal – construction of communism. Society was identified with the state. In the mid-1930s, the opposition that had existed until then was repressed and dissidence was severely persecuted. There was no division of powers into legislative, executive, and judicial; the mass media were monopolized and social organizations were subject to rigid control. In the first half of the 1960s (the so-called thaw period), when the cruelties of the mass repressions of Stalin's regime were officially acknowledged, timid attempts were made by top Party leadership to reform the totalitarian system without changing its basis – state property.

The years 1965–85 were marked by a retreat from reforms and the intensification of economic problems connected with the exhaustion of the possibilities of extensive economic development. Centralized planning led to major disproportions in the economy; prices played a subordinate role; wages tended to be equalized; and the state apparatus became increasingly bureaucratized. Due to a growing shortage of goods and services, state control over the quality and quantity of labour and rationing of consumption grew widespread. By the end of the 1980s, shortages had reached a disastrous level, leading to a strengthening of the state's distributive functions, both overt and covert, through a system of special supply for the post-1930 elite; for labourers, depending on which economic sector and enterprise they were working in; and for special groups – war veterans, disabled persons, large families. Coupon rationing was introduced on a sporadic basis in some regions in 1960 and lasted for many years.

By the 1980s, the totalitarian state began to weaken: embezzlement and mismanagement grew. The society became uncontrollable and the economy was bankrupt.

In 1991, the Soviet Union began to break down into separate states; Russia became an independent federation. The USSR was created in 1922, on the basis of the military-political union of four republics headed by the Russian Soviet Federative Socialist Republic; by the 1940s, the USSR included 15 republics. Russia was the largest republic by territory, by population, and by economic potential within this strictly centralized entity. The question of the degree of independence of the republics was first addressed in the Constitution of 1977, but this document did not record a demarcation between the central and other power organs. The divisions of territories into republics, areas, regions, and districts changed many times, independently of an expression of the will of population.

In 1990, Russia adopted a Declaration of Sovereignty within the limits of the USSR, and it became an independent state in 1991. At that time, because of the economic crisis, the central power's ability to administer its territories and to find funds for its own maintenance appears to have been questionable. Centrifugal tendencies become obvious, and autonomy discourse emerged in the regions. In 1994, regional leaders and the central government signed the Social Consensus Agreement. Centrifugal tendencies became most evident in Chechnya and culminated in war involving heavy human losses in 1994–95. This revealed the inability of the principal state leaders to reach consensus and made evident the inefficiency of the Russian armed forces. On the other hand, certain republics of the former USSR, mainly the less developed ones, tried to co-operate with Russia.

In the 1990s, Russia underwent a transition from Soviet state to parliamentary and presidential republic. Formally, representative democracy existed in the country beginning in the 1920s, after the "war communism" period that was connected with the civil war after the 1917 October Revolution. Soviets of labourers' deputies, from local soviets to the Supreme Soviet, concentrated power within themselves. This resulted in an underdevelopment of state juridical norms and institutions and in an absence of due process in the relations between the state and individuals. Within the political sphere, everything was subordinate to the state; social organizations were regarded as parts of the state mechanism and controlled by state-appointed officials. Elections were held, but with no alternatives to choose from, and were in fact subordinated to Communist Party control. Important state decisions were made by the Political Bureau of the Central Committee of the CPSU, and always confirmed by the Supreme Soviet. In the late 1980s, the situation changed: there was a choice of candidates in elections, the position of president was introduced, and elections and a referendum were held in 1991. Institution of the division of powers into legislative and executive functions led to conflicts that resulted in bloody clashes in 1991 and 1993.

The state monopoly over the economy was limited in the 1980s. Since the 1920s, the state had been considered the only entity with a right to property. There was a system of hypercentralized and rigid management of enterprises and organizations. State led to distortions in the economy, resulting in constant anomalies – overproduction of some goods and shortages of others. Several hundred enterprises produced between 35% and 100% of the total Russian output of some kinds of products ([171]). A system of centralized distribution of credits and goods devoid of market-value criteria came into being. In fact, state property became the property of certain ministries, which were able to concentrate the enormous material, human, natural, and financial resources at their disposal. The concept of monopolistic state property gave rise to enterprises and production for which no one was responsible. Theft of state (or "no one's") property was not considered to be a serious crime by public opinion; the explanation was "everyone's property is my property." In the 1990s, with the "denationalization" of enterprises, the state withdrew from direct management of the economy (see table 1). By 1994, 70% of all small enterprises and more than half of all large and medium-sized enterprises had been privatized ([313a]). In a country in which all property had been state owned not so long ago, there were 40 million landowners by 1994 ([11e]).

The number of workers at state enterprises, which had comprised more than 90% of all employees from the 1960s to the 1980s, fell rapidly by the 1990s. In the "state of working people," work had been regarded as a right and duty for all. In the 1930s, the system of state compulsion to work was strengthened (in the form of

Table 1
Privatization of industrial enterprises, Russia, 1991

	Number of enterprises	(%)	Total sales (million roubles)	(%)	Number of personnel (000)	(%)
State and municipal	26,328	94.0	1,090,830	97.00	18,109.0	97.00
Federal property	23,790	85.0	1,042,642	93.00	17,245.0	92.00
Property of CIS states	48	0.2	884	0.07	11.1	0.06
Property of republics, areas, regions, and districts of RF	1,472	5.3	24,637	2.20	403.0	2.20
Municipal property	927	3.3	11,226	1.00	307.0	1.60
Property of business associations	89	0.3	11,441	1.00	143.0	0.80
Private	1,366	4.9	28,650	2.50	493.0	2.60
All industry	28,023	100.0	1,123,758	100.00	18,743.0	100.00

Source: [171], p. 68.

criminal punishment of absence from or tardiness at work). In the 1950s, the system of sanctions for parasitism, unscrupulous attitude toward work, tardiness, and so on, was relaxed. In the 1970s, drinking, a lack of spirituality and social vitality, and corruption became more evident among the population. Almost all employees worked at state enterprises, since collective farms (*kolkhozes*) and other co-operatives were nonstate in name only. In the 1990s, with the appearance of enterprises under other forms of property, the number of workers at state enterprises fell (see table 2).

State paternalism and the consequent social infantilism of the population existed for a long while, but were gradually being eliminated in the 1990s. Under the socialist state, individuals were alienated from the main social institutions, from property, from power and management, from the value of labour, and from the very possibility of gratifying work and adequate income, a high level of professionalism became superfluous. The state itself decided to pay a certain minimum income to workers, and redistributed the rest in the form of free housing, medical service, education, and pensions, benefits, and provisions to the elderly and disabled. However, all of these free goods and services were of extremely low quality and were distributed not so much as a function of a person's labour contribution but according to need or enterprise affiliation and personal access to the distribution system for those goods and services.

Human rights and interests were considered unimportant compared to social interests and were inevitably subordinate to them. As a result, most individuals'

Table 2
Distribution of the population by employment sector, Russia, 1980–91

	1980	1985[a]	1990	1991
At state and municipal enterprises and organizations	90.4	91.1	82.8	75.5
At "rented" enterprises	–	–	3.7	7.6
In "joint-stock" companies	–	–	0.2	1.4
In economic associations	–	–	0.1	1.1
In special associations	–	–	0.8	0.9
At joint ventures	–	0.1	0.2	1.4
In collective farms (*kolkhozes*)	6.6	6.0	5.3	5.3
In consumer co-operatives	1.9	1.9	2.0	2.0
In goods-and services-producing co-operatives	–	–	3.4	3.4
In individual and private business	1.1	1.0	1.6	2.6

Source: [171], p. 122.

motivations were not personal but were determined largely by juridical and political constraints – that is, fear of being punished – and, to a lesser extent, economic constraints. The official drive to turn people into interchangeable cogs in the machinery of the state was most intense in the 1920s and 1930s, but this determination existed, to some extent, up to the 1970s. In fact, the only matter left to the individual's discretion at that time was the choice of life or death; however, unsuccessful attempts of suicide in the 1970s and 1980s were punished by compulsory psychiatric treatment.

Totalitarianism and nationalization of property led to an emptying of rural communities due to the suppression of the most successful farmers in the early 1930s and of the most motivated workers in urban communities due to equalization of wages in the 1960s and 1970s. All responsibility for employment, education, health care, security, and so on was turned over to the state. This gave rise to a rather infantile, superstitious, and awed attittude toward the state. Social indifference grew and, for the most part, endured into the 1990s (mostly among representatives of the older generation). Simultaneously, people's confidence in social protection by the state was falling.

Formation of a legal system and the institution of the rule of law began in the 1990s. Under socialism, individuals owned nothing and the state owned everything, so many people expected much from it. The law was perceived as an alien force. Juridical information was inaccessible to both ordinary citizens and professionals; *juridical* offices did not provide adequate protection of civil rights and freedoms. Only a few rights and freedoms were defined, and they were far from being uniformly implemented. In public opinion, judging someone according to the "law" became a complete contradiction to judging according to conscience. In the 1990s, laws were adopted but not obeyed, and the expression of the will of the majority of the population was not taken into account by state authorities.

The personnel in the reigning state elite remained constant. The USSR of the 1970s and 1980s was often regarded as a bureaucratic oligarchy. The state apparatus served the interests of political unity. The politico-administrative system was controlled from the top down. The economy was administered by sector, and was consequently divided into departmental jurisdictions. Professional administrators, as a rule, were not trained, except at schools of Communist Party activists.

The most important and abrupt turnover of leading state bureaucrats took place after Stalin's death (1953). Leaders appointed to their positions in the 1960s and especially in the 1970s remained there for 15 to 20 years. Their average age when they were appointed was 56.6 years in the early 1980s, and even higher in 1985–88. Under Gorbachev, the higher administrative strata included few who had studied the humanities or had a background in law(see table 3). This determined, to a great degree, the technocratic orientation of the state administration as a whole. Unlike their predecessors, some state leaders in the 1990s had had academic degrees bestowed upon themselves.

Within years, and especially with the disintegration of the USSR (1991), the number of ministries and departments fell, but the numbers of administrative staff in enterprises and organizations grew by 700,000 between 1985 and 1988 ([181]; see table 4). In 1994, 2% of the total national budget was spent on this apparatus (Arguments, 1994).

The "upper class" was not so much a new class or stratum as a caste, which it was as difficult to leave as to enter. This situation persisted into the mid-1990s.

The state, which had been militaristic since the 1920s, very gradually demilitarized in the 1990s. A large portion of national revenue was spent on the military-industrial complex. In the 1920s and 1930s, "socialist development" was imposed by the USSR upon several states in Asia; in the 1940s, on states in Eastern Europe; in 1961, in Cuba.

Within the state education system, basic military training was obligatory for all *schoolchildren* and most *students* (this was abolished in the 1990s), and for many years all everyday vocabulary was militarized: waging a "battle" for crops, for discipline, for product quality, and so on, was a standard expression.

The state agreed to a rapprochement with the church, which was formally separated from the state. In the early 1990s, replacing the political (ideological supervisors (*commissars*), chaplains were introduced into the Russian army; the government head and the president publicly attended church services, and Orthodox

Easter and Christmas were declared national holidays. In 1988, priests entered the Supreme Soviet as deputies; the church later forbade priests from holding such positions.

Table 3
Type of education of heads of ministries and departments, Russia, 1960–88

Years appointed	Engineering and technical	Agrarian	Humanities (inc. medicine)	Party and political	Military	No data
1960–1970s	50	5	27	3	7	8
1984	66	7	15	3	2	7
1986–88	63	10	17	3	2	5

Source: [37], p. 37.

Table 4
Personnel in ruling administrative organs, USSR and Russia (000)

	1970	1980	1985	1988	1990	1991
In the USSR, total	1,724	2,231	2,376	1,831	–	–
Ministries and departments	1,217	1,531	1,623	1,080	–	–
Apparatus of the USSR	88	104	107	85	–	·
Republican apparatus	116	134	140	108	–	–
Ministries of autonomous republics, local and regional departments and sections	201	251	280	265	–	–
District (*okrug*), area, city, and town departments and sections	351	413	450	477	–	–
Procurement offices	460	629	646	145	–	–
Apparatus of presidiums of the Supreme Soviet and executive committees of Soviets of people's deputies	261	297	312	311	–	–
Judicial and juridical offices	70	849	92	99	–	–
Apparatus of administrative organs of co-operative and social organizations	176	319	349	341	–	–
In Russia, total administrative apparatus financing, and state insurance	–	1,719	1,809	–	2,169	2,479
% of all employed	–	2.3	2.4	–	2.9	3.3

Sources: [171], p. 122; [182], p. 395.

I.A. Boutenko

9 Mobilizing Institutions

9.1 Labour Unions

From the 1960s to the 1990s, trade unions were the largest nonparty organizations; in the 1990s, other forms of workers' organizations appeared. In 1980s, trade-union membership became almost routine, and its prestige fell. Alternative labour organizations arose.

Throughout their history, Soviet trade unions were the largest nonparty organizations. From the 1960s to the 1980s, the number of members of trade unions affiliated with the All-Union Central Council of Trade Unions and the proportion of working people who were members of trade-union organizations in the USSR (and in Russia) rapidly increased (see also section 10.2). For example, in 1960, 93.7% of those employed belonged to a union. During the 1970s and 1980s, this number reached almost 100%. Most of the rural population – collective farmers – were accepted into trade unions beginning in the late 1970s, considerably increasing the number of trade-union members (see tables 1 and 2). When workers retired, this usually ended their contact with the enterprise and the trade-union organization, thus also ending their union membership.

Between 1937 and 1959, the number of people employed at state-owned enterprises increased by a factor of 2.5, due mainly to urbanization, which peaked in the 1960s. In the 1960s and 1970s, workers or students who wanted to join a trade union had to submit a written application. Trade-union members paid dues and had membership cards on which their monthly dues payments were recorded. By the 1980s, admission to a trade union was automatic: when a person took a job, he or she simultaneously became a trade-union member; the dues (1% of the wage before taxes) were automatically calculated by the enterprise and transferred to the account of the trade-union committee. Restoration of less formal membership began only in the first half of the 1990s, when people wanting to join a trade union again had to write and submit a personal application.

Beginning in 1990–91, the number and proportion of trade-union members decreased noticeably. An investigation of the elasticity of the labour market in

Table 1
Trade-union membership, USSR, 1937–77

	Members (million)	% of total employed
1937	21.8	84.3
1959	52.8	93.1
1977	123.0[a]	98.2

Source: [152], p.18.
[a] Includes agricultural workers.

Table 2
Changes in trade-union membership, Russia, as at 1 January, 1993

	(million)	(%)
Total membership (including non-working pensioners)	64.4	100.0
Left union during fiscal year	2.4	3.7
suspended membership by choice	1.7	2.6

Source: [3], p. 18.

Russian industry was conducted in 1993 in four regions by the Institute of Economics (of the Russian Academy of Sciences). It showed that the proportion of trade-union members among employees in industrial enterprises was 85.5%. The greatest decreases in trade-union members were in the machine-building sector (to 82%) and in light industry (to 84%) – that is, in sectors that were suffering the most from the economic recession. Over the same period, the smallest decrease took place in the food industry (to 91%) and metallurgy (to 89%), where the economic situation was the most stable. According to preliminary data from a similar investigation in 1994, the proportion of trade-union members in various industrial sectors decreased by a further 10–20%.

When collective agreements were discussed, attendance at the meetings was usually less than 40% of the workers affected ([3]).

The prestige of trade union organizations decreased. Length of service at a given enterprise or industrial sector permitted an ordinary worker to receive some social goods, distributed by the trade-union leaders, and at any rate to receive social protection in the form of positive social sanction in the workplace. By the beginning of the 1990s, the situation had changed. In 1992, 7.5% of working people felt that they could rely on the trade unions for help; 47.9% were not sure that trade unions could help them; and 22% felt that they would not help ([238]).

In 1989, people did not distinguish between the activity of trade unions, directed at improving working and living conditions (see table 3), and that of the administration and party organization. The crisis of faith in traditional trade unions due to their inability to guarantee and defend the rights of working people in their fight with the employers (see table 4) gave rise to a number of alternative trade unions in the late 1980s and early 1990s.

The fact that trade unions were diverted from their activity on behalf of workers in the late 1980s resulted in the spontaneous emergence of workers' self-help organizations. An attempt to organize the first non-official trade union in 1977 was connected with the fact that official trade unions could not effectively defend the rights of working people, because they were responsible only for the fulfilment of economic plans. But this and other attempts were very soon stopped by persecution of these new union leaders ([3]). At the beginning of the 1980s, soviets (councils) of working collectives (SWCs) were formed at many enterprises, with participation by administration representatives and workers. SWCs took part in formulating both short-term and long-term production plans at these enterprises. In the mid-1980s, legislation was enacted concerning SWCs, but they very soon stopped playing any significant role at enterprises because the administration actively opposed them and workers had a passive relationship with them.

Table 3

Evaluation of effectiveness of company management, Communist Party committees, and trade-union committees in improving labour conditions and everyday life, Russia, 1989 (%)*

	Good	Satisfactory	Bad	No answer
Company management	11.5	44.0	22.5	22.0
Party committees	9.0	39.5	23.0	28.0
Trade-union committees	10.0	44.0	23.5	22.5

Source: [327], p. 171.
* Survey of employees of Moscow enterprises, 1989.

Table 4

Opinion of union members on the capacity of their trade union to defend their interests, Russia, 1991–92 (%)

	1991	1992
Quite well	1.6	0.5
Partially	18.9	16.7
Not at all	55.5	72.8
No answer	24.0	10.0

Source: [238], p. 89.

Trade unions adapted to the changing socio-political situation of the 1990s primarily by mobilizing their members to strike (see section 10.2).

E.G. Meshkova and P.G. Smirnov

9.2 Religious Institutions

In the state of "militant atheism" that lasted until the end of the 1980s, the activities of religious institutions were regulated indirectly by the state. Since the institution of religion was not officially approved, it was difficult to calculate the number of religious persons, which was deliberately underrated. Starting in the early 1990s, there was a religious boom and a definite reinstitutionalization of religious values.

In the Soviet state, which declared atheism to be its official ideology, the position of the church in social life was determined by Party directives until the end of the 1980s. After the period of repression of and total war against religion in the 1930s, relations between the church and the state began to be normalized in the 1940s and 1950s, in many respects because of diplomatic efforts and an evaluation of the contribution made by the church and the religious to the victory in the Great Patriotic War of 1941–45. More opportunities were presented to religious organizations to broaden religious practice. The number of Orthodox parishes increased fivefold from 1941 to 1959, reaching 14,500. The number of people performing religious rites increased: in the country as a whole, 30% of people born in 1959 were baptized; in some central European regions, this proportion reached 40% to 60%. One third of the deceased had church funeral services ([1]).

In the late 1950s and early 1960s, there were other religious denominations besides the Russian Orthodox church. There were 2,114 Baptist churches, 1,244 Catholic parishes, and 4 ecclesiastical boards of Moslems. In addition, there were many illegal, unregistered denominations. According to estimates, by the early 1960s there were 11,000 non-Orthodox religious associations in the USSR, of which only 4,424 were registered with the state ([1]).

In the 1960s, a second wave of religious suppression began, disguised in increasingly bureaucratic forms, although the character of atheistic propaganda harkened back to the severe repression of the 1930s. The religious affiliation of part of the population was declared, in Party documents of the time, to be one of the most serious obstacles to rapid construction of a communist society in the USSR, and the state actively interfered in the activities of religious institutions. In 1961, bowing to pressure from the power structures, the Bishop's Council of the Russian Orthodox Church adopted new rules (which were in force until 1988) concerning the organization of parish administration, which impeded the normal institutionalization of religion. Appointments of upper and middle church hierarchy and parish administration were to be confirmed by the state and the details of church affairs were to be transparent to the secret service. The practice of noting those who initiated religious rituals and informing the secret service was thus instituted. For the religious, this posed a threat to their career, especially for CPSU members. Every year, under different pretexts, churches were closed and parishes ceased to function (see table 1). By 1966, the number of Orthodox churches and parishes had dropped by half from its 1959 level ([322]).

In the 1970s, the Orthodox Church, which remained the most significant religious association, extended its foreign links. It joined the World Council of Churches, organized international religious colloquia, attended international conferences of European churches, and worked out a new approach to the ecumenical movement. UNESCO's support of the celebration of the thousandth anniversary of the introduction of Christianity to Russia (1988) was of great significance for strengthening the church's position in society.

The clergy were under close surveillance by the government throughout the Soviet period. After the separation of church and state in 1918, the clergy suffered pressure from the new political power: the repression of the 1920s and 1930s,

Table 1
Number of parishes and monasteries in the Russian Orthodox Church, 1959–94

	Parishes	*Monasteries*
1959	14,000	47
1961	8,000	–
1966	7,523	16
1971	7,274	–
1976	7,038	–
1981	7,007	–
1986	6,794	–
1988	7,798	18
1989	10,000*	–
1993	14,113	242
1994	15,810	269

Sources: [113], p. 3; [156], p. 2; [322], pp. 154, 160, 165, 18Ê7, 188, 192.
* Estimate.

Khrushchev's persecutions of the 1960s, when 1,234 people were convicted for religious motives ([1]). The number of clergy was decreasing by attrition. It was more and more difficult to get a religious education: during the 1960s, five seminaries were closed. In the 1990s, some of them were reopened and new ones created. In 1988, more than a thousand Orthodox parishes, ecclesiastical colleges, and seminaries opened ([322]). The number of religious students increased (see table 2). But the problem of personnel (see table 3) remained acute: in 14,113 Orthodox churches active in 1993, there were only 12,013 clergymen ([113]). The situation was aggravated by the fact that among the students at seminaries, there were always some who were not planning to become clergymen: from 1972 to 1974, only two thirds of seminary graduates went to serve in parishes ([322]). Nevertheless, the popularity of religious education increased considerably among young people. Thus, in 1992, for the first time since the revolution, two people were applying for every place in religious schools ([206]).

In the first years of perestroika, not only did the church support political reforms, but clergymen were among the leaders of the reform movement and were members of Parliament. The exacerbation of political struggles led the Patriarch to declare political activities incompatible with ecclesiastical dignity. Nonetheless, without participating directly in the political debate, the Orthodox church maintained a constant dialogue with the power structures and became an influential social force. Laws on freedom of religion and religious organizations, adopted in 1990, reflected a change in the church's position in society and put religious institutions on an equal footing with other social organizations.

The change in the church's position in society was reflected in rapid growth of religious observance. In the early 1990s, there was a boom in religion, with up to 39% of the population declaring themselves to be religious. In January, 1993, the Ministry of Justice registered a total of 8,612 religious organizations (see table 4) ([311]). However, attendance at services and religious ceremonies, which would

Table 2
Number of students at Orthodox ecclesiastical schools, Russia, 1975–94

	Students
1975	756
1985	1,200
1994	2,548

Sources: [156], p. 3; [322], p. 190.

Table 3
Number of clergy, Russia, 1961–94

	Number of clergy	Number of deacons
1961	8,252	809
1966	6,694	653
1971	6,234	618
1976	5,994	594
1993	12,013*	
1994	12,707	1,380

Sources: [113], p. 1; [156], p. 2; [322], pp. 154, 160, 165.
* Total of clergy and deacons.

Table 4
Largest religious organizations in Russia (according to the Department of Justice of Russian Federation, 1 Jan. 1993)

	Places of worship	Regional centres	Societies	Monas- teries	Educa- tional insittutions	Communal groups or "brotherhoods"	Missions
Russian Orthodox	4,566	54	4,357	81	7	54	19
Roman Catholic	73	3	65	2	1	–	2
Moslem	2,537	23	2,440	–	69	–	5
Buddhist	52	2	46	–	1	–	3
Jewish	40	1	34	1	4	1	–
Old believers*	108	4	102	1	1	–	–
Russian Orthodox Free Church subordinate to Russian Orthodox Church abroad	57	1	54	–	–	1	1
Lutheran	75	3	72	–	–	–	–
Gospel Christian Baptist	433	21	387	–	–	–	25
Council of the Church of Gospel Christian Baptists	11	–	8	–	–	–	3
Seventh-day Adventists	114	6	107	–	1	–	–
Christians of the Gospel Religion	114	6	83	–	1	1	23
Charismatic churches	52	–	41	–	–	–	11

Source: [311], pp. 14–15.
* Those who do not follow the church rules adopted in the seventeenth century.

indicate active, rather than passive, participation in religious institutions, remained at a low level: churches were attended weekly by only 10% of the religious, with 50% attendance on holidays. Other rites were observed regularly by 10% of the religious and not performed at all by 31% ([163]).

Interreligious tension and competition were growing, a consequence of the proliferation of various denominations. The Orthodox church accused other denomination of proselytizing in its territory. Religious representatives were very aware of the situation: up to 61% of those interviewed in 1993 advocated creation of a special organization consisting of representatives of different denominations to deal with interreligious conflicts ([163]). In 1994, the Orthodox church, the largest religious institution in Russia, whose authority was acknowledged by other religions, organized a negotiation process that helped to normalize interreligious relations but led to a confrontation with pseudo-Christian, occult, and charismatic sects.

In connection with the increase in the number of religious organizations, the state implemented a policy of returning churches, temples, and mosques, and cult objects to their respective religious adherents. In Moscow alone, from 1989 to 1994, 269 orthodox churches were returned, of which 164 are already active ([113]), along with 269 monasteries ([156]). Because of a rapid increase in the number of adherents to Catholicism from 1992 to 1994, more than 120 parishes were formed in the European and Siberian regions, and 10 churches and several chapels were placed at their disposal (estimated by information from the magazine *Truth and Life*). From 1988 to 1994, the Ministry of Culture turned over about 50,000 icons and more than 10,000 other cult objects from the state reserve stocks to various religions, including Orthodox, Buddhist, and Jewish ([143]).

A priority of religious institutions is attracting new members. From the 1960s to the 1980s, sacred books were almost completely inaccessible, even to the religious. The Bible was published only in 1976, 1979, and 1983, with a total print run of 300,000. Ignorance of religious matters resulted in a phenomenon noted by sociologists in the early 1990s: up to 47% of the religious identified with no single denomination but regarded themselves as Christians in a general sense ([312]). In the 1990s, TV, newspapers, and magazines willingly gave broadcast time or pages to representatives of different religions. Churches were responsible for publishing about 50 periodicals; the Moscow Patriarchate alone publishes five magazines and three newspapers as central Orthodox editions. Many Sunday schools have opened, at which catechism lessons are conducted; in Moscow alone, there were about 70 Orthodox Sunday schools in 1993 ([113]).

L.Y. Petrunina

9.3 Armed Forces

In the postwar armed forces of the USSR and Russia, there were close links between structural and quantitative reorganizations and military and strategic changes.

The organization and size of the Russian military forces underwent major changes. The transition to peace after the end of World War Two brought about significant changes in administrative structures and troop organization in the Russian army and navy. As a result, the Ministry of Defence of the USSR was set up in March, 1953. From 1945 to 1948, 8.5 million people were demobilized from the armed forces. Later, the number was reduced further (see table 1).

During World War Two, the Air Defence Forces acquired an independent status and became a separate organization of the armed forces. In 1960, a similar status was acquired by the Strategic Rocket Troops, which had become a crucial part of the armed forces.

Table 1
Personnel in the USSR Armed Forces, 1945–95 (000)

1945	11,365
1948	2,874
1950	5,763
1953	3,623
1960	2,423
1964	3,300
1970	3,305
1975	3,575
1980	3,658
1984	5,300
1988	4,257
1990	3,760
1992	2,800
1994	2,302
1995	1,900*

Sources: [12j]; [162g]; [204], p. 16; [229], p. 357.
* Including 1.1 million soldiers, among them 350,000 on contract.

Prior to the 1990s, the armed forces of the country comprised the following services: the Strategic Rocket Troops, the Land Forces, the Air Defence Forces, the Air Force, the Navy, the Civil Defence Troops, the Frontier Protection Forces, and the Internal Defence Troops. Unified principles and regulations on personnel training and promotion were established within the framework of the armed forces.

In the 1990s, the armed forces were theoretically being converted into an institution of a democratic state. They ceased to be affected directly by political bodies. The veil of secrecy over many aspects of the military was lifted. The overall strength of the army and its armaments diminished. Military expenditures were cut, while the role of the government in directing the armed forces was circumscribed. The Warsaw Armed Forces Pact was dissolved. The withdrawal of military units and formations from other states and from former republics of the USSR was under way.

Essential changes took place in the numbers of top military administrators and in the functions they fulfilled. In April, 1992, a civilian was appointed first vice-minister of the Ministry of Defence. One feature of the new Ministry of Defence was that all of its large-scale plans and major activities were to be discussed in Parliament and, hence, covered by the media.

In September, 1992, the country's first law on defence organization was passed. It specified the organization and size of the armed forces, the basis of personnel mobilization, the rights of the civil personnel, the administrative bodies and systems, the functions of the Ministry of Defence and the General Headquarters, and so on.

The Central Political Administration with a political control function in the army and navy, was replaced by organs whose main task was to take care of military personnel, involving sociologists, chaplains, lawyers, and recreational specialists.

The period of the 1960s to the 1980s was characterized by changes in the numbers, proportions, and kinds of both strategic nuclear-weapon carrier systems and nuclear warheads (see tables 1 and 2). The most intensive growth in the number of nuclear-weapon carrier systems took place from the early 1960s to the mid-1970s, with further growth in the number of nuclear warheads (see tables 2 and 3).

The foundation of the fighting strength of the armed forces of Russia, and that of the USSR, was its strategic offensive weapons; in the mid-1980s, there were 10,000 warheads on strategic carriers. At the same time, efforts by the military and political administration were focused on designing launch pads for land-based intercontinental ballistic missiles. There were a number of reasons for this, including the geographical position of the country, with extensive land borders, the presence of the strongest probable enemy stationed in Western Europe (NATO bloc).

Table 2
Number of strategic nuclear weapons on missiles, 1955–91

1955	1960	1965	1970	1975	1980	1986	1991
20	300	600	1,800	2,800	6,000	10,000	10,271

Source: [232], p. 167.

Table 3
Number of nuclear weapon delivery systems, 1960–91

	1960	1965	1970	1975	1979	1986	1991
Total	500	1,475	–	2,446	2,504	2,480	2,500
submarines	15	25	300	784	950	912	940
bombers	150	215	115	135	156	160	162
ICBMs	150	250	1,300	1,527	1,398	–	1,398

Sources: [232], p. 166.

The fighting strength of troops depended on the geopolitical conditions that prevailed in the world and on the antagonisms between ideological systems. The most rapid growth in numbers of nuclear missiles took place in the 1960s and 1970s, when the Cold War policy was pursued by both the NATO bloc and the Warsaw Pact countries. A relaxation of international tensions started in the 1970s; as a consequence, there was tangible stabilization in all aspects of nuclear-missile deployment.

After 1972, talks were held to set limits on strategic nuclear weapons. In 1990–91, the USSR completed decommissioning of a total of 809 mid-range missiles, including 654 RMD-10 missiles, 149 R-12 and R-14 missiles, and 408 missiles in stationary launch pads. In addition, 2,725 units of auxiliary equipment and 84 stationary units were liquidated. In the 1990s, there was a trend toward further reduction in the numbers of Russian nuclear weapons.

Since 1992, a mixed method of recruiting military personnel has been introduced. Previously, every man over eighteen years of age was conscripted for military service, and students' service took the form of service after graduating from high school or special officer training as a complement to their education. In the 1990s, there was a move toward voluntary recruitment and a certain reliance on civilian personnel as opposed to career military personnel. In accordance with plans drawn up by the Russian military and the government, the armed forces were to comprise reserve troops and one million civilian employees working under contract. Earlier, the number of this category of employees was not specified with such accuracy.

The transition to a mixed form of recruiting is regarded as a positive change by military personnel as well as by the civilian population. Polls carried out by the

Centre of Military, Social, and Juridical Research among persons working under contract, those who have been and or will be drafted, and officers dealing with volunteer recruiting show a positive attitude toward this measure. The possibility of a civil-service corps has been put forward. Among young people, this is considered to be an alternative to the traditional and unpopular draft. It is attractive because it gives them a chance to make an independent choice regarding the form of their duty ([205]).

The duration of military service tended to get shorter. In the 1960s, obligatory military service in the land forces was set at two years; in the Navy, three years. Since 1992, the term for the former has been set at 18 months, and that for the latter at 24 months. In 1995, there was an adjustment in favour of longer service.

The numerical strength of the Russian armed forces has constantly dropped. In 1992, the total number of military personnel was reduced by 200,000. According to plans drawn up by the military and political leadership, the number of military personnel will be 2.1 million by 1995 and 1.5 million by the end of 1999.

V.A. Frolov and F.I. Makarov

9.4 Public Associations and Political Parties

Until the end of 1980s there was only one political party in Russia, the Communist Party. In the early 1990s, there was an explosion of public associations and political parties. In 1991–92, Russia had about 7,000 registered public associations, many of which later became political parties.

The one-party system of Soviet society, by definition, did not permit the existence of any political party except the Communist Party of the Soviet Union. Membership in the CPSU provided better career opportunities; the number of communists grew until 1990 (see table 1). Two other organizations calling themselves political parties, the Democratic Union and the Union of Civil Rights Fighters, had to operate completely underground. Dissidents were considered to be mentally ill or criminals.

The need to create a Communist Party of Russia (as opposed to the Communist Party of the USSR) was openly discussed for the first time at the beginning of perestroika in the late 1980s. The reformers of that period were suffering with an acute inferiority complex, since the largest Soviet republic did not have such attributes of its own statehood as an academy of sciences, a Communist Party, or a secret-police force. The Russian Communist Party (RCP) was created in early 1991, and it existed only until the putsch in August of that year. Within this short period, this party was unable to solve the problem of its membership. Many of those who lived in the Russian Federation and were automatically enlisted in its ranks refused to recognize the status quo. A considerable proportion of radical communists, who rejected the conservative direction of the leadership, formed a splinter group, which soon became an independent party, the Democratic Party of the Communists of Russia (DPCR).

Membership in some associations had been compulsory (see section 2.5). It is very hard to imagine how a scientist could refuse to join Znanie ("Knowledge") or a state employee could refrain from registering in the Voluntary Society for Assisting the Army, Air Force and Navy (DOSAAF). A person could be registered in the DOSAAF, Friends of Forests, the Red Cross, and other such organizations through absolutely no doing of his or her own, and people often had no idea that they were members of such organizations, but from time to time paid dues in a perfunctory fashion to these organizations.

There were few exceptions to this general rule. For a new voluntary association to be created by public initiative was incredibly difficult, for those in power were suspicious of any initiative of this kind. The spontaneous creation of any association was considered a serious threat to the existing political leadership. The authorities in power did not take the trouble to establish new public associations. The main issue was the mass nature of the membership in existing public associations, which had to be expanded by any means possible. In the 1960s and 1970s, however, membership was often expanded mainly by distorting figures. As a result, the number of members in public associations grew steadily, but the number such associations stayed the same.

Public life in the Soviet Union was organized so that when children entered first grade, they automatically became an *oktyabryonok* (October is the month when the 1917 revolution took place): when they were a bit older, they took an oath of loyalty to the Communist Party and entered the Pioneer League. In fact, becoming a Pioneer was mandatory, and it was perceived as an initiation of sorts, or as part of the educational process. The only children who were not admitted were those who were religious (1930–1950s) and serious juvenile delinquents.

In the early 1990s, there was an explosion in the number of associations and political parties formed. About 7,000 public associations were registered in Russia in 1991–92 (see table 2). As a rule, all kinds of activities, including commercial, were mentioned in the charters of these associations. According to Russian legis-

Table 1
Number of members of the CPSU and the Communist Party, 1960–90

	USSR	Russian Federation	% RF to USSR
1960	8,708,667	–	
1965	11,758,169	–	
1967	12,684,133	8,225,033	64.8
1970	14,011,784	–	
1973	14,821,031	9,378,066	63.3
1975	15,294,803	–	
1977	15,994,476	10,002,935	62.7
1980	17,082,289	–	
1983	18,117,903	11,220,340	61.9
1985	18,700,000	–	
1987	19,267,715	11,842,496	61.5
1988	19,486,786	–	
1989	19,487,822	–	
1990	19,228,217	–	

Source: [208], p. 3.

Table 2
Public associations registered in Russia 1991–92

International	231
All-Russian	648
Inter-regional	496
Republican	468
Krai (region)	435
Oblast	2,267
Local (part of Oblast)	249
City	1,952
Local	106
District	92
Municipal	13
District (part of city)	390
Settlement	37
Village	14
Cossack village	12
Total	7,424

Source: [234], p. 18.

lation, public associations enjoy certain tax exemptions. In fact, this is one of the main reasons for the enormous number of public associations in Russia.

In 1993, 37 national political parties were registered in the Russian Federation. In addition, there were about 20 unregistered organizations that called themselves parties. It is nearly impossible to determine membership in these parties in the mid-1990s, because most of them preferred not to reveal how many members they had. Those who did publish these data most likely inflated the figures. Moreover, the number of members in a particular party bore no particular relationship to public support for it. The survey data can be an eloquent illustration of this (see table 3).

These data did not reflect the situation in the whole of Russia. Moscow was the most politicized city in the country; in the rest of Russia, attitudes toward parties were more critical or indifferent. According to various sociological data, in 1994 the overwhelming majority of the population knew about the existence of no more than two or three parties.

The role that parties and their leaders played in political life in the mid-1990s did not depend directly on how many members they had but on the image of their respective leaders.

It is also difficult to discern whose interests each party expressed. There were representatives from very different groups and strata, from the new owner classes to the proletariat, from retired people to young people, among the members of every major party.

Table 3
Members of political parties* and proportion of the population who expressed a preference for a party, Moscow, 1993

	(n)	(%)
Democratic Party of Russia	60,000	5.4
People's Party Free Russia	60,000	2.4
Socialist Party of Working People	60,000	0.0
Russian Christian-Democratic Movement	1,500	0.0
Communist Party of Russian Federation	450,000	1.5
Russian Communist Workers Party	100,000	0.3

Source: [50], p. 11.
* According to respective party leaders.

A.T. Gasparishvily

9.5 Mass Media

Information media became more diversified; at the end of 1980s censorship was ended. The development of the Russian – and Soviet – mass media followed global technological trends, though lagging behind Western standards. Some experts evaluated this lag at ten years, others at twenty.

The first television sets appeared in the USSR toward the end of the 1930s, but they came into homes only twenty years later, and then only into a small number of households. Every family had a television set only in the late 1980s – and Russia possessed more TV sets than other Soviet republics (see table 1).

The number of Russian television stations grew by a factor of 38.9 in just 30 years (from 157 in 1960 to 6,774 in 1990). Television became the leader in mass media, and in the 1990s was watched far more often than radio is listened to or newspapers are read. In Moscow and the Moscow region in 1991, television took up 44.4% and 47.8% of leisure time, respectively, while newspapers took up 5.8% and 5.2%, respectively, and radio 0.3% ([213]). Nevertheless, the number of radio sets reached 50.7 million in 1991, compared to 17.5 million in 1960 (see table 2). Sales of radio sets grew (see table 3).

The number of tape recorders grew from 8% of households in 1970 to 58% of households in 1991. These appliances were of great importance for the free-thinking public under conditions of severe Soviet censorship, when they were used to circulate recordings by dissidents, and lost their significance after freedom of speech came to Russia.

The 1980s were marked by the appearance of the VCR in private business and home entertainment. Soviet manufacturing of VCRs started in this decade. The total number was estimated at roughly three million in 1990, but there were no official statistics.

Filmmakers and video-salon owners owned about a half of this number. According to VCIOM data, 3.4% of households possessed VCRs in 1992, and ownership of this appliance was spreading more quickly than had record players and tape or cassette recorders. A CD player remains a luxury article.

Cable television appeared in the late 1980s on a local scale as new housing developments got narrow-cast stations, which, like use of VCRs, were used mainly for pirated American movies. Last, but not least, the 1990s brought satellite dishes not only to posh hotels but to many government-owned, co-operatively owned, and privately owned apartment houses.

Table 1
Audiovisual appliances, Russia, 1965–91 (per 100 households)

	TV sets	Radio sets	Tape recorders
1965	27	53	–
1970	52	74	8
1975	79	86	–
1976	82	88	–
1977	86	90	–
1978	88	92	–
1979	90	92	–
1980	91	92	28
1985	103	101	40
1986	105	101	43
1987	107	101	47
1988	109	101	50
1989	110	98	54
1990	111	99	58
1991	112	100	58

Source: [176], p. 217.

The media revolution dramatically increased domestic and foreign information sources. Between the 1960s and the 1990s, the number of national and local television channels doubled (from three to six), as did the number of radio stations (from five to ten). Some regions received foreign programmes, which were highly popular, though official statistics did not mention them.

Russian-language programming on Voice of America, Radio Liberty, and other Russian-language radio stations had very limited audiences because of jamming, which stopped in the mid-1980s. With social and economic changes, audiences multiplied, and national and local stations turned to US, West European, and Latin American entertainment programming.

The disintegration of the Soviet Union brought the confrontation between federal and local (and ethnic) interests to a head, and the repercussions were seen immediately in the mass media. Thus, the political stances of Central and Russian television channels changed visibly between 1986 and 1991; they shared similar opinions after the abortive coup of August, 1991, though local political leaders had many Moscow broadcasts and even certain channels blocked. Sociological probes and the first semi-official ratings partly reflected this tug-of-war.

The mass media had another salient feature – the use of different languages in the multi-ethnic Russian community. It would be natural that the new official status of

Table 2
Audiovisual mass media, Russia, 1960–91

	TV stations	TV and radio audience (million)	TV sets (million)	Radio sets (million)
1960	157	39.3	3.4	18.4
1965	372	54.3	–	–
1970	720	77.6	20.4	27.8
1975	1,099	106.2	–	–
1976	1,201	111.0	–	–
1977	1,295	115.9	–	–
19781	4,761	20.6	–	–
1979	1,790	124.7	–	–
1980	2,107	129.3	39.5	49.4
1981	2,640	135.8	–	–
1982	3,050	142.0	–	–
1983	3,650	148.4	–	–
1984	4,090	153.1	–	–
1985	4,598	156.9	48.3	60.8
1986	5,096	161.0	49.9	63.2
1987	5,543	164.9	51.2	65.9
1988	6,041	169.1	52.4	68.5
1989	6,479	172.6	53.7	70.1
1990	6,774	176.7	55.0	72.0
1991	6,780	187.2	56.5	80.0

Source: [171], p. 217.

former Soviet republics would be a factor encouraging multi-lingualism. Statistics, however, do not bear this out, at least in Russia, where the number of Russian-language editions and broadcasts underwent only a negligible change within the period under review. Moreover, many local-language periodicals with limited readership folded when government financing stopped.

The authorities eased their grip on the media in the mid-1990s. Television was the only exception, as control of this medium became even tighter during the repeated political crises (1993).

Official Soviet control over the press was very tight in the 1960s, and even well into the 1980s because of its powerful levers – government allocations, absence of advertising, coercively limited circulations of popular publications, and bloated ones in the case of their Communist Party counterparts. The official choice of news was the same at all levels from federal to local, and dailies were no longer than four

Table 3
Television and radio sets: Sales per 1,000 population, Russia, 1960–91

	Population	TV sets	Radio sets	Tape recorders
1960	119.9	7.5	17.6	–
1965	126.7	15.2	22.6	–
1970	130.4	23.7	25.1	4.2
1975	134.2	26.3	31.3	–
1976	135.2	26.2	26.2	–
1977	136.1	26.6	26.8	–
1978	137.1	28.3	26.9	–
1979	138.0	26.3	26.0	–
1980	138.8	25.4	24.5	11.2
1981	139.6	25.8	22.8	11.6
1982	140.5	27.3	22.1	12.7
1983	141.6	28.7	22.0	12.3
1984	142.6	31.5	21.7	15.5
1985	143.6	31.6	24.6	17.7
1986	144.7	33.6	24.3	20.1
1987	145.8	31.2	27.3	20.7
1988	146.6	31.1	25.9	21.5
1989	147.5	31.6	26.6	23.2
1990	148.3	32.3	31.5	25.1
1991	148.7	22.3	27.3	21.0

Source: [176], p. 218.

pages, or six pages for the few lucky exceptions. Several weeklies published by professional unions, such as the Writers' Union's *Literaturnaya Gazeta*, rose above the drab standards and were rewarded with a huge readership because they debated social problems.

There was another salient feature in the Russian press: an unique role played by thick monthlies that combined fiction, literary criticism, and topical social and cultural journalism under one cover. The most courageous of them faced even higher barriers than the rest of the press. In particular, they were banished from public libraries.

As censorship became progressively more lenient and the public poorer and more preoccupied, readers and viewers were attracted by the easily predictable themes of sex and violence, with an emphasis on erotic and crime thrillers.

In the mid-1990s, the financial sources of mass media changed. Though most television stations were still run by the government, the budget it allocated to this function was shrinking. It was charging more and more for commercials, which, in

Table 4
Printed media, Russia, 1960–90

	Periodicals	Russian-language	Circulation (million/year)	Newspapers	Circulation (million)
1960	2,361	2,227	649	4,474	46
1965	2,603	2,463	1,304	3,991	73
1970	4,133	3,945	2,060	4,445	94
1975	3,521	3,325	2,293	4,226	113
1976	3,672	3,462	2,301	4,253	113
1977	3,480	3,262	2,331	4,311	114
1978	3,640	3,415	2,342	4,328	115
1979	4,005	3,782	2,475	4,370	117
1980	3,960	3,715	2,488	4,413	120
1981	3,909	3,643	2,365	4,436	122
1982	3,927	3,662	2,414	4,498	121
1983	3,994	3,722	2,603	4,501	122
1984	3,921	3,640	2,629	4,546	128
1985	3,869	3,587	2,726	4,567	132
1986	3,961	3,682	2,946	4,652	137
1987	3,966	3,666	3,107	4,647	145
1988	4,060	3,759	3,462	4,696	153
1989	3,781	3,504	4,265	4,772	162
1990	3,681	3,392	5,010	4,808	166

Source: [171], p. 217.

1993, took up 15% of the time in every programme as per an officially determined pattern.

The attempted economic reforms of the late 1980s and especially the early 1990s penalized cultural activities. The mass media were strongly affected, and the press was hit the hardest.

Circulation of newspapers and magazines rose until 1990 (see table 4), but began falling dramatically in 1992, as paper prices, printers' fees, and postal rates became exorbitantly expensive for state-sponsored and private periodicals alike. The 15 most influential dailies lost a total of 18 million subscribers, and leading magazines lost 7 million. At six major weeklies, subscription dropped by a factor of 3.5. In the first six months of 1993, subscription prices ballooned by a factor of 26.5 against 1992 prices, and by a factor of 90 against 1991 prices, and circulation dropped by a factor of between 3 and 9, in comparison to those years ([52]).

The relative drop in radio and TV audiences was due to many people holding down a second job, which cut into their leisure time. Present wear and tear on radio and TV sets will present a formidable problem in the future, when the owners find new ones unaffordable.

Public preferences slowly shifted from news and educational programmes to domestic, US, and Latin American entertainment, earlier banned for political reasons or too expensive to import. This trend, observed over the last thirty years or so, reached its peak quite recently.

Public preferences for feature films and, to a lesser extent, talk shows and game shows rose from the late 1950s to the mid-1980s. Throughout this period, information was constantly in second place among media preferences. The round-the-clock Mayak radio station, set up in the 1960s in a format of music with short news breaks, quickly broke all popularity records, and now ranks second to Europe Plus (Moscow), a Western station with the same format.

Males were enthusiastic about sport programmes on radio and TV. However, the popularity of this type of programming has dropped drastically, with the exception of world football championships and, to a somewhat lesser extent, the Olympics.

TV news rose in popularity between 1985 and 1991, and public interest peaked in August of 1991 and October of 1993. In times of peace, their ratings dropped in favour of soap operas, the new ratings leaders, which appeared on Russian television only recently.

The Soviet Union and the newly independent countries that appeared with its disintegration were not signatories to the Bern Convention until 1995, so government and private channels had broad access to foreign films, which they got free of charge. If this pirate bonanza were cut off, the number of foreign entertainment programmes would be likely to fall. New ways to the settle this problem are being proposed.

K.E. Razlogov

10 Institutionalization of Social Forces

10.1 Dispute Settlement

From the 1960s to the 1980s, owing to the latent nature of labour conflicts, there was no admitted need to settle them. In the 1990s, this need became extremely urgent. The transition to market relations led to the creation of social mechanism to ensure stability and balance in society. Social partnerships were formed to overcome acute contradictions and conflict situations by co-ordinating the interests and actions of main social groups in the labour relations sphere. Institutionalization of the settling of labour disputes settling was being realized through improvement of legislation and establishment of specialized conciliation bodies within government departments.

At the beginning of the 1990s, a trend toward intense, more open conflicts in labour relations became obvious. In view of the latent character of labour conflicts in the "state of working people," there was no recognized need to settle such conflicts from the 1960s to the 1980s; also in this period, mass protests and open forms of workers' struggle for their rights were extremely rare. In 1991–92, most legal strikes occurred in the services sector and had to do with low wages and delayed payment in state enterprises to account for inflation and indexation. However, as of the second half of 1993, the absolute numbers of the strikes and participants in them increased, particularly in industry. In the first five months of 1994, a total of about 125,000 people participated in strikes – that is, almost as many as in all of 1993 (see table 1).

The system of fixed-term contracts, after expiration of which workers were automatically discharged, became widespread in the 1990s. Redistribution of property also caused serious labour conflicts. When privatization began, many labour collectives were poorly informed about the conditions prescribed by the State Privatization Programme. Such ignorance also led to greater tension in relations with management and was behind a number of conflict situations. It was not by chance that Russian industry was the sector with the most strikes among enterprises, organizations, and institutions in 1993–94 (see table 2).

Table 1
Strikes in the Russian Federation, 1990–94

	Enterprises affected	Participants		Work-time losses (000 person-days)	Person-days per individual in strike
		(000)	per enterprise		
1990	260	99.5	383	207.7	2.1
1991	1,755	237.7	135	2,314.2	9.7
1992	6,273	357.6	571	893.3	5.3
1994*	400	135.0	333	540.0	4.0

Source: [192], p. 23.
* First nine months.

Table 2
Distribution of strikes per economic sector, Russian Federation, 1990–94

	1990	1991	1992	1993	1994
Industry	1,991	324	63	176	177
Transport	10	44	68	13	10
Construction	10	17	14	45	8
Health	6	173	943	1	–
Education	7	1,177	4,929	–	197
Science	–	–	–	3	-
Other	28	21	256	26	8
Total	2,512	1,756	6,273	264	400

Source: [192], p. 23.

By the mid-1990s, the Russian "social partnership" system was well rooted and had a declared political character. Parties of various political stripes, which insisted that political demands be included in agreements during negotiations on social-labour disputes, contributed to the cost of negotiations. In many respects, the political character of the "social partnership" is explained by the weakness of the Russian trade-union movement; as of the first half of the 1990s, most trade unions were not yet independent organizations formed to defend the interests of workers. In the 1990s, as well as under the command economy system of the 1970s and 1980s, trade unions strove to solve the social problems of workers by appealing to the government and federal executive authorities, not by means of negotiations with the employers. Quite often, attempts were made to solve these problems simply by increasing wages, without taking into account the overall configuration of social relations. At best, this postponed conflicts but did not settle them. As a result, there was a drop in the number of collective contracts concluded in the mid-1990s: one third fewer enterprises concluded collective agreements in 1994 than in 1993. Surveys showed that 35% of the workers at Russian enterprises regarded collective agreements as insignificant in defending their rights, while 35% felt that they had no effect at all. Most respondents felt strongly that such agreements defended the interests of management better than it defended the interests of the workers ([192]).

Signing of collective contracts and general agreements was the main result of negotiations in the "social partnership" system. In 1994, the Russian Three-Party Commission for regulation of social-labour relations, which was founded in 1992, concluded a general agreement and 48 agreements in industrial sectors among employers' associations, trade unions, and the Russian Federation government. At the same time, this official body helped to solve a number of labour disputes by the signing of wage agreements in several economic sectors (light, textiles, coal mining, etc.).

By the mid-1990s, there was an acute need to create effective mechanisms to settle labour disputes and strikes out of court and to conduct conciliation procedures, including mediation and labour arbitration. In the 1994 debate on the new law on settling labour disputes and conflicts, trade unions paid special attention to consolidation of workers' right to strike. However, such institutions for dispute regulation as labour arbitration, new to Russia, were not questioned.

Gradually, official institutions replaced the command economy system dictates of the 1960s to 1980s applicable to the regulation of acute labour disputes between workers and management. A certain practical experience of the Service for Labour Conflicts Settlement (created as part of the Russian Ministry of Labour in 1994) showed considerable practical possibilities for the strategy of peaceful regulation of labour conflicts. A number of successful pre-strike procedures were instigated. In the first nine months of 1994, regional offices of this service helped to prepare pre-strike conciliation procedures in more than 70 enterprises and organizations ([192]).

In 1993–94, the number of labour disputes that did not develop into strikes but were manifested in other forms increased (see table 3), including making demands regarding the conflict to the government, the president, executive authorities, at meetings and demonstrations, and picketing the central and regional authorities. Strike committees at enterprises and a few independent trade unions (Independent Miners' Trade Union, Social Trade Union, Air Controllers' Trade Union, etc.) organized these actions and were the main representatives of the strikers' interests in the official negotiations with the administration in the first stage of the workers' movement (1989–94). In 1993–94, trade-union associations in different economic sectors, which were under the umbrella of the Federation of the Independent Russian Trade Unions, organized open protests more often.

Table 3
Labour conflicts and strikes by economic zone, Russia, September 1993–September 1994

	Conflicts	Strikes
North	136	80
Northwest	125	12
Central Russian Regions covered by the Service for Labour Conflict Settlement	266	21
Central-Chernozemnoye	288	1
Volga	31	10
Northern Caucasus	194	106
Volga-Viatskoye	104	2
Ural	2,188	37
Western Siberia	2,878	99
Eastern Siberia	256	176
Far East	96	39
Total	6,502	583

Source: [192], p. 23.

V.N. Shalenko

10.2 Trade Unions

Until the end of the 1980s, trade unions functioned under the guidance of the CPSU and were practically state organizations. In the 1990s, however, they lost their exclusive mandate to defend formally workers' interests, became independent from the CPSU, changed their functions, and turned to real defence of workers' interests.

In Russia trade unions were created in 1905–07, at a time when the Russian Bolshevik social-democratic workers' party had been organized and was beginning actively to fight to protect workers' interests. In the socialist state, trade unions were called upon to propagate the communist ideology among the working masses.

The structure of Soviet trade unions imitated the Party structure: they were built on the production–territorial principle and were quite stable (see tables 1 and 2). Enterprises contained so-called triangles, consisting of representatives from management, the Party, and the trade union, and every decision had to be discussed and approved by this triangle. The participation of trade unions in solving a wide

Table 1
Number of central and local trade unions, USSR, 1981–88

	1981	1988
Central	31	31
Republican, regional	172	173
Territorial	2,634	2,671
City and district	22,045	22,705

Source: [280], p. 312.

Table 2
Types of trade unions, Russia, 1993

Russian branch of trade unions	36
Republican, regional councils, federations, confederations	78
Republican (included in the RSFSR), regional, sectoral committees of trade unions	1,212
Regional, sectoral councils of chairpersons of trade-union committees and organizations	697
City and district trade union committees, corresponding to sectoral trade union	8,849
Primary trade-union organizations (at work place)	423,000

Source: [185a], p. 13.

range of important production problems very often was subordinated to the Party and the enterprise's managers. In addition to this tight control by the Party, nearly every trade-union leader had to be a Party member; as well, managers of an enterprise would be members of the same trade unions and, quite naturally, could influence the decision-making process. According to the 1977 Constitution of the USSR, trade unions were independent units, functioning on the basis of their own regulations and aims; neither state nor party organizations, they operated under the leadership of the CPSU. This Constitution clearly emphasized that both trade unions and the state equally expressed the interests of one and the same class – the working class – and the interests of its vanguard, communists, and the people as a whole, with aims in common.

Trade unions liberated themselves from CPSU control only when the ban on activities by any party or movement in enterprises was adopted in 1991.

The main functions of trade unions in socialist society were to organize production and defend workers' interests. For decades, trade unions organized "socialist competitions" for the best and the most productive work at enterprises and organizations, and oversaw vocational training of young people and workers; they were in charge of other public organizations, such as the All-Union Society of

Inventors and Equipment Improvement and the Scientific-Technical Society. Trade unions also helped to organize councils of work collectives, public and construction bureaus, associations of production-quality initiatives, and so on.

Theoretically, trade unions had the right to defend the interests of workers when management violated labour legislation, the obligations of the collective agreement, and so on. It was impossible to dismiss anybody, change norms and prices, or distribute flats in a new apartment building without the consent of the trade-union committee . But in fact, trade unions, and especially their leaders at the regional and all-Union levels, who directly depended on the highest local authorities and on the government, stopped performing their main duty – to defend the interests of the workers.

In the 1960s and 1970s, along with the CPSU, trade unions actively participated in organizing and conducting *subbotniks* (days of voluntary labour), festive manifestations, and so on. The number of people taking part in such activities was the criterion of their success. Trade unions arranged for help to other enterprises (agrarian construction, etc.) free of charge. A primary use of this assistance was the mass mobilization of citizens (students and workers) to gather harvest agricultural products, perform temporary labour in building projects, operate food depots, and so on. In 1985 alone, according to official data, about 0.8 million people were sent to perform such work every day – that is, 0.6% of the total number of the employed. In reality, such disruptions involved even more people. However, employed people were not drawn into participation in management.

In the 1970s and 1980s, the redistribution function of trade unions increased and began to take precedence over their production functions. Trade unions directed social-insurance funds, from which temporary disability allowances were paid. Also under the authority of trade unions were a considerable number of rest homes, stadiums, tourist resorts, and so on. These institutions were 70% to 90% subsidized by trade unions, and therefore they were theoretically available to all the workers (in fact, they were available primarily to leaders and the needy). Quotas for passes to convalescence homes and rest homes were distributed by the trade-union committee of enterprises through regional and branch associations. Considerable subsidies were committed by trade unions of enterprises for the organization of summer camp for the children of those working at the respective enterprise). Through much of the 1980s, when there was a shortage of various everyday products and goods, trade unions played a leading role in their distribution among the employed according to seniority, work input, neediness, and so on. This role was especially important in distributing such social goods as flats and cars, which were always in short supply. Control over scheduling and periodic reports increased the role of trade-union committees at enterprises and sometimes prevented violations and abuse on the part of management. Because of the widespread shortages, this role intensified in the late 1980s and the early 1990s. As a result of the economic reforms in 1990s, shortages of many goods and products became less widespread and stopped in 1994, and consequently this function gradually faded from the trade unions' mandate or was passed to social services of enterprises and organizations.

At the end of the 1980s, informal alternative trade unions sprang up, as a first result of spontaneous strikes. Though the main reason for these strikes was the deterioration of working and living conditions (problems that were within the mandate of the trade union), none of the official (old) trade unions supported these strikes. The alternative, or "independent" unions (as opposed to the traditional ones) more consistently supported reforms and defended workers, and this made them more popular. These trade unions were not organized on the basis of industry type or geographical grouping, but on the basis of the mode of property of the enterprise (state, co-operative, private).

During the 1990s, trade unions also lost their legislative function. According to the USSR Constitution of 1977, the state guaranteed the conditions of fulfilment of the main aims of social organizations, consolidating their right of legislative initiative. According to this right, the All Union Central Committee of Trade Unions took part in the elaboration of laws connected with production, labour, everyday life, and culture, and it did so primarily in terms of state interests rather than the interests of individuals. Trade unions were to help the state by participating in ruling state and social affairs, and by solving political, economical, and socio-cultural problems.

From the 1960s to the 1980s, there was no law regarding the rights and guarantees of trade unions. According to the Constitution of Russia (1993), trade-union committees of enterprises and organizations had no right to solve labour disputes between employees and management. No trade union – either official or independent – had the right to take a legislative initiative.

Before 1992, attaining a collective agreement on working conditions was a formality that took place between management of an enterprise and the trade-union leadership once a year. Sanctions for its violation were not foreseen; going beyond the scope of the standard agreement was not encouraged or practised.

The emergence of a considerable number of new "independent" trade unions at the beginning of the 1990s and their fight for the rights and interests of workers stimulated a general increase in trade-union activity. In 1993–94, an informal campaign for collective agreements at the country-wide, economic-sector, and regional levels, as well as within some certain enterprises, was a result of long discussions between representatives of the trade unions, employers, and the state.

The defence of workers' interests became the unions' most important function only during the 1990s. From the 1960s to the 1980s, unions had two main activities. First, any dismissal from an enterprise (except for gross violation of discipline) was to be confirmed through the trade union. Trade-union committees did not often refuse to give consent for the dismissal, but they could sometimes raise barriers to block management arrogance. Second, trade unions had the opportunity to suggest to a higher body that particular enterprise managers be dismissed. These managers were state employees, and so such suggestions could influence their methods of management, and in some cases they resulted in a change of manager.

The transition of the workers' movement to active forms of protest and to strikes, at the end of the 1980s, was not supported by trade unions at first. In 1989–90, strikes were organized by independent trade unions – by enterprise councils (see section 9.1) and strike committees. Later, on the basis of such committees, new independent trade unions were organized.

The first acts of protest were organized by the Federation of Independent Trade Unions of Russia and took place in 1992. During discussions regarding the General Tariff Agreement on Wages and Salaries, in the mid-1990s, the government obviously preferred to have FITUR, which was more respected by the workers, as a partner in these talks.

From 1992 to 1994, trade-union activities were directed mainly to fighting with the state bodies for better pay. In some cases, trade unions were successful in increasing wages to match inflation.

E.G. Meshkova, N.A. Rostegaeva, and P.G. Smirnov

10.3 Social Movements

The emergence of social movements in the late 1950s and early 1960s was directly connected with the Khrushchev thaw. In the stagnation period that ensued, all such movements were crushed, although officially inspired ones persisted. In 1990s, the latter faded, and spontaneous movements, with diversified activities and forms, became widespread.

Economic-patriotic movements such as the Movement for the Communist Approach to Labour, the Creation of the Material-and-Technical Basis of Communism, and the Movement for Creation of the Communist Personality

ceased to exist by the mid-1980s. These movements, which appeared during the "thaw," reflected hopes for construction of a communist society and the romantic memories of the heroic spirit of 1920s and 1930s. They were all created to invent moral stimuli for work.

The Movement for the Communist Approach to Labour was grafted onto the working class in the lead-up to the 21st CPSU congress, in 1958. According to All-Union Trade Council data, by January 1, 1972, almost 42.5 million people were taking part in the movement, which comprised 50.3% of all workers. In the years of perestroika, the movement quickly came to naught.

The Tselinnik movement emerged as a response by broad strata of the population who still believed in communist ideals to calls by the Party to take part in developing virgin lands. It ended, in a natural way, as the virgin-land-development program was completed. Since then, the Party has been unable to repeat this success. In the 1970s, the official ideology definitely lost its effectiveness, and propaganda attempts to revitalize a movement of ideologically reliable activists whose purpose was to participate in construction of the "project of the century," the Baikal-Amur railway line, proved absolutely futile.

The Student Construction Team movement arose without involvement of the Party or any other ideological bodies; only after some time was it recognized by the authorities. The first two student teams were organized in 1958; in 1960s and early 1970s it degenerated and was turned into an obligatory form of productive work in construction in the countryside, mainly during summer vacations, for some, and a way to earn money, for others.

Youth movements have ranged from opposition to support of official ideology. The Youth Residential Complexes Movement, sparked by the poor living conditions of young families, started in the late 1960s and involved young people trying independently to solve their housing problems without the help of the state. Then, in the early 1980s, the sphere of their activities expanded to included the issues of creating housing for young families, kindergartens, recreation sites, sports installations, and so on – everything created by them and according to their own plans. The movement was still alive in the mid-1990s, although not on as large a scale as in the 1980s; it was overtaken and rendered ineffective by the overall rise in cost of living.

The hippie movement in the 1960s was brief but spectacular; it languished because its appeal was limited except in some large cities. It took on the outward attributes of the movement in the West, but not its ideology. In the late 1980s, there was a small revival, but it did not last long; in the 1990s, it had disappeared almost completely.

The Movement of Amateur Student Song began in the 1960s. Young intellectuals tried to create a culture in opposition to the establishment. Rallies were regularly held in the countryside in which up to several tens of thousands of young people took part. The movement ended in the late 1980s, first, because there was no longer a need for such a form of protest; second, because a new generation was turning to a fairly different musical culture.

In the late 1980s, a youth movement arose in some large Russian cities to protest against the unfairness of the social regime. These groups professed a variety of ideologies, ranging from creative Marxism, criticism of practice of socialism in the USSR, and a return to genuine Marxism (*Sotsyazvists*), to young people from Moscow workers' suburbs anxious to dissuade their contemporaries from adopting Western consumer patterns (*Lyubers*). In the 1990s, there was virtually no youth protest or youth-rights movement. For example, the Russian Parliament has not yet passed a law on youth, but young people themselves do not seem to be very worried by this. There have been some scantily attended youth demonstrations, picket lines, and rallies, which cannot be called a youth movement proper.

The women's movement has been on the rise. In the early 1980s, women's councils started to re-emerge (they had been quite active in the 1920s). In the 1990s, organizations once designed as a form of ideological control acquired quite a different content. Now that women are distanced from the political management of society (while in pre-perestroika times about 50% of the deputies at various levels of Soviets were women, in the 1990s this proportion was under 5%), exploitation of women is increasing and taking on new shapes. A feminist movement is gaining strength, while other women's movements are becoming institutionalized. The Women's Union of Russia was set up in 1990, while Missiya, Women for Social Renovation, and the Soldiers' Mothers Committee were set up in 1991. The latter has a pronounced anti-war bent.

Anti-war movements became institutionalized almost immediately after they were created. Under socialism in Russia, the fight for peace was referred to as one of the major tasks of the Party and of government strategy. Any public anti-war undertaking from the 1960s to the 1980s could be held only within the framework set by official bodies. True, there were the Soviet Peace Protection Committee and the Peace Foundation, but both of these organizations were semi-official. Public peace movements were rather reduced to collecting donations to the Peace Foundation and agreeing to participate in the rare demonstrations held under the slogan, "We approve of the peace-loving policy of the Communist Party."

A real peace movement came into existence in the late 1980s, during perestroika, to protest against the war in Afghanistan. Until the troops were withdrawn, the movement kept expanding and gathering strength. At present, the anti-war movement has been more or less institutionalized. Various public organizations have emerged, such as Peace without Violence (1991), Peace Child (1990), and so on.

Patriotic, regionalistic, and nationalistic movements were on the rise in the 1990s. "Patriotic movements" includes organizations whose aim is to strengthen the state of Russia or even restore the USSR. Kossacks plays an active role in the patriotic movement.

Nationalistic movements now stand up for the exclusive rights of a certain nation, nationality, or ethnic group. The word "nationalist" in Russian acquired negative connotations in the 1990s, and spokespersons of such movements prefer to call themselves patriots. The Pamyat (Remembrance) Society is the best-known representative of nationalism in Russia (it arose in the late 1980s). Its members are not very numerous, but it is very active.

Unlike patriotic and nationalistic movements, regionalistic movements have some tradition in post-revolution Russia. For example, the Crimea Tartar movement arose at the time of the Khrushchev thaw in the 1960s. During the stagnation period, part of this movement was dissolved and part went underground. In the late 1980s, regionalistic movements in Russian autonomous republics started to emerge with the aim of changing the respective region's status or even seceding from Russia and gaining independence. Among these was Birlik, the organization of the Nogai people (1991); Sadval, the movement of the Lezghin people (1991); and Djamat, a society of the Avar people (1990). The movements in Tatarstan and Chechnya proved to be very powerful: Tatarstan proclaimed its independence in 1992, while Chechnya not only proclaimed independence but struggled for it in a real war in 1994-95.

The environmentalist movement is an important political force in the 1980s. It can apparently be considered the first public movement in the country that not only had superficial traits similar to those of movements in other countries, but was essentially the same. It emerged naturally in the 1960s, when the scale of adverse human impact on the environment became especially noticeable and the totalitarian state was not strong enough to nip the movement in the bud.

The first public environmental committee in Russia was set up in 1967 to protect Lake Baikal. Among other achievements by the environmental movement have been cancellation of the diversion of northern rivers to Central Asia and cancellation of construction of a nuclear power station in Krasnodar Province. In the late 1980s, numerous environmental organizations and associations were created. Most were small, comprising 15 to 100 persons. According to surveys, environmental movements were composed mostly of middle-income intellectuals and individuals from artistic and literary circles. There were approximately equal proportions of young and old people.

After the mid-1960s, the environmentalist ideology changed. In the early stages, its major aim was an attempt to control the certain state decisions. Later, the focus shifted to criticism of state planning, financing, and labour-force distribution – that is, criticism of the regime itself. The Chernobyl disaster (1986) greatly boosted the reputation of the environmental groups.

In the 1990s, environmental movements began to lose their popularity. First, an overriding concern for maintaining existing living standards resulted in a decline in interest in such matters among the population; second, there was a marginalization of human values such as maintenance and recreation of destroyed ecosystems, awareness of the importance of the environmental quality for the survival of human civilization, and so on.

The democratic movement is the most influential and popular movement in Russia in the 1990s. In the late 1980s, associations began to emerge that were openly advocating the elimination of the existing regime by peaceful means.

At the same time, various "fronts" came to prominence in Russian cities. In the beginning, most of them said that their goals were development of socialist democracy, support for perestroika, and solidification of socialism. Active participation in the defence of the constitutional regime at the time of the August coup attempt (1991) was the apotheosis for the democratic movement.

A.T. Gasparishvily

10.4 Interest Groups

From the mid-1980s to the mid-1990s, a great number of associations arose, setting themselves the task of expressing group interests. Different forms of representation of interests began to develop rapidly. Lobbying became widespread, interest groups began to co-operate with political parties, and other forms of indirect interaction of organized interests with the state were evolving.

Until the mid-1980s, the Soviet political system left practically no room for the creation, on initiative from below, of organizations expressing the interests of any group. In the 1960s and 1970s, such initiatives, as a rule, were brutally suppressed. Creation of organizations of this type from above was quite a rare thing for the period. Thus, for example, in the 1970s, only one organization was created: the All-Union Book-Lovers' Association (1974). According to the official viewpoint, existing social organizations (see sections 2.5, 9.4) were sufficient to express the interests of all classes, strata, and groups, whose interests were believed to coincide. A notion such as "corporative interest" usually had a negative connotation and was used only for condemnation of a particular group.

Almost all of the working population was associated in sectoral trade unions, artistic unions, or scientific-educational, cultural, scientific, scientific-technical, sports, defence, and assistance societies. Nonetheless, only professional and artistic unions dealt with the defence of interests (openly corporative in the case of artistic unions). Once they got a job, citizens automatically became members of a trade union.

The process of entering artistic unions was extremely complicated. Members of such unions (Writers' Union, Journalists' Union, Composers' Union, etc.) enjoyed rather substantial privileges, which were very important under conditions of widespread shortage. Army personnel had no professional associations at all.

By the mid-1980s, a fairly complex network of voluntary societies existed (there were more than a hundred all-Union societies alone), which were intended to reflect the wide spectrum of citizens' interests. These societies were strongly influenced by the Soviet bureaucratic system and, as a rule, were not seen by citizens as expressing their interests.

A great number of new associations arose in the late 1980s, when limitations concerning associations were abolished. Different group interests, which had remained unexpressed for many years, managed to find expression. In 1987–88, organizations arose that were formed and developing indirectly under the influence of the processes of democratization and *glasnost* (freedom of speech): school and students' self-government clubs fought for students' interests; groups of citizens anxious about the critical state of municipal economies created "communalists'" associations. Various religious associations arose, including the Society of Christian Public and the Believing Christians-Socialists. For the first time in the Soviet period, religious associations openly expressed a desire to influence the political realm by achieving a certain transformation of the society according to their group values. Distinguishing features of group associations during this period were their anti-bureaucratic orientations and appeals to democratic values. Discussion was their main activity.

In 1989, the number of organizations defending group interests exploded. The phenomenon had two specific causes. First, the regulations for the election of deputies to the Congress of Soviets in 1989 practically guaranteed that representatives of professional and social associations would be elected to the top organs of the legislative power of the country. It turned out, after the elections, that most of these associations had been fictitious; by the mid-1990s, most of them had ceased to exist. Second, the course of the economic reform in Russia. Current law presupposes favourable taxation for social organizations. It is not difficult to create and register them. Most probably, rather than the extraordinary political and social activity of the population, it is the possibility of procuring such advantages that is the main reason for the great number of social organizations in Russia. Information from the Ministry of Justice leads us to believe that in the mid-1990s there are no fewer than 300 organizations expressing or defending individuals' occupational and group interests. However, state bodies possess practically no reliable statistical data about membership in these organizations. Data made available by organizations themselves often do not correspond with reality.

In the 1990s, new groups arose in Russian society that organized to defend their respective interests. With the policy of perestroika, social life became more complex and fundamentally new social groups arose: business people, farmers, the unemployed. New occupations appeared, which were completely unknown during the socialist period: brokers, dealers, travel agents, and so on. For the first time, Russian consumers became aware of their rights; according to data from the Russian consumers' association, about 1% of purchasers have already appealed to court in connection with unscrupulous practices.

During the short period of formation of a new political system in Russia, different forms of representation of interests began to develop rapidly. Lobbying became widespread, interest groups are co-operating with political parties, and other forms of indirect interaction of organized interests with the state are developing.

Analysts usually distinguish four main interest groups in Russian society of the mid-1990s: state bureaucracy – representatives of state apparatus not connected with economy; old economic elites – state officials connected with the economy, directors of industrial enterprises; new economic elites – mostly business people; and the fourth estate – urban workers and other mass strata of the population. The conflict of interests among these groups is preconditioned by the different nature of corporative interests, different evaluations of the fate of such interests during the reform process, and claims made by each group professing to be concerned with the general interests of the state.

Interest groups try to influence political power. More and more attention is paid to selecting and training candidates for elective bodies. Simultaneously, activities of interest groups are becoming compartmentalized. This is manifested most clearly in the creation of business parties: one or another business group plays the role of a core, around which a party is formed.

Up to the mid-1990s, it was difficult to establish indirect connections between interest groups and the state. Committees and consultative councils created under the president, the government, and the parliament covered only a small part of organized interests and were incapable of providing successful interaction with the state. The power of these committees was not defined, so they could not substantially influence the process of making state decisions.

The most widespread form of co-ordination of interests in Russia in the 1990s is lobbying. Practically all groups of businessmen are trying to carry on lobbying activities, but the most powerful lobbies are oil and gas and the military-industrial complex.

A.T. Gasparishvily

11 Ideologies

11.1 Political Differentiation

From the 1960s to the 1980s, there was no political differentiation in socialist society. In the 1990s, such differentiation has existed only in an embryonic state. Political parties formed in the 1990s are marginal, their social base is amorphous, and all of them are "parties of leaders": the population supports and votes for the leader of a party, remaining unaware of and uninterested in its programme and goals.

It is difficult to say anything definite about political differentiation in Soviet society in the 1960s and 1970s. The class structure of the society in this period was summarized in an ideological formula: two friendly classes – working class and *kolkhoz* (collective farm) peasantry – and the intelligentsia, which was regarded not as a class but as a "layer." Since all three groups were considered to have common interests, there were not supposed to be any grounds for political differentiation.

The Communist Party, according to the ruling ideology, expressed the interests of everyone, and during elections communists acted in an inviolable bloc with nonmembers of the Party. There was practically no opportunity for different groups to express their political interests.

What political differentiation did exist manifested itself in forms specific to Soviet society, and usually only in the higher power echelon. The most characteristic examples of political differentiation over the period under study were the removal of N. Khrushchev from power in 1964 and Y. Andropov's attempts to turn the country back to "true socialism" (1982–83).

Political differentiation began manifesting itself on a national scale only in connection with the beginning of Gorbachev's policy of perestroika (1985). The first stages of Gorbachev's political leadership, an "acceleration in scientific and technical progress," and an attempt to dislodge the "braking mechanism" that prevented scientific progress caused no dissension in society, but the reaction to *glasnost* was taken rather more equivocally. What is more, *glasnost* led to freedom of thought for many citizens, making expression of personal interests and an open display of political sympathies possible. It is only since this time that it is possible to speak about political differentiation in Russian society.

Publication of formerly prohibited literature and freedom of access to various information led larger and larger portions of the population to reject communist values and, simultaneously, evoked protest and resistance among another portion. The publication, in *Sovetskaya Rossiya* (Soviet Russia), one of the largest-circulation Russian daily newspapers of the time, of an article entitled "I cannot forsake principles," by N. Andreeva (1988), evoked wide social debate. In the article, the process of democratization in the country was condemned from a position of left-wing radicalism, and a demand was made to return to traditional Bolshevik values. The article turned out to be a catalyst of differentiation among those who supported and rejected major changes in society.

At the time, ideological differentiation concerning a wide variety of issues began to deepen. Disintegration of the USSR (1991) and formation of nation states, national relations, privatization of state property, and other topics gave rise to differences of opinion and were discussed vehemently in society.

Political differentiation revealed itself during the elections to the Russian Congress of People's Deputies and to local Soviets in March, 1990. The victory of democrats in the elections of delegates of the Congress was only partial. It took three votes to elect the chairman of the Supreme Soviet, and B. Yeltsin, the personification of democratic forces, won with only a small majority. At the local level, democrats had a majority in only three city Soviets: Moscow, Leningrad (St Petersburg), and Sverdlovsk (Ekaterinburg).

On opposite political poles in the Russian Congress were the Reform Coalition and the Party of Russian Unity. The centrist position was occupied by two coalitions: the Democratic Centre and the Bloc of Constructive Forces. The main differences between these groups were in their attitude toward President Yeltsin, toward the market economy, and toward different models of privatization. The Reform Coalition (in favour of Yeltsin, the market, and the most radical privatization *model*) included such factions as the Democratic Russia Party (72 members), the Radical Democrats (54 members), and some other deputies' groups. In total, the coalition comprised about 250 deputies. The Party of Russian Unity took exactly the opposite positions. This coalition included the following parties: Russia (54 members), Fatherland (54 members), Communists of Russia (59 members), Civil Society (9 members), the Agrarian Union (121 members), and others, for a total of about 350 members.

The Bloc of Constructive Forces included The Change–"New Policy" (51 members), the Industrial Union (72 members), and the Workers' Union (41 members), and totalled about 140 members. The Democratic Centre was known above all for its moderation and was as unorganized as the Bloc of Constructive Forces. It comprised non-party deputies (44 members), Free Russia (64 members), the Left Centre (68), for a total of about 200 members.

By the beginning of the 1993 election campaign, about forty political parties had been registered. The conflict between the power blocs, reflected in the stand-off between the executive branch and the Parliament, led to tragic consequences, resulting in the bloody events of October, 1993.

The elections to a new supreme organ of legislative power, the State Duma, in December, 1993, showed that Russian citizens are not active supporters of the reforms or of the politicians leading them in that direction. By December, 1993, almost all of the parties, created in 1990–91 and oriented toward reforms, began to deteriorate. The deepening economic crisis in 1992–93 was to the advantage of parties such as the Communists and the Agrarians.

Political parties and social movements united in 35 electoral blocs to campaign for the election. To be eligible for elections, each party had to present 100,000 signatures. Twenty-one of the blocs managed to qualify. Eight unions, representing the pro-communist and nationalistic parties and movements that had linked up with the opposition forces were stripped of their party status for the election ([50]) because of their participation in the failed coup in 1993.

The ten main parties and blocs in the elections were the Agrarian Party of Russia; The Civil Union for Stability, Justice, and Progress; the Democratic Party of Russia; Women of Russia; The Communist Party of the Russian Federation; the Liberal-Democratic Party of Russia; the Party of Russian Unity and Consensus; the Russian Movement of Democratic Reforms; the bloc of Yavlinsky, Boldyrev, Lukin, and the Choice of Russia. These parties and blocs attracted a total of 94.5% of the vote.

During the December elections, almost all participating political parties called themselves centrist. The Liberal-Democratic Party of Russia received the largest plurality of votes, 23.5% (see table 1). The LDPR is one of the largest and the influential parties in Russia today. Its slogans and goals are extremely pliable, which may in part explain its popularity. The party's greatest successes were achieved in small and medium-sized towns in the far east, Siberia, and the northwest. The lowest proportions of votes for the LDPR were in Moscow, St Petersburg, and Ekaterinburg.

The second choice of the electorate (with 15.0% of the vote) was the Choice of Russia, which was openly pro-presidential at the time. The main plank in its platform was carrying out democratic reforms. The Choice of Russia was most successful in major cities: Moscow, St Petersburg, Sverdlovsk, Pyerm, and Chelyabinsk. It was not supported by the population in many regions of central Russia, in Siberia, or in the far east.

Table 1
Results of elections to the State Duma, December 12, 1993 (% of voters)

Liberal-Democratic Party of Russia	23.5
Choice of Russia	15.0
Communist Party of Russia	13.0
Agrarian Party of Russia	8.5
Women of Russia	8.5
Bloc of Yavlinsky Boldyrev Lukin	7.5
Party of Russian Unity and Consensus	7.0
Democratic Party of Russia	5.5
Russian Movement of Democratic Reforms	4.0
Civil Union for Stability and Progress	2.0
Other blocs	5.5

Source: [51], p. 18.

The Communist Party of the Russian Federation came in third (13.0%). This was a major success and a revelation. Fourth place was a tie between the Agrarian Party and Women of Russia (8.5%). The Communists and Agrarians had the greatest success in agrarian regions and the least support in major cities, Siberia, and the far eastern regions.

It is not completely clear what is an "extremist" party in Russia. The Liberal-Democratic Party enjoys special popularity among extremist and marginal strata of society. Other extremist parties and organizations, such as Russian National Unity and the Union of Resistance, do not have many members, nor do they take part in elections. Their representatives are present only in few local organs of self-government.

In the mid-1990s, the notion of marginalization applied to practically all Russian society, including its elite groups. Opinion is widespread that the social base of extremist parties and movements is found in the lower-class elements. With the deterioration of the economy, the crisis in industry and agriculture, and the abrupt drop in living standards for the majority of the population, marginal strata have grown immensely. Hence, in essence, all parties of Russia were marginal, their social base was amorphous, and they are all "parties of leaders." The population supports and votes for the leader of a party, not for its programme and goals. Thus, political differentiation did not exist in the conventional sense and was in an embryonic state. It did not matter how and on what scale parties defined themselves; their self-definition could change at any moment. Society is differentiated today not on the basis of goals, interests, or programmes, but on the basis of sympathies and antipathies to leaders' personalities.

A.T. Gasparishvily

11.2 Confidence in Institutions

In the 1960s and 1970s, the idea of "confidence" or "lack of confidence" in state institutions in Russia would have sounded rather strange. In the late 1980s and early 1990s, confidence in almost all institutions in Russia was dropping.

In the 1960s and 1970s, public opinion on social problems was not an object of study. The results of government elections from the 1960s to the mid-1980s cannot be considered a reliable indicator of confidence, because elections to Soviets at all levels included no alternatives and election days represented anything from a tedious duty to a brief holiday. The election results always demonstrated the victory of the "inviolable bloc of Communists and of the non-Party people." Ninety-five percent of the electorate voted, and 98% of them voted for candidates nominated by the CPSU.

It was unusual and very rare for deputies to be recalled. This indicated the failure of the respective individual, but not disapproval of state institutions.

Until the end of the 1980s the confidence in the ruling party was taken for granted. The authorities were not very concerned with the population's confidence in the state health system, education, trade unions, and the mass media, but here we can rely only upon indirect evidence. Over the period, people's attitude toward state institutions was contradictory and covert. On the one hand, most people were under the influence of official propaganda and considered themselves to be living in the best of worlds; on the other hand, there was a certain scepticism arising from the evidence of everyday life and from counter-cultural political anecdotes about this "best world."

Criticism in the press concerning schools, hospitals, local militia offices, and so on was aimed neither at the authority nor at the system, but at particular cases. Open disapproval was expressed by a very small number of dissidents, and their criticisms were not widely circulated.

When a gradual reform of the political system was undertaken in the mid-1980s, the result was growing social tension. There was a crisis of confidence in the Communist Party, as evidenced by a 50% drop in CPSU membership in the second half of the 1980s. In 1990, people began resigning from the CPSU en masse (see table 1); this trend increased each year.

There was increasing pessimism, and reorganization (perestroika) was met with apathy and disbelief, leading to a disillusionment with the viability and effectiveness

Table 1
CPSU members, Russia, 1960–90

	CPSU members	Increase
1960	8,708,667	
1965	11,758,169	3,049,592
1967	12,684,133	925,964
1970	14,011,784	1,327,651
1973	14,821,031	809,247
1975	15,294,803	473,772
1977	15,994,476	629,673
1980	17,082,289	1,087,813
1983	18,117,903	1,035,694
1985	18,700,000	582,097
1987	19,267,715	567,715
1988	19,486,786	219,071
1989	19,487,822	1,036
1990	19,228,217	−259,605

Source: [208], p. 18.

of socialism as a social system. Between 1987 and 1990, many public-opinion polls on major social problems showed people's alienation from communistic values.

We can measure confidence in Soviet institutions by the press during this period. The popularity of newspapers and magazines that criticized the Soviet social system began to grow, and the mass media, which had supported old socialist values, began to lose subscribers and readers.

In 1991, a new state institution – the position of president – was introduced in Russia. The majority of the population supported both this idea and the first Russian president. In the presidential elections, 57.3% voted for B. Yeltsin; after the first 100 days of his rule, his popularity increased. With his decisive actions during the putsch in August, 1991, his popularity increased even more. In October, 1991, 64.2% of respondents to a survey said that they had confidence in the President: 11.9% had complete confidence, 52.3% had confidence; 23.2% did not have much confidence, while 7.9% had no confidence at all ([259]). According to data from the Institute of Social-Political Research of the Russian Academy of Science, in March of 1992 the level of confidence in the President was the same, at 64%.

After the beginning of 1992, the President's popularity gradually dropped. In April, 1993, during the National Referendum, 57.8% of those who took part approved of the President's actions and 39.2% disapproved. In December, 1993, 35.6% of Russians completely or partially approved of the President's actions (completely approved, 8.5%; approved on the whole, 27.5%; didn't approve on the whole, 27.8%; didn't approve very much, 25.3%; didn't know or refused to answer, 11.1%).

The drop in confidence in the institution of the presidency is associated with the present president becoming a dictator being seen as the most serious political threat in Russia by 32.6%; with establishment of a too-powerful parliament by 7.9%; 16.4% felt that no political danger exists in this respect, and 43.2% could not or did not answer ([50]).

Attitudes toward the Supreme Soviet changed rapidly after 1990. Under the Soviet regime it played the insignificant role of affirming the decisions of the CPSU. In the autumn of 1991, the Supreme Soviet (parliament) of the Russian Federation was regarded in public opinion as a symbol of a new society and democratic changes, and the level of confidence in it was quite high (see table 2). At the end of 1991, the population's confidence in legislative institutions fell abruptly, apparently because of contradictions between the Supreme Soviet and the President. In 1992, 37% of the population wanted dissolution of the Supreme Soviet of People's Deputies before its term was up; in the spring of, 1993 45% held this opinion ([164]).

In the 1990s it is difficult to evaluate the degree of people's confidence in the church. Citizens of the USSR were not able to express their confidence in the church openly. For example, the 19 million members of the CPSU had to be atheists according to Communist Party rules, as did members of the Union of Young Communists. In the late 1980s, attitudes toward the church began to change; several priests were even elected to the top legislative bodies of the USSR and Russia. However, in the 1990s, confidence in the church as an institution declined.

Between 1990 and 1992, the number of those who considered themselves to be Christians increased by a factor of 2.5, while the number of those who supported the official church dropped by a factor of 3 ([312]). The main distinction was not between Christianity and other religions, but between church-goers and the growing numbers of religious people with no concrete identification with a denomination (see table 3). Analysts usually connected this trend with the conservatism of the Russian Orthodox Church and its inability to find a place in a changing society.

In the 1990s, confidence in the army began to drop sharply. New Soviet and, later, Russian leaders repudiated the ideological doctrine about hostile opposition of two systems that had dominated throughout the Soviet regime and the army's role in Russian society began to be reviewed. At the end of the 1980s, the public was of the opinion that it was too expensive to maintain the army. The mass media exposed criminality and poor organization in the army, poor living conditions for officers, and the army's previous improper role in suppression of public protest in Russia and abroad. Debates on the need for reforming the army, the introduction

Table 2
Confidence in selected institutions, 1991, 1994 (%)*

	Believe		Don't believe	
	1991	*1994*	*1991*	*1994*
Trade unions	24.7	16.0	66.1	45.0
Judges	22.0	14.0	65.0	46.0
Office of Public Prosecutor	20.6	14.0	63.2	46.0
Militia	16.9	13.0	75.8	56.0
Church	49.2	–	27.2	–
Supreme Soviet of the RSFSR	48.0	16.0	42.6	41.0
TV and radio	32.0	19.0	62.5	40.0
Press	29.7	19.0	62.2	4.0
Army	–	32.0	–	28.0

Source: [236], p. 49[[239], p. 2.
* Without responses of "don't know" and no responses.

Table 3
Religious affiliation, 1990–92 (%)[a]

	1990	*1991*	*1992*
Christian generally	22	47	52
Orthodox	46	19	15
Catholic	0	1	1
Old believer[b]	0	1	1
Protestant	0	0	1
Buddhist, Hindu, other	1	2	1
Atheist	24	14	8
No answer	7	16	22

Source: [235], p. 16.
[a] Survey carried out in 15 large and small towns.
[b] See section 9.2.

of voluntary recruitment, and a reduction of military forces were held at all levels of society.

In 1982, 70% of young men questioned the day before they were recruited into the army considered military service to be an honourable duty and regarded army service as prestigious; in 1992, only 20% expressed the same opinion. As well, a decreasing number of people believed in the fighting efficiency of the Russian army (see table 4).

Confidence in the mass media is falling. The late 1980s could be called the "golden age" of Soviet mass media. Although they still belonged to the state at this time, control had been relaxed to a minimum. They did not have to worry about surviving, so their attention could be concentrated on the content of their publications, resulting in larger numbers of readers and increased confidence. In 1993, however, confidence in the largest Russian newspapers and the main TV news programs fell approximately by half (see tables 5, 6).

Confidence in legal institutions fell constantly. Between the end of 1980s and the mid-1990s, crime was on a constant increase. Legal institutions were not able to control the situation. There were many reasons for this, such as insufficient experience with fighting organized crime, the absence of necessary laws, low wages, poor equipment, low wages in the justice system, corruption, and even the romanticizing of criminal life in contemporary art.

This problem was reinforced by increased stratification of society and rise in all forms of social inequality. People perceived that only the state could protect them. In 1994, the people's confidence that legal institutions would protect their interests decreased even further (see table 7).

Table 4
Opinion of fighting efficiency of Russian army, 1993–94 (%)

	1993	1994
Efficient	40.0	32.1
Not efficient	35.9	45.2
No answer	24.1	22.7

Source: [50], p. 12.

Table 5
Confidence in the largest Russian newspapers, 1993–94 (%)

	1993	1994
Arguments and Facts	22.9	10.6
Izvestia	7.8	5.8
Komsomolskaya pravda	3.3	1.8
Trud	6.3	4.1

Source: [50], p. 14.

Table 6
Confidence in the major national TV news programs, 1993–94 (%)

	1993	1994
Vesty	30.5	16.4
Itogy	14.1	11.7
Novosty	20.6	12.9

Source: [50], p. 18.

Table 7
Answers to the question "Do you think that the legal institutions of Russia protect interests of all citizens equally, or they protect only those who possess the state power?," 1993–94 (%)

	1993	1994
Everybody	5.1	4.4
Those who possess power	79.0	82.6
No answer	5.9	13.0

Source: [50], p. 19.

A.T. Gasparishvily

11.3 Economic Orientations

Russians' attitudes toward business, economic inequality, social justice, and the property of others have been changing rapidly in the 1990s, under the influence of socio-economic reforms.

Economic topics (such as income, investment, disposition of savings, etc.), which were not much discussed from the 1960s to the 1980s, became very urgent for all strata of population in the 1990s. In the 1980s and 1990s, as national wealth began to decrease, the number of unprofitable enterprises and bankruptcies increased, as did the share of national revenue used for consumption (see tables 1, 2), but at the same time there was an obvious drop in the amount of national revenue connected being generated by foreign trade, a drop in production of material goods, and the higher cost of raw materials.

Table 1
Average economic indexes, Russian Federation, 1981–91 (annual increase, %)

	1981–85	1986–90	1991
Gross national product	3.1	1.9	(9.8)
National revenue	3.0	1.1	(11.0)
Use of national revenue	2.7	1.4	(10.2)
for consumption	2.8	3.0	(2.7)
for investment	2.5	(3.9)	(36.2)

Source: [121], p. 17.

Table 2
Proportion of national revenue used for non-investment purposes, 1980–91 (%)

1980	1985	1986	1987	1988	1989	1990	1991
74.4	72.2	73.0	74.4	72.7	75.1	77.8	79.6

Sources: [171, p. 20; [175], p. 17.

As the economic reforms began, an abrupt stratification of the population took place. In the early 1980s, about one third of the population had difficulty obtaining clothing; but this proportion reached one half in the late 1980s; the proportion of those for whom the purchase of durable goods was not a problem decreased from 23% to 16% ([222]).

Negative and irreverent attitudes toward others' property and wealth were characteristic of social consciousness and behaviour from after the revolution to the early 1990s. Under the regime of exclusive state control of property, which was regarded as belonging to everyone, any business operations involving foreign currency or resale of goods were considered to be economic crimes against the state. Misappropriations of state property were punished more severely than were other thefts. Any aspiration to personal wealth was regarded as a "vestige of the past," as evidence of deception, and was to be extirpated.

Many working people and pensioners saw their poverty as an object of special pride, and regarded it as an indication of unselfish service to the state. People's aspiration to a comfortable everyday life and ownership of beautiful things was treated by official propaganda in the 1960s as *meschanstvo* (middle-class convention-ality) and in the 1970s and 1980s as *veshchizm* (possessiveness). An individual's aspiration to get more through honest labour often provoked negative and contemptu-ous attitudes, and "workaholics" aroused suspicions.

In conditions under which all property, except personal-consumption items, was state property, it was actually treated as if it belonged to no one; a variety of devious practices with regard to state property became the norm. Pilferage of production, equipment, and materials from enterprises was increasing, and many did not see it as a serious crime; a person who stole from his or her place of work was considered not a thief, but a *nesun* (carrier). During the first half of 1988, more than 7,000 thieves were detained in Moscow, twice the number as during the same period in 1987. In one poll, 97% of respondents did not approve of buying goods from a person who had stolen them from someone else; 62% disapproved of buying items stolen from the workplace; and 50% approved of selling goods through irregular channels to those who do not want to queue up for them ([259]).

For many years, social justice was associated with equal distribution of goods among all citizens. According to the Constitution of the USSR, the right to work was also a duty, and employment income was the main and basic source of wealth. The level of remuneration of different categories of personnel was determined on the basis of state-established economic and political priorities through the system of wage rates and, for workers, according to grades (see section 5.1).

For different socio-professional groups, there were strict limits on income levels that were not at all linked to the results of work or to the demand for the goods being produced. Consequently, the level of individual wealth was not necessarily connected with the individual's labour contribution, because the state, rather than demand, dictated the importance of various kinds of work. This is why, with the introduction of the market economy, much of the population (26%) believed that an individual's wealth depended not so much upon the individual himself or herself, but on the degree of social justice prevailing in the society ([146]).

In the 1990s, a major source of dissatisfaction, as a VP poll showed, was differences in income, which were regarded as an injustice. Although 63% of respondents believed that in a market economy the state gives everyone an opportunity to earn as much as he or she can, 42% nevertheless felt that differences in levels of individual earnings should be reduced. The polarization between the supporters of economic differentiation and supporters of egalitarianism (45% and 42%, respectively) reveled that an egalitarian spirit still existed in the society ([91]). In 1994, 81% felt that the present distribution of income in the society was unjust ([146]).

In 1994, according to surveys carried out by VCIOM, people were most preoccupied with high prices (34% of men and 45% of women), increases in crime (30% and 32%), low incomes (30% and 32%), uncertainty about the future (28% for both men and women), and social injustice (11% also for both men and women) ([343b]). Persons who had been more successful during the economic reforms were much more positive about the reforms than were those who were less successful (see table 3).

In the 1990s, being the recipient money and other goods was being gradually replaced by earning them. On the one hand, from the 1960s to the 1990s, egalitarian precepts served to justify socio-economic privileges for the less well off. On the other hand, the fact that education and health services were free failed to stimulate highly productive work and, on the contrary, began impeding it. Deliberately impeding productivity as a reaction to egalitarianism became more and more frequent.

In 1986, 88% of workers in industrial enterprises and 82% of managers expressed a readiness to work more efficiently. At the same time, however, 60% of workers expressed doubt that improving their work would lead to an increase in their remuneration, while only 37% felt that a deterioration in their work would reduce it ([297]). During the same period, in the course of discussions on how wages could be increased, it did not occur to the majority of workers in industrial enterprises that the production of modern and better-quality goods or increased efficiency might be a means to this end. Rather, they were inclined to see an increase in physical effort on their part as the means.

An established stereotype of insufficient payment took root in workers' consciousness, and further wage increases did not encourage them to work harder, since they believed that they would always be deceived by the employer (the state). In the 1990s, this attitude toward wages in many respects determined the choice of preferred forms of privatization of state enterprises. Since it was a common belief that an honest individual could not have enough money to purchase shares in a company, and because the workers in enterprises were convinced that they had contributed a great deal to their enterprises, they were inclined to believe that shares should be given to employees in enterprises. In a survey about how small commercial and service should be privatized, 53% of respondents supported privatization by selling to employees, 16% wanted a sale by auction, and 18% did not want any privatization at all ([91]). In the 1990s, income opportunities grew considerably, but a belief persisted that high wages are not connected with hard intensive or competent work, and this was actually true because of previous distortions in the economy.

One of the most acute issues in the economic reform was the right to own land, which, on the whole, was of limited interest to rural inhabitants. Practically throughout its entire existence, the Soviet state had paid special attention to agriculture and agrarian production, proposing various forms of collective work organization. In the late 1980s, leasing was proposed, and in the 1990s, at last, came the first experiences with privatization.

Table 3
Satisfaction with economic reform in Russia, 1991 (VCIOM survey, % among satisfied and not satisfied with their own life)

Attitude toward economic reforms	Quite satisfied with life	Not satisfied at all with life
Satisfied	10	4
Needs some readjustment	29	17
Should be carried out in a basically different way	16	28
Should return to system before 1985	17	21

Source: [134], p. 164.

Alienation of agrarian workers from the results of their labour led to complete degradation both of the sector and of those working within it. During that period, newly introduced forms of labour organization interested very few workers. In 1984, when asked why they participated in the asset "rent" arrangements (see section 5.1), 36% of rural respondents answered that they had been forced to, and 17% that they were persuaded to by their leaders ([2], 1990; see tables 4, 5). Two years later, when asked whether widespread development of farming while maintaining *kolkhozes* and *sovkhozes* (state farms) was possible, 46% answered positively, 37% answered negatively. On the whole, rural inhabitants considered such eventualities impossible more often ([99r]).

This ambiguity was reflected in a 1993 survey, which found that the proportion of rural inhabitants wanting radical reform of the agrarian sector, the introduction of a land market, and the introduction of private ownership of land fluctuated between 10% and 25% ([199]).

In the 1990s, doing business evolved from being an activity punishable under the criminal code into a phenomenon that evoked quite different reactions. The proportion of those expressing a desire to go into business grew abruptly (in various regions, from 16%–18% in 1986 to 57% in 1992 ([308]). When asked what factors impeded private business, 30% of respondents mentioned people's lack of readiness to get involved in a new, unfamiliar activity; 26%, the absence of adequate technology and resources for private business; 25%, the absence of laws; 15%, the indecisiveness and inertia of authorities; 15%, sabotage by higher party and state officials; 11%, unwillingness of the masses to change their lives; and 11%, envy, racketeering, and threats ([91e]).

In 1992, 80% of Muscovites disapproved of new businesspeople ([264]). The opinion that those active in the underground economy would be the first to become businesspeople was expressed by 23% of respondents, and 11% felt that heads of

Table 4
Evaluation of leasing and co-operative forms of property, Russia, 1989 (%)

	Workers in:	
	Agriculture	*Service sector*
Leases and co-operatives are temporary, just another campaign	24	25
Hiring of workers by leaseholders and co-operatives should be allowed	37	40
Incomes of leaseholders must be limited	16	30
Land leasing should be allowed	24	49
Nationalization of farms should be reinstituted	30	33

Source: [2], p. 54.

Table 5
Evaluation of the social consequences of leasing and co-operative property, Russia, 1989 (%)

	Workers in:	
	Agriculture	*Service sector*
The people's life will improve	18	59
The country, on the whole, will become prosperous	18	59
The number of poor will increase	23	38
There will be less mercy and kindness	29	39
Crime will increase	35	48
There will be more greedy people	39	53

Source: [2], p. 54.
Note: multiple answers were possible. Source: [2], p. 54.

state enterprise and of *nomenklatura* would be the first to get into business ([91e]). In 1992, 85% of respondents felt tat businesses were making a fortune at their expense, and that the words "profit" and "gain" had an ideological connotation ([91g]). Businesspeople and other representatives of the new economy were named as their main enemies by 4% of Muscovites ([91l]). According to the VCIOM poll, in 1994, 36% considered wealthy people to be neither better nor worse than others, while 19% were suspicious, 14% interested, 10% disgusted, 6% respectful, 3% envious, and 10% weren't sure. At the same time, those advocating privatization of all types of state enterprises was growing. When asked whether the government should allow citizens to be private owners of large enterprises, 31% answered in the affirmative in 1991, and 39% did so in 1992 ([91o]); 75% felt that it was all right for people to become wealthy by honest means, and 70% felt that the state should permit the opportunity to earn as much as the individual wants ([91d]).

An education in economics was felt to be necessary and desirable by many people only in the mid-1990s. Various forms of complementary education in economics had been directed periodically to much of the labour force, but it was formal in character. In the mid-1980s, only one out of every ten workers who had received such instruction found it useful in his or her work ([297]). With the formation of the market economy, economics courses and schools became very popular; competition for entry to institutes and faculties of economics was intense, and the fees for studying at these institutions were much higher than for others.

I.A. Boutenko

11.4 Radicalism

Open manifestation of political and national radicalism during the 1960s and 1970s was practically impossible in Russia. Radical movements of various types appeared before the 1990s, but it was quite difficult to define to what extent radical ideas were supported by the population.

In the 1960s and 1970s, it was rare for people openly to express any opinion that differed greatly from the official ones, and it was impossible to carry out sociological studies that might reveal radical consciousness among Russians. The so-called everyday nationalism of that time might be classified as a type of radicalism – that is, a hostile or scornful attitude of the representatives of one nationality toward another. Officially, the Communist Party blamed nationalism for everything, but in reality the party allowed it to continue in a latent form. During the 1970s national intolerance was manifested openly in some autonomous republics of the Northern Caucasus.

Manifestation of political radicalism in the form of extreme dissidence, ranging from appeals to return to the roots of Marxism to calls for a religious revival, were very rare and were cruelly punished by the authorities.

Only at the end of the 1980s did radicalism more or less come out into the open in connection with a new politics of glasnost (freedom of speech). Under USSR national policy at the end of the 1980s, nationalistic radicalism began to grow rapidly, and ethnic conflicts broke out in many regions of Russia. Movements for state independence and for withdrawal from the Russian Federation intensified in some autonomous regions.

A radical youth movement of *sotsyazvists* appeared in Russia, comprising small groups of young people who systematically studied the works of classic Marxism-Leninism and using this philosophy, attempted to reveal the defects in society and to combat them. This movement quickly faded; some members joined new radical parties, some simply stopped being active.

The return to Russia of dissidents who had emigrated and publication of their works helped many people to dissociate themselves from CPSU official ideology. Studies from 1987 to 1993 revealed that an increasing proportion of the population was retreating from communist values. After the coup in August, 1991, many people assumed that hostility toward the communist ideology was total. This belief (or a profession to this effect) was very strong among Russian leaders. With the help of a great galaxy of journalists and social scientists, the notion that democratic values were winning a complete victory was formulated and propagated. At the end of 1993, however, it "unexpectedly" appeared that popular support for the reform policy and for the leaders who were conducting them was not so unanimous and absolute as thought.

Before 1995, 60 political parties were registered in Russia; just over 20 of them were defined as radical. But at the same time, it was practically impossible to distinguish the orientation of some of them. Moreover, sometimes it was impossible to distinguish, even roughly, whose interest they represent and what their social base is.

About 10 organizations are classified as right-wing radical parties, or "browns." They comprise a variety of nationalistic, patriotic, and monarchist parties. Some of them profess an ideology very close to fascism, and even use corresponding symbols. The Liberal Democratic Party of Russia (LDPR), which is headed by B.B. Zhirinovsky, one of the largest and most influential parties in Russia in the mid-1990s, was usually classified as right-wing radical, but this classification was quite provisional; its values and slogans encompassed, at one and the same time, bourgeois and technocratic, nationalistic and neo-communist proclamations. In fact, the volatility of its slogans and goals can be regarded as one of the important reasons for its popularity. But if Liberal Democrats are considered right wing, it would nevertheless be a mistake to explain their success in the elections to the State Duma in 1993 by the popularity of right-wing radical values in Russian society. A plurality of voters (23.5%) voted for the LDPR, but many competent analysts considered this success to be not a result of the support of wide strata of the society but of the general disillusionment of people with leadership policies. Votes for the LDPR were more likely to be a protest against the leaders' actions during the events of October, 1993, than evidence of deliberate devotion to the goals and methods of this party. The LDPR declared itself to be in opposition to the regime, but unlike other parties and blocs it organized its election campaign quite skilfully. There were no exact data about membership in similar parties, but indirect data indicated that they were small organizations, which, as a rule, did not play an important political role. The size of their membership stated by their leaders was usually overstated. Before the mid-1990s, such ideas as "Russia for Russians" had few supporters. In the 1993 election, nationalists did not win any seats in the State Duma. In general, right-wing radical parties represent a rather interesting phenomenon: in spite of their different titles all of them are equally anti-bourgeois and constantly appeal to the working people.

In 1991–92, the idea of autocracy was viewed positively by only 9% of respondents and negatively by 40%. One in ten Russians were in favour of restoration of the monarchy, while 41% were opposed. In October, 1994, the Party of the Majority, which had in no way been suspected of radicalism, was able to gather the one million signatures needed to call a referendum on restoration of the monarchy in Russia.

There were also about 10 left-wing radical (or reds) parties and organizations. They were small and do not noticeably influence policy. Unlike the Russian right-wing radicals, the left-wing groups had the same criteria as did similar organizations throughout the world: anti-capitalism, internationalism, appeals to the forcible overthrow of the system, constant calls to a new, victorious socialist revolution.

There was one noteworthy exception: one of the largest Russian parties, the Communist Party of the Russian Federation (CPRF). Judging by published data, this might have been the largest party in the country in the mid-1990s, when the communist press claimed that it had about 550,000 members. It was also one of the most influential factions in the State Duma: in the 1993 elections, it came in third place, with 13% of votes. All parties of a communist nature, the CPRF included, have a stable bloc of voters.

In the mid-1990s, both left-wing and right-wing parties easily found a common language and, as a rule, were not hostile toward each other. At anti-government meetings and demonstrations, supporters of Bolshevik, nationalistic and monarchistic parties participate in complete unity. Thus, it is not surprising that these radical groups have been dubbed with a collective name: "red-and-browns."

In addition to traditional radicals, there are so-called democratic radicals in Russian society in the mid-1990s. The first to appear was the Democratic Union, a small but extremely active organization. Supporters of the Democratic Union (mainly part of the intelligentsia) are characterized by extreme intolerance of their opponents, including demanding prohibition of communist and right-wing radical parties.

The Democratic Russia movement gave rise to a new party, Democratic Choice of Russia, which was the largest pro-presidential party, organized in 1993. Even before it was officially organized, representatives of this party were the second most popular (15%) in elections to the State Duma. The Choice of Russia was seen as radical because of its unlimited commitment to market values in society and, especially, because of the methods it advocated to achieve its economic (shock therapy) and political (e.g., destruction of the Soviet Union) goals. People who had voted for the Choice of Russia supported an unconstitutional decision by the president to dissolve the Supreme Soviet and to use the army to attack the House of Soviets, in October, 1993.

Readiness to radical actions is one more feature connected with the spread of radicalism in Russian society. The level of this readiness was high in the early 1990s (see table 1). According to polls carried out by "Public Opinion," in July of 1994 fewer than one third of Russians (27%) did not want to participate in mass protest demonstrations under any circumstances, one fifth (21%) had no opinion, and the rest were ready to take part in them (see table 2).

Table 1

Degree of readiness to participate in different actions, Russia, 1992 (%)

	Absolutely ready	Ready	Perhaps not ready	Not ready
Collecting signatures for petitions, demands	24	30	16	30
Participating in meetings, demonstrations	16	27	21	36
Participating in forms of civil disobedience	16	24	24	36
Setting up blockades or occupying buildings	15	25	21	34
Participating in strikes	4	10	23	53
Protecting oneself by any means, including revolt	19	20	17	44

Source: [236], p. 113.

Table 2

Readiness to participate in a protest demonstration by personal life event, Russia, 1994 (%)

Lack of money for food	26
Loss of job and inability to find another	18
Lack of money for clothes and footwear for selves and children	15
Shortage of money to buy medicine for selves and family	15
Unpaid wages for months	10
Ready to participate right away	7
Other reason	3
No answer	21

Source: [12j].

Note: respondents could give up to three answers.

A.T. Gasparishvily

11.5 Religious Beliefs

During the Second World War and the postwar period, the anti-religion strictures were relaxed. In the late 1970s and early 1980s, a slow growth of religiosity began. In the late 1980s and early 1990s, the spread of religion became an avalanche.

After the 1960s, a second wave of anti-religion strictures began after a period of normalization in relations between the church and the state in the late 1940s and early 1950s. It acquired a formal and bureaucratic character as compared with the intensity of the total war against religion in the 1930s. According to the results of sociological investigations (which at that time were carried out under strict ideological constraints and were designed mainly to confirm the official point of view), religiosity was at a low level: in the mid-1960s, it stood at 15% of the population ([291]); in the mid-1970s, at 11.5% ([142]); in regions where Islam dominated, the level of religiosity was about 32% ([254]).

The highest proportion of religious people, 30-40%, were pensioners, and 3 or 4 times more women than men were religious ([121]). Nation-wide forced migration organized by the state (development of virgin land and some agrarian territories, urbanization), which separated younger and older generations and violated cultural traditions, contributed to the decrease in numbers of religious people. There was labour discrimination against the religious; as a result, people kept their true attitude toward the church hidden. In the absence of normal institutionalization of religion, there was an obviously manifested trend toward syncretism with folk pagan beliefs.

The Soviet state declared religion a hostile world-outlook and tried to replace it with Marxism-Leninism, which it endowed with religious features. Just as, before the revolution, religion was taught at all educational establishments, in Soviet times, Marxism-Leninism was an obligatory subject in all educational institutions; portraits of leaders hung even in kindergartens.

In the late 1980s, there was a rapid growth of religiosity, combined with a rapid decline in atheism. In 1988 10% of respondents defined themselves as believers ([91a]); this proportion rose to 39% in 1993 ([163]). The trend toward growth of religiosity (see table 1) developed in the context of a transformation of state, political, and ideological institutions and was, in many respects, determined by them.

By the mid-1990s, the religion boom began to abate. The characteristic ripple effect, in which trends appear in the centre first and travel to outlying areas, which

Table 1
Reliious belief among urban dwellers, Russia, 1971, 1991 (%)

	1971	1991
Religious	7.6	30.2
Unsure	7.2	27.6
Indifferent	21.6	–
Nonreligious	42.1	21.2
Atheists	20.4	10.7
No Answer	1.1	10.2

Calculated from [121], p. 19; [142], p. 19; [312], p. 14.

took place for atheism in the 1930s and also for the religious boom of the early 1990s, was evident for this latest trend as well. In Moscow, the proportion of religious people fell by 3% from 24% in 1990, to 21% in 1991 ([312]).

In a time of fundamental changes in value orientations about 61% of Russian citizens began to regard religion as a way of preserving national identity ([91a]). Religious holidays and rites were seen as a national heritage and part of spiritual wealth. The equation of nationality with religious belief (e.g., Russian: Orthodox; Tatar: Muslim) took root in the popular consciousness. In 1990, religion was seen as a guardian of moral norms by up to 60% of the religious and 48% of the nonreligious ([91a]).

Neglecting religious rituals and norms is a characteristic feature of the new enthusiasm for religion. Under the atheistic dictatorship, conducting religious rituals had been impeded, among other reasons, by a lack of functioning churches, mosques, and temples and by a lack of professionally educated clergy; thus, in the 1970s, churches were attended monthly just by 1.5% of the religious ([142]). In the 1990s, a mass transfer of church buildings from the state to the churches began to take place, and the number of functioning churches increased greatly. For instance, there were 46 functioning churches in Moscow in 1988, and 198 in 1993 (not including 100 transferred but not yet functioning) ([113]). However, an extremely low proportion of the religious manifest their belief in activities (see table 2): Up to 42% of the religious were not ready to accept church discipline and to execute rituals ([311]). In the mid-1990s, only 1% of the religious went to church every day; 23% did not attend services at all. Other rituals were conducted regularly by only 10% of the religious, while 31% did not conduct them at all ([163]).

In the early 1990s, turning to faith was often a nod to fashion or a response to a political situation, or a consequence of an ideological vacuum. Religiosity had an almost symbolic character, showing a person's belief in general humanistic ideals;

Table 2
Church attendance, Russia, 1971, 1991, 1993 (%)

	1971	1991	1993
Once a month	1.5	5.0	5.0
1 to 10 times a year	8.8	20.0	35.0
Never	89.7	65.0	45.0

Calculated from [36], p. 5; [142], p. 24.

the result of this was increased attention to external attributes to the detriment of belief.

Interreligious tension was on the rise in the 1990s. In a multi-religious society with official atheism for 70 years, the law entitled "On the Freedom of Religions" (1990) opened various opportunities for competition between religions for potential members. According to a 1991 poll, 35% of Muslims, 47% of Protestants, and 63% of Catholics felt that the Orthodox church was favoured by the state. Nevertheless, the Russian Orthodox church was losing strength: it had half as many members in 1991 as in 1990 ([312]). A series of articles in the popular press about corruption in the patriarchate and recent links between the clergy and the KGB helped to discredit the Russian Orthodox church in the public mind.

The highest degree of intolerance toward other religions was demonstrated by Catholics. Among Catholics polled in different regions of Russia, 87% expressed a negative attitude toward Islam; 84%, toward Protestantism; 75%, toward Russian Orthodoxy ([163]). Up to 34% of respondents felt that a religion should be propagated where it is traditionally rooted, which indirectly reflected a negative attitude toward proselytization activities by foreign missionaries.

In the 1990s, the number of different religions increased. Up to 50% of respondents regarded themselves as members of the Orthodox church, while about 5% adhered to other religions ([36]; see table 3), among them Catholicism (about 1%), Oriental religions (2%), and Baptist (1%) ([312]). There are numerous Christian sects. Many new non-Christian sects arose; by 1993, there were 52 groups and 41 communities ([311]).

By the 1990s, the number of eclectic religions was growing. The category of Christians in general, of people not regarding themselves as belonging to any of world confessions, was increasingly rapidly; in 1991 alone, their proportion grew from 22% to 46% ([312]), mostly at the expense of members of the Russian Orthodox church. But their religiosity was a form of transition from non-believing to faith or vice versa. These people combined formal belonging to a branch of the

Christian church with a superseding interest in and involvement with Buddhism, Hinduism, and other non-Christian faiths. This was connected with the global trend toward "dedogmatization" and a growth in tolerance.

Investigations of the early 1990s noted a substantial rejuvenation among the religious (see table 4) and shed some light on the importance of education. Sociological investigations in the 1970s had provided data on a heavy preponderance of people over 50 among the religious ([121]). Surveys conducted in 1993 showed that the level of religiosity among 16–17-years-old people was about 64%, higher by half than the average level of religiosity in the country ([163]).

Throughout the period under study, there was a trend toward dropping religiosity as educational level increased (see Table 5). Nontraditional forms of religious belief attracted people with a higher education, mainly creative intellectuals. In 1994, nontraditional beliefs were professed by 10% of respondents, most of them young people ([163]).

Table 3
Self-assessment of beliefs and degree of religiosity, Russia, 1989, 1993 (%)

	1989	1993
Nonreligious	65	40
Russian Orthodox	30	50
Other faith	3	5

Source: Borzenko, 1993, p. 5.

Table 4
Proportion of religious people by age group, Russia, 1965–91 (%)

Age	1965	1971	1991
16	-	-	12
18–20	3	-	13
21–25	8	4	9
26–30	-	-	10
31–40	9	5	10
41–50	14	6	9
51–60	28	20	9
61 and over	38	65	28

Calculated from [142], p. 24; [291], p. 138; [312], p. 4

Table 5
Education level of self-assessed religious people, Russia, 1971, 1991 (%)

	1971	1991
Higher and incomplete higher	2	11
Secondary	6	14
Special secondary	4	17
7-8 grades	7	25
Primary	81	33

Sources: [142], p. 29; [163], p. 29.

L.Y. Petrunina

12 Household Resources

12.1 Personal and Family Income

Before 1990, degree of wealth enjoyed by the population of Russia had been growing constantly. From 1990 to 1993, the spectacular increase in nominal incomes was paralleled by a drop by more than half in real incomes. The drop in living standards resulted in radical polarization of the society between rich and poor, at the expense of the middle strata.

Salaries and wages are the main sources of family income (see table 1). Between 1960 and 1994, nominal wages increased by a factor of a few thousand. Before 1990, the annual rate of increase was around 5–10%; however, between 1990 and 1994, with the transition to the market economy, average annual wages increased by a factor of 500. Wages in the state service sector adapted much more slowly and with considerable delay. As a result, in the 1990s incomes were redistributed in favour of workers in industrial sectors at the expense of employees in the education, medical services, culture, and science sectors.

Beginning in 1989 the increase in prices resulted in anticipatory buying, which fueled inflation, with the result that nominal wages no longer reflected the level of well-being. Before 1989, prices for goods and services were more or less frozen, which is why the rise in absolute wages resulted in a rise in real incomes. From 1989 to 1991, wage increases were ahead of price increases; as well, real wages continued to rise (see table 2). Liberalization of prices in January, 1992, resulted in a sharp (practically twofold) drop in real incomes. This trend continued in 1993 and 1994.

Changes in wage and salary parameters resulted in similar transformations in per capita incomes. In 1993 average per capita real incomes fell to the 1970 level (see table 3). Between 1989 and 1994, changes in average wages and level of real income did not always coincide. In 1991, real wages continued to grow and per capita incomes began to decrease. At the same time, in 1992, both wages and incomes fell in real terms, but wages fell more quickly.

Table 1
Average monthly wages, 1960–94 (in roubles and %)

	1960	1970	1980	1985	1989	1990	1991	1992	1993	1994 (Aug.)
Roubles	83.1	126.1	177.7	201.4	258.6	297.0	552.0	6,127.0	47,800.0	183,500.0
%	100	152	214	242	311	357	664	7,373	57,521	2,208,818

Sources: [171], p.157; [175], p. 370; [176], p. 135; [242], p. 90; [277], p. 61.

Table 2
Wages (at end of year), 1989–94

	Nominal wages	Consumer price index	In constant roubles (1989)
1989	259	1.0	259
1990	297	1.1	269
1990 (December)	412	1.1	362
1991	1,195	3.0	405
1992	16,071	77.0	208
1993	141,218	723.4	195
1994	207,500	1,288.8	161

Sources: [242], pp. 90–1; [277], p. 91.

Table 3
Real Incomes, 1970–89 (%)

Basis of calculation	1970	1987	1985	1989	1990	1991	1992	1993	1994
1970=100%	100	151	168	176	228	226	110	97	107
1989=100%	57	86	96	100	130	128	62	55	61

Sources: [112]; [175], p. 287; [242], p. 94.

Beginning in 1991, increases in nominal incomes and pensions and the minimum wage failed to compensate for inflation. Before 1989, the lower limit of wages was set according to the supposition that it should be no less than 1.5 times the minimum cost of living (it should ensure the cost of living for one employee and one half of the cost of living for one dependent). Similarly, the minimum pension was defined in terms of the cost of a minimum pensioner's consumer basket. From 1990 on, this principle of co-ordination of minimum wages and pensions was disregarded. In 1989, a minimum pension amounted to 60% of the minimum wage; in

1991 they were equal in absolute terms, and beginning in 1992 the minimum wage amounted to only half of the minimum pension level (see table 4). By the end of 1994, the minimum pension represented 37% of the minimum cost of living.

The decrease in real incomes in the mid-1990s was accompanied by a radical polarization. Under the old administrative system, inequality of incomes was seen as a quite undesirable but inevitable necessity, flowing from the principle of "everyone according to his or her work contribution." Correspondingly, state policy in the sphere of distributive relations was based on elimination of income differences. This is why income differentiation during the Soviet period was much lower than it was in the countries with a market economy. From 1991 to 1994, the decile coefficient of income differentiation grew by a factor of 2.5 (see table 5).

Before the 1980s, the domination of public property in the Soviet Union predetermined that a high share of goods would be received from the state free of charge. Social consumption funds provided the population with expenses for

Table 4
Minimum wages and pensions, 1987–94 (roubles)

	Minimum wage	Minimum pension
1987	80	50
1988	80	50
1989	80	50
1990	80	50
1991 March	80	80
1991 June	130	120
1991 September	130	140
1991 December	180	342
1992 May	900	900
1992 November	900	2,250
1993 January	2,250	2,250
1993 February	2,250	4,275
1993 April	4,275	8,122
1993 July	7,740	8,122
1993 August	7,740	14,620
1993 November	7,740	26,320
1993 December	14,620	26,320
1994 May	14,620	38,700
1994 July	20,500	38,700
1994 August	20,500	41,550
1994 September	20,500	44,400

Calculated from [277], p. 61; [344], p. 91.

Table 5
Decile coefficients of income differentiation, 1965–93

1965	1975	1980	1985	1989	1990	1991*	1992	1993
3.9	3.0	4.1	4.3	4.2	4.1	4.5	8.0	11.0

Calculated from: [176], p. 135; [344].

Table 6
Payments and concessions received per capita from social consumption funds, 1960–90 (roubles)

1960	1970	1980	1985	1986	1990
143	288	489	594	620	760

Sources: [175], p. 282; [176], p. 139.

education and qualification improvement, medical services, and maintenance of children in preschool institutions. The average per capita payments and concessions received from the social consumption funds were practically double the average wages (compare tables 1 and 2). After 1991, the social consumption funds no longer played their decisive role (see section 6.2).

L.N. Ovcharova

12.2 Informal Economy

The informal economy, which is, naturally, illegal, is very difficult to measure. It is considered to have been formed in the 1960s, when the rate of growth in consumer commodities and services began to fall far behind growth in personal incomes. After that, the scale and structure of informal economy broadened and the proportion of persons involved in it grew constantly.

Over thirty years, the scale of the informal economy increased immensely. The Russian informal economy covered production, distribution, exchange, and consumption of commodities and services, including legal economic activities that are left out of the official account of commodities and services produced and are thus sheltered from taxation; the illicit economy, comprising activities such as embezzlement, false accounting, and bribery; and outright llegal economic activities such as production and sale of narcotics and weapons. Calculations show that in 1960 the informal economy produced 5 billion roubles' worth of commodities and services, while at the beginning of the 1990s turnover was estimated as being anywhere from 100 to 150 billion roubles in constant prices ([66]; [133]).

From 1960 to 1990, turnover in the informal economy grew considerably, with an average increase by a factor of eighteen in different sectors (see table 1).

Nearly all sectors of the national economy were penetrated by informal economic relations. In the beginning of the 1990s, with respect to absolute volume, agriculture had the highest penetration rate, trade and food-catering serviceswas second, construction was third, and industry was fourth. In terms of growth, however, the informal economy grew most intensively in construction (by a factor of 60), transportation (by a factor of 40), and agriculture (by a factor of 30). The development of informal structures in these sectors occurred mainly through upward distortions and pilfering ([290]).

The services sector was the obvious leader in the informal economy's influence on existing socio-economic and political processes. In 1990, the share of the informal economy in this sector was approximately one third; in services to households and domestic maintenance, informal structures provided approximately one half of services ([133]).

Table 1
Structure and scale of informal economy, 1960–61, 1989–90 (billion roubles per year)

	1960–61	1989–90
Contribution to the informal economy by economic sector	590	
Industry	0.3	10.0
Agriculture (including collective farms)	0.6	23.0
Transport and communications	0.2	8.0
Construction	0.2	12.0
Trade and food-catering services	–	17.0
Other kinds of production	–	1.0
Nonindustrial sector	2.5	17.0
Housing maintenance and consumer services	1.6	6.7
Health care, sports, and fitness	0.5	6.2
Education	0.3	1.5
Culture and art	–	0.3
Science and scientific services	–	0.3
Banking and insurance	–	0.1
Management offices	0.1	1.6

Source: [344], p. 16.

Since 1989, the shortage of consumers' commodities stimulated the growth of illegal commercial activity. According to a poll carried out at the end of 1990, 30% of the population bought provisions, clothes, and household utensils on the black market, and 44% intended to obtain them from this source ([344]). Black-market prices were, on average, three times higher than were state ones (see table 2); moreover, the value of commodities exchanged in the black market was tax exempt.

In January, 1992, price liberalization virtually eliminated this kind of black market, but the informal economy continued to grow. New structures – legally functioning economic units – began to spring up to ensure the transition of production activity in state resources into the private sector. At the beginning of 1990, nearly 80% of industrial non-state associations and joint ventures were functioning as parts of state enterprises, the latter realizing 70% of their production through these new types of units ([74]). The creation of such "pocket" economic structures was a convenient way to solve many financial problems (such as effecting transactions, sheltering income from taxation) for the administration of the state enterprises. Hence, since the moment they were created, these economic units wsere designed to conceal information about various economic activities.

In 1993, when mass privatization began, the structures pumping capital from the state sector into the private sector contained both commercial and financial entities (banks, investment companies, and funds). During the privatization process, firms in the informal economy acquired up to 50% of the ownership of many enterprises. Furthermore, although their direct ownership may have represented no more than 20% of stock, their indirect control amounted to 50% of Russian industrial potential ([105]).

According to some calculations, over the 30-year period, the number of persons engaged in the informal economy doubled ([133]; [338]). The majority of economists who studied the question of the informal economy considered the number of employed to have comprised about 10% of total able-bodied population in 1960 and about 20% at the beginning of the 1990s ([66]; [133]; [338]). In 1989, strict limitations on supplementary earnings and moonlighting were eliminated. The liberalization of the control of labour activities and the introduction of progressive income tax created the prerequisites for misrepresentation of information incomes. According to a survey of urban populations carried out in 1992–93 by the Institute of Socio-economic Problems of the Russian Academy of Science that included a comparison of family revenue and expenditure, 15–20% of family income is concealed from taxation ([110]).

Table 2
Black-market prices compared to state prices, December 1990 (state prices = 1.00)

Commodity	Price
Foodstuffs:	
Meat	4.8
Cooked meat	3.2
Instant coffee	3.0
Tea	3.0
Salmon caviar	4.0
Exotic fish	3.0
Boxed sweets	4.4
Vodka	2.2
Champagne	3.1
Wine	3.0
Clothes:	
Woman's winter overcoat	2.8
Man's winter overcoat	3.4
Man's sweater	2.5
Man's & woman's clothes	3.0
Jacket	3.2
Footwear:	
Man's winter boots	4.8
Woman's winter boots	4.5
Woman's dress shoes	4.4
Shoes for teenagers	3.7
Girls' shoes	3.1
Boys' shoes	3.6
Household articles:	
Carpets	2.6
Dish sets	3.3
Cut-glass ware	3.1
Sewing machine	2.8
Knitting machine	4.0
Refrigerator	2.6
Washing machine	2.6
Vacuum cleaner	2.8
Coffee grinder	3.0
Iron	5.6
Televisions and VCRs:	
TV set, black-and-white	2.6
TV set, colour	2.5
VCR	2.6

Source: [344], p. 7.

L.N. Ovcharova

12.3 Wealth

Until the 1990s, social consumption funds played a very important role in distributing national wealth according to need. Shortages of goods caused them to be redistributed according to need, but not according to income. A gradual rise of wealth among the population during the1990s resulted in the emergence of a radical income differentiation and consequent impoverishment of the bulk of the population; formerly subsidized services, such as housing, became too expensive. In the mid-1990s, property differentiation became more closely linked to income differentiation.

Before the 1980s, the state monopoly on property was such that a wide variety of goods were distributed to the population free of charge. Free flats, free education, and free medicine were ensured by the social consumption funds. The quality and availability of many goods and services were almost completely independent of income for the majority of population. This resulted from the absence of private property, the shortage of goods and services, and distribution networks that resulted in those who were closest to the sources of supply and the most needy being served first. This situation caused growth in deferred demand, a growth in savings, and an informal consumer market.

Before the 1990s, medical services were provided free of charge, except for some dental and cosmetic ones. In 1985, 0.5% of medical services supplied to the population were paid for; in 1990, 0.9%; in 1991, 1.2% ([171]). A considerable proportion of payments for other medical services became legalized in the1990s, terminating black-market medical services. Medical insurance was introduced at that time, but it developed slowly because of low profits realized by the enterprises constrained to pay for this kind of insurance coverage.

In the 1990s, the level of individual medical care began to be dependent upon the level of family income.

Until the 1990s, level and quality of education did not depend directly on personal or family wealth; private schools did not exist. Before the mid-1990s, the quality of education in both paid and free institutions of primary and higher education depended neither on the existence nor the amount of fees, but was a function of the number of students per class and, in high schools, sometimes of the level of discipline, which was lower in the paid institutions. Access to the best educational resources was very much a matter of chance and degree of commitment on the part of the parents.

Up to the end of the 1980s, expenditures by the population were far below income. The main feature of the structure of consumer expenditures in Russia was the dominant proportion spent on food: 35% in 1980 and 50% in 1993 (see tables 1, 2, 3; [93]). In 1992, almost all indicators showed a drop in living conditions.

Table 1
Usage of total income by workers' and employees' families, 1980–90 (%)

	1980	1985	1989	1990
Food	35.0	32.8	29.2	50.0
Noncomestible goods	30.6	31.3	32.7	–
Alcoholic beverages	3.9	3.3	3.0	7.0
Entertainment and household maintenance (including tobacco)	10.7	10.5	10.3	–
Taxes, duties, rent	9.4	9.7	10.3	–
Other expenses	4.9	4.7	4.5	–
Savings	5.5	7.7	10.0	–

Sources: [93]; [176], p. 143.

Table 2
Structure of income and expenses, Russia compared to selected countries, 1993 (%)

	Russia	US	Japan	Germany	France	Great Britain	Italy
Incomes:							
Salary/wages	73.5	64.5	58.5	57.5	53.5	60.5	42.5
Profits by an individual businessperson[a]	5.0	8.0	12.0	4.5	5.0	12.5	28.0
Dividends and profits	5.0	15.5	11.0	17.5	15.0	13.5	10.5
Pensions and grants	16.5	12.0	18.5	20.5	27.0	13.5	19.5
Usage of incomes:							
Direct taxes[b]	8.0	20.2	18.0	27.0	26.3	19.9	23.0
% for financing	–	3.5	5.0	7.0	8.5	9.9	9.8
Savings	19.0	5.0	16.5	9.0	4.0	3.5	6.5
Purchasing of goods and services	73.0	71.3	60.5	57.0	61.2	66.7	60.7

Source: [93].

[a] Farmers, craftsmen, tradesmen included.

[b] Obligatory payments to the state funds of social development included.

Table 3
Food consumption per capita, 1989–93 (kg per year)

	1989	1991	1992	1993*
Carbohydrates:				
Wheaten bread	68.7	73.0	71.5	70.5
Rye bread	23.6	24.7	6.7	26.7
Potatoes	93.8	98.1	106.7	117.6
Vegetables and legumes	91.0	87.0	83.0	74.0
Fruit and berries	41.0	37.0	34.0	37.0
Sugar and confectionery	33.0	29.0	28.0	33.0
Meat and meat products	75.0	65.0	54.0	58.0
Beef	18.9	15.6	14.1	16.6
Mutton	2.2	1.5	1.4	1.2
Pork	10.4	9.5	10.3	11.0
Poultry	13.6	12.6	10.3	18.7
Sausage	14.4	13.0	10.4	10.5
Fish	16.1	14.1	11.6	12.0
Milk and dairy products:				
Unskimmed milk	116.6	118,0	106.4	99.5
Sour cream and cream	14.1	13.3	6.5	6.5
Butter	7.1	5.5	5.6	5.8
Eggs	237.0	229.0	243.0	255.0
Oil, margarine	6.9	6.1	6.5	7.2

Source: [343b].
* Data for first six months extrapolated to a year.

Consumption of goods and services was reduced because of price liberalization, and the population became able to satisfy only basic needs. Incomes rose more slowly than did prices. Income differentiation became sharper. In 1993, average per capita consumption of non-food products by low-income groups in 1993 was 12 times lower than was similar consumption by high-income groups; consumption of durable goods was 20 times lower ([343a]). Nevertheless, in 1993 the general volume of trade in durable goods increased by 2%, and specifically the volume of trade in television sets rose by 34%, in radio sets by 45%, and in refrigerators by 60% ([111h]).

In 1993, there was a certain amount of growth in consumer purchasing, but it was not yet stable and was directly connected to indexation of wages, salaries, and pensions. For example, in January 1992, 90% of an average salary had to be spent to purchase a set of 19 main food products; in January 1993, this proportion was 52%; in December 1993, it was 26% ([111f]). Well-off population groups increased their purchasing power, while that of low-income groups decreased ([111g]).

The rise in income of some groups was not accompanied by a rise in investments. Private consumption increased, and money was being sent abroad: in 1992, 35.9% of the gross national product was spent on private consumption; in 1993, 40.5% ([111f]).

Before the mid-1990s, ownership and size of flats were not indicators of a family's wealth. Even after a considerable increase of housing construction in the 1960s and 1970s, living conditions improved very slowly. From 1985 to 1994, the average level of housing remained practically unchanged (16.4–16.8 square metres per capita); a 1985 state programme to provide every family with a separate flat (with 18.9–19 square metres per capita) was entirely forgotten as a result of major changes in the social and economic situation in the 1990s.

Ninety percent of urban flats were owned by the municipality (see table 4), and rent was quite low. In order to buy a flat in a housing co-operative, a citizen had to prove his or her family's housing need. Before the 1990s, to become a member of a housing co-operative, or to be on a waiting list for those wanting a better flat, one also had to bring a reference from his or her place of work. The only people who could move into a larger municipal (rarely co-operative) flat were those with very poor living conditions (less than 5 square metres per capita) and families living in workers' hostels or unsafe housing. Families on a waiting list for better housing (see table 5) comprised 19% of all families in the country in 1993 ([111e]).

State subsidies for housing maintenance, which resulted in low expenditures on such services by the occupants themselves (see table 6), were gradually repealed before the mid-1990s.

Privatization of flats began in the1990s, and the rise of housing markets led to the redistribution of many flats from pensioners and socially weak groups to the wealthy.

At the end of the 1980s, every fourth flat in cities had no in-flat water supply, sewage system, or heating; in villages, over 60% of houses had no such conveniences. The level of amenities in rural houses had been the lowest (see table 7). Housing amenities had not been improved for many years; the size of kitchens, bathrooms, corridors, built-in cupboards, and other additional space also had not increased; such amenities represented 40% of the overall living space in a flat for decades ([176]).

In spite of inflation in the 1990s, the population's savings as reflected in bank deposits increased. Before the 1990s, this revealed primarily postponed demand, linked to shortages of goods (see tables 8 and 9). From 1971 to 1986, deposits increased by a factor of 5.2, whereas the volume of purchases had increased by a factor of 2.5 between 1970 and 1986 ([176]).

Table 4

Number of flats built by the state (municipal) and by housing co-operatives, 1976–91 (000)

	1976–80	1981–85	1986–89	1990	1991
By the state	5,033	4,795	4,168	852	658
By housing co-operatives	317	333	353	52	42

Sources: [176], p. 228, [171], p. 224.

Table 5

Number of families on waiting lists for flats and improved living conditions, 1989–92

	1989	1990	1991	1992
Total number of families (000)	95.6	99.6	100.3	96.5[a]
Proportion of families on waiting lists (%)	19	20	20	–
Among families on waiting lists, those living (%):				
In communal flats[b]	16	15	15	14
In hostels	12	12	12	12
In unsafe houses	5	6	4	4
Waiting more than 10 years	13	13	13	13

Sources: [111e]; [171], p.227.

[a] In connection with the reduction in state housing construction, the queues of department employees to receive flats (housing standards for them were somewhat higher than average) disappeared (0% in 1992, compared to 24% in 1991).

[b] Flats where more than one family lives.

Table 6

Share of expenses for rent, communal services, and maintenance of private houses, 1980–93 (% of total family income)

	1980	1985	1990	1991	1993*
In workers' and employees' families	3.0	3.0	2.5	1.5	–
In families of collective farmers	2.0	2.0	1.7	1.2	–
Total families	–	–	–	–	5.0

Sources: [171], p. 146, 147; 94

Table 7
Housing accommodations and services, 1980–91

	1980	1985	1990	1991
Total housing area (million square metres)	1,861	2,138	2,465	2,449
Average per urban dweller (square metre)	13.3	14.4	15.7	16.0
Average per rural dweller (square metre)	13.7	16.2	18.2	17.9
Urban houses equipped with (%):				
Water supply	90	92	94	94
Sewage system	88	90	92	92
Central heating	88	90	92	63
Gas	75	73	72	72
Electric stove	61	62	2121	
Hot water	60	73	79	80
Bath (%)	80	83	87	87
Rural houses equipped with (%):				
Water supply	29	39	49	50
Sewage system	22	29	37	38
Central heating	28	32	37	38
Gas	61	73	78	78
Electric stove	0.2	2.0	3.0	4.0
Hot water	9	13	19	19
Bath	19	24	32	33

Source: [171], p. 225.

Table 8
Deposits in state savings banks of the Russian Federation, 1980–91

	1980	1985	1990	1991
Number of deposits (million)	83.1	97.5	124.9	141.0
Sum of deposits (billion roubles)	89.4	124.7	216.4	372.3
Average deposit (roubles)	1,075	1,280	1,733	2,640

Source: [171], p. 140.

With regard to bank deposits, the largest deposits were registered as anonymous. Changing modes of deposit registration introduced in 1978 coincided with a decrease in number of deposits and sums deposited. This fact indicated to some researchers that anonymous deposits had been a convenient way to accumulate illegal incomes. In any case, deposits increased more rapidly than did wages and salaries ([10]).

Table 9
End use of family savings, 1987 (% among families with savings)*

	Workers and employees	Collective farmers	Pensioners Workers and employees	Pensioners Collective farmers
Anticipating major expenses	28.9	24.5	4.5	3.6
Help to children	41.4	48.2	21.1	32.6
Supporting standard of living after retirement	20.0	27.9	57.0	64.1
Unexpected expenses and other	55.4	51.2	55.4	46.5
For no particular reason	9.1	6.7	3.7	5.6

Source: [75], p. 83.
* More than one answer possible.

The possibility of having several savings accounts resulted in the fact that, for example, in the Gorky region, every worker had an average of 1.25 of these accounts, which is why it was impossible to consider average size of a deposit to be an indicator of savings among different social groups.

After 1992, cash savings depreciated by approximately half due to inflation ([171]); by 1993, they had depreciated by a factor of 10 ([111g]). In 1994, however, the number of depositors drastically increased; the share of savings as a proportion of income rose to 18%, compared to 6% in 1980 ([162a]). But these deposits did not constitute deferred demand, as had formerly been the case; a considerable proportion represented a decision to withdraw income from consumption to invest in dividend-bearing deposits.

Under socialism, property differentiation in the context of redistribution of social goods was not directly linked to income; this differentiation appears in the mid-1990s, but often due to the informal economy. Housing and many essential goods could not be legally bought until the1990s. During the 1970s and 1980s, a person was considered prosperous if he or she enjoyed the use of a flat, a car, and a country house.

In the 1990s property differentiation became more important, although it was based not only on a function of income or enjoyment of durable goods acquired under previously prevailing conditions. For this reason, if we compare families with incomes below the cost of living with those of the population in general, only 8% more of the former were without refrigerators, 11% more did not have a washing machine; 26% more did not have a colour television set, 20% more did not have a sewing machine, and 25% more did not have tape recorders or new furniture ([242]).

Although the supply of durable goods increased (see table 10), changes in life style were insignificant. In 1993 60% of families had tape recorders, 58% had sewing machines, 52% had vacuum cleaners, and 22% had motorcycles. About 30%–40% of these durable goods, however, had been acquired more than 10 years previously. In the1990s, consumption of the most expensive goods (such as private cars, country houses, and so on) increased rapidly in a context of drastic differentiation of consumption. For example, the number of those with private cars rose by 8% in 1992, and by 9% in 1993 ([111h]).

In the 1990s, there were new phenomena relating to the question of consumption versus savings and investment. The advent of unexpected or sudden gains in the absence of culturally internalized strategies for long-term personal investments, such as education or family wealth, resulted in much conspicuous consumption of "luxury" items (entertainment, dining, expensive travel abroad, and so on). This kind of behaviour was not limited to the most prosperous sector of the population, but extended to all those experiencing ephemeral and substantial gain from their legal or illegal economic activities.

Table 10
Distribution of household appliances and means of transportation, 1980–90 (per 100 families; per 1,000 population)

	1980	1985	1990	1980	1985	1990
Urban dwellers:						
Television sets	95	113	121	318	358	391
Radio sets	105	111	110	314	359	358
Refrigerators and freezers	103	106	106	315	345	345
Sewing machines	78	78	79	123	166	199
Automobiles	10	14	17	30	43	56
Motorcycles and scooters	41	45	47	131	143	154
Rural dwellers						
Television sets	71	80	88	203	264	296
Tadio sets	70	75	73	220	242	243
Refrigerators and freezers	59	66	66	168	210	210
Sewing machines	62	66	68	204	207	223
Cars	9	17	25	29	48	65
Motorcycles and scooters	14	20	25	39	66	89

Source: [171], pp. 188–9.

Table 11
Distribution of household appliances, means of transportation, and country house, 1993 and 1994*
(per 100 families)

	1993	*1994*
Colour TVs	70.0	72.0
Freezers	12.0	12.0
Microwave stoves	2.0	3.0
Video recorders	5.0	9.0
Video cameras	0.2	1.2
Personal computers	2.0	6.0
Pianos	–	7.0
Second car	0.2	1.0
Country house	29.0	29.0

Source: [12i]; [171], pp. 188–9.

* Distribution of answers to the question: What do you have in your family? from VCIOM polls.

I.A. Boutenko

13 Lifestyle

13.1 Consumer Market

The 1960s, 1970s, and 1980s were characterized by increasing shortages of goods and services, which led to the rationing system that was widespread until the end of 1980s. The late 1980s and early 1990s saw an accelerated slowdown in production of consumer goods. In the mid-1990s, the imbalance between demand and supply began to correct itself, due mainly to imports and lack of purchasing power.

From the 1960s to the 1990s, there was a constant imbalance between demand and supply of goods and services. A considerable surfeit in demand for goods and services over supply arose in 1965, when the first attempts at economic reforms began during the "thaw" period. This imbalance was manifested in a classic form: the population had money and there was nothing to buy, resulting in a forced excess of savings.

Before the end of the 1970s, the situation appeared to improve. The imbalance between demand and supply diminished slightly, thanks to periodic increases in nominal prices for so-called nonbasic (luxury) goods and rates for paid services. Direct price increases were intensified by a considerable hidden rise, growing out of a manipulation of the types and quality of products available.

One of the main reasons for the hidden rise in prices was structural shifts in trade. The growth in the proportion of goods with relatively higher retail prices in the shops also led to rises in prices. For example, before the mid-1980s the relative cost of protein foods (mainly meats and processed meats) decreased, while the relative cost of luxury goods such as crystal, jewellery, carpets, and so on, increased. In 1986, the index of retail prices for all goods compared to 1960 was 112%, whereas the price index not including alcoholic beverages was 104% ([177]); this was due to the fact that there was an increase in sales of alcohol after the the anti-alcohol campaign in 1985 (see section 16.3).

A growth in imports also contributed to hidden price rises. The influence of the import factor was especially great at the end of the 1960s and beginning of the

1970s, when importing of retail goods increased by 250%, while the volume of non-comestible products more than tripled ([338]).

In the 1980s, the imbalance continued, becoming more acute by 1989–90. Shortages of consumer goods became widespread and intensified the distortion of demand, which, in its turn, began to have a negative influence on the market. This was a consequence of a considerable rise in income among the population and an unsatisfied or postponed demand for consumer goods and services In 1989, the annual rise in prices reached 9%, whereas in previous years the average annual rise had been between 3% and 5% ([123]). As a result, the gap between money supply and supply of goods increased even more (see table 1).

Production of consumer goods increased slowly (see table 2). The transition to a market economy in the 1990s was accompanied by a sharp increase in prices (see table 3), which brought many consumer goods back onto the market.

For the first time in 30 years, a shortage of money, not of goods, became typical for most families. The increase in income lagged behind the rise in prices by a factor of five on the average, and the population began to spend their money on food and the most necessary consumer goods and services.

With the transition to a market economy, important changes took place in the structure of spending (see table 4). Due to the sharp differentiation in incomes, the growth in cash income surpassed by a greater and greater margin the growth in expenses for consumer goods and services. In 1993, the total excess of cash income over cash expenses was 6.7 billion roubles. A large portion of cash incomes therefore became savings. At the end of 1993, the cash surplus in the hands of the general public exceeded 7.8 billion roubles, much of which had been converted into foreign currency.

In the 1990s, the proportion of expenses for nutrition began to increase, reaching 47% in 1992 and 46% in 1993; as a result, the expenses for noncomestible goods and services decreased substantially. The share of expenses for noncomestible goods was 41% in 1992 and 44% in 1993; for services, these shares were 7.7% and 7.5%, respectively ([278]).

Before the 1990s, consumption of practically all types of foodstuffs decreased markedly, and the level of consumption of many foodstuffs corresponded to that at the beginning of the 1970s (see table 5). In 1993, three times fewer noncomestible goods were sold than in 1990. Sales of basic clothing, footwear, and entertainment and everyday goods decreased by half, linked with the decrease in income level; most income was being spent for the most basic essential goods or kept in savings.

From the 1960s to the 1990s, the range of services for which people had to pay broadened, though it was always underdeveloped and one-sided (see table 6).

Table 1
Changes in sales of consumer goods and cash incomes, Russia, 1988–93 (in % of 1985 levels)

	1988	1989	1990	1991	1992	1993
Sales of consumer goods	107	116	127	118	76	–
Cash incomes	118	133	157	340	2,561	–
Retail trade (including restaurants)	107	116	127	118	76	78

Sources: [171], pp. 15, 177; [189].

Table 2
Production of consumer goods, Russia, 1988–92 (in % of 1985 levels)

	1988	1989	1990	1991	1992
Food	–	–	127	116	95
Alcoholic beverages	–	–	93	98	92
Noncomestible goods	–	–	138	145	125
Goods of light industry	–	–	117	121	98
Total consumer goods	109	119	127	126	107

Source: [171], pp. 15, 149.

Table 3
Increases in consumer-goods prices (from December to December) (ratio), Russia, 1990–92

	1991 to 1990	1992 to 1991	1993 to 1992
Consolidated indexes of consumer-goods prices	2.6	26.1	9.4
Foodstuffs (including alcoholic beverages)	2.4	22.1	9.0
Noncomestible goods	3.1	26.7	7.4
Paid services	1.8	33.6	24.1

Sources: [171], p. 205; [278], p. 127.

Table 4
Expenses (% of total income), Russia, 1985–93

	1985	1990	1992	1993
Goods and services	83	75	73	69
Payments to financial and credit system	12	12	9	8
Increase in savings and purchase of foreign currency	7	5	1	4
Cash on hand	5	1	4	9

Sources: [171], p. 133; [278], pp. 149, 157.

Table 5
Consumption of goods, Russia, 1960–92 (per capita, in kg)

	1960	1970	1980	1990	1991	1992
Meat and processed meat	41	50	59	69	63	55
Milk and dairy products	255	331	328	386	347	281
Eggs	128	182	279	297	288	263
Fish and seafood	12	19	22	20	16	13
Vegetables and legumes	69	82	94	89	86	77
Sugar	31	42	47	47	38	34
Cooking oil	6	7	9	10	8	6
Bread and pastry	164	144	126	119	120	125

Sources: [171], p. 187; [177], pp. 310, 312.

Table 6
Volume and structure of paid services, Russia, 1985–92 (in %)

	1985	1990	1992
Domestic services	25.0	27.0	23.0
Public transportation	33.0	29.0	34.0
Communications	6.0	6.0	7.0
Housework	20.0	18.0	15.0
Pre-school tuition	3.0	2.0	3.0
Culture	4.0	4.0	2.0
Tourism and excursions	3.0	5.0	3.0
Physical fitness and sports	0.2	0.3	0.2
Health	0.5	0.9	2.0
Convalescence and health resorts	3.0	4.0	6.0
Legal and banking	0.4	0.9	1.0
Other	2.0	4.0	2.0

Source: [171], p. 145.

In the 1990s, it also included some medical and educational services that had previously been mainly free. In the services sector, such material services as laundries household-appliance repair, transportation, and home-maintenance services dominated. In 1992, these kinds of services comprised 79% of the total volume of paid services, the other 21% being services connected with the satisfaction of socio-cultural needs. However, demand for such services increased faster than did supply. Unsatisfied demand was much higher than was the unsatisfied demand for consumer goods.

However, liberalization of prices led to a moderation of demand for many forms of services. In 1992, the volume of tourist services diminished by 48% in comparison to 1991; sanatorium and health-resort services, by 40%; cultural services, by 43%; domestic services, by 54% ([171]). The standards of services for rural populations were much lower than were those for urban populations, because the social infrastructure and the material and technical bases for rural services are weak, the assortment and quality of these services are insufficient, and there is a shortage of trained personnel.

L.N. Sivashenkova

13.2 Consumption of Mass Information

The amount of time spent consuming information has been constantly increasing. There was a marked growth in media use up to 1988, and then a distinct drop, particularly in the use of print media. Television is becoming the main source of information. The decrease in consumption of other types of mass media has not only been caused by the expansion of television viewing, but is closely linked to sharp changes in life styles.

The role of the mass media in daily life is constantly growing, as indicated by the constant rise in expenditures on media equipment, which has outstripped the rise in expenditures for other noncomestible goods (except for clothing and footwear). From 1975 to 1985, expenditures on the mass media increased by 1.6 times among urban dwellers and remained stable among rural populations. Urban dwellers spent 0.5% of their annual family budget on books and newspapers in 1975 and 0.8% in 1980 and 1985; for rural dwellers, these proportions were 0.4%, 0.3%, and 0.4%, respectively ([177]).

Consumer fees for radio and TV reception (payments for radio and TV antennas) comprised an insignificant proportion of expenditures on housing and continued to do so up to the mid-1990s. Prices for print media, however, increased greatly in 1991, and were one of the main causes of the drop in public interest in newspapers and magazines.

The availability of different types of mass media is increasing. From 1960 to 1990, the number of telephones increased from 2.8 million to 23.4 million (including private telephones in apartments, which went from 6.4 million in 1980 to 14.6 million in 1990). By 1990, every third urban family and every eighth rural family had a telephone. In the 1990s, use of cellular telephones began to rise. In general, however, the rate and level of telephone penetration was still extremely low (see table 1).

During and after the Second World War, many radio sets were situated in streets and parks. By the 1980s, they had disappeared from these locations but were an invariable attribute of any office, to be replaced in the 1990s by television sets. Production of radio sets increased from from 17.5 million units in 1960 to 44.7 million in 1991 (see table 2). The importation of radio and television sets increased immensely in the 1990s.

Listening to radio programmes, which was the main source of information in the early 1960s, became a secondary and complementary occupation in the 1990s.

Television and radio progamming, which had been a monopoly and a means of ideological influence, began to be transformed into a means of diversification of information sources and entertainment in the late 1980s. At this time, although the television network remained a state body, state allocations played a smaller part in its budget. In the 1990s, independent commercial radio stations and television channels began to operate.

The number of television sets per 100 families increased by 400% between 1960 and 1990, and the television set came to be seen as an essential appliance. By 1985, almost all urban families had one television set, and some had purchased a second set. According to a 1994 VCIOM poll, 72% of families had a colour television set ([12i]). The availability of television channels was on the rise (see table 3). Since 1986, cable television has developed particularly in large cities.

In the 1980s, television became the main source of information and its use was constantly increasing: people watched television more than they listened to the radio or read newspapers. Among adults living in Moscow in 1991, watching television accounted for 44% of leisure time, while among those living in Moscow suburbs, it accounted for 47.8%; reading newspapers took up 5.8% and 5.2%, respectively; listening to the radio took up 0.3% among both groups ([213]). According to polls taken in the late 1980s, people spent between 30% and 50% of their leisure time (7–15 hours a week) in front of a TV set. Men watched television a bit more than did women ([211]) and spent two to three times less time reading (see table 4).The number of regular television viewers increased in all age groups from 1970 to 1985 (see table 5), although transmission of soap operas, in combination with increased employment of men, at the beginning of the 1990s has slightly influenced the gender composition of the audience in favour of women.

In 1991, 25% of TV viewers were interested in entertainment programs, 25% preferred cultural-educational programs and entertainment shows; 21% watched

Table 1
Telephone penetration, Russia, 1980–90

	Telephones (million)	Phones per 100 families	
		Urban	Rural
1980	13.5	18.1	5.3
1985	17.6	24.5	8.2
1990	23.4	35.7	13.9

Source: [176], p. 209.

Table 2
Distribution of televisions, radios, and tape recorders, Russia, 1960–91 (per 100 families)

	Total population			Urban			Rural		
	TV	Radio	Tape recorder	TV	Radio	Tape recorder	TV	Radio	Tape recorder
1960	27	53	–	–	–	–	–	–	–
1970	52	74	86	48	81	22	9	50	–
1975	79	86	18	87	99	23	56	59	8
1980	91	92	28	96	105	40	71	70	16
1985	113	101	40	113	111	47	80	75	22
1990	121	100	59	122	110	65	88	73	36
1991	122	100	122	111	65	89	74	37	–

Source: [171], pp. 187–9; [176], p. 210.

Table 3
Proportion of population receiving television channels, Russia, 1980–92 (%)

	Number of channels:			
	0	1	2	3+
1980	13.4	22.9	46.9	16.8
1985	7.3	13.8	61.2	17.7
1990	2.1	4.0	57.5	36.4
1991	1.6	3.2	50.7	44.5
1992	1.3	3.0	45.9	49.8

Source: [285b], p. 36.

Table 4

Duration and frequency of use of different media by the populations of Pskov (1965) and Kertch (1982)

	Men				Women			
	1965		1982		1965		1982	
	Min.	%	Min.	%	Min.	%	Min.	%
Total media use	123.0	100.0	156.0	100.0	7.4	100.0	99.0	100.0
Watching TV	45.8	37.0	95.8	60.0	26.4	35.0	76.0	76.0
Listening to radio	11.7	9.0	0.8	4.0	8.4	11.0	0.5	1.0
Reading newspapers	23.9	19.0	18.9	11.0	9.5	13.0	4.2	4.0
Reading magazines	6.0	5.0	20.4	12.0	4.7	6.0	1.4	1.0
Reading books	35.7	30.0	20.4	12.0	25.0	34.0	17.3	18.0

Estimated from: [210], p. 189.

Table 5

Proportion of regular television viewers by age group (%)

	1970	1980	1987
18–19	71	80	89
20–24	71	88	80
25–29	74	82	82
30–39	81	89	87
40–49	83	82	83
50–59	76	79	88
60 and over	59	78	85

Source: [249], p. 259.

public affairs; 16% preferred news shows and folk arts; 13% watched theatre performances and movies ([200]).

For many years before perestroika, circulation of newspapers and magazines had very little link to real demand and reflected the state ideology. Party members were obliged to subscribe to a number of All-Union publications that were under cpsu direction. Subscription to some journals, magazines, and newspapers was restricted because of limited circulation, which made these publications difficult to obtain. It was necessary, in many cases, to subscribe to ideologically approved editions in order to get access to the popular publications. It was only in 1988, with abolition of such subscription restrictions, that the real demand for certain publications became evident and was satisfied.

Newspapers were the mainstay of news for many years. From 1960 to the 1990s total newspaper circulation increased by 360%, and the number of newspapers publishing increased by 107%.

At first glance, the variety of registered newspapers and magazines increased insignificantly over the period (see tables 6 and 7). It should be remembered, however, that a considerable number of periodicals published by plants, collective farms, and state departments ended publication because of the transition to the market economy. At the same time, daily and weekly newspapers and magazines began reflecting various nonprofessional interests (politics, hobbies, and so on) began to appear. In the mid-1990s, circulation of periodicals dropped, but many newspapers and magazines carrying advertisements were delivered to residences in large centres.

Over 30 years, the number of journals, mainly on scientific and professional topics, increased by a factor of 4.4 (see table 7). Unlimited access to magazines, which in turn made their survival dependent on readership, resulted in major changes in circulation of magazines with various ideological orientations. In general, demand for magazines (mainly those on literature and politics) had increased by 50 million copies by 1990, when circulation peaked at 125% that of 1980. Due to regular exchanges among readers, there were several readers per magazine copy. After 1990, there was a sharp drop of almost 30% in subscriptions and reading activity, and this decline continued in the following years. By 1992, the 15 leading newspapers had lost 18 million readers and popular magazines had lost 7 million readers; the readership of 6 weeklies declined by 350%. This drop was due to two factors. First, there had been an excessive burst of attention to social and political life in the previous several years, and this had fallen back to a more normal level. Second, subscription prices for daily newspapers increased by a factor of 26.5 in 1993 compared with 1992, and by a factor of 90 compared with 1990, causing a drop in circulation to about one third of its 1992 level. This trend strengthened in 1995. The number of different scientific journals, once considerable, dropped, and others cut back to one issue a year, rather than several.

Book publishing (as measured by circulation) more than doubled from 1950 to 1990, and the number of titles almost doubled (although there were many repetitions among these titles because of re-issues; see table 8). This exhibits a relative decline in the diversity of book publishing.

There was a book boom in the 1960s and early 1970s. In 1985, 8 out of 10 urban families and one half of rural familes had collections of books in the home; the average number of books was 3.5 times less among rural families ([334]). A 1988 survey revealed that only 10% of families did not have a private book collection at

Table 6
Newspaper publishing, 1950–93

	Number of titles	Circulation per issue for all titles (000)	Annual circulation of all issues of all titles (billion)
1950	5,021	2,545	15.1
1960	4,474	45,629	10.1
1970	4,445	93,715	21.1
1980	4,413	119,574	29.1
1990	4,808	165,546	34.4
1991	4,863	160,224	32.8
1992	4,837	144,044	29.8
1993	4,650	82,201	18.5

Source: [215], p. 90.

Table 7
Magazine and journal publishing, 1950–93

	Number of titles	Number of issues printed	Annual circulation (000)
1950	295	3,470	123,219
1960	600	6,731	501,980
1970	788	8,729	1,683,854
1980	954	10,291	2,025,725
1990	1,140	11,332	2,687,102
1991	1,301	10,434	1,483,674
1992	1,287	8,332	713,958
1993	1,385	8,779	290,429

Source: [215], p. 81.

Table 8
Book publishing, 1940–93

	1940	1950	1960	1970	1980	1990	1992	1993
Total number of titles	32,545	28,486	48,940	50,040	49,563	41,234	28,716	29,017
Circulation (000)	353,505	646,798	990,228	1,005,785	1,393,227	1,553,096	1,312,964	949,860
Number of books per person	–	633	827	771	1.004	1,047	833	640

Source: [215], p. 6.

home. In 1987, urban families had an average of 325 books at home ([120]). From 1970 to 1980, there was a book shortage, and a considerable proportion of the population took part in informal book exchanges. As well, there were long queues for popular books in the public libraries, and a black market in books was born and flourished.

When publishing houses became independent in the late 1980s, the market became saturated with best-sellers.

Reading habits have changed considerably. Reading as an activity was constant until the mid-1980s, when it started to decline rapidly. In 1965, men spent 24.5% of their leisure time reading newspapers and magazines, while they spent 25% of their time on this activity in 1985; for women, the figures were 19% and 17%, respectively. The latter prefer reading books, especially fiction ([43]).

It should always be remembered that ideological censorship existed until the late 1980s, and there was a widespread opinion that the population of the USSR was the most literate in the world. Censors primarily determined the content of the mass media, as well as access (the opportunity to subscribe) to some newspapers and magazines. Thus, we cannot determine true readerhsip of the print media through circulation figures.

However, public interest in the print media picked up twice during the period under study: in the mid-1960s and late 1980s, and it concerned mainly publications dealing with social and political problems. This was connected with rapid changes in the social and political situations during both periods and the weakening (in the 1960s) and abolition (in the 1980s) of censorship. The number of publications was growing during this period, and, for the first time, more rapidly among magazines than newspapers. In the 1990s, though, there was a rapid decline.

In general, reading magazines did not play an important role in consumption of information; however, in nineteenth-century Russia, substantial literary and political-commentary magazines with ideological orientations played a special role in intellectual life. Though all print media were supervised by the Party in the Soviet period, some differences could still be discerned, and these were responsible for the popularity of different publications. One example of this was in the 1960s, when numerous liberal-democratic forces rallied around the literary/politic-commentary magazine *Novy mir*. Similar phenomena occurred in the late 1980s, when a subscription to this or that magazine or newspaper was essential and sometimes was the only means by which the electorate could obtain accurate information on candidates for the Supreme Soviet of the USSR in 1989 and of the Russian Federation in 1990.

The transition to a market economy, changes in life styles, abolition of censorship, and the impoverishment of much of the intelligentsia created a situation in which the "fourth power" – mainly the print media – having accomplished one of the greatest revolutions in the century, was transformed into a marginal market with a weakly developed infrastructure and a low profit level, with an over-supply of semi-professional personnel infused with nostalgia for their lost power.

In the mid-1990s, the media accumulated considerable wealth from advertising, which was controlled by criminal influences.

I.A.Boutenko

13.3 Health and Beauty Care

The typical state paternalistic patterns in social life that led to an indifferent attitude to personal health from the 1960s to the 1980s gave way, in the 1990s, to a more personal concern with fitness. A number of national health standards fell with the transition to a market economy. Choice of health-care services grew and became more differentiated. A market for beauty and fitness services, new to Russians, was emerging.

Soviet society viewed health as social property, and so health care was seen as a state, rather than a personal, problem. Mottos like "Keep fit for the Army" appealed to citizens to stay in shape for community work, with free health service in exchange. Workers on sick leave were entitled to 80–100% of their wages, while the time of temporary disability had very little effect on their career or vocational status. Neglect of health and a disregard for life itself accounted for a lack of fitness and safety precautions. Inadequate industrial safety and bad habits brought life expectancy down, especially among males, and deteriorated the nation's health.

The social and economic reforms of the 1980s and 1990s gradually changed public attitudes toward health and personal appearance, especially among such elite groups as private entrepreneurs, financiers, political activists and also among young women ([49]).

With the social and economic changes of the 1990s, health problems came to the forefront and part of the population became interested in a new range of services in fitness and recreation. Alternative folk medicine, witchcraft, and extrasensorial and other kinds of healers acquired a status alongside established medicine. Bio-energy methods and shamanism became widespread treatments, available in clinics, at public sessions and in television programs. A questionnaire administered by the author of this section revealed that these methods owed their attractiveness to profoundly sceptical attitudes toward established medicine, and to promises of results that were instantaneous and required little effort, as evidenced in an advertisement with the tag line, "Cure alcoholism in one day!"

In the mid-1990s, physical exercise remained neglected in Russia. According to many surveys, 70% of the population did not play any sports, and 50% to 80% of those in the 11–17 age bracket did not get sufficient physical exercise; the same could be said for high-school students. Sports as an active pursuit (as opposed to a spectator sport) ranged from fourth to eleventh on the scale of leisure activities among these groups, depending on future occupation ([310]).

Opportunities for physical self-improvement grew spectacularly in terms of quality and quantity—but only in urban settlements, with their new beauty parlours, massage rooms, and bodybuilding and fitness clubs. For the most part, these facilities were not officially registered, so statistics (see table 1) are not completely reliable.

In the mid-1980s, a trend started toward reducing the amount and nutritive value in food. A great number of books on curative diets were circulated unofficially via informal associations. All of these associations were later granted official status. A popular joke of the 1980s ironically described the situation: "A Soviet woman has two problems: to find food and to lose weight."

Up to the 1990s, Russians have kept to their habitual diet, which oversteps World Health Organization recommendations by 200 kilocalories and 10% of fat per day. Skyrocketing prices reduced consumption of milk, meat, fish, vegetables, and fruit (the latter having always comprised a small part of the diet anyway), and bread and potatoes became the staples of an average diet, whose daily nutritive value dropped 300 kilocalories, falling below the medical norm in 1992 (see table 2).

Table 1
Barber and hairdresser revenues (current prices, million roubles), 1980–89

	1980	1985	1989
Rural population	26	38	51
Total population	382	514	634

Source: [175], pp. 214, 215.

Table 2
Average daily diet: composition and nutritive value, Russia, 1989–92

	1989	1991	1992
Proteins, gr	81.8	76.9	71.8
Fats, gr	96.7	87.9	79.1
Vegetable fats, gr	21.0	20.5	20.6
Carbohydrates, gr	346.2	329.5	323.4
Daily nutritive value, kcal	2,599.0	2,433.0	2,305.0
Vitamin C, mg	41.0	39.0	38.0

Source: [115], p. 26.

In 1993, 37–41% of respondents said that their family diet had not changed, while 51–57% reported a deterioration (342h). Only a few well-to-do people think about the ecological appropriateness of what they eat.

High evaluations of personal health went hand in hand with a deplorable real situation. The awareness of lower longevity and higher morbidity did not cure bad personal habits. Habitual smokers accounted for over a half of the male population; in Russian cities, between 27% and 59% of boys and between 11% and 36% of girls below the age of 14 have begun to smoke (116). According to surveys, many smokers, drinkers, and drug addicts knew that their habits were destructive, according to surveys ([116]). In a VCIOM poll, half of the respondents said that they were satisfied with their health; 31% said that they were not very satisfied with their health; and 15% said that they were not at all satisfied ([342i]).

I.M. Bykhovskaya

13.4 Time Use

In spite of increasing numbers of days off and holidays, total work load remained constant or even grew for some parts of the population, because of the increased amount of time spent on housekeeping. Less time was spent on education and retraining. Differences in time use between urban and rural dwellers and males and females were maintained.

The official work week shrank throughout the period under study. Between 1960 and 1990 the duration of the work week changed repeatedly. In 1956–60, the work day was established at six to seven hours in a six-day week. In 1966, most enterprises moved to a five-day, 41-hour work week. As a consequence, there were 32.3 fewer work days in 1970 than in 1965. Between 1955 and 1970, the work day was reduced to 7.2 hours ([151]), at which level it remained stable for a number of years (see table 1).

Since the early 1960s, part-time work became more widespread. From 1972 to 1980, there was some reduction in work time, particularly in the service sector, where most women were employed. Taking into account the shorter work day before holidays and holidays in addition to usual days off, the average duration of the work week in the industrial sector comprised 39.8 hours, while that for the total economy (including shorter work days for teachers, medical personnel, and others) was 39.2 hours ([177]).

Work time for urban dwellers was constant since 1963, consisting of one fourth of the daily time-budget (see table 2). A decrease in work load from 1975 to 1986, at least for rural populations in the winter (see table 3), is also evident. According to the Central Statistics Committee, work time dropped for all employees, especially males, between 1985 and 1990.

The use of work time itself was ineffective as a result of poor organization of labour and production. As a result, 1.7 work days per worker per year in 1980, 1.06 in 1985, and 1.2 in 1989 were spent idle ([177]). The difference between real and total working time was 12.4% in 1960 and 14% in 1970; in the latter year, this meant that industrial workers had a 42-hour work week and collective farmers had a 50-hour work week ([289]). These figures exceeded the legislative norm (40 hours per week), but this fact was ignored because of the exigencies of production and the ideological thesis about conserving the desirability of reducing the gap between towns and villages.

As a result of poor work organization, a need for overtime work emerged. From 1965 to 1972 overtime work per industrial worker increased by a factor of 1.6. This figure exceeded the overtime load set in a labour code by factor of 4.2 ([14]).

Paid absence from work increased constantly from the mid-1950s: a major rise in absences was noted in 1990 in connection with the new phenomenon of strikes (see table 4).

In the mid-1980s, office workers were the most likely to be disrupted from their regular job by ad hoc mobilization for short-term labour priorities (see table 4): in 1985, this loss amounted to 2.2 days per worker; in 1989, 1.4 days. This was equivalent to 300,000 person-days of work lost annually ([175]). This practice ended in the 1990s.

Table 1
Average duration of work week for adult workers, Russia, 1955–87 (hours)

1955	1979	1983	1987
47.8	40.6	40.7	40.7

Source: [177], p. 57.

Table 2
Structure of time use for workers in large cities, 1963–90 (%)

	1963	1977	1986	1988	1990
Work	24.0	25.4	25.5	24.8	25.5
Work-related activities	5.4	2.3	4.5	5.5	3.9
Housekeeping	15.4	14.3	12.3	15.6	14.2
Rotal work load	44.8	42.1	42.3	45.9	43.6
Satisfaction of physiological needs	38.6	39.2	36.8	34.4	38.2
Leisure activities	14.8	16.0	20.0	19.7	18.2
Other	0.8	2.8	0.9	–	–

Source: [212], p. 6.

Table 3
Structure of time use for agricultural workers 1975, 1986 (%)

	Summer				Winter			
	Men		Women		Men		Women	
	1975	1986	1975	1986	1975	1986	1975	1986
Work in state (collective) enterprises	58.2	52.2	47.8	46.1	62.6	68.8	48.4	44.0
Work-related activities	3.6	4.9	5.1	4.8	4.1	4.0	5.1	7.5
Home labour	3.6	3.3	23.3	25.5	4.4	2.7	18.4	23.0
Work in private kitchen garden	8.9	11.4	11.3	8.7	10.6	19.4	22.3	29.1
Child care	1.4	2.4	4.1	3.0	1.0	1.0	2.7	2.4
Total work load (child care included)	75.7	77.2	91.6	86.7	82.3	94.8	96.5	105.8
Satisfaction of physiological needs	69.1	65.9	61.1	65.0	63.5	56.0	57.1	52.0
Free time	23.1	27.5	14.8	14.2	20.9	16.4	12.9	9.1

Source: [14] p. 72.

248   Lifestyle

Table 4
Disruption of urban workers from their main professional activity for compulsory short-term labour
activities, 1985–89 (%)

Activity	1985	1986	1987	1988	1989
Agricultural work	49.8	48.5	50.1	44.1	40.5
Vegetable storage	5.9	5.4	5.5	3.6	
Construction	15.9	17.2	16.2	17.7	18.0
Work in pioneer camps	4.3	4.4	4.8	6.0	6.6
Amateur theatre, sports	1.0	1.0	0.8	0.9	1.2
Conferences and seminars, service sector	1.3	1.2	1.2	1.5	1.8
Attendance at military agencies, court, etc.	9.5	9.5	10.4	13.3	14.6
Municipal militia	4.0	4.5	2.1	0.9	1.2
Other	8.3	8.3	8.9	10.9	12.5

Sources: [175], p. 125; [177], p. 88.

Up to the end of 1980s the deepening of the economic crisis resulted in a great number of state enterprises imposing work stoppages; workers in these enterprises were forced to accept a shorter work day or week and to take unpaid vacations.

Holding down a second job was subject to numerous restrictions, which were abolished in late 1980s. In 1982, 2% of those employed practised job-sharing; in 1988, 2.2% did so. ([181]). According to official statistics, in 1989 second jobs accounted for 0.3% of vacation time for both urban and rural dwellers; in 1990, it account for an average 0.3% for urban dwellers. In 1992, 12.6% of workers had a second job ([111b]). In reality, this number is swollen due to informal employment. In 1992–93, many more people began to look for extra income and turned to employment services, but most of these occupations are carried out at the informal limits of the law because of legal loopholes. In 1995, many more people wanted and had such jobs.

The number of holidays and days off increased. Between 1950 and 1990, one official holiday was added to the calendar. But in 1991, the celebrating of holidays was changed, resulting in a real increase in holidays when a holiday coincided with the day off. The number of days off increased over the 40-year period by a factor of 1.6 (see table 5).

Time spent on labour, travelling to work, and meals at the work place decreased in the 1970s and 1980s by 2–6%, due mainly to improvements in the public transportation system ([13]). Time-budget surveys showed that the increase in time used by women for transportation to and from the work place – from a half-hour to three hours – led to 8.5 less time being spent child-rearing, 4 times less time

Table 5
Use of time over the calendar year by industrial workers, 1950–91 (average per worker, days)

	1950	1960	1970	1985	1989	1990	1991
Holidays and days off	15.2	16.2	25.9	26.5	21.8	27.9	28.7
Work days	75.0	79.8	64.9	62.4	65.4	67.5	60.3
Absences from work*	7.7	9.8	9.8	10.9	9.6	-	10.4
Work stoppages	0.1	0.2	0.2	0.2	0.2	0.2	0.2

Calculated from [171], p. 56; [177], p. 128.
* Since 1989, women's maternity leave has not been counted as absence.

spent watching television, 3 times less time spent reading, and half as much time spent on education and job training ([289]).

Time spent on child-rearing was insignificant: men began paying more attention to it, but still did it less then women. According to statistics, caring for and bringing up children had been included in the time for housekeeping and leisure time and began to be considered separately only recently. The trends in this field are estimated in different ways: time spent purely on this activity (usually connected with providing personal hygiene and nourishment) and time spent by working women who send their children to kindergartens at the age of 1.5 years. Moreover, in the 1960s and 1980s, a number of kindergartens were open 24 hours a day with a break for days off. In 1985, women devoted twice as much time to child care as did men; in 1990, they spent 1.6 times more; thus, time spent by women and by men on this activity tended to equalize. In quantitative terms, women spent 17 minutes a day on this activity; men spent 10 minutes ([175]). The general decrease in the birth rate kept this activity very insignificant in terms of time, even though fewer children have attended kindergartens since the end of 1980s.

Time spent on housekeeping is increasing. Time spent on shopping, cooking, cleaning, and caring for clothes has tended to increase throughout the period under study. Men's participation increased slightly until 1985 and then began declining.

Total work load (including housekeeping) is evaluated in various ways. According to some sources, it remained constant or even increased throughout the period under study ([59]). Other sources show that from 1960 to 1970, the work load of urban workers decreased by 3 to 3.7 hours a week, due to less time spent on kitchen gardens and housekeeping. For rural dwellers, time spent working in the kitchen-garden and other subsidiary work decreased by 2.5 hours a week for men and by 7 hours for women. On the average, however, the decline was small; for male industrial workers the total work load at the end of 1970s was 65 hours a week and for female industrial workers, it was about 80; for male collective farmers, it was 80 hours a week, and for female farmers it was 90 ([289]). In the mid-1980s, men's work load increased greatly in summer and decreased slightly in winter (see table 3).

According to other sources, the work load was constant in the 1960s and 1970s, while in 1980s there was a growth in total work load, mainly because more time was spent housekeeping. According to the State Statistics Committee, in general, the work load of men and women increased about equally from 1985 to the 1990s.

Men spent more time on satisfaction of physiological requirements (sleeping, eating, personal hygiene) than did women throughout the period under study. According to some sources, time spent on this activity from 1960 to 1975 declined for men and grew for women. According to other sources, it grew by 3 to 5 hours for both ([289]). Some research shows that from 1965 to 1986, it was constant for men and increased for working women by 2 hours a week ([211]).

Surveys show that among rural populations the increase in time spent satisfying physiological requirements and self-care in winter was insignificant and dropped considerably in summer (see table 3).

Education and retraining took up less and less time. This activity was compulsory for many years, and some additional time expenditures for retraining were included in work time (see table 5). Usually, it is considered in the structure of leisure time, which makes evaluation difficult. Adoption of the Law on Compulsory Secondary Education resulted in a reduction by a factor of four in attendance by workers at night school; the number of pupils dropped by a factor of 2.1 from 1970 to 1987. The number of workers who were retrained or trained for a different vocation increased by 220% from 1960 to the 1980s and then began declining, first bit by bit and then more quickly ([175]).

From 1965 to 1986, time spent by male workers on education decreased from 51 to 17 minutes per day; time spent by female workers on this activity decreased from 30 to 19 minutes per day ([212]). Since the mid-1980s, a number of short-term courses, including correspondence courses, have been made available, which would lead us to assume that more time has been spent on education during the most recent part of the period under study, at least for urban dwellers under 40.

Time spent on leisure is diminishing. In general, time-use studies are difficult to conduct due to the fact that a number of activities are realized simultaneously, such as television viewing and cooking, or cleaning and radio listening. The reduction in work time for some socio-demographic groups led not to a growth in leisure time, but mainly to an increase in time spent on housekeeping. The difference between men and women in amount of leisure time grew in the 1960s and 1970s, then decreased significantly up to 1986: in 1965 men had 63% more leisure than did women, while in 1986 this figure was 30% ([59]).

As men's housework was reduced by one hour their leisure time increased by 37 minutes; women's leisure time under these circumstances increased by 42 minutes ([289]).

Physical activities take up an extremely small part of leisure time.

Consumption of information via the media is growing. Collective farmers doubled to tripled their information consumption between 1961 and 1976. Between 1965 and 1986 men's consumption of information increased by 210%, while women's grew by 290%, mostly due to watching television and reading ([211]).

I.A.Boutenko

13.5 Daily Mobility

The slow increase in mobility was limited by the increase in the total work time (employment and housework) and unsatisfactory transportation conditions.

The mobility of the population increased slowly from 1965 to 1986 by 6 minutes a day ([59]), as cities and towns grew. Among the employed, travel to and from work was the predominant reason for mobility, with mobility time consistently higher among men than among women (see table 1).

Mobility not connected with work decreased from 1965 to 1986. Much of it was devoted to shopping and obtaining services (see tables 2 and 3). This was due to shortages of consumer goods and food, and an uneven supply of these commodities between cities, small towns, and villages. People who lived in the country and small towns were more frequently forced to travel to large cities to shop before the 1980s; this trend decreased noticeably in the 1990s, when market relations were introduced. This type of mobility was characteristic mainly of women.

Mobility connected with cultural interests and recreation decreased in the 1980s, but later it began to increase in some groups of the population. The growth in the total work time and the need to deploy more effort to make essential purchases shortened the amount of time spent on various forms of leisure outside the home (see table 4).

Price increases for tourist and excursion services and the drop in demand for them led to a sudden decrease in pleasure travel during the 1990s: in 1985, tourist and excursion services comprised 2.8% of all services; in 1990, they comprised 4.9%; in 1991, 3.8%; in 1992, they dropped to 49% of the 1991 volume ([171]; see tables 4

Table 1

Time taken to travel to and from work, Pskov, 1965, 1985 (minutes per day)

	1965	1986	Change
Men	48	60	+12
Women	42	50	+8

Source: [59], p. 77.

Table 2

Use of transportation time budget, Pskov, 1965–86 (per person per hour for 1 week)

	Total population			Working men			Working women		
	1965	1986	growth	1965	1986	growth	1965	1986	growth
Trips not connected with work	5.6	5.2	–0.4	5.6	4.6	–1.0	5.6	5.1	–0.5

Source: [59], p.12.

Table 3

Time spent on travel by workers and employees in industry and agriculture, 1985 (hours and minutes)

	Industry				Agriculture			
	Men		Women		Men		Women	
	Work day	Rest day	Work day	Rest day	Work day	Rest day	Work day	Rest day
Production (including travel to work, beginning and ending shifts)	1:51	–	1:38	–	0:58	–	0:51	–
Shopping and obtaining services	0:16	0:58	0:46	1:25	0:10	0:35	0:29	0:52
Shopping for food	0:10	0:44	0:32	1:00	0:07	0:26	0:20	0:38

Source: [280], pp. 261, 264.

Table 4

Time spent on out-of-home leisure, 1965, 1986 (per person per minute per day)

	1965	1986
Visits to cultural institutions and rest	4.9	1.4
Excursions, tourism	13.8	11.7

Source: [349], p. 72.

and 5). In the 1990s, a high degree of mobility appeared to be not only available, but also prestigious, for the most prosperous people.

On the other hand, as a result of an increase in the number of urban owners of kitchen gardens in the country (see table 6), the mobility of urban citizens increased considerably in the spring, summer, and autumn.

The load on public transportation increased. Public transit appeared to be the main means of transportation throughout the period under study, whether for work or for other needs (see table 7). Urban transit (subways, trolleys, trains) were used more and more intensively, taxis and buses being the exception (see tables 8, 9). The situation changed in 1991: as a result of the age of the vehicles and their heavy usage, the number of bus runs decreased by 12%; of tram runs, by 4%; and of trolleys, by 2% ([171]). In 1993, taxi services practically disappeared (as a result of privatization of car ownership); taxicab owners worked for organizations and firms but could not be hailed on the street. They returned to the streets in 1995.

Individual transport played an important role in everyday mobility for only a small number of urban dwellers. There are few car owners: in 1991 only 19% of families had their own cars. Car ownership is more common among rural dwellers (see table 10); in towns and cities many private cars are out of use in the winter. Gasoline sales increased (see table 11). In the 1990s, the number of private cars suddenly increased, related to increased imports of automobiles, especially second-hand ones, which made the population more mobile.

Table 5

Where industrial and office workers and collective farmers spend their days off in different seasons, 1985 (%)

| | Industrial/office workers | | | | Collective farmers | | | |
| | Men | | Women | | Men | | Women | |
	Summer	Winter	Summer	Winter	Summer	Winter	Summer	Winter
At home	50.9	78.5	55.9	80.2	88.8	92.8	90.8	93.6
Visiting relatives, friends	15.6	13.2	18.7	14.8	4.3	5.8	4.7	6.0
Weekend rest	0.3	0.2	0.5	0.3	–	–	–	–
Excursion, tourism	1.5	0.9	1.7	0.8	0.2	0.1	0.2	0.1
In country house	11.2	0.6	8.5	0.3	–	–	–	–
Hiking, fishing, mushroom picking	20.5	6.6	14.7	63.6	6.7	1.3	4.3	0.2

Source: [280], p. 189.

Table 6
Collective gardening and kitchen garden owners, 1980–91

	1980	1985	1990	1991
Citizens owning gardens (number of families, 000)	3,155	4,711	8,534	11,618
Citizens owning vegetable allotments (number of families, 000)	3,731	4,207	5,086	7,353

Source: [171], p. 461.

Table 7
Means of transportation used by workers in Pskov on their way to and from work, 1965, 1986 (%)

	1965	1986
Foot	62.6	47.6
Bicycle	1.0	0.1
Moped, motorcycle, scooter	1.2	0.2
Personal car	0.1	0.5
Public transport	34.1	41.5
Other, departmental transport included	0.9	10.1

Source: [60], p. 75.

Table 8
Passenger use of urban transport, 1980–91 (millions of persons)

	1980	1985	1990	1991
Bus	17,503	19,818	22,869	21,359
Taxi	684	680	557	526
Trolleybus	4,739	5,314	6,020	8,005
Tram	5,695	5,997	6,000	7,619
Subway	3,036	3,319	3,695	3,229

Source: [171], p. 555.

Table 9
Kilometres travelled on different types of public transport, 1980–91 (billions of passengers/km)

	1980	1985	1990	1991
Bus	209.7	240.3	262.2	250.7
Taxi	9.0	9.9	8.0	7.9
Trolleybus	16.2	18.1	20.5	27.3
Railway	227.3	246.3	274.4	254.7
Subway	29.4	36.7	41.0	35.6
Tram	18.1	19.1	19.1	24.2
Airplane	102.3	121.5	159.5	150.4
Inland water transport	5.3	5.1	4.8	3.7
Sea transport	1.0	0.9	0.6	0.5
Total	618.1	697.9	791.0	755.0

Source: [171], p. 555.

Table 10
Car ownership, 1970–93

	Per 100 families				Per 1,000 population				
	1970	1980	1986	1991	1970	1980	1986	1991	1993
In cities	2	10	14	19	6	30	45	62	–
In villages	2	9	16	26	4	29	53	67	–
Total	2	10	15	19	5	30	47	64	180

Source: [12d] (VCIOM polls); [171], p. 189; [177], p. 312.

Table 11
Gasoline sales to the public, 1980–86 (000 metric tonnes)

1980	1985	1986
1,441	1,539	2,103

Source: [177], p. 312.

I.A. Boutenko

13.6 Housework

Household work was becoming more time-consuming and increasing the total work load. The largest proportion of time was spent on meal preparation, cleaning and washing. Men and women still do an unequal amount of housework. The services network has an insignificant effect on this phenomenon.

Time expenditures on housework are increasing. The transition to a five-day work week in the mid-1960s and the development of services resulted in less time being spent on housework. Later, however, the reduction in the work week by an average of 2.5 hours was accompanied by an increase in time spent on housework of the same number of hours. This was possible in part because time spent on leisure and, for men, sleeping, was declining.

Since 1970, the time needed to satisfy basic needs increased, which resulted in changes to the structure of and increase in the total work load of the population. According to some acconts, in the 1970s, housework took up 180 billion person-hours annually. To carry out this work would have required about 100 million people – that is, the total number of employees in the USSR at the time ([20]).

Rural dwellers spent more on housework than did urban dwellers, but for both groups the amount of time spent increased (see tables 1, 2). Two thirds of all time spent on housekeeping fell on women's shoulders. In 1986, men performed 10.5 hours of housework per week, while women performed 22 hours ([59]).

The higher the educational level of an individual, the lower the value accorded to housework ([72]).

Housekeeping is done mostly by women. In urban settings, men do about one third the amount of housework as do women; in rural settings, the difference is even more significant: in 1985, the housework load of men comprised 12% of women's, and in 1990, it comprised 16.5%. Men gradually took on a greater number of housework duties, but they did a smaller share of these duties – much less than their share in the amount of services they consumed ([72]).

Cooking takes up the largest amount of time in housework. An overwhelming majority of meals in urban areas and an absolute majority of meals in rural areas are prepared at home. In the 1970s and 1980s, the amount of time spent on this activity increased because of difficulties obtaining food. Increased sales of food, modern conveniences, and a greater number of food shops and cafeterias turned out not to have a significant influence on time spent cooking. This was confirmed by the fact that more refrigerators than any other appliance were purchased (see table 3).

Table 1

Time use for housework and kitchen gardens by urban employees, men and women, 1986, 1990 (hours:minutes per day)

	Men				Women			
	1986		1990		1986		1990	
	Work day	Day off	Work day	Day off	Work day	Day off	Work day	Day off
Shopping and services	0:15	0:58	0:13	0:34	0:46	1:26	0:39	0:56
Housework	0:44	1:46	0:59	2:17	2:25	2:47	2:48	5:44
Kitchen garden	0:04	0:17	0:19	0:55	0:01	0:05	0:07	0:23
Total	0:59	2:44	1:12	2:51	3:11	6:13	3:27	6:40

Sources: [171], p. 132; [175], p. 275.

Table 2

Time use for housework and kitchen gardens by collective farmers, 1986, 1990 (hours:minutes per day)

	Men				Women			
	1986		1990		1986		1990	
	Work day	Day off	Work day	Day off	Work day	Day off	Work day	Day off
Shopping and services	0:07	0:24	0:06	0:14	0:32	0:48	0:28	0:33
Housework	0:38	1:41	1:18	2:50	3:17	5:35	3:41	6:43
Kitchen garden	0:18	1:30	1:32	2:23	0:10	0:50	1:05	1:39
Total	0:45	2:05	1:24	3:04	3:49	6:23	4:09	7:16

Sources: [171], p. 132; [175], p. 275.

Table 3

Electrical Household Appliances, 1965–91 (per 100 families)

			1980		1990		1991	
	1965	1970	Urban	Rural	Urban	Rural	Urban	Rural
Refrigerator	10	30	103	59	106	66	106	66
Washing machine	21	52	78	62	79	68	80	69
Vacuum cleaner	7	11	39	14	59	27	60	28

Sources: [171], p. 188; [175], p. 312.

For 30 years, house-cleaning took second place, after cooking, in time spent on housework, although this proportion has declined slightly. The significance of this activity did not change either with the proliferation of home appliances or with some improvements in living conditions: in 1989, more than one third of the population had a living space of 5 to 8 square metres per person; 20.7% had 9 to 10 square metres per person ([175]).

Men are more active in house-cleaning in urban areas than in rural areas; nevertheless, in 1985 men spent 52% of the time women spent on this activity; in 1990, they spent 25%.

With some decrease in time spent on house cleaning, time spent on taking care of clothes and footwear is increasing ([13]), connected mainly with the shortage of goods. This was the activity most exclusively carried out by women. The use of laundries and dry-cleaners remained steady and then declined by the mid-1990s, due to the higher cost of these services.

In other types of housework (kitchen gardening, repairs), men are much more active in performing minor repairs, particularly in rural areas, but their share in housekeeping is minimum (see tables 1, 2).

Time spent on the kitchen garden declined and then increased. Over the period under study, characterized by an increase in the number of urban owners of kitchen gardens for whom a certain proportion of production went to personal consumption, with the rest being sold, there was a trend toward less time spent on this activity, followed in the 1980s by an increase in time spent. The main reason for the increase was food shortages.

In 1977, 25% of all collective farmers' incomes consisted of profits from kitchen gardens; in 1979, this figure was 27%; in 1980, 20.5%. For urban dwellers, this activity took up 2.5% of time in 1980, and 2% in 1990 ([171]); for some urban dwellers, kitchen gardening was not only a means of sustenance but a form of leisure.

Shopping took up more and more time because of the increasing general shortages in the consumer sector and the spread of the rationing system; since 1990, this trend has weakened. In the 1960s and 1970s, the amount of time spent on shopping grew from 12% to 17% of total housework time for women ([269]); in 1986, this activity took up 20% of all household activity for women and 22% for men ([59]).

It should be noted that in the 1980s it was common for rural dwellers to travel to the city to shop because there were more supplies there, but this situation was not reflected in available statistical measures. According to available data, villagers did half only of their shopping in cities ([175]).

With the transition to a market economy, privatization of commerce, sharp changes in family incomes, and a growing number of shops and other retail outlets, the time spent shoppint dropped, especially in rural areas.

Some researchers found that in the late 1970s and early 1980s men spent more time shopping. In the 1990s this situation had changed and seemed to drop in parallel with changes in the contemporary neopatriarchal stereotype of the distribution of men's and women's roles, according to which men were seen as providing financial support to the family and women were seen as housekeepers.

In 1994, women were more inclined to buy goods at supermarkets and from acquaintances, while men shopped in private commercial stores ([321]).

The development of distribution networks and services lagged behind the population's needs. This situation began developing rapidly in the 1960s, particularly in urban areas; supermarkets, laundries, and cleaners were the primary services offered. However, despite this, the population's needs were not satisfied; the number of enterprises did not increase (see table 4), the assortment of services grew no broader, the quality was not perceived as high. There was a considerable variation in the degree of satisfaction of the population's needs according to the types of paid services (see table 5); about 70% consisted of repairing and cleaning, housing maintenance, and transportation services. There were no tourism, leisure, or health services, nor was demand for house repair and construction, transportation, or repair of electronic equipment satisfied. Of all complaints received by these service shops, 40% were due to the repair not being effected on time; 30%, by bad quality of service; 11%, by refusal to provide service. This is why, in spite of the fact that personal income grew by 17.2% from 1986 to 1988, expenditures on goods and services grew by only 12.3% over the period ([241]).

Expenditures on services up to the beginning of the 1990s took up an insignificant part of the budget among the overwhelming majority of families, and this is why differences in income level were not very important. As of 1990, however, the diversity of available services increased rapidly and the rise in their cost resulted in a drop in demand. In the mid-1990s, there was a large variety of services available, but accessible mostly to those with higher incomes.

Eating out was increasing slowly, but did not result in a decrease in time spent by women to prepare food. In spite of an increase in the number of cafeterias and the number of seats (the number of cafeterias per 100,000 people doubled from 1960 to 1970 and grew by a factor of 1.5 up to 1985), the number of people who ate at these establishments during their work day represented half of the adult population, rising from 64 million people in 1980 to 89 million in 1988 ([175]). In the 1990s, the combination of low quality of food served and high prices lessened the

Table 4
Numbers of Service Enterprises, 1970–93

	1970	1980	1985	1989	1990	1991	1992	1993
Number of enterprises	113	120	128	142	139	127	91	16
Change from previous period (%)	–	6.2	6.7	10.9	–3.8	–9.1	–39.5	–468.7

Sources: [111k]; [171], p. 195; [175], p. 333.

Table 5
Structure of paid services, 1985–91 (%)

	1985	1989	1990	1991
Domestic services	21.1	21.5	26.8	27.3
Public transit	34.2	30.2	29.0	33.4
Communications	6.7	6.2	6.4	6.6
Housing and maintenance	21.3	17.6	17.9	13.8
Tourism and travelling	3.8	5.4	4.9	3.9
Other	14.9	19.1	15.0	15.1

Source: [171], p. 195.

demand. Most people use cafeterias only for lunches during the work week; although the number of restaurants and cafés rose in the mid-1990s, there were still very few and most of them were accessible only to very well-to-do people. As well, many people avoid these establishments because they are known for harbouring criminal activities.

I.A. Boutenko

13.7 Forms of Erotic Expression

During the Soviet period, there existed underground eroticism alongside the underground economy; at the end of the 1980s, the former was legalized. Attitudes toward sexual contacts before marriage became more and more tolerant. Liberalization of sexual morals, emancipation from double standards, and little sex education led to an increasing number of early abortions and the transmutation of sex from being a principle part of the mystery of love to being, in many cases, a mere question of sexual techniques.

Before the mid-1980s, censorship, which was intolerant of eroticism, was being replaced by complete permissiveness; in the mid-1990s, attempts were made to control eroticism and pornography.

In the first years of its existence the Soviet state propagated a hypocritically virtuous attitude toward sex, limiting it exclusively to the reproductive function within the limits of monogamy. Repressive sexual morals and anti-sexual propaganda, vividly expressed in publications such as *The 12 Sexual Commandments of a Party Member* ([95]), made abstention and asceticism officially obligatory for literature, the arts, and everyday life. Under censorship, introduced in the 1930s, pictures of naked bodies and descriptions or hints of sexual acts were cut from books and, later, from films and TV programs. For example, in works of fiction words such as "breast" were stricken out and works by Arab poets addressed to boys were readdressed to girls when translated into Russian ([147]). Up to the end of the 1980s, those who made pornographic films available were prosecuted as criminals. Until the beginning of the 1990s, homosexual relations were also prosecuted as criminal.

The mid-1980s were characterized by a rapid withdrawal of various bans. For the first time sexual intercourse was shown in the Russian cinema at the end of the 1980s in the film "Little Vera." The notion of a "non-printed word" (in the Russian language a "non-printed word" is usually connected with description of genitals or the sexual act) disappeared. At the same time, nudism and sexual minorities were legalized; they began to publish newspapers and to demonstrate for their rights. However, public interest in these people, as well as in open discussion of sexual questions, quickly vanished.

After a long period of shortage of sources of information about sexuality, in the mid-1980s they became more and more varied and available. Up to the mid-1980s, the theme of sexual intercourse was practically prohibited. A school course called "Ethics and Psychology of Family Relations," introduced in the early 1980s, was limited to the exposition of the institution of marriage and child care, as opposed to sex education; children, teachers, and parents were disappointed and the course was quickly cancelled.

The long period during which there was a dearth of sexual information resulted in the appearance of a special adolescent literary tradition: for at least two generations of Soviet people, the works of the French writers Guy de Maupassant and Émile Zola, with their open description of sexuality and some elements of coitus, enjoyed enduring popularity. As well, young people regularly circulated among themselves homemade instructions and descriptions and some fiction about sexual relations. This represented another form of compensation for the lack of information, created by adolescents independently of adults. In 1988, 80% of female students in one pedagogical institute said that they had had an oppportunity to read illegally distributed manuscripts of an indecent, pornographic character; they first saw such literature when they were about 12 years old ([38]). It was a tradition for girls to keep diaries in which they wrote adolescent urban folk love poetry and speculated on their involvement in traditional courting rituals and practices. In these diaries, popular in the 1930s, 1950s and 1980s, special attention was paid to the romantic dimension of love ([41]).

In the 1990s, every second schoolchild mentioned television and the press as a main source of information about sexuality; 22% mentioned their schoolmates; 12% mentioned their parents ([160]). More than two thirds of parents never spoke to their children about sexuality. In the year before the poll carried out by VCIOM in 1992, 67% of girls and 77% of boys never asked questions about sex. In the mid-1990s, some attention was paid to sexual problems in families. This represented some progress: parents in fact discuss sex with their children four times more frequently than their own parents did with them ([160]).

People began their sexual life earlier and the difference in age at first sexual experience between men and women diminished. In the 1920s, men began their sexual life between the ages of 16 and 18, while women began later; as a main reason for sexual contact women noted love (46%), passing passion (30%), and curiosity (20%); men mentioned sexual need (54%); passing passion (28%), and curiosity (19%) ([68]). No studies were carried out from the 1930s to the 1950s; they started to be carried out again in the 1960s, and they revealed the gap between the age of men and of women at first sexual contact was diminishing. In the 1970s, the gap continued to diminish, and among students, boys overtook girls (see table 1). The same results were obtained in polls among Leningrad workers ([152]). In the 1990s, 15% of girls and 22% of boys admitted that they had sexual experience; among those younger than 14, 2% admitted this; among those 14 and 15 years old, 13% did, among those 16 and 17 years old, 36% did. Among sexually experienced adolescents, the proportion of boys is higher than that of girls in all age groups ([160]).

In the 1920s and 1930s, couples used not to register their marriage, but in the 1950s, the state began to control this side of life as well as all others. From the 1960s to the 1980s, it was difficult for unmarried couples to live together; until the 1990s, a single room in a hotel could be obtained only by those who had special indications in their passports showing that they were married to one another. As a result, weekend rest and convalescence homes became the most popular places for sexual adventures with new acquaintances. Sexual affairs, officially frowned upon, were regarded by part of the population as a type of sport or a form of protest against prevailing social conformity.

Table 1
Age at first sexual intercourse, Leningrad students, 1957–71 (%)

	1957		1964		1971	
	Men	Women	Men	Women	Men	Women
Under 16	7.0	1.0	10.3	1.7	11.7	3.7
16–18	22.0	8.0	42.2	12.8	37.8	20.9
19–21	30.0	40.0	32.8	50.4	38.8	54.5
22–24	31.0	34.0	13.1	27.3	11.7	19.0
Above 24	10.0	17.0	1.6	7.8	–	1.9

Source: [132], p. 171.

In the 1970s and 1980s, a wife could complain about her husband's behaviour to the secretary of the cpsu or to a trade-union chairperson at her husband's workplace and at a special meeting of communists or colleagues, where the problem of adultery could be discussed in public. In the 1990s, this side of life became an exclusively personal affair.

The attitude toward sexual cohabitation before marriage became more and more tolerant. In the 1920s, the question of free love was actively discussed; 85–95% of men and 48–62% of women had sexual relations before marriage. In the 1970s, there was a trend toward a convergence in the positions of men and women rearding cohabitation([69]; see table 2). At the same time, however, a double standard continued to exist. All respondents make different claims for men and for women (see table 3). When asked who was responsible for using contraception, teachers and doctors more often answered women than men (see table 4). Public opinion, especially men, was more tolerant toward men. Among women, the youngest are the most permissive (see table 5).

A revolution in attitudes toward sexual relations took place in the 1970s, carried out by the contemporary generations of 40-year old persons when they were young, but not for the youth of the 1990s, who see it as expected practice.

Young women were the most tolerant of sexual minorities ([39]).

The appraisals of women appeared to be changing more quickly. Love-making for the sake of intimacy became, to a considerable degree, independent of matrimonial plans. In the 1970s and 1980s, almost nine out of ten men and 95% of women considered it permissible to have sexual relations someone they loved; 56% of men and 11% of women felt that it was permissible to have sexual relations with someone they did not know ([69]). Over one third of respondents, boys and girls, felt that the main reason for their sexual relations was mutual love, 15.4% felt that it was pleasant pastime, 14.2% stated the wish to experience pleasure; 9.8% wanted emotional

Table 2
Attitudes of students toward sexual intercourse before marriage, 1965, 1972 (%)

	Total		Men		Women	
	1965	1972	1965	1972	1965	1972
Approve	45	47	53	51	38	42
Disapprove	22	14	16	11	27	18
No answer	33	39	–	–	–	–

Source: [69], p. 66.

Table 3
Opinion on permissibility of extra-marital sexual intercourse among men and women respondents, 1990 (%)

	Premarital contacts for women		Premarital contacts for men	
Opinion of:	Men	Women	Men	Women
Permissible with any pleasant partner	15	10	42	19
Permissible only with someone loved	35	43	25	40
Permissible only with future spouse	14	19	11	16
Never permissible	13	5	8	3
Difficulty answering	23	23	14	22

Source: [46], p. 78.

Table 4
Doctors' and teachers' responses to the question "Who is responsible for using contraception?" 1990 (%)

	Doctors	Teachers, skill upgrading	Teachers, district
Both partners	53	37	11
Man	–	15	18
Woman	7	15	28
Other replies*	28	22	31
Difficulty answering	12	11	28

Source: [46], p. 79.

* Among other replies, mention of the state and its organs – health services and educational institutions – prevailed.

Table 5
Attitudes toward premarital sexual relations, 1991 (%)

	Intolerable		Tolerable only with future spouse		Tolerable with any partner	
	For girls	For boys	For girls	For boys	For girls	For boys
Men	19	12	39	27	27	46
16–25 years	13	6	44	22	30	60
26–40 years	13	7	37	25	33	56
Women	30	22	33	29	29	29
16–25 years	8	13	35	19	48	64
26-40 years	20	22	33	29	22	35

Source: [39], p. 102.

interaction; 7% supposed that marriage would follow; 5.5% stated that curiosity was their motivation ([132]).

In the 1970s and 1980s, frequency of sexual intercourse with strangers increased, from 11% to 16%. According to polls, the level of emotional involvement of women decreased, leading to the spread of cool, often passing and pragmatic relations. From the point of view of men, on the countrary, the value of emotionality and intimacy increased ([69]). Up to the mid-1990s, sexual relations in general became more and more a mere mechanical act, simplifying the problem of sexual and gender identification and making it more relative in the context of the increased technical possibilities for sexual pleasure.

Liberalization of sexual morals, in the context of the absence of sexual education, resulted in several negative consequences, such as early pregnancy. In the town of Perm in 1981, for each 1,000 pregnancies among women who had not yet given birth, there were 272 abortions, 140 births out of wedlock, 271 born during the first month of marriage, 317 babies conceived in wedlock ([294]). From 1989 to 1994 the number of girls under 17 who had abortions more than doubled; the mortality of women connected with abortions at an early age reached 25–26%, a level at which it remained stable ([162d]).

Prohibition of pornography and of provision of sexual services was removed in the 1990s. Before that time, pornography was imported illegally. At the end of the 1980s, the first sex-shops were opened and erotic magazines for men and women began to be published. In the 1990s, newspapers began to carry a great number of advertisements offering different kinds of erotic massage, "leisure activities for men," and jobs for "beautiful girls without prejudices." If during the 1920s the majority of women who became prostitutes were forced to do so by hunger and extreme poverty, in the 1980s the reason was a desire for especially lucrative earnings ([69]). In 1991, over 5,000 prostitutes were registered by police 15% of them 12 and 13 years old ([145]). In the mid-1990s, there was an attempt to license different sexual services in an effort to contain criminal activity and maintain health standards.

Of male consumers of telephone-sex services (a dialogue on sexual themes) in 1993 in Moscow, 53% were under 25; 25% were aged from 25 to 30; and 4% were over 40; 65% requested the description of a sexual act. Reasons given for such telephone calls, starting with the most frequently stated, were the wish to relieve sexual tension; to realize an erotic fantasy; to satisfy curiosity. Other reasons mentioned were to overcome loneliness; to unburden oneself; for self-affirmation; to gain sexual experience ([104]).

In the 1990s, there was a rapid decline in public interest in moral problems connected with eroticism. In 1990, 31% of VCIOM respondents evaluating public morals stated that radical moral degradation had set in (most expressing this opinion were elderly people, women, chiefs of enterprises and institutions, cpsu members, and military personnel). More than one third felt that previously hidden immorality had come out in the open, while 21% felt that morals and manners had changed and that each generation had its own moral norms. In response to a question about the meaning of "degradation of public morals," 11% (13% of women and 8.5% of men) mentioned the spread of eroticism and pornography. The appearance of a naked body at the movies or on TV screens was seen negatively by 49% of respondents; among people younger than 30 only 14% felt this way and among those 60 years of age, 60% felt this way. Almost 30% of respondents (mainly the elderly and military personnel) felt that free discussions of sexual problems in popular newspapers and magazines negatively influenced public morals ([111a]).

I.A. Boutenko

13.8 Consumption of Psychotropic Substances

There was a distinct trend toward an increase and variety in use of psychotropic substances, and toward a penetration into younger age groups.

Beginning in the late 1980s, a general rise in anxiety level was evident in the population, where at least one-third of the adult population was living under emotionally stressful conditions. This indicator was on the rise, reaching 45% in more polluted regions. Another one-third of the Russian population lived under conditions of chronic stress ([223]); that is, about 70% of the population experienced the effects of persistent stress and anxiety.

Monitoring of stress revealed its main causes: lack of a feeling of security; anxiety caused by the widespread presence of criminal elements; low level of economic well-being; harmful ecological situation; fear of the future, tension both in family life and at work. Roughly one third of the adult population was in need of psychological assistance for treatment of stress.

Under these conditions, a trend toward an increasing variety of forms of addictive behaviour among growing numbers of people became obvious and increasingly understandable. The desire to alter one's mood through the use of certain substances or through diversion by immersion in an object or activity was manifested in wide use of tranquillizers, addiction to musical rhythms of a special kind (psychedelic music), and escape into the world of virtual reality (not to mention alcoholism, narcomania, and toxicomania).

These patterns of behaviour, provoked by conditions of psychological discomfort associated with breaking down of central values, marginalization, yearning for immediate solutions to problems, and so on, are becoming predominant in Russian society.

Tobacco smoking is a widespread attribute of the Russian way of life. Tobacco consumption is on the increase (see table 1) and there is no effective anti-smoking education. There was no sign of a decrease in smoking among adults: 50–65% of the men in large cities are regular smokers. Surveys conducted in Moscow in 1979, 1983, and 1987 among the population aged 20–69 years, showed how markedly stable this widespread habit was (see table 2): nearly 60% of men in this age group were smokers. Every fourth to fifth woman aged 20–39 smoked ([223]). Survey data obtained on the relationship between smoking and mortality over a long period (1977–89) are given in table 3.

In the 1980s, there was a clear indication of an increase in smoking among children and teenagers. In Moscow, 14% of boys 10–11 years old smoked; 35% of boys and 14% of girls 14–15 years old smoked. When they were 16–17 years old, 53% of boys and 28% of girls became smokers. Results of surveys conducted in other cities and towns showed that prevalence of smoking vacillates between 27% and 59% among boys and between 11% and 36% among girls ([223]).

Consumption of alcohol is a persistent and obligatory aspect of social life. It is part and parcel of social rituals, an attribute of official ceremonies, festive occasions, a prerequisite for "cultural" communications with friends, a means of escaping

Table 1
Production and consumption of tobacco products, 1960–90

	1960	1970	1980	1985	1990
Production:					
Cigarettes (billion)	126	172	181	179	151
Filter cigarettes (billion)	–	–	98	122	115
Loose tobacco (ton)	131	137	120	105	144
Consumption:					
Tobacco items (billion units)	55.5	208.0	248.5	249.3	245.8
Per capita (thousand)	–	–	1.8	1.7	1.7

Sources: [171, p. 183; [177], p. 172.

Table 2
Distribution of smokers by age and sex

	20–29	30–39	40–49	50–59	60–69	Total
Men	65	67	58	57	29	59
Women	21	27	13	7	4	15

Source: [223], p. 18.

Table 3
Death rate due to smoking, 1977–87 (per 1,000 male citizens)

	No risk factors	Smoking plus other factors	Smoking only
Cause:			
Various reasons	96	218	158
Heart disease	20	113	46
Cancer	53	–	80

Source: [116], p. 30.

personal problems. Russians are characterized as drinkers of hard liquor – in this case, vodka – as opposed to beer or wine. The features of this type of drinking are: 50% or more of total alcohol consumption involves hard liquor; existence of groups characterized by excessive use of alcohol and by asocial forms of behaviour caused by this abuse; drunkenness as a deliberate and conscious objective of alcohol consumption.

Increasingly, both the quantity and manner of alcohol consumption influenced social attributes such as age, gender, and occupation (see tables 4, 5, 6, and 7). One consequence of this is that alcohol consumption per se reflects only indirectly the extent of heavy drinking.

004BA E

Table 4
Moscow teenagers who do not consume alcohol (%)

	1987	1992
Boys	39.5	20.8
Girls	39.2	25.5

Source: [88], p. 72.

Table 5
Production and consumption of commercial and homemade liquor, 1981–91 (litres per of conventional alcohol per person per year)

	1981	1983	1985	1987	1989	1991
Commercial	10.7	16.6	9.1	4.2	5.6	6.3
Homemade production	3.0	3.5	4.1	6.5	6.2	6.3
Consumption	13.7	14.1	13.3	10.7	11.6	12.3

Source: [116], p. 40.

Table 6
Demographic characteristics of patients suffering from alcoholism (%)

	Aged 20–29 years	Women
1981	11.5	18.3
1992	18.7	14.3

Source: [195], p. 18.

A rise in the proportion of wine and beer consumed did not lead to a reduction in vodka consumption, but to an overall rise in volume consumed. Around one third of the adult male population and one tenth of the adult female population use alcohol immoderately.

It can be posited that there was a trend toward the lowering of the age of alcohol consumers. A survey conducted in a number of cities and towns of Russia showed that 8% of all teenagers drank alcohol, and among this group 17.1% consumed alcohol once a week or more often ([191]; see table 4). In the 1990s, the acuteness of the alcoholism problem in the both European and Asian parts of Russia was on the rise, spreading from south to north.

Public opinion on issues associated with alcohol consumption revealed contradictions in attitudes. On the one hand, an overwhelming majority of respondents considered alcoholism to be a great evil, but at the same time, this majority drank like everybody else. Approximately 50% of respondents would not want a non-drinking man or woman among their friends; 40% believed that alcohol

Table 7
Beer consumers by marital and professional status, 1993 (%)

	Number of litres per month			
	Less than 0.5	Less than 3	Less than 10	More than 10
Marital status:				
Married	17.0	15.7	5.2	2.0
Divorced	21.9	9.4	6.3	6.3
Single	7.7	7.7	5.1	0.0
Professional status:				
Executive	9.0	6.0	3.0	1.6
Businessperson	7.1	7.1	14.3	0.0
High-ranking employee	4.8	9.5	4.8	0.0
Medium-ranking employee	20.5	19.3	8.0	1.1
Militia member	26.3	10.5	0.0	0.0
Skilled worker	10.6	10.0	2.8	1.9
Unskilled worker	7.7	7.7	4.6	0.0
Peasant	5.1	6.4	0.0	2.6

Source: [216] (VCIOM poll).

consumption is not harmful if one knows one's limits; and 20% thought it normal for a drunk person to appear in public ([335]).

For a long period, drug addiction, as a social phenomenon, was thought to be nonexistent in Russia. In the 1990s, its prevalence in the life style in certain social groups became obvious. "Traditional" types of addiction were prevalent: consumption of cocaine, morphine, opium, hashish, and a wide spectrum of drug preparations were consumed with the aim of becoing intoxicated.

The number of persons registered as suffering from addiction induced by different intoxicating drugs was continually growing. From estimates, real numbers of addicts exceeded the figure obtained by official statistics by five- to tenfold. Both narcomania and toxicomania are prevalent in urban areas rather than rural ones (by as much as three times in 1990) ([191]).

The tendency for consumers of drugs and toxic substances to be younger is noticeable. In the 1990s, surveys of students aged 14–17 years showed that 10.2% of pupils tried narcotics at least once in their life and 9.8% took toxic substances ([61]). Prevalence of toxicomania among teenagers was 31.6 cases per 100,000, as compared to 4.5 cases among the population as a whole. Nearly 30% of those suffering from toxicomania were teenagers; 7% are children under 14 years old.

Knowledge about the consequences of drug consumption has considerably increased and remains at a high level, which, however, does not essentially affect the extent of the phenomenon. A considerable proportion of the those who consumed drugs expressed a negative judgment of their own addiction (over 66%), while 12.2% considered it extremely harmful ([61]).

According to sociological studies, the main motives behind the drug consumption are a desire for strong sensations, pleasurable experiences, and escape from a dull life. First experience with drugs, as studies showed, took place in the company of other people – an explanation given by over 77% of those polled.

I.M. Byhovskaya

14 Leisure

14.1 Amount and Use of Free Time

Free time of working people, particularly women, was decreasing. Throughout the period studied, there were significant differences in the amount of free time available to urban dwellers and rural dwellers. There was a temporary trend toward an increase in cultural activity. Television viewing became the main type of leisure, with a mainly recreational function.

In the last 30 years, net free time has increased by 3 hours a week due to a reduction in time spent at work, shorter workdays, more days off and holidays, and longer vacations. In the 1970s, the annual amount of free time reached and, for some groups, exceeded the annual amount of work time ([289]). The transition, in the mid-1960s, to the five-day work week, with two days off, markedly changed the type of use made of free days, which now comprised more than half of the free time available in a week.

Nevertheless, the amount of free time available to working men and women dropped because of an increase in total work load. The difference between the amount of free time for men and for women vacillated but never disappeared. In 1924, men had twice as much free time as women; in 1959, 1.5 times more. When work time was reduced by one hour per day in 1959–63, free time increased by 7%, but most of this accrued to men ([201]), whose free time rose from 3.5 to 4.8 hours a day, while women's free time rose from 2.8 to 3 hours. In 1965 men had 65% more free time than women; in 1985, 30% ([59]); in 1990, about 50% ([171]).

The differences in the amount of free time between urban and rural populations persisted until the mid-1990s. In the 1970s, industrial workers and employees had 4.6 hours of free time per week, technical specialists had 5.2 hours, and agricultural workers had 3.5 hours ([289]). From 1985 to 1990, free time for employed people on the whole dropped by more than one third: for urban men, by 18%; for urban women, by 33%; for rural men, by 37%; and for rural women, by 44% (see table 1).

Table 1
Use of free time according to sex, 1985, 1990 (per worker per day)

	1985				1990			
	Urban		Rural		Urban		Rural	
	Man	Woman	Man	Woman	Man	Woman	Man	Woman
Total free time (minutes)	275	187	267	148	227	126	169	83
Spent on:								
TV and radio (%)	48	47	44	61	51	46	59	61
Reading (%)	17	13	16	12	13	17	17	13
Movies, concerts, theatres, sports events	5	7	5	6	4	7	4	4
Walking and playing sports	13	13	5	6	7	8	6	3
Hobbies	2	3	10	2	2	1	3	2
Other	17	12	11	11	8	12	7	8

Source: [176], p. 226.

On the other hand, free time has been enriched due to a increasing variety and combinations of activities available outside of the work-place, such as listening to the radio while eating, conversing while doing housework, listening to a personal stereo system while travelling, and so on. The combination of free time with other types of activity tends to grow.

The main occupation of the overwhelming majority of the population in their leisure time has become watching television. From 1965 to 1985, time spent on this activity increased by a factor of 2.6–3. Initially, this was a result of increasing audiences and, after 1985, with growing duration of viewing time. In 1995, urban dwellers spent almost 50%, and rural dwellers spent more than 60%, of their free time watching TV; the figures were almost the same in 1990. Television viewing took up 20 times more time than that spent in cultural institutions ([59]).

Given the slightly greater amount of free time available to rural populations in the winter, time spent watching TV and on athletic and hobby activities increased among men ([14]), but insignificantly and temporarily.

Reading proved to be the most stable activity, in terms of the amount of free time spent on it, up to the 1990s. Women preferred reading fiction, while men read more magazines and newspapers ([42]).

The most popular leisure activities in the 1960s were reading books and newspapers, then watching TV, then sports and athletics, and, finally, just relaxing. From 1985 on, TV rose first place, ahead of reading, walking, and sports and athletic activities, in that order. Hence, the main location for spending leisure time was in one's flat: on workdays, 70–80% and on days off 50% of free time was spent there. The ability of the population to deploy their use of available free time creatively was developing extremely slowly ([349]).

Active leisure, on the increase until the 1970s (see table 2), later became marginal. From 1961 to 1976, with the growth in amount of free time, the rate of use of cultural activities, communication, and sports was rising and time spent on inactive leisure was declining. In the following years, however, there was an obvious trend toward passive leisure ([201]).

From 1961 to 1976, time spent on rest and entertainment increased, taking from 67% to 84% of men's free time and from 68% to 81% of women's free time. Between 1965 and 1985, men's leisure time increased by four hours a week, although the total amount of free time remained almost constant. This took place because of a sharp (4.2 hours) drop in time spent on education. For women, the decrease of time spent on education was 1.3 hours ([349]).

Leisure institutions (stadiums, sports clubs, beer parlours) were extremely rare and mainly oriented toward men. The ratio between leisure time spent publicly and individually was 1:21 for men and 1:30 for women, and this ratio did not change for many years ([59]). In the 1990s, nightclubs became popular among the very wealthy in large cities.

In 1980, individuals spent an average of 65 minutes per week at performances, films, sporting events, and concerts ([337]), and 16 minutes in 1985; in 1990, urban dwellers spent 11 minutes and rural dwellers spent 9 minutes ([176]).

Time spent on creative activities and hobbies throughout the period under study was almost insignificant; by 1990, almost no time was spent on these activities due to a general increase in total work load.

Table 2
Time spent on active leisure, 1963–71 (per worker per week, hours)

	1963		1968		1971	
	Man	Woman	Man	Woman	Man	Woman
Sports	0.7	0.5	1.4	0.7	3.3	2.3
Hobbies	-	-	1.5	1.0	2.3	3.4
Other	32.0	20.0	33.5	14.0	35.8	29.8
Free time	32.7	20.5	36.4	15.8	41.4	35.5

Source: [33], p. 102.

I.A. Boutenko

14.2 Vacations

The duration of annual paid vacations increased up to 1989 and then decreased. Most of the population continued to spend vacations at home. In the 1970s and 1980s, this was connected with a lack of institutions and inconvenient transportation; in the 1990s, with a shortage of money. However, more people are travelling abroad.

Vacations became longer. After the mid-1960s, the minimum duration of an annual paid vacation was 15 work days. More then 80% of workers and employees (practically all of whom worked for state enterprises till the end of 1980s) had longer vacations. In the past 30 years, the average length of vacation increased from 20.3 to 22.8 work days (including Saturdays) a year (see table 1). Until the 1980s, these vacations turned out to be 2–3 days shorter in reality, mainly due to money compensation received upon the occasion of changing job, for unused vacation time. Workers and employees younger than 18 were given a one-month annual vacation.

In addition to annual vacations from state enterprises, there were other types of paid vacations: for studying or medical treatment, to compensate for overtime, and maternity leaves. In 1956, the length of paid maternity leave increased from 77 to 112 days. In 1981 a partly paid one-year leave for baby-care was introduced.

Table 1
Length of vacation for workers and employees, 1964–87 (%)

	1964	1968	1977	1983	1987
Length of vacation (days):					
12	34.8	–	–	–	–
15	11.8	39.0	30.1	22.5	17.6
16–17	–	0.5	0.9	4.5	3.4
18	13.5	16.3	17.8	17.5	20.8
19–20	–	0.2	0.6	0.9	1.1
21	5.1	5.1	5.1	5.4	5.5
22–23	–	0.4	0.4	0.6	0.8
24	20.4	23.3	28.2	30.4	31.0
Above 24	19.5	21.1	21.9	22.2	22.9
Average	20.3	21.9	22.5	22.6	22.8

Source: [175], p. 275.

The development of market relations did not change the existing legislative privileges, but the real duration of vacations decreased. In 1987, some urban and rural dwellers had to work during their vacation longer than they had intended in order to obtain additional income (see table 2); in 1995, the number of people working during their vacation increased considerably.

Most people regularly spent their vacations and holidays at home or visiting relatives (78% of workers and employees and 91% of collective farmers). Some urban dwellers also own a summer house with garden in the country. From 1985 to 1992, the number of people who own a plot of land for gardening and kitchen-gardening increased by a factor of 2.8 ([171]). Traditionally, a considerable number of urban families, particularly those with children, spent most of the summer in the country living in their own, their parents', or rented dwellings. Construction of summer houses stopped almost completely in the 1970s and 1980s, and was revived in 1990s, but creation of gardening co-operatives with summer houses increased constantly.

Another traditional vacation type among urban dwellers is visiting (usually with children) to relatives – mostly older – in the country. In the 1990s, the situation had not changed significantly: almost one third of urban dwellers spent their vacations this way.

Over a 30-year period, passes to convalescent homes and resort hotels were nearly unattainable for many working people: from 1960 to the 1980s due to a shortage of places; in the 1990s mainly due to high prices. This situation led some people to take vacation trips abroad, which were not cheaper but were much more comfortable. Only 35% of the demand among urban dwellers for resort hotels and rental apartments at beach resorts was satisfied; only 10% of rural dwellers' demand for the possibility of a vacation away from home (not including visits to relatives and acquaintances and gardening) was satisfied. In 1986 and 1988, 27% of the population spent their vacations in resort hotels, camping, on tourist excursions, and in sanatoriums ([177]); 19.5% had recourse to health care in convalescent homes; 3.3% went on excursions lasting one or two days. In 1989, such types of vacations – sanatoriums, rest cure, tourist excursions – were available only to every sixth urban dweller and every tenth rural dweller among those who had expressed a desire for such a vacation (see table 2).

The main preoccupation of the state was the rest and treatment of individual workers. The growth in the number of convalescent homes and resort hotels and of the number of places in them fell substantially behind the demand for these services; in fact, since 1980, in fact, the number of these institutions decreased (see table 3). This situation led people to rent private houses and flats in the country, thus

Table 2
Desired and actual vacation destination, workers and families, 1989 (%)

	Workers and employees			Collective farmers		
	Desired	Actual	Actual to desired	Desired	Actual	Actual to desired
At home	7.0	47.3	487.0	32.1	81.3	253.6
At a convalescent home	13.4	3.4	25.0	15.0	2.5	16.6
At a resort hotel	9.5	3.3	35.0	9.6	0.7	7.3
At a family resort hotel	23.1	2.4	10.3	12.7	0.2	1.6
At summer cottage or gardening plot	2.7	5.2	192.0	20.2	0.3	150.0
Visiting relatives and acquaintances	13.3	30.2	227.0	15.1	9.9	65.6
Hiking	7.1	2.4	33.4	3.9	0.6	15.4
At beach resort	7.3	2.6	35.6	4.0	0.6	15.0
Other types of vacations	13.8	2.5	18.1	7.2	0.8	11.1
Extra work	0.1	0.7	700.0	0.2	3.1	1,550.0

Calculated from [175], p. 308.

Table 3
Number of convalescent homes and resort hotels, 1980–91

	1980	1985	1990	1991
Number of convalsecent homes	607	601	542	546
Places (000)	195	190	172	168
Number of organized camp sites	2,459	2,901	2,969	2,888
Places (000)	316	360	387	381
Number of campgrounds	514	490	497	465
Places (000)	208	221	255	185
Total establishments	6,572	7,263	7,431	7,356
Total places (000)	1,135	1,237	1,299	1,218

Source: [171], p. 298.

providing more individualized rest or vacation that was more affordable but much less comfortable. Unfortunately, statistics about this phenomenon are not available.

Demand for family vacations in specially created facilities (camp grunds, resort hotels) was unsatisfied in the mid-1990s. Opportunities for family vacations (rooms for couples, admission for children) grew only slightly faster than did opportunities to spend vacations in resorts and hotels (see table 4).

Table 4
Lodgings for couples and for families with children, 1986, 1989

	1986	1989
Lodgings for couples, places (000)	436	445
Lodgings for parents with children	833	1,839
Weekend rest institutions, places (000)	134	143

Source: [177], p. 420.

There were 21% fewer summer camps for schoolchildren in 1992 than in 1991, and the number of children convalescing declined by 30% (111h).

Recreation in resort hotels and health care were the most desirable types of vacation. Most urban dwellers and more than half of all rural dwellers preferred this type of vacation; the former preferred to stay in family rest organizations and the latter preferred to visit relatives and acquaintances. Accommodation in convalescent homes ranked second for both groups. Rural dwellers expressed a desire to spend their vacation away home three times less often than did urban dwellers, probably due to the fact that they were not able to leave their private farm plot (see table 2). There were no particular differences between men and women as to how they actually spent their vacation (see table 5).

Vacation mobility for most of the population, already low, decreased rapidly because of the social and economic changes going on in the country and border shifts from 1985 to the 1990s. On the other hand, the variety of geographic sites available for summer vacations expanded in the mid-1990s, as did opportunities to travel abroad.

Among the main reasons mentioned for dissatisfaction with organization of vacations were difficulties in getting accommodation passes, accommodation of families, lack of money, and the fact that family members' vacation time did not occur at the same time. According to one poll, 18% could not buy long-distance train tickets and 15% could not buy airline tickets in advance; according to a 1989 estimate, about 18 million people who had the money could not obtain airline tickets. Bus transportation is not well developed: more than half of rural settlements are not served by local buses, and three quarters are not served by intercity buses ([175]).

There was obvious unequal distribution of accommodation passes to working and non-working people (the latter as a rule had to pay full price, whereas the former had access to them at a discount in the workplace), and differences in distribution among working people. Work position affected both the price of the accommodation pass (for managers it was practically free of charge) and the location of the vacation (beachside for managers; suburban resort hotels for ordinary workers). The share

Table 5
Type of vacation for industrial workers and clerks, 1989

	At home	At a convalescent home, resort hotel or country home	On a tour	Hiking	Visiting relatives
Men:					
16–19 years	48.2	3.2	4.9	5.2	27.1
20–24 years	52.2	2.5	2.5	3.6	28.2
25–29 years	44.6	5.0	2.4	2.4	39.9
30–44 years	48.4	7.4	5.9	2.1	32.0
45–54 years	48.4	11.5	11.4	1.5	23.2
55–59 years	51.9	9.2	15.0	0.1	21.1
60 and over	53.5	13.9	17.6	0.3	13.9
total	48.4	7.5	6.8	2.2	29.9
Women:					
16–19 years	44.9	6.3	4.6	3.6	28.9
20–24 years	38.0	4.9	0.9	5.1	42.5
25–29 years	38.1	8.9	1.8	2.8	42.2
30–44 years	42.7	11.9	5.1	2.5	33.3
45–54 years	44.5	17.3	8.3	1.9	24.6
55–59 years	49.7	15.1	6.5	0.5	24.7
60 and more	48.5	16.9	8.5	-	24.3
Total	42.7	11.9	5.1	2.5	32.6

Source: [175], p. 309.

received from the social consumption funds was directly connected with an individual's position at the enterprise ([11]); in the 1990s, vacation patterns depended more on income level and on the the opportunity to travel abroad.

In the 1980s the population had more mobility for various short-distance excursions; this mobility decreased in the 1990s. On average, in 1989, 78.3% of the population took part in weekend excursions once a year, compared to 17% in 1970 ([175]). The absence of formerly available trade-union subsidies made this kind of vacation practically unaffordable for large strata of population in the 1990s.

The overwhelming majority of tourist trips before 1990 were within the USSR. They were not widely available due to the lack of hotel rooms, poor transportation, and so on. The number of hotels and motels for individual and group excursions and trips increased extremely slowly (see table 6). In the 1990s, the distinction between hotels for domestic and for foreign guests was abolished; many foreign corporations began constructing hotels; and, increasingly, flats were rented out to visitors. Due to all of these factors, the shortage was practically over.

Table 6
Hotels, motels, guest houses, and number of available places, 1980–87*

	1980	1985	1987
Number of hotels, motels, and guest houses	7,823	8,139	8,240
Available places (000)	544.4	583.1	769.0

Source: [75], p. 158.

* Foreign tourists were accommodated in special hotels, and are not included in these figures.

Foreign travel for vacations began in the 1960s, but it was extremely limited and available only to a very small group, as it was used to reward workers and was accompanied by numerous ideological tests. In 1987, 0.5% of the population travelled abroad; 834,000 people went to eastern Europe; 63,000 travelled to western Europe and other developed countries, and 23,000 people went to other countries. The number of foreign visitors to the USSR exceeded the number of Soviets going abroad: in 1987, 991,000 tourists from Eastern Europe, 1.1 million tourists from industrialized countries, and 25000 from other countries visited the USSR ([75]).

In the 1990s, the procedure for leaving the country become considerably easier and so-called shopping tourism became very popular. Business trips became widespread and travel destinations became more varied; trips were used not only for recreation and tourism, but also for in-service training, language training, and other aims connected with self-improvement and work.

The preferred means of transport for long trips were train and airplane. Travel by automobile was extremely limited because of bad roads and services and a lack of gas stations. By the 1990s, due to high prices for domestic flights, train service was preferred; the number of flights and travellers declined as prices rose sharply.

I.A. Boutenko

14.3 Athletics and Sports

After 1960, there was an obvious increase in the number of people engaged in different types of sports. This was a result of the construction of numerous stadiums and other sports venues from the 1960s to the 1980s and a more definite concern with physical fitness. Simultaneously, there was a growing practice of passive attendance at sports events and a decrease in outdoor activities. Since the end of 1980s, a social differentiation in the sports sphere and in types of physical leisure activities has been manifested.

There was an increase in the number of people regularly engaging in sports from the 1960s to the 1990s. However, there was a slow-down in this increase, as well as a decline in participation in sports clubs – that is, those who practised sport in institutional ways (see table 1). Before the mid-1980s, the main official indicator of what was going on in the sphere of sports was membership of different sport clubs and training groups. Frequently, the authories had manufactured nonexistent sports clubs and membership in them. It is feasible that since the end of 1980s there was not a new trend in participation in sports (a decrease in the number of people regularly engaging in sport) but more reliable statistics available.

According to other sources, there was an obvious trend toward declining participation in sports clubs in the 1980s, especially after 1985, though the decline in the number of clubs was not as noticeable. This trend was associated with the process of deinstitutionalization in different spheres and with the growing interest in more personalized forms of physical activity. The latter was compounded by commercialization of the recreational sphere and by greater financial difficulties faced by organizers of recreational activity in any institutional context ([19]; [49]).

Throughout the 1980s, participation in physical fitness activities was quite low. It varied, according to age group, from 6% to 87%, with an average of 30% ([310]). The number of the people engaged in different kinds of organized recreation decreased from 23.9 million to 10.1 million between 1983 and 1992. It should be noted that these figures include students, who were required to take part in sports once or twice a week ([116], 1994).

The number of males and females involved in sports differed greatly throughout the period under study: according to some surveys, men spent three times as much time participating in sports than did women ([309]). However, according to leisure-time budget surveys, active involvement in sports decreased slightly for both men

Table 1
Participation in sports, 1960–92

	1960	1970	1980	1985	1989	1992
Regularly engaged in sports						
(million)	27.7	31.7	37.4	45.5	45.8	43.2
Women	10.5	13.0	16.6	17.9	16.7	-
Number of sport clubs (000)	90.0	105.0	117.0	138.0	135.0	132.0
Sport-club members (% of adults)	24.0	26.0	-	19.0	6.7	6.8

Sources: [171], p. 413; [177], p. 537; [203], p. 118.

and women from 1987 to 1991, although time spent by women on individual types of athletics (aerobics, body building, self-defence) increased. In general, the level of interest in sports events (passive consumption of sports) constantly exceeded the level of active involvement ([203]).

An important factor governing involvment in sport activities and preferences for this or that type of sport is social position and profession. For example, among young people, students are the most avid participants in sport activities (aside from the forms of activity that are included in curricula); second come young workers, followed by intellectual workers. Among the latter, the aesthetic types of sports and the hedonistic orientation present in them are more popular, whereas among people with a low educational level and professional qualification the most popular activities are those associated with muscle development and gaining strength ([49], [309]).

The advent of the market economy brought with it a new prestige to certain kinds of new sports associated with organized facilities. Interest in some types of recreational activity was a reflection of new forms of social differentiation. Incomes influenced the variety of service and equipment and the location of participation (public sports field or elite tennis court, golf club, ski resort, etc.). This differentiation manifested itself also in terms of motivation: elite groups had a more hedonistic orientation toward physical recreation, while less well-to-do groups had a more pragmatic approach to staying fit and becoming stronger. In addiiton, the growth of social tensions and crime stimulated women to engage in the self-defence types of sports.

Up to the mid-1990s, amateur and professional sports were not distinguished in the statistical indicators because professional sports were not ideologically acknowledged.

Traditionally, the most popular types of organized sports were those that do not require any special equipment or infrastructure (see table 2). The existing system of sports and athletic facilities is characterized by low quality and quantity and chaotic deployment of sports facilities. According to statistical reports up to 1990, only 52% of the population's demand for gymnasiums and arenas was satisfied; 58% of demand for stadiums, tennis courts, skating rinks and other facilities was satisfied; and 16% of requests for indoor swimming pools and 5% of requests for outdoor swimming pools was satisfied.

The overall number of stadiums, gymnasiums, arenas, and swimming pools increased, as did other elements of the sports infrastructure (see table 3). However, after the end of 1980s a new trend became apparent following commercialization of sports institutions and infrastructure. On the one hand, many stadiums and other facilities have been transformed into commercial facilities; on the other hand, some of them became commercial clubs – expensive and elite.

Polls in the 1990s showed that many people feel that work in country gardens is the most valuable and useful way to send leisure time that presupposes physical activity.

Table 2
Participation in recreational activities (% of registered participants and/or sport-club members), 1965–90

	1965	1975	1985	1990
Basketball	7.4	8.2	11.0	9.4
Volleyball	16.0	12.5	11.9	11.6
Bicycling	2.3	2.1	1.3	0.5
Gorodki	0.9	0.6	0.4	0.4
Aerobics and athletics	–	–	5.4	5.9
Skating	2.8	–	0.6	0.5
Track and field, including running	14.3	12.9	9.7	7.8
Skiing	18.9	14.5	10.3	9.5
Orienteering	–	–	1.1	1.3
Swimming	6.2	7.3	5.1	4.2
Tabletennis	–	–	6.1	5.2
Football	11.7	16.3	11.2	10.9
Hockey	–	4.7	–	3.4
Chess	3.5	3.9	4.2	4.9

Sources: [116]; [203], p. 23; [310], p. 42.

Table 3
Sports and athletics infrastructure, 1960–92

	1960	1970	1980	1985	1990	1992
Stadiums	1,118	1,573	1,941	1,946	2,216	2,208
Gymnasiums and arenas	8,700	25,600	41,100	44,300	48,400	49,700
Swimming pools	289	378	793	1,302	2,059	2,194

Sources: [171, p. 414; [177], p. 537.

I.M. Bykhovskaya

14.4 Cultural Activities

Attendance at most cultural institutions dropped, partly as a result of the overall decrease in available leisure time in the 1980s and 1990s. There was a reduction in the number of cultural institutions and changes in their activities. The cultural activity of the population decreased: more than 60% spent their free time at home, a trend that intensified up to 1990.

Opportunities for cultural activities in towns and rural regions differed. At the beginning of 1988, 59 towns with a population of 100,000 to 150,000 did not have theatres, 42% of rural settlements had no cultural institutions at all; 56% of rural settlements, where 20% of the rural population lived, had no movie theatres. In 1985, 15 million people could not receive TV programs ([209]). Urban dwellers spent twice as much on theatre, movies, and museums as did rural dwellers, and the amount spent decreased gradually between 1975 and 1990 for both groups (see table 1). The economic crisis caused the closure of 1,162 cultural centres that had, collectively, a seating capacity of 145,000; three quarters of these were situated in the countryside. Because of lack of funds, 161 libraries for children, serving 540,700 readers, were closed in 1991–92 ([111h]). Under these circumstances, television and video became strong competitors for cultural centres, theatres, and libraries, many of which could not weather the changing financial situation and closed their doors, while some tried to find additional funding, experimented with new kinds of activities, sometimes putting commercial interests above social and cultural ends.

Movie attendance peaked in the 1970s and dropped abruptly in the 1990s. From 1960 to 1970, movie attendance increased by 23%, peaking in 1970, but from 1970 to 1975 it grew only by 5.8%. Attendance began dropping in 1975; by the 1990s it had declined to 29%. Average annual per capita movie attendance decreased from 22 to 9 visits from 1970 to the 1990s. Although they did not lose their interest in the cinema, most people had stopped going to the movies by 1993. The cinema network itself declined more gradually: from 1970 to 1975, the number of movie showings dropped by 6%; from 1985 to 1990, by 9% (see table 2).

Audience preference for foreign films was obvious: in 1990, 35% of movie goers preferred them, while 25% preferred Soviet productions, and 27% said that they had no preference with regard to films unknown to them ([221]).

Attendance at theatres and concerts gradually grew, peaking in 1985, but from 1985 to 1990 it declined by 23% in spite of the fact that the number of theatres

Table 1
Expenditures on books, newspapers, and performances, 1975–89 (%)

| | Urban dwellers | | Rural dwellers | |
	Books, newspapers	Films, theatre, museums	Books, newspapers	Films, theatre, museums
1975	0.5	0.8	0.4	0.4
1980	0.6	0.8	0.3	0.3
1985	0.8	0.7	0.4	0.2
1989	n/a	0.7	n/a	0.7

Calculated from [171], p. 216.

Table 2
Selected annual statistics on movies, 1960–91

	Number of screenings (000)	Attendance at theatres (million)	Average annual attendance per theatre (million)	Average per capita annual attendance
1960	64.3	2,279	35.4	19
1965	92.5	2,610	28.2	21
1970	96.7	2,804	29.0	21
1975	91.8	2,640	28.8	18
1980	87.8	2,430	27.7	18
1985	84.4	2,263	26.8	16
1990	77.2	1,609	20.8	11
1991	68.2	1,323	19.4	9

Source: [176], p. 219.

rose by 13% between 1985 and 1990. Almost 70% of the population did not attend theatres at all, so theatre audiences comprised a relatively stable group of theatre lovers. The rate of decrease in audiences exceeded the decrease in the number of performances, which was 15% between 1985 and 1990.

Concert audience started decreasing after 1978. Between 1978 and 1990, the number of listeners dropped by a factor of 1.5; the number of concerts almost halved. Average attendance per concert was lowest in 1978 then increased up to the 1990s (see table 3).

The number of visitors to museums remained relatively stable. Over all, museum attendance increased from 1960 to 1990. However, according to polls, for instance, in 1980 about 78% of the population had not been to a museum. The number of museum visits grew due to more assiduous visits by the same people who

Table 3
Selected statistics on theatre and concert organizations, 1966–93

	1966	1970	1978	1980	1985	1990	1993
Total number of theatres	292	302	319	324	333	375	427
Performances (000)	152.7	156.0	155.7	156.4	163.4	139.3	105.6
Total attendance (000)	62,220	64,921	66,224	66,710	69,658	53,310	41,212
Average audience per performance	423	415	426	426	426	383	390
Total number of concerts (000)	229.4	273.6	412.2	430.1	317.9	225.8	126.6
Total attendance (000)	81,046	93,385	99,881	95,131	89,774	66,785	37,471
Average audience per concert	358	341	242	221	282	296	295

Source: [345], p. 34.

attended museums more than once a year ([346]). Over a 30-year period, the network of museums grew by 180% (see table 4).

Library attendance peaked in 1985, then decreased abruptly by 20% from 1985 to 1991. Between 1965 and 1990, the average number of books per library increased by 93%, then decreased by 8% between 1990 and 1993. The network of libraries contracted by 50%. The proportion of the population that visited a library decreased from 57% in 1985 to 42% in 1993 (see table 5).

Reading books was one of the most important leisure-time activities throughout the period under study. In urban areas, 8 out of 10 families had home libraries; 50% of rural families also had books at home, but their collections were 3.5 times smaller than urban families' ([334]).

Information about readers' preferences showed that reading was considered a form of recreation, a kind of escape from everyday life. In the 1980s, almost half of adult Russians were in the habit of reading books more or less regularly: 19% read regularly, 25% read two or more books a month, 35% read one or two books a year, and 21% did not read at all.

A very small proportion of the population was interested in "serious literature." This interest increased in periods of social changes in the 1960s and mid-1980s, when the public's attention to social, political, and historical topics was at its peak. From the 1960s to the 1980s, these readers were interested mainly in military and rural topics: they were trying to discern lasting values (as opposed to the officially imposed ones) in certain books under censorship ([40]).

From 1960 to 1991, there were quantitative changes in amateur clubs and in organized creative activity. Growth in such activities was particularly noticeable from 1970 to 1975, when the number of participants in amateur art groups increased

Table 4
Selected statistics on museums, 1960–93

	Total number of museums and branches	Total visits (million)	Number of visits per 000	% of visitors to total population
1960	492	34.0	89.4	36.4
1965	494	49.0	98.2	38.1
1970	582	65.0	116.7	49.8
1975	646	82.0	130.0	60.9
1980	740	88.0	126.7	63.0
1985	964	104.0	107.9	72.4
1990	1,315	144.0	90.8	97.1
1991	1,379	114.4	83.0	77.0
1993	1,978	–	–	–

Source: [171], p. 49; [221], p. 49.

Table 5
Selected statistics on libraries and readers, 1965–93

	Number of libraries (000)	Number of books (000)	Number of readers per book	Number of members per library	% of readers to total population
1965	58,756	596,723	–	–	–
1970	60,140	729,593	–	–	–
1975	61,399	868,470	–	–	–
1980	61,536	981,677	78,100	1,269	56.1
1985	62,118	1,132,193	82,140	1,322	57.0
1990	62,234	1,153,705	71,900	1,155	48.4
1991	59,145	1,082,552	65,400	1,106	44.0
1993	56,985	1,060,638	61,754	1,084	41.6

Source: [171], p. 530; [220], p. 42.

by 27% and the number of groups themselves grew by 35%. By 1985, this trend had reversed itself: the number of club members dropped by 35% from 1985 to 1993, and the number of cultural interest groups dropped by 28%. The share of people in the overall population who participatied in amateur clubs declined from 1980 to 1991 from 4.8% to 3.0% (see table 6). Women are more active in the field of amateur art activities than men.

Table 6
Amateur clubs and participants, 1960–91

	Number of participants (000)	Number of clubs (000)	% of participants to total population
1960	2,660.7	168.5	2.2
1970	3,481.6	222.4	2.7
1975	4,421.8	299.5	3.2
1980	6,757.0	385.0	4.8
1985	6,757.6	395.8	4.7
1990	5,037.0	324.3	3.4
1991	4,397.8	284.1	3.0

Sources: [174], p. 23; [346], p. 18.

The ideological inspiration of the educational function of cultural institutions, and the centralization of forms and supervision of their activities that resulted from administrative pressure, brought about a drop in public interest. In addition, starting in the mid-1970s, opportunities to satisfy cultural aspirations at home began growing (improvements in living conditions, the spread of television, the perfection of video and audio equipment, and so on).

Changes in the political and economic context in the second half of 1980s resulted in changes in the sphere of culture, including a reduction in state subsidies, decentralization of finances and administration and increased operating expenses for cultural organizations. There were also considerable changes in life style of the working population, who were inclined to seek opportunities to earn additional income at the expense of free time. In the 1990s, this resulted in a situation in which most free time is spent on relaxation, as opposed to perusing cultural interest.

In 1992, according to VCIOM data, Russians read newspapers half as much as in 1990, and magazines one quarter as much ([342g]). These changes were paralleled by a drop in attendance at cultural events.

Table 7
Reasons for not visiting cultural institutions near the home, Moscow, 1994 (%)*

	All respondents	Women	Men
No interest	25	20	33
Not enough money	25	26	24
No free time	23	25	24
Not well, too tired	10	14	5
Dangerous to leave home in the evening	7	8	3
Too far away	5	5	5
Other	5	2	6

Source: [45], p. 18.
* Multiple answers possible.

I.A. Boutenko and E.V. Bykova

15 Educational Attainment

15.1 Basic Education

The trend toward an increase in educational level and attainment of higher education was predominant until the mid-1980s. This trend abated somewhat in the early 1990s, but returned in the mid-1990s.

The reform of the school system after 1917, along with the separation of schools from the church, led to the creation of a unified educational system. Subsequent reforms of public education were regulated by resolutions passed by the Central Committee of the cpsu, the Council of Ministers, and regional departments. The 1958 reform emphasized vocational education, aiming at involving schoolchildren in useful work. This resulted in a hypertrophy of the technical emphasis, which intensified professional and vocational training of students in the senior grades at workshops and shops, and brigades of schoolchildren participated directly in production plants and factories one day a week.

Compulsory school education for everyone was a consistent goal. Its first objective was elementary education (grades one to four, in the 1920 and 1930s), then the initial stages of secondary education (grades one to seven, since 1949; grades one to eight, since 1958), and, finally, compulsory complete secondary education (grades one to ten, since 1966, and grades one to eleven after 1984; at the senior grade level students could either continue their general education at school or go to technical and vocational school). The primary and initial stages of secondary school ceased to be independent; no longer considered to be autonomous stages in education, they became sequences in the system of over-all secondary education. Primary education was switched to a three-year course in the 1970s but returned to a four-year term in accordance with the 1984 reform, with the prospect of making a gradual transition to primary education beginning at the age of 6, instead of 7.

The number of schools providing general education dropped by half between 1960 and 1992, after a relatively stable growth up to the year 1960 (see table 1). This was due to school amalgamations and closings, predominantly of primary schools in rural localities that had very few students. In the 1990s, some schools were closed and replaced them by commercial ventures through illegal privatization.

Table 1
School systems and attendance at beginning of school year, 1960–94

	1960–61	1970–71	1980–81	1985–86	1990–91	1991–92	1992–93	1993–94
Number of general-education schools (million)	129.1	104.1	74.8	71.7	69.7	69.9	70.2	70.0
Number of students (million)	20.4	25.4	20.8	20.2	20.8	20.9	21.0	21.0
Students in grades 1–3 (million)	7.9	7.5	6.0	6.6	7.6	7.7	7.8	7.8
Students in grades 4–4 (million)	10.0	13.1	9.0	9.8	10.3	10.3	10.4	10.5
Students in grades 9–12 (million)	0.7	2.4	2.3	1.8	2.0	2.0	1.9	1.9

Sources: [171] 1992, pp. 234–37; [172], pp. 353, 354, 257; [197], pp. 57, 130.

In 1992, 28% of occupied school buildings were in need of capital repairs, 7% of them urgently; in 1993, these figures were, respectively, 33% and 9.1% ([197]).

In the late 1980s, educational institutions referred to as lyceums and gymnasiums came into being, laying claim to educational specificity. Like schools dedicated to comprehensive study of certain subjects (mathematics, foreign languages, etc.) that began to appear as early as the 1950s, they made efforts to work out their own specific curricula. From data supplied by the Ministry of Education of the Russian Federation, in the 1992–93 school year around 1,000 lyceums and gymnasiums were in operation, serving over 600,000 students ([168]).

The number of students in schools providing general education stabilized after reaching a zenith in 1970 (see table 1). Between 1950 and 1970, the total number of pupils rose by 24.5%, whereas it rose by 3.8% between 1980 and 1992 (see table 1). The number of children in the senior two grades diminished by 20.8% from 1970 to 1993. On the one hand, this was accounted for by an opportunity to receive secondary general education not only at general education schools but also at specialized educational institutions and in vocational and technical schools that, since the 1970s, commenced providing secondary general education along with a professional education. On the other hand, senior-grade students began dropping out in the late 1980s because of the introduction of a new scheme according to which students were to be transferred to the senior grades on the basis of a competition. Hence, pupils with better marks had a better opportunity to continue their education.

A loss in the prestige of education, which manifested itself during the crisis, also had an effect on the drop-out rate. From 1985 to 1989, the proportion of students who continued their studies after graduating from secondary school dropped by nearly 2%. The proportion of school graduates who went to work increased somewhat, but the proportion of those who neither worked nor studied doubled in 1989. In 1993, 4.2% of secondary-school graduates and 2.6% of those who had graduated from lyceums and gymnasiums that provided the same level of education were neither working nor in school (see table 2) ([250]).

From 1987 to 1990, the number of schoolchildren aged 6 years rose by 18%. They studied both at schools providing general education or in preparatory groups based in kindergartens. Their number dropped by 21.5% in 1990–92. By the end of 1993, the proportion of 6-year-old schoolchildren comprised almost one quarter of all children of that age (see table 3). This testifies to the fact that the task of universal school entrance at age 6 is far from completed; not all families are in favour of it.

The overall number of teachers engaged in the general education system rose by 44.9% between 1960 and 1991 and fell by 2% between 1991 and 1993. The educational level of these teachers was gradually falling (see table 4). The proportion of certified teachers dropped from 75.1% in 1985 to 74.2% in 1992. However, the proportion of teachers possessing higher non-pedagogical certificates grew, and and the number with a secondary general-education certificate tripled from 1980 to 1992. Low salary and a drop in prestige of the teaching profession drew teachers away from the education sector. The number of graduates from higher, secondary, and specialized educational institutions that prepare teachers failed to make up for the shortage in personnel. For example, in 1993, there were 4,400 teacher vacancies for the subject of Russian language and literature in full-time general-education schools (grades 5 to 11), 6,800 for the subject of foreign languages, and 2,800 for mathematics. Personnel turnover was increasing. More men left teaching, thus increasing feminization of school personnel. In the 1960–61 academic year, women accounted for 76% of all teachers; in 1993–94, they accounted for 84.1% ([197]). In the mid-1990s, the situation began to change because of unemployment.

The total number of students attending higher and secondary specialized vocational and technical institutions rose between 1960 and 1980; however, this trend turned downward between 1980 and 1992. Despite some increase in the number of higher educational institutions, including universities, amounting to about 36% between 1960 and 1993, the number of students attending them dropped. From 1980 to 1993, the number of students attending institutes of higher education fell by 8.4%, while those in secondary institutions dropped by 19.6%, despite the fact that the number of both types of institutions had doubled from 1960 to 1980. As well, the number of students dropped per 10,000 of total population (see table 5). This trend continued in 1993, testifying to the fact that there was a drop in the prestige of education. One reason for this was that graduates did not find jobs, which, in turn, contributed to an increase in the number of unemployed. There were other factors contributing to this, such as: low salaries, particularly for graduates in education, science, health care, and the opportunity to earn high profits in the activities that do

Table 2
Occupation of secondary-school graduates, 1981–89 (%)

	1981	1985	1989
Continued studying, not working	63.4	69.9	68.2
Working, not studying	33.6	27.3	29.2
Neither working nor studying	0.7	0.6	1.4

Sources: [169], pp. 234–7; [174], p. 257.

Table 3
Number of children aged 6 years attending grade one, 1987–94

	1987–88	1988–89	1989–90	1990–91	1991–92	1992–93	1993–94
Number of children aged 6 (000)	665	773	767	785	699	616	580
attending school (000)	437	473	517	539	479	428	373
attending kindergarten (000)	228	260	250	246	220	188	207
% among all children	30	32	33	33	29	25	24

Source: [197], 1993, p. 90.

not require (in the current social and economic context) any specialized training. According to sociological research, only every third young person under 25 gave priority to education ([122]).

Until 1990, students were taught free of charge and received allowances if they were able to do their homework and met other mandatory requirements. In the mid-1990s, a centralized obligatory streaming of graduates to a definite working place was discontinued. In a 1990 survey conducted by the Central Statistics Committee, it was found that 9% of graduates from higher educational institutions could indeed find a job on their own. In 1991, the number of such young graduates (in a survey of 189,000 persons) amounted to 16% ([171]). New mechanisms of job allocation began to emerge after 1990, including special bilateral arrangements between school institutions and employers. In 1993, only 46.4% of high-school graduates were able to find jobs ([197]).

The professional structure of the group of future graduates shows an overemphasis on vocational and technical education. Instruction provided at institutes and at specialized secondary educational institutions was aimed primarily at the needs of industry under the planned, governmental economic system (see table 6). Among all graduates, the greatest proportion were engineers with higher- and medium-level qualification trained to work in industry, construction, transportation,

Table 4
Teachers in general-education schools, 1960–94

	1960–61	1970–71	1980–81	1985–86	1990–91	1991–92	1992–93	1993–94
Total number of teachers (000)	1,077	1,301	1,067	1,171	1,442	1,497	1,411	1,465
By education level, day schools (%):								
With higher education	–	49.1	–	75.1	74.6	74.4	74.2	74.2
With incomplete higher education	–	1.2	–	2.9	3.1	3.1	3.2	3.0
With secondary pedagogical education	–	30.7	–	19.4	19.4	19.4	19.5	19.6
With secondary non-pedagogical and secondary general education	–	1.0	–	2.6	2.7	3.1	3.1	3.2

Sources: [169], p. 105; [171], p. 253; [172], p. 364; National education..., 1993, p. 105; [242], p. 274.

Table 5
Specialized educational institutions and attendance (at beginning of school year), 1960–94

	1960–61	1970–71	1980–81	1985–86	1990–91	1991–92	1992–93	1993–94
Number of higher-education institutions	430	457	494	502	514	519	535	548
Number of students (million)	1.5	2.7	3.0	2.9	2.8	2.8	2.6	2.6
Universities	14	28	40	40	42	48	52	57
Number of students (000)	81.5	228.4	303.6	294.8	328.1	382.3	389.6	393.1
Number of secondary specialized educational institutions	1,961	2,423	2,505	2,566	2,603	2,605	2,609	2,607
Number of students (million)	1.3	2.6	2.6	2.5	2.3	2.2	2.0	2.0
Number of students at higher education institutions (per 10,000 total population)	124	204	219	206	190	186	178	171
Number of students at specialized secondary-education institution (per 10,000 total population)	104	199	190	172	153	148	141	134

Sources: [171], p. 255; [172], p. 364; [174], p. 370; [197], pp. 177, 184, 211, 216; [242], p. 276.

Table 6
Proportion of students at institutions in different sectors, 1960–94 (%)

	1960–61	1980–81	1991–92	1992–93	1993–94
At high schools:					
Industry and construction	42.6	44.2	38.3	36.0	35.9
Agriculture	8.3	9.1	8.8	8.9	9.4
Transport and communications	6.9	6.5	6.0	5.9	5.8
Economy and law	8.2	7.6	6.5	6.9	7.5
Health care, sports	6.7	6.8	7.9	7.8	7.7
Public education	26.3	25.0	31.6	32.5	32.9
Arts and cinematography	0.7	0.7	0.8	0.8	0.9
At secondary specialized educational institutions:					
Industry and construction	51.6	43.6	37.9	36.6	37.4
Agriculture	11.3	16.2	13.4	14.0	11.4
Transport and communications	8.4	9.3	7.9	8.1	8.3
Economy and law	9.5	10.2	9.5	10.3	10.3
Health care, sports	8.2	9.4	14.2	13.3	12.0
Public education	8.7	9.1	15.6	15.4	15.1
Arts and cinematography	1.7	2.4	2.3	2.5	2.5

Sources: [171], p. 256; [174], p. 373; [197], pp. 178, 212; [242], pp. 214, 277.

and communications. They accounted for roughly 50% of all students in the 1992–93 academic year.

The proportion of graduates intending to specialize in economics and law was not large. Between 1960 and 1993, the proportion of would-be economists and lawyers already possessing a higher education dropped from 8.2% to 7.5%, whereas that of those with a lower level of qualification increased slightly, from 9.5% to 10.3%, despite the fact demand for these specialists rose rapidly since the mid-1980s.

The proportion of graduates being prepared at higher education institutions to work in the school system grew from 26.3% to 32.5% between 1960 and 1993, while the proportion being prepared in secondary educational institutions grew from 8.7% to 15.7%. The proportion of those who were studying health care, sports, arts, and cinematography was low, though there was a slight upward trend.

A shortage of accountants, economists, lawyers, and other professions that emerged in the 1990s was effectively compensated for by various courses, seminars, and so on, most of which cost money and were offered as complementary education ([197]).

E.V. Bykova

15.2 Vocational Training

The number of vocational-technical and technical schools and attendance at them rose between 1960 and 1987, followed by a decline from 1987 to 1991.

In the 1980s, various kinds of vocational-technical schools started to emerge. Vocational-technical education was a constituent part of the state centralized hierarchical system that was called on to train qualified personnel for different sectors of the planned economy.

In the 1960s, vocational education was ensured by professional-technical schools (PTSs) working on the basis of shortened (eight grades) schooling, with a program of 1 to 2 years, and by technical schools giving for graduates from general-education secondary schools (grades 10 and 11), with a program lasting two years. After the introduction of universal, compulsory, full-time, secondary education in the late 1960s, secondary professional-technical schools (sptss), with programs of three to four years were instituted. These provided general, full-time, secondary education, simultaneous with acquisition of professional qualification, and their curricula were based on standards created by the Ministry of Education and the State Committee For Professional And Technical Education.

As a result of the 1984 reform applied to both general and vocational schools, all vocational-technical educational institutions (PTSs and SPTSs) were transformed into secondary vocational-technical educational institutions structured according to industry sector; for students who did not have ninth grade, the duration of the program was three to four years; for secondary-school graduates it was one or two years long.

The number of vocational-technical educational institutions and of students attending them increased gradually. Between 1960 and 1991, the number of educational institutions almost doubled, while the number of students more than tripled. After reaching a peak in 1987, quantitative growth was replaced by a slight drop, obviously caused by the economic crisis and an overall drop in production. Between 1987 and 1993, the number of educational institutions fell by 3.4%, while the number of students dropped by 21.6% (see table 1).

Future workers in heavy industry (machinery manufacturing, metalworking, mining, etc.) were predominant in the occupational structure of students at PTSs and SPTSs from 1960 to 1991, constituting over one third of graduates (see table 2). In 1980, over one fourth of all trained workers were assigned to work in agriculture.

Table 1
Number of vocational-technical educational institutions and attendance, 1960–93

	1960	1970	1980	1985	1987	1990	1991	1992	1993
Number of schools	2,317	3,257	4,045	4,196	4,419	4,328	4,321	4,269	4,273
Number of students (000)	677	1,406	1,947	1,987	2,223	1,867	1,841	1,773	1,772

Sources: [171], p. 125; [174], p. 272; [196], p. 165; [197], p. 163.

Table 2
Number of students who graduated from vocational-technical schools per industrial sector, 1980–92

	Number (000)					%			
	1980	1985	1990	1992	1993	1980	1990	1992	1993
Total number of students	1399.3	1378.1	1271.5	1038.9	1,038.9	100.0	100.0	100.0	100.0
Heavy industry	487.9	507.3	428.4	360.0	319.0	34.9	33.7	33.7	30.7
Light industry	90.0	86.8	101.9	94.9	96.4	6.9	6.4	9.1	9.3
Food industry	22.4	19.4	17.7	14.7	3.2	1.6	1.4	1.4	0.4
Construction	255.8	238.1	241.6	170.9	147.3	18.3	19.0	16.4	14.2
Transportation	155.1	143.7	182.6	137.3	101.5	11.1	14.4	13.2	9.7
Agriculture	383.3	312.9	194.3	170.0	163.9	27.4	15.3	16.4	15.8
Trade and public food catering	49.1	57.9	116.5	105.0	99.8	3.5	9.2	10.1	9.6
Housing and community services	15.5	15.1	13.6	10.8	12.2	1.1	1.1	1.0	1.2

Source: [196], p. 168; [197], p. 173.

The proportion of students trained for industry between 1980 and 1993 changed slightly, dropping by 3.0%, while 2.3 times fewer students were trained for agriculture in 1993 as in 1980. The number trained for trade and food-catering services rose in 1993 to almost double that of 1980. The proportion of graduates in light and food industries is not large; together, they constitute less than 10%. This reflects a general structure of manufacturing production that is biased in favour of heavy industry.

In-plant training of workers continued to be the most important means of vocational education, despite some reduction in proportion of the total number of workers trained this way by the beginning of 1990. This training was of two types: training through courses and individualized in-plant training. Courses for personnel were held at educational training centres, technical schools, and continuing-education courses. These programs lasted 6 to 12 months. Theoretical aspects were discussed and learned in group settings or at educational training centres, while industrial training was more individualized and had two stages: the first under the supervision of a tutor at the educational institution, the second at the workplace, under the supervision of a highly qualified worker (an instructor of industrial training).

As important as vocational and technical schools might be, the emphasis was placed on training at the workplace. Thus, in 1980 77.0% of skilled workers were trained at their workplace – factories, plants, etc. – while 23% were trained at professional-technical schools; in 1990, these figures stood at 71.0% and 29.0% respectively; in 1992, at 68% and 32%, respectively ([197]).

Paid education based on short- and long-term courses and even primary schools began expanding in the 1990s.

E.V. Bykova

15.3 Continuing Education

A relatively stable rise in the numbers of students enrolled in different forms of supplementary education, including part-time and extra-mural education, in the 1960s and 1970s was followed by a decline in the 1980s and an upturn in the mid-1990s.

Continuing education, concurrent with work, was carried on at evening classes and by correspondence with educational institutions. Evening and correspondence education introduced the basis of unified requirements for content and body of knowledge corresponding curricula adopted in force at full-time educational institutions. This form of education were promoted at the governmental level via a number of benefits offered to students, such as annual paid leaves (20 days off) calculated on a mean month salary or wage; a much shorter work week or day, paid at half the salary rate; and an opportunity to take a temporary unpaid leave from work. It was characterized by an increase in the number of students from the 1960s to the 1980s, followed by a decrease in the 1980s. This type of education permitted a rise in the educational level with respect to both general and specialized education. It was aimed at persons who had to earn a living and were self-supporting. The numbers of this type of student increased, from 1960 to 1980, reaching a peak of 64.3% in 1980. From 1980 to 1992, there was a virtual collapse, the number of students dropping by a factor of 2.4.

The largest drop in student numbers occurred in evening and correspondence general education courses. The number of students had increased by 55% from 1960 to 1980, only to experience a fivefold drop between 1980 and 1991. The drop in demand for these kinds of general education was due to substantially broadened curricula in secondary education at technical, secondary professional, and technical schools.

The greatest drop was seen in evening and off-campus departments of high schools. Here, the drop in attendance began in 1985 and comprised 24.7% from 1985 to 1993. The rate of admission to these departments suffered markedly.

On the whole, between 1980 and 1992 the proportion of those who studied without interrupting their work fell from 18.1% to 8.1% of the total number of students at the educational institutions of all kinds (see table 1).

Supplementary professional education, including that aimed at improving qualifications and retraining workers and employees, expanded up to 1985, followed by an appreciable contraction. This system was regulated by an interdepartmental council that functioned under the USSR Ministry of Higher and Secondary Specialized Education. The principal task of this sector was to co-ordinate trained labour with the current level of production, technology, science, and so on.

Improvement of qualifications for managers and skilled workers took place at special ministerial training institutes in respective economic sectors. In accordance with the requirements of long-term planning, all trained personnel were expected to take such upgrading courses every 5 to 6 years.

Workers mastered new skills or took retraining courses in industry, agriculture, and other sectors at technical educational institutions, technical, continuing education courses, or work on probation in the workplace. The duration of these courses was 6 to 12 months, depending on whether or not work was interrupted.

Table 1
Attendance at night and off-campus schools, 1960–92 (per 000)

	1960	1970	1980	1985	1990	1991	1992
Students at evening and extramural schools	1,663	2,137	2,578	1,578	523	509	487
Students at evening and extramural departments of high schools	798	1,189	1,178	1,219	1,082	1,031	1,000
Students at evening and extramural departments of secondary specialized educational institutions	628	1,154	1,063	942	796	702	600
Students at evening PTSs and SPTSs	–	171	256	326	205	184	122
Total students	3,088	4,651	5,075	4,065	2,606	2,426	2,237
Share in overall number of students attending educational institutions of all types (%)	–	14.3	18.1	14.6	9.4	8.7	6.1

Sources: [171], pp. 125, 235, 255; [175], pp. 272, 357, 370; [242], pp. 127, 270, 276.

Up to 1985, numbers of students, specifications of objectives, tasks, and setting of requirements and norms were centrally planned by government ministries and departments and the State Committee for Labour. These bodies controlled activities at educational institutions in the domain of supplementary professional and technical education via certification, inspection, and so on. Subsequently, educational institutions dictated curricula and course content and methods to be followed by enterprises, educational centres, and other concerned bodies without taking into account the needs of the latter or of the workers themselves.

All of this, combined with an absence of any connection between skill upgrading and retraining, on the one hand, and compensation for work, on the other hand, combined with official reshuffling, led to red tape, bureaucracy, and a lack of interest in continuing education among both enterprises and workers. Persons who were surplus for some reason or other were being shunted off to retraining.

After 1985, management was decentralized, resulting in increased autonomy of educational institutions and enhancement of their responsibility for the results of their work; abolition of the system of centralized planning; creation of self-supporting relationships between educational institutions and industrial enterprises, organizations, and other bodies, and bilateral arrangements between them. Tuition fees were to be paid from the funds destined for development of manufacturing production rather than from centralized funds, and according to contracts, arrangements per individual trainee. Thus, the entire structure of the academic plan, the pattern of studies, and the nature of specialization became dependent on the educational consumer.

In the 1990s, efforts were made by the government to interest workers in raising their professional competence acquiring new knowledge and skills through linking salary level to achievements and competence.

Along with the government (ministerial) educational institutions that existed in the system of continuing professional and technical education in the late 1980s, there appeared other types of education. Chief among these were user-paid programs that were being introduced by educational centres, educational information centres. Such short-term courses were designed to give a comprehensive and concentrated overview of certain subjects, such as tax policy, management, marketing, and so on.

Between 1960 and 1985, the total number of individuals trained in the continuing education system rose by a factor of 4.2, followed by a drop by a factor of 3.2 from 1985 to 1992. At the same time, there was a fivefold increase in the number of those who improved their qualification from 1960 to 1985, and an increase by a factor of 3.5 from 1985 to 1991 (see table 2).

A collapse in the system of continuing education was evident in the late 1980s and early 1990s.

In the 1960s, in the wake of rapid expansion of interests of the population, concurrent with the growth of state educational institutions that provided continuous education opportunities, there arose, under official sanction, the so-called people's universities. Until 1987, attendance at these institutions grew and they were deemed to represent a variant of continuous adult education that provided opportunities for self-improvement. People's universities were considered to be generally accessible educational institutions for both working and nonworking students, and admittance did not depend on previous level of education, specialty, age, sex, and so on. The principal task of the people's universities was to meet individual aspirations for greater knowledge and a higher educational level, whether or not it was associated with one's main profession. The people's universities covered a great variety of subjects and provided students with an opportunity to gain knowledge in medicine, history, law, economy, ecology, and so on. Courses of study varied in duration from one to three years. These institutions were not government financed and functioned under the auspices of the founding organizations, remaining apart from the centralized planning system. Schools, higher educational institutions, club institutions, cultural centres were the founders, providing the people's universities with classrooms for studies, and supporting them financially. Tuition was free.

According to data from surveys on people's universities, conducted occasionally by the USSR Central Statistics Committee, their number rose nearly eightfold (see table 3), with the number of students increasing by a factor of 12.5, between 1961 and 1987. These educational institutions involved different strata of the population.

Table 2
Numbers of students in the supplementary professional education system, 1960–92 (million)

	1960	1970	1980	1985	1990	1991	1992
Students in qualification upgrading and retraining	6.9	11.4	24.3	29.1	20.4	9.7	7.5
Improvement of qualification for workers and employees	4.6	7.5	19.4	24.7	17.2	7.0	5.4
Mastering new skills	2.3	3.9	4.9	4.4	3.2	2.7	2.1

Sources: [171], p. 126; [174], p. 273; [242], p. 128.

Table 3
Number of people's universities and attendance, 1961–87

	1961	1964	1969	1973	1980	1987
Number of people's universities	6,357	9,629	15,788	28,815	47,534	47,657
Number of students (000)	1,494	1,925	3,218	6,870	13,838	18,687

Sources: [138], p. 327.

By 1987, 11.3% of the country's inhabitants had attended people's universities. Among them were people under the age of 29 (41.2%), students with secondary general education (over 60%), and students with higher education (21%) (Kuptsov et al., 1989).

As it was decentralized, in the late 1980s, the continuing education sector could react with more flexibility to changes in interests and requirements by adapting academic curricula, introducing new disciplines, and so on, without obtaining approval special agreements from higher instances.

Since the late 1960s, the cpsu and public organizations have been entrusted with administering the affairs of people's universities. The Ministry of Culture, the Ministry of Education, and industrial ministries chose representatives to sit on the All-Union Central Council of People's Universities. These organizations ceased to exist in the late 1980s. In subsequent years, departmental and territorial councils were established to co-ordinate and improve activities at people's universities.

However, in the 1980s the forms and types of their main activities were brought strictly into accord with the "Exemplary Statement on Peoples' Universities," which led to inevitable unification. Meeting quotas, implementing different kinds of ideological work, lecturing, club work, and thematic meetings were tasks that began to be assigned to people's universities.

Changes in the economic situation in the country in the late 1980s strongly affected the status of people's universities. The founding organizations were no longer in a position to support them, except in some rare cases. There was a rapid decrease in their number and a sharp transformation of their nature.

Centres of continuing education, information educational centres, educational centres for young people, and other institutions were established in their place. The latter were often set up on the premises of night schools to provide general and professional education and to prepare young people for entrance to high schools or technical schools. These centres set tuition rates (for both groups and individuals) based on a contract system and became self-supporting institutions. A new generation of educational and consulting institutions rendered services for fees, especially in the areas of computerization and education as well as in upgrading of qualifications – in other words, acquisition of skills needed for work, for every day life, for the development of creative capacities, and so on.

Thus, continuous, continuing, general, and vocational education are converging. Government agencies were now attempting to introduce standardization and licensing for these educational institutions. This substantially changed the nature of public continuing and adult education.

E.V. Bykova

16 Integration and Marginalization

16.1 Immigrants and Ethnic Minorities

In the 1980s, on the territory of the USSR, centrifugal forces were being super-seded by centripetal ones. Urbanization was in decline. The problem of refugees arose and became dramatically aggravated. As well, more and more people from the southern and Asian republics of the former USSR came to settle in Russia.

The idea of a "new community" – the "Soviet people" – greatly hampered analysis of real problems associated with migration and national minorities. From the 1950s to the 1980s, the state was the main organizer of migration, especially that of working youth. Deployment of these young people was determined as a function of economic and production considerations as well as by the need to correct the imbalance in labour resources and differences in living standards. The state stimulated the settling of virgin territory in Kazakhstan in the 1950s and 1960s and construction of the Baikal-Amur Main railway line in the 1970s and organized various Komsomol construction projects in some regions of Central Russia.

From the 1960s to the 1980s, migration was strictly regulated by means of passport registration, on the one hand, and by means of different privileges and a differential wage rates in some regions of the country, on the other. Until the 1970s, the low rate of retention of new residents was the most serious migration problem, attracting the attention of scientists and authorities. At this time, representative portions of some ethnic groups formerly (under Stalin's régime) evacuated from the European districts of the country returned home, and this migration wave was the last resulting from the war ([252]). Due mainly to this fact, in the second half of the 1970s and the beginning of the 1980s a positive balance in inter-regional migration was achieved in Siberia, and in some of the newly reclaimed territories the level of retention rose.

Seasonal migration, resulting mainly from the lack of sources of supplementary income in villages and small towns, underwent structural rather than quantitative changes. From the end of 1970s to the 1990s, a considerable portion of the unskilled labour force was recruited from Vietnam and North Korea to do nonprestigious heavy manual labour at Russian industrial enterprises. By the end of 1989 there were more than 100,000 foreign workers, of whom nearly 90,000 were Vietnamese. This process was stopped only when mass unemployment arose among the Russian population. In the 1990s, unemployment became a factor influencing Russians' migrational mobility. But this influence appeared to be not as important as had been expected ([159]).

Urbanization was intensive in the late 1940s and the 1950s, and began to decline in the 1980s (see table 1); in 1992 there was a limited but increasing outflow of urban population (mainly the first urban generation) back to rural areas. At the same time, migration from rural central regions to cities is still taking place, in most cases, simultaneously with a negative natural increase in rural areas. In general, between 1979 and 1988, a negative natural increase was noted in all rural Central regions.

One main reason for migration to cities was the better social-cultural living conditions to be found in them. By the 1960s, 7.5% of migrants stated their desire to be where there were other young people; in the mid-1980s, this figure had risen to 22.9%. This was closely connected with the ageing of the rural population and with the desire of young people to improve their living conditions, but also their desire to start a family, which became difficult in rural settlements because they were now thinly populated and demographically unbalanced. Before 1968, only 3.8% of migrants expressed the wish to move to a settlement with more commodities. In the 1980s, 9% gave this reason. An increasing need for domestic comfort caused the rise in migration from 3% in 1953–57 to 14% in 1968–69 and to 24% in the mid-1980s. The wish to continue studies or to acquire a profession decreased as a motive for migration to cities from the 1970 to the 1990s ([202]).

The number of both rural and urban migrants began to decline at the end of the 1980s and the beginning of the 1990s (see table 2), mostly as a result of the economic difficulties of settling in a new place.

From the 1930s to the 1960s, it was mainly Russians who actively populated the territories of other Soviet republics and Russian virgin lands; by the 1970s, they were gradually losing this role. In the mid-1970s Russia had a positive migrational balance for the first time in the period from the 1950s to the 1970s. Simultaneously, the inflow of migrants from the central regions of Russia and Siberia to central Asia declined, and from 1975 Siberia had a positive migrational balance in the population interchange with all the Central Asian republics. From 1979 to 1989, the number of Russians living in the republics of Central Asia declined markedly.

Table 1
Percentage of urban and rural populations, Russia, 1959–92

	Urban	Rural
1959	52	48
1970	62	38
1979	69	31
1989	74	26
1990	74	26
1992	74	26

Sources: [171], p. 81; [176], p. 57.

Table 2
Migration to urban and rural regions, 1989–91

	To urban region	To rural region
1989	1,212,496	883,385
1990	1,051,529	889,155
1991	847,000	802,000

Source: [12a], p. 8.

According to the 1989 population census, 17.4% of Russians lived beyond the borders of Russia, including 25 million who lived in the Ukraine, constituting 22% of its population; 6 million lived in Kazakhstan (38%); 1.7 million lived in the Baltic republics. From 1979 on, the annual inflow of Russians to other republics of the USSR decreased by a factor of between two and five, including to the Ukraine by 3.8 and to Belorussia by 2.4 ([159]).

There was an obvious acceleration in the process of exclusion of Russian-speaking populations from different republics of the USSR and their return to Russia; the problem of refugees, previously latent, came into particular prominence. In 1980, the number of Russians living in Russia increased by 1.2 million, including 872,000 as a result of assimilation, and there was a positive natural migration balance of 317,000 from 1979 to 1989 ([295]).

The refugee problem, in latent form, sprang up in the mid-1970s, involving the outflow of non-native populations (mostly Slavic-speaking) from several Soviet republics: in the 1970s, there was a considerable decline in the number of Russians, Ukrainians, and Belorussians in Georgia and Azerbaijan. Over 30 years, 359,000 Russians left these republics; by the 1980s, the intensity of their migration increased, reaching 16.8%. In the 1980s, the number of Russians who left Kazakhstan and

Central Asia was about 700,000 more than the number who arrived. Aggravation of national conflicts at the end of the 1980s led to a mass flight of Russians to Russia, and so the problem of refugees mushroomed ([159]).

In the second half of the 1980s, streams of refugees appeared. During the winter of 1988–89, there were 422,000 refugees, and before the autumn of 1990, 700,000 people were registered as having been forced to leave their dwellings because of violent ethnic conflicts ([159]). According to other data, there were 500,000 such persons in 1990, and one million in 1991. USSR military personnel returning from abroad also joined this stream; 70% of them were from Russia. Forced migration from the Asian and Baltic republics is the most intense, with about 30% of the Russian-language population wanting to return to Russia ([296]). In 1993, 390,000 refugees arrived in Russia, more than one third of them from Tadjikistan ([12j]).

In the 1980s and 1990s, due to glasnost and to the general increase in ecological awareness among the population, hundreds of thousands of refugees left such ecologically dangerous regions as Chernobyl, Semipalatinsk, Arkhangelsk, Novaya Ziemlya, and the Urals (Chelyabinsk, Ust-Kamenogorsk).

Natural calamities such as earthquakes and floods also gave rise to a considerable number of refugees at the end of the 1980s. With the generalized economic crisis, it was not possible to provide them with much support. Their impoverishment forced them to consider emigrating.

Russia increasingly became the centre of attraction for nationalities from the South and Asian republics of the former USSR. From 1959 to 1969, non-Russians accounted for 125,000 immigrants; from 1970 to 1978, for 1.38 million; and from 1979 to 1989, 1.43 million. As a result of migration, the number of Ukrainians living in Russia rose by 11.3%, and the number of Belorussians rose by 6.6%. From 1979 to 1988, the inflow of migrants from Transcaucasus and Central Asia increased as well. The number of Azerbaijani migrants increased by a factor of 4.5 compared to the 1970s; Armenian migrants, by a factor of 7.9; Georgian migrants, by a factor of 2. The total number of Caucasians settling in Russia increased by a factor of 1.5, and their proportion in the total population of Russia increased from 0.9% in 1979 to 1.3% in 1989.

Simultaneously, there was a rapid growth in aboriginals from Central Asia who came to Russia. From 1979 to 1988, the number of Kirgizis and Tadjikis in Russia increased by a factor of 1.7, while the number of Uzbekis and Turkmens increased by a factor of between 2.1 and 2.8, due to intensive migration to Russia ([252]; see table 3).

Since a person's nationality was registered by self-identification and children of mixed couples preferred to register themselves as Russian, the positive assimilation balance in Russia from 1979 to 1988 was 872,000 people, or 11.2% of the total increase in the Russian population ([295]).

In the mid-1980s, internal migration predominated. Later, external immigration grew (see table 4). A new law passed in 1987 making it easier to enter and leave Russia provoked an outflow of the population to economically developed countries. From 1945 to 1990, 2.5 million people left the USSR for another country, including 1 million who left in 1988 and 1989; this can be characterized as mass emigration. The outflow increased thereafter; in 1991 it doubled ([159]). According to the Ministry of Foreign Affairs, emigration from Russia in 1992 was 34 times greater than immigration ([12f]; see table 5). Well represented among the emigrants were representatives of the creative intelligentsia and skilled workers, thus raising a critical concern about a "brain drain."

Almost half of the emigrants were Jews emigrating to Israel; 42% were Germans emigrating to Germany; 6% were Armenians emigrating to the United States; and 5% were Greeks emigrating to Greece (see table 6). People of other nationalities who were members of the families of these ethnic emigrants were also leaving the country. Indeed, in 1990, 35% of the 186,000 Soviet citizens emigrating to Israel were not Jewish ([159]).

The data show that in coming years the number of Germans leaving Russia may reach one million – that is, nearly half of the German population who were living in the former USSR in the 1990s. The largest losses were suffered by Kazakhstan and Russia, especially Western Siberia.

Table 3
Percentage of Russians in the USSR living in Russia, 1959–89

1959	1979	1989
85.6	82.6	82.6

Source: [295], p. 36.

Table 4
Number of registered migrants and refugees by region, 1993–94

	1993	*1994*
Tadjikistan	65,448	134,046
Azerbaijan	32,680	77,339
Georgia	24,817	90,880
Russia	21,860	69,951
Moldova	10,341	14,664
Uzbekistan	3,247	21,613
Kirghizia	897	20,971
Kazakhstan	283	7,948
Armenia	126	1,990
Latvia	85	4,245
Estonia	60	2,050
Turkmenistan	54	504
Ukraine	19	281
Belorussia	17	–
Lithuania	14	540
Not mentioned	243	924

Source: [100], p. 9.

Table 5
Emigration from Russia, 1987–92

	Emigrants: *Number*	*Per 10,000*	*Annual proportion of emigrants (%)*	*Changes 1987=1*
1987	9,697	0.1	2.6	1.0
1988	20,705	0.1	5.6	2.1
1989	47,521	0.3	12.7	4.9
1990	103,614	0.7	27.8	10.7
1991	88,281	0.6	23.7	9.1
1992	102,910	0.7	27.6	10.6
total	372,728	1.9	100.0	

Source: [55], p. 40.

Table 6
Emigration from Russia by country of destination, 1987–92

	Germany	Greece	Israel	US	Other	Total
1987	3,866	87	3,523	235	1,986	9,697
1988	9,988	198	8,088	667	1,784	20,705
1989	21,128	1,831	21,956	676	1,930	47,521
1990	33,753	4,177	61,022	2,317	2,345	103,614
1991	33,697	2,088	38,742	11,016	2,738	88,281
1992	62,690	1,855	21,975	12,200	3,190	102,910

Source: [55], p. 40.

I.A. Boutenko

16.2 Crime

The crime rate rose. The state attempted to solve a certain number of economic problems by introducing various types of prohibitions, including the criminal prescriptions. The toughening of legislation in the mid-1980s and considerable revisions in the 1990s influenced the interpretation of such notions as "crime" and "criminal"; moreover, new types of crime emerged related to the development of the market economy.

There was a constant increase in crime, with a peak in mid-1950s due to the amnesty after Stalin's death in 1953, and another peak caused by the destruction of the socialist system in the late 1980s (see table 1). From the 1960s to the 1980s, it was believed that rising criminality was a characteristic only of capitalist countries; there was no public access to statistical data in Russia, and the ideologists insisted that it was declining.

It became known after the fact that between 1973 and 1983 the total number of crimes doubled in number; serious offences against the person increased by 58%; robberies and thefts doubled in number; the number of burglaries and briberies tripled in number ([282]); the number of registered offences rose from 1.4 million to 1.6 million ([175]). In 1993, more than 2.5 million crimes were registered ([12f]).

There were some noticeable changes in the structure of crime, related, among other reasons, to changes in registration. The number of offences against civil order

Table 1
Criminality in Russia, 1987–93 (000)

	1987	1988	1989	1990	1991	1992	1993	1994
Reported crimes	2,278	2,354	2,666	2,696	2,978	–	–	–
Registered crimes	1,186	1,220	1,619	1,839	2,168	2,761	2,800	2,600
Solved cases (arrests)	969	835	848	897	956	1,149	1,263	–
Convictions	580	427	437	538	594	686	814	925
Acquittals	–	–	–	–	–	–	2,699	3,557

Source: [111o].

and the person dropped between 1985 and 1991 (see table 2) but grew thereafter, while the number of crimes against personal and state property increased in 1989 and 1990: serious bodily injury increased by 15%; premeditated murders and attempted murders, by 20%; state and common property theft, by 37%; rapes and attempted rapes, by 7%; robberies, by 25%; theft of individual property, by 18%; burglaries, by 25%, armed robberies, by 30%; misappropriation of weapons and ammunition, by 58%; offences against foreign citizens, by 29%. There were 16,765 recorded rape cases in 1987; in 1988, there were 17,658 – that is, one officially reported rape every 30 minutes – but actually rape was much more frequent ([218]). In 1989, every seventh crime was serious ([175]). There was an increase of so-called occasional crime caused by drinking. In 1993, 70% of registered crimes were robberies and the bribery rate rose by a factor of 15 ([12f]).

Two thirds of recorded crimes took place in republican, regional, and territorial centres; one third, in agricultural areas ([282]).

The level of crime investigation was extremely low. The gap between recorded and latent criminality was increasing. In 1989, one third of the recorded crimes were not solved; in 1992, the number of unsolved crimes rose to one half of the total ([171]).

The low level of crime solution resulted in an expanding gap between recorded and latent criminality. According to experts' estimates, only about one half of the total number of bodily and sexual assaults were recorded; not more than 10% of economic crimes – misappropriations, bribery, etc. – were recorded ([282]).

VCIOM poll results showed that the rise of criminality ranked second (51%) (following the rise of prices) among internal problems of Russian society that concern the population ([111f]).

There was a professionalization of everyday and economic crime. Organized crime, the existence of which was officially recognized only at the end of the 1980s, is rising. The number of criminal groups increased by 17% between 1988 and 1989,

Table 2
Structure of registered crimes, Russia, 1985–91 (%)

	1985	1987	1989	1991
Against public safety, norms, personal health	27.4	27.5	23.6	18.4
Against private property	27.4	27.2	41.5	45.6
Against state, common property	19.4	17.6	18.2	22.9
Against the person	10.3	8.1	7.7	6.2
Economic crimes	8.4	13.4	5.0	3.5
Against the official administrative norms	5.0	3.6	2.7	2.2
Other	1.7	1.4	1.3	1.2

Source: [241], p. 300.

the number of people involved was 175,000, representing one fifth of all solved crimes ([176]).

A rise in female criminality from 12% to 22% was noted between 1977 and 1987; in the category of economic crime, the female and male crime rates were about the same; 60% of those responsible for brewing liquor at home were women ([282]). The number of girls among juvenile criminals doubled between 1976 and 1990 ([9]). However, after 1985, women comprised a decreasing proportion of total criminals (see table 3).

Juvenile delinquency increased by 28% in the 1980s, and this trend continued in the 1990s (see table 4). The proportion of those under 14 years old among juvenile delinquents was 15% in the early 1990s, compared to 10% in the early 1980s. Juvenile delinquency rose by 21% in the country in general. The proportion of schoolchildren among criminals grew markedly (by 46%). The crime rate among girls tripled in 1989 alone, and there was an increase in female teenage drug addicts. Among all juvenile delinquents, the proportion of those under 14 years old who committed serious crime (rape, robbery, looting, etc.) remained stable and high, at about 70% ([175]).

The most characteristic features of juvenile delinquency of the end of 1980s were the following: there was an increase of more than 25% in very dangerous crimes; the crime rate among criminals under 14 years of age doubled compared with that of criminality in general; the number of 14- to 17-year old criminals increased by a factor of 1.5; the number of persons who had committed a socially dangerous crime before they reached the age of 14 years increased ([18]); every sixth crime among the under-age criminals was serious ([175]).

Organized crime was not associated with juvenile delinquency in 1990s, despite the fact that almost 40% of offences committed by teenagers in the second half of the

Table 3
Gender characteristics of criminals, Russia, 1985–92

	1985	1988	1989	1992
Men (000)	–	695.3	725.8	834.3
Women (000)	–	139.4	121.8	122.0
Proportion of women (%)	13.5	16.6	14.4	12.3

Source: [171], p. 305.

Table 4
Age of convicted criminals, Russia, 1985–91 (%)

	1985	1987	1989	1991
14–17	9.3	10.3	14.3	14.3
18–24	32.0	21.5	23.7	22.9
24–29	20.3	20.6	21.1	18.8
30–49	39.5	37.8	35.3	38.2
50 and over	7.9	9.8	5.6	5.8

Source: [171], p. 310.

1980s had an organized, group character. New types of juvenile criminality emerged, including extortion. Recidivism among under-age criminals was 9% in 1992 ([171]).

Throughout the history of the socialist state, penal educational measures consisted of punitive repressive measures, which only served to increase the social isolation of the individual. Such repression was not successful and criminality and recidivism rates remained high, especially among young people (see table 5), growing by 10% in 1988 and 1989 ([282]).

In the 1980s, there was a trend toward milder punishment and a liberalization of the attitude toward criminals (see table 6). Measures other than imprisonment were being used for women and adolescent criminals. Thus the number of those convicted sentenced to corrective labour colonies dropped by 40% after 1987.

Under-age wrongdoers were given considerable privileges. Half of them were absolved of criminal liability during the investigation. They were also often freed from serving their sentence and given conditional sentences. Thus, only one third of adolescent wrongdoers were actually punished. The personnel who dealt with juvenile offenders (inspectors and the staff at juvenile detention centres) maintained that the corrective measures used to date had never worked ([117]).

The corrective institutions (correction with the help of obligatory labour) served only to improve the skills of criminals due to the strict social stratification inside these institutions. Every newcomer faced a powerful, cruel system of

Table 5
Recidivism rate and proportion of those who neither worked nor studied before committing the crime
(% among sentenced)

	1985	1990	1991
Recidivists	38.1	39.6	37.9
Those able to work who neither worked nor studied before committing the crime	23.1	20.3	21.3

Sources: [171], p. 306; [175], p. 354.

Table 6
Sentencing, Russia, 1985–94 (%)

	1985	1990	1991	1994
Prison	47.4	37.8	34.9	40.0
Conventional imprisonment	7.5	6.6	6.7	18.0
Probation	9.6	13.4	14.0	–
Obligatory labour without imprisonment	21.8	21.8	27.1	–
Conventional imprisonment or obligatory labour	4.3	8.4	10.1	–
Fine	8.7	11.6	12.2	10.0
Other	0.7	0.4	0.4	–

Source: [171], p. 306.

repression. A shared social situation and the impossibility of changing existing communication channels forced convicts to acquiesce to existing norms, though identification with these norms varied in different groups.

The community of convicts is characterized by some formal labour organization – detachments, brigades, etc. At the same time, there are spontaneous processes of sharing social self-organization: layers and strata are formed that occupy different positions and have different rights and obligations in the sphere of informal communication. Five hierarchical groups can be distinguished: "very privileged" – informal leaders, arbitrators in arguments and conflicts; "privileged" – advisors to the former, executors of their will (not more than 5–10% of the total number of convicts); "neutral" – the majority; "nonprivileged" – the persons whose authority was seriously undermined either by infringement of the norms or by some compromising information about their previous life and who do all the dirty work and are used as a means to mockery; "offensive," who are bereft of any privileges because they are oppressed, subjected to passive homosexuality and other compromising behaviour, and are used as an object of mockery (about 10%).

Vertical mobility in the social structure of the convicts is controlled mainly from the top down; access to the upper layers is very difficult, and absolutely impossible for the "offensives" ([139]).

I.A. Boutenko

16.3 Emotional Disorders

In spite of numerous prohibitions and severe punishments, the number of people with various emotional disorders grew constantly, though the prevalence of certain types of behaviour changed. Public opinion became more tolerant of delinquent behaviour.

The number of mentally ill increased constantly (see table 1), **though at the end of the 1980s the diagnostic criteria changed**. On the one hand, psychological diseases were considered shameful; on the other, in the 1970s they were seen, mainly among the intelligentsia, almost as prestigious, because the authorities tended to interpret any manifestation of dissident thought as a criminal act or as madness. The compulsory health care at mental hospitals and in the medical-and-labour dispensaries (the so-called houses for prophylactics closed in 1993) for alcoholics can be compared only with living conditions in prisons.

Statistics on mental illness were collected in conjunction with the general population census since 1839, which indicated that 0.37% of the population suffered from such illnesses. There were four general population censuses – 1839, 1897, 1920, and 1926 – that included a question about mental health.

The data show the incidence of serious psychological pathologies (such as psychosis and different types of imbecility) in Russia was quite similar to that of the other European countries, but marginal cases were much less frequent. This was connected with the fact that, for different reasons, only 25–30% of those who needed psychiatric help got treatment. In 1990, only 4% of the population sought psychiatric help ([108]). In 1993, because of anonymity for patients and more tolerant attitudes among the population, psychiatric assistance was sought 3.3 million times ([108]), a figure equivalent to 21% of the population.

In 1989, 5.5 million mentally ill were registered ([175]. In 1991, 5.1 million mentally ill people were suffering from alcoholism; 2.5 million, from drug addiction ([171]).

Table 1
Rate and number of first diagnoses of mental illness, 1985–91 (000)

	1985	1990	1991
Number of first diagnoses	678.6	627.9	543.9
Patients registered with:			
Psychosis	78.5	68.6	60.7
Age-related senility	17.9	19.4	16.2
Schizophrenia	29.8	22.3	21.0
Mental disorder	157.2	272.6	273.1
Mentally disability	59.2	55.3	50.2

Source: [171], p. 282.

In 1993, 688,000 people were considered invalids owing to mental illness. There were 200,000 places in mental hospitals; 17% of these were not occupied in 1992–93 not because of a decrease in the number of patients but because of new legislation on psychiatry and a change in the approach to compulsory treatment. Almost 700,000 children under 14 years and 300,000 teenagers (14–18 years) were under psychiatric observation in 1993, among them more than 200,000 with mental disabilities ([12h])

In spite of the widespread opinion that emotional disorders are closely associated with psychiatric disorders, in Moscow in 1989, for example, only 15% of suicides had been diagnosed as mentally ill. The proportion of drug addicts who were schizophrenic was only slightly higher than among the general population ([109]).

The sale and consumption of alcohol drinks increased (see tables 2, 3, and 4), but there is a lack of official statistics concerning homemade alcohol production. Sales dropped, but this was more than compensated for by homemade alcohol, and in the 1990s also by imports. In the structure of the household expenditures, the proportion spent on alcohol (see table 5) reflects not a reduction in alcohol consumption, but an increase and then relative stability in prices for alcohol. In the mid-1990s alcohol prices were lower than ever before compared to those for other foods.

In rural areas, as a result of the unsatisfactory commercial distribution, prolonged shortage of food products and liquor, irregularities in salary payments, and so on, a strong tradition of making homemade liquor for personal consumption and under-the-table sales arose and flourished. In spite of the criminal nature of such activities, they became a widespread practice. From the 1970s to the 1990s, a bottle of vodka or of home-brew compensated for the lack of leisure activities and the paucity of interpersonal communication. Consequently, it became a hard currency of sorts – first in rural areas and, in the mid-1970s, in cities – for settling accounts for communal and other services.

Table 2
Production of alcoholic beverages, 1960–93 (million decalitres)

	1960	1970	1980	1989	1991	1993
Vodka and liqueur	101.5	164.7	207.2	99.0	154.0	112.3
Grape wine	32.9	161.0	193.6	106.4	64.7	–
Fruit-and-apple wine	13.8	92.1	81.8	10.7	–	–
Cognac	0.8	4.1	5.2	5.9	3.7	–
Champagne	1.7	3.9	7.6	11.9	7.4	–
Beer	143.3	244.4	334.6	251.8	333.0	–

Sources: [93b], p. 8; [171], p. 171; [175], pp. 154–56.

Table 3
Consumption of 100% conventional alcohol per capita, 1913–80 (litres)

Russia			USSR		
1913	1928–32	1940	1960	1970	1980
3.4	1.0	41.9	3.9	6.8	8.6

Source: [282], p. 177.

Table 4
Expenses on alcohol in selected family budgets 1970–91 (%)

	1970	1980	1985	1986	1990	1991
Workers and employees	3.6	3.3	3.3	2.3	3.5	3.0
Collective farmers	5.1	5.5	5.2	2.9	4.3	3.1

Sources: [171], pp. 146–47; [175], p. 288.

Table 5
Sales of alcohol* (constant roubles, % to 1985)

1986	1987	1988	1989	1990	1991
62	53	60	74	79	83

Source: [171], p. 177.
* Sales of imported alcohol not included.

In 1985, the government tried to strengthen the crusade against alcoholism by reducing liquor production, destroying vineyards, and reinforcing disciplinary and criminal measures against home production and sale of hard liquor. State sales dropped by 63% between 1984 and 1987 (see table 5), but in 1987 consumption of unregistered liquor, and especially of home-brew, nearly doubled, exceeding state sales. According to some data, the result of the campaign was a decrease in the consumption of approved alcohol by 25.1% ([188]); according to other sources, home-made alcohol more than compensated for the drop in state sales ([282]). For example, opinion polls in Cheliabinsk in 1985 show that over 25% of respondents drink homemade liquor. Not everyone would make such confessions, even anonymously, and so the proportion of such people was probably higher. This kind of hard liquor was used mainly by young people and the elderly, both groups belonging to less prosperous strata ([319]).

The anti-alcoholic campaign brought about a temporary drop in short-term incapacity and in the rate of death due to trauma and poisoning (see table 6). Beginning in 1987, consumption of alcohol began to rise, as did the number of violent deaths among drinkers.

The number of alcoholic psychoses and deaths from cirrhosis of the liver increased, despite the fact that statistics showed a drop in number of patients (see table 7); in fact, this drop was an artifact of changes in registration rules. Evidence indicates that anti-alcoholic measures actually adversely affected people's health. Since 1985, the proportion of people committing crimes in a drunken state grew constantly, from 24.3% in 1986 to 39.9% in 1992 ([188]).

Consumption of alcoholic drinks rose steeply until 1991, reaching the 1984 level of an average of 14 litres of conventional 100% alcohol per person per year. This is closely connected with, among other things, extensive importation of cheap liquor, its greater accessibility, and an inadequate social network.

Consumption of alcohol rose among teenagers, who were more often seen drunk in public (see table 8). These teenagers were mainly from less prosperous and less educated sectors of society, who finished their secondary education not at general secondary schools, but at vocational schools. From 1984 to 1989, the gap in alcohol consumption between students at general schools and those at vocational schools widened. Among the former, the number of non-drinkers began to decline in 1988, a trend that lasted until 1991. Those at general schools began experimenting with liquor at age 13–14 with champagne and wine, while vocational-school students began at age 11–12, and by the age of 15–16 they were already drinking hard liquor (see table 9). In 1984, 27.2% of vocational-school students said that they had been drunk several times; in 1988, 29.2% admitted this; in 1991, 38.1%; for students at

Table 6
Mortality due to alcohol drinking, 1980–91 (number deaths per 100,000 population)

	1980	1985	1989	1990	1991
Total deaths*	26.4	19.3	9.9	12.3	12.6
working age	11.3	10.9	14.2	17.0	18.2

Sources: [171], p. 116; [175], p. 102.

* Due to alcohol poisoning, chronic alcoholism, alcoholic psychosis, alcoholic cirrhosis of the liver.

Table 7
Alcoholism and narcotism, 1980–91

	Number of patients with total diagnosed (000)	Number of registered first-time patients (per 100,000 population)
1980	338.2	244.0
1985	380.7	265.4
1986	349.5	241.8
1987	325.7	223.4
1988	291.4	198.5
1989	280.1	190.6
1990	224.9	152.0
1991	154.2	104.0

Source: [171], p. 281.

Table 8
Number of adolescents arrested for public
drunkenness, 1981–89

1981	1987	1989
43,109	45,567	49,517

Source: [175], p. 321.

Table 9
Age (in years) at first experience with alcohol, 1984–91 (%)

	Under 10	11–12	13–14	15–16	17–18	Never	No answer
General-education students							
1984	5.7	14.2	27.2	19.5	0.9	31.9	0.6
1988	5.8	6.8	27.5	19.1	0.4	33.5	6.9
1991	3.4	5.8	28.1	21.6	0.9	34.9	5.3
Vocational school students:							
1984	5.5	15.0	28.0	12.1	0.3	30.0	0.1
1988	4.6	5.4	33.2	34.6	3.4	16.9	1.9
1991	7.5	14.7	26.1	34.8	0.8	14.8	1.3

Source: [118], p. 37.

general secondary schools, the figures were 8.2%, 6.8%, and 11.7%, respectively. In 1991, teenagers began to drink somewhat less in comparison with 1988, but they drank stronger liquor and got dead drunk ([118]).

Drug addiction moved from being a latent phenomenon, usually interpreted as an unavoidable result of the Western system, to the proportions of a serious social disaster Originally it was popular among criminals. Until 1986, the market network of the drug trade existed without obstacles, but its peak was in the late 1960s, when social and political stagnation pushed more and more people to seek such solace ([225]). The peak was caused, in the opinion of some experts, by the termination of the political "thaw" and the ensuing social and political stagnation. In 1984, the proportion of patients diagnosed with drug addiction was 13.7 per 100,000; in 1986, 17.1; in 1987, 21.5. In 1989, 2.8 million alcoholics and drug addicts were registered in medical-preventive institutions, and their number was on the rise ([175]).

According to the data from the late 1980s, 80% of the drugs used were prepared from wild hemp and opium poppy; 20% were medical preparations. Before the 1990s, narcotics prepared in factories and imported narcotics were more widespread.

Beginning in the mid-1980s, as result of the anti-alcoholic campaign, different medications containing alcohol, eau-de-cologne, glues, and combinations of alcohol with tranquillizers and other drugs began to be used more often. Stupefaction by means of breathing in benzene, acetone, the vapours of certain sorts of glue, various aerosols, and so on became very popular among some children and teenagers. This fad then dropped off because of greater access to alcoholic beverages.

Narcotics consumers became younger, and the social basis of narcotism broadened. In the late 1980s, teenagers were very well informed about narcotics and addictive substances. Most frequently mentioned by young people were different domestic and industrial chemical preparations, poppies and opium-containing plants, hemp, and hashish; cocaine was the least frequently mentioned ([80]). In the 1970s teenagers were usually 16–17 years old when they first tried narcotics; in the 1908s, 10–12 years old Among students aged 14–17, between 10% and 35% had tried narcotic drugs, even if only once. A survey of students at general and professional-technical schools showed that in 1986 6.8% had used narcotics at least once; in 1987, 12% had done so.

The following reasons were given for trying narcotics: it was interesting to try (39%); the influence of friends (20%); nothing interesting to do (18%); misfortune in the family, low spirits (12.2%); conflicts in the family (5%) ([78]). The lack of such experience is explained not by concern over the consequences for one's health, but by lack of access to narcotics ([148]).

In 1992, 11% to 15% of urban dwellers used nonprescribed narcotics at least once. Among them, the newly rich strata of society rank first (32%), workers and the unemployed rank second (20–23%), then students (11–15%) and housewives (11%). Most people who are drug addicts are completely satisfied with their present status ([260]).

Over a long period, the rate of suicide rose, then it decreased, but in the 1990s it began to rise once more. In comparison with 1926 the rate of suicide more than quadrupled until the 1980s ([282]), but from 1980 to 1990 it dropped by a factor of 1.3 (see table 10). In 1989. 56,500 people were murdered or committed suicide – that is, 30% of the total who died from accidents, poisoning, and trauma ([175]).

Suicides were more frequent among villagers, which was blamed on the more unfavourable social and economic situation in the countryside. The highest suicide rate was found in towns with a population of between 500,000 and one million. Economic and geographical situation appeared to be the most important factors in defining the character of distribution and level of suicide. The situation improved from the northeast to southwest regions of the country ([263]).

The rates of and reasons for suicide did not change. Usually, suicides occurred as a result of family conflicts; ranking second were conflicts connected with state of health; next came antisocial behaviour (fear of criminal prosecution, shame, etc.); followed by conflicts at work and at school. In the 1980s, a small number of people who had committed suicide had economic reasons ([282]). An analysis of suicide dates leads to the following conclusion: men are pushed toward a fatal step by alcohol on paydays; women, by hard drinking of their husbands ([64]).

At the end of the 1980s, more women began to commit suicide, though male suicides prevailed by a considerable degree. Male mortality due to suicide was 4

Table 10
Mortality from murder and suicide, 1980–94

	Thousands of persons		Per 100,000 population	
	Murders	Suicides	Murders	Suicides
1980	17.8	47.9	12.9	34.5
1985	14.9	44.6	10.4	31.0
1989	18.5	38.0	12.5	25.7
1990	21.1	39.2	14.3	26.4
1991	22.6	39.4	15.2	26.5
1993	–	–	–	31.0
1994	–	–	–	38.0

Sources: [111i]; [171], p. 117; [175], p. 103.

times higher over all, and 8 times higher between the ages of 25 and 39 ([263]). In 1989, the proportion of female suicides began to rise, comprising one quarter of all suicides, mainly due to an increase among younger women – from 22.2% to 30% among the women below 20 years old and from 14.3% to 20% among women 20–24 years old (see table 11). In 1991, the proportion of women committing suicide dropped.

Suicides became younger. There was a marked rise in the suicide rate among children. The number of suicides gradually increased, beginning at age 14, and reached a maximum among those aged 40–49 years. The new peak was observed among people over 60. The average age of suicides among men and women was more or less the same, and recently it dropped. In 1980 in Moscow, for example, for men it was 46.4 years, for women 47 years; in 1985, the ages were 43.7 and 43.4, respectively. High suicide rate among those aged 40–49 years, especially men, was connected with the fact, that this was a time of life when people summed up their lives, reappraised their values, and searched for a new aim in life. The age over 70 years became critical for women. At this group the intensity of suicide among women was three times higher than among men in the same age group; the main reason was loneliness and poverty ([64]).

Among attempted suicides the number of insincere attempts or imitations decreased with increasing age. Most attempts at suicide were made between the ages of 16 and 24 years.

One survey showed that in 1985 all suicides in Moscow were either native Muscovites or had lived in Moscow for more than 20 years. This contradicts the conventional wisdom that it was migrants, the most unsettled, with no stable living and working conditions, that were more likely to commit suicide ([182]).

Table 11
Mortality rate from suicide, 1984–89 (number per 100,000 persons of corresponding gender and age group)

	1984			1989			1991*		
	Men	Women	Share of women (%)	Men	Women	Share of women (%)	Men	Women	Share of women (%)
Under 20	8.8	2.0	22.0	7.5	2.3	30.0	7.0	1.8	25.0
20–24	53.9	7.7	14.3	33.1	6.7	20.0	35.3	6.7	19.0
25–29	80.2	9.2	11.5	49.2	6.0	12.0	49.6	7.1	14.0
30–39	88.7	13.2	14.8	59.8	8.0	13.3	63.6	8.4	13.0
40–49	117.4	21.0	17.8	66.8	12.7	19.0	67.3	12.2	18.0
50–59	116.9	22.8	19.5	72.6	15.7	21.6	71.0	15.5	22.0
60–69	81.7	24.3	29.7	60.1	19.2	31.9	65.7	18.8	28.0
70 and over	105.4	31.0	29.5	95.9	32.1	33.4	87.9	28.8	32.0
Total	65.6	14.2	21.0	42.9	10.9	25.4	44.5	10.8	24.0

Calculated from [171], p. 117; [175], p. 103.

I.A. Boutenko

16.4 Poverty

The proportion of the population that was poor was rising. Over the long term, poverty was a function of household structure, age, and marital status. A substantial proportion of the poor were working. Poverty as a phenomenon was not very present in the popular consciousness until the mid-1990s.

Until the 1990s, poor people were at an advantage, to a certain extent. In the 1920s, the practice of calculating a minimum subsistence level was stopped; it was resumed only in the 1990s. "The poor" as a term was shunned in a country that was striving for general economic equality. In the 1960s, the term "not sufficiently provided for" was introduced. In the 1970s and 1980s, poor people in Russia comprised a small segment of the population. They were not characterized by a particular mode of social reproduction, activities, or access to material wealth. In certain cases, they actually gained an advantage due to the policy of selective philanthropy conducted by trade unions; the main criterion for distributing accommodations, material assistance, bonuses, and plots for kitchen-gardens was need, rather than work contribution.

In the 1960s, wages rose by 150%, whereas the level of benefits from the social consumption funds rose by 230%. Thus, aggregate income was rising for the poor in the framework of the public consumption funds. In the overall income structure in the 1980s, payment for work constituted 70% of income; this figure declined in the 1990s ([175]; see table 1).

With the development of the market economy, the number of poor rose substantially. The gap between the richest and the poorest widened. It was possible systematically to assess the number of poor (those whose income was below living wage; see table 2), only after 1975, when allowances for those who were "not sufficiently provided for" were introduced. Different experts apply different methodologies, but they all record mass impoverishment of the population (see table 3). The proportion of poor increased from 2% in 1989 to 6% in 1990 ([198c]). In accordance with the State Statistics Committee, in 1992 40.3% of the population of Russia had incomes lower than the minimum consumption threshold; in 1993, this figure was 32% ([111h]). In 1992, around 50% of all working people had lower than average incomes, and 2% had salaries below the minimum standard ([171]). Almost one third of families thought that their material situation was very poor in 1993 (see table 4). However, in 1994 as compared to 1993, the number of people earning less than a living wage dropped by 0.5%, and the number of poor dropped by 2% ([342f]).

Until 1990, the gap between the poor and the wealthy narrowed (see table 3).In 1993, the average salary for the best-paid 10% of workers rose by a factor of 27 compared to that of the lowest-paid 10% of workers. According to other data, the ratio was 1:10 in 1970 and 1:50 in 1993 ([326]; see table 5). In 1993, 1.6% of aggregate cash income went to the lowest decile and 30% to the highest; in 1994 , these figures were 1% and 34.2%, respectively ([111g]).

In Russia, poverty was caused by family and demographic factors; the majority of poor were employed. Poverty was never of a professional or class nature; low-income groups were present in all social and professional strata. The state institutions that carry out social policy provided an administrative and statistical definition of poverty and consider that certain population categories had a greater risk of impoverishment: large families, single people, pensioners (see tables 6–8).

The demographics of poor people remained relatively constant up to the late 1980s: large families, young couples, lonely pensioners. According to some data, large families (with three or more children) constituted the largest proportion: according to VCIOM data, such families comprised 12% in the total population, but 59% of poor people in 1993 ([326]). Other data show that among the poor were young families with one or two children, in which one parent, the mother as a rule, was temporarily not working. A 1993 survey showed that alimony accounted for only 20% of per capita income in one-parent families ([111h]).

Table 1
Aggregate income of workers and employees, 1940–92 (%)

	1940	1960	1970	1980	1985	1989	1991	1992
Salary, wages	71.3	75.2	74.4	82.4	80.9	82.2	74.5	57.0
Pensions, stipends, subsidies	–	–	–	9.9	9.6	7.1	12.0	–

Sources: [171], p. 133; [172], p. 562; [175], p. 144.

Table 2
Proportion of low-income families (%)

1975	1985	1988	1990	1992	1993
16.0	11.3	15.0	11–12	33–40	33–40*

Sources: [12c]; [281], p. 327; [325], p. 54.
* Including 10% with income at half of subsistence minimum.

Table 3
Per capita income, 1980–93

	1980	1985	1990	1992	1993
Average (roubles per year)	1,454	1,704	2,584	42,117	528
Minimum (roubles per year)	818	975	1,545	21,600	270
Maximum (roubles per year	3,465	3,711	5,470	175,500	1,534
Ratio of maximum to minimum	4.24	3.81	3.54	8.13	5.68
Ratio of maximum to average	2.38	2.18	2.12	4.17	2.90
Rate of minimum increase	1.00	1.19	1.89	26.40	330.20
Rate of maximum increase	1.00	1.07	1.58	50.60	442.70

Source: [31], p. 4.

Table 4
Distribution of answers to question "How would you characterize the financial position of your family?," 1990–93 (%)

	1990	1992	1993
Hardly make ends meet	35	54	48
Very poor	–	–	7
Poor	–	–	31
Live more or less decently	46	31	53
Below subsistence level	6	9	–
No financial difficulties	7	4	–
Good, very good	–	–	6
No answer	6	2	2

Source: [288], p. 66.

Table 5
Income difference between the 10% best-off persons and the 10% lowest-income persons,
1980–94 (%)

1980	1989	1991	1992	1993	1994
3.0	5.0	4.5	7.5	11.0	12.0

Sources: [111h]; [162c]; [281]; [343a].

Table 6
Old-age pensioners with minimal pensions, 1980–89

	1980	1985	1989
Total (million)	4.0	3.5	6.8
% of total of old-age pensioners	21	16	27

Source: [175], p. 144.

Table 7
Amount of social welfare payments by different types of pension provision, 1980–92 (roubles)

	1980		1985		1986		1989	1992
	Workers	Farmers	Workers	Farmers	Workers	Farmers		
Average	63.8	35.2	78.7	47.0	81.2	48.0	92.1	419.2
Old age	71.6	35.2	87.2	47.2	89.4	48.2	–	438.0
Work-related-illness								
pension	52.7	34.6	57.6	40.6	58.8	41.7	–	–
Disability	53.4	36.6	64.4	48.5	66.2	49.5	–	404.5
loss of breadwinner	37.7	31.3	46.1	38.7	46.9	39.1	–	279.5

Sources: [75a], p. 114; [171], p. 143; [175], p. 141.

Table 8
Number of large families and single mothers receiving
monthly state subsidies, 1980–89 (000 individuals)

1980	1985	1989
779	1,268	1,592

Source: [175], p. 140.

Different data show that 80% to 88% of young people under 25 and 68% of those under 30 systematically received financial assistance from their parents ([281]), whereas the majority of the poor comprised working people aged over 28, with one of two children; the birth of a child forces one of the parents to stop working or change jobs. When parents retired and stopped helping young families, the latter's grew poorer. Hence, an especially high proportion of the poor were aged 30–34.

In 1981, 58% of those in the "poor" category were employed; in 1987, this figure was 63%; in 1992, it was 50%. The main reason for poverty was concealed unemployment ([155]). In 1989, people with intellectual and office jobs were most frequently categorized as poor ([326]).

In rural areas, poverty assumed larger proportions. In the 1980s, 15% of the rural population including old-age pensioners living apart from relatives were below the poverty level ([281]).

When the transition to the market economy occurred, the following groups were vulnerable to poverty: people with low incomes; people with a low level of education (training), who lost their jobs; families with elderly, sick parents; one-parent families; and psychologically fragile people who found it difficult to adapt ([47]).

What was generally perceived as an acceptable living standard – below which one was poor – was more a function of income than of actual material well-being. In the late 1980s, rather than being obscured by socialist pride, as was previously the case, poverty became something that gave rise to complaints and claims on the government. In the public eye, the subsistence level represented an income level that provided for a decent, acceptable standard of living: as few as 20% of the population perceived poverty as the lack of means to provide material needs. In other words, the minimum was perceived as a social minimum rather than a physiological one, which testified to a phenomenon of egalitarianism; public opinion did not distinguish the poor in society.

In 1994, a substantial proportion of respondents thought of themselves as "not sufficiently provided for"; at the same time, they believed that their material position was satisfactory. Many poor people did not believe that it was possible to improve their material position by working hard ([146]).

In the late 1980s, the number of people who stated that they had experienced a worsening of living conditions rose. However, as the state had for a long time appropriated everything earned in order to redistribute money "justly," the number of those in this group who wished to find a second job did not increase, which testified to economic passivity. In the early 1990s, it could easily be seen in the VCIOM data that the poorer the respondent, the more inert he or she was. Fewer poor people made attempts to look for jobs than did those with medium incomes (25% versus 29%) ([326]).

Poor people exhibited signs of marginalization: they were much more likely to be unemployed than were others; they suffered from several kinds of deprivation; their major values in life were family, an interesting job, and stable living conditions. In 1990, every fifth poor person sold off his or her property to support the standard of living to which he or she had formerly been accustomed. Trying to save mony by purchasing the cheapest food, making various repairs themselves, not using any paid services, working hard in their kitchen gardens – that is, doing everything themselves and not relying on professional contributions – are characteristic of poor people.

Poor people, more than others, attached importance to psychological factors such as inconsolability, hopelessness, lack of future prospects. They did not believe that it is possible to provide their children with a good education. Finding a solution to future problems was more often pushed into the background in the struggle for survival.

I.A. Boutenko

17 Attitudes and Values

17.1 Satisfaction

For a long time, official thinking had it that Soviet people had "feelings of legitimate pride and deep satisfaction." This definition made it difficult to deal with a satisfaction problem. Judging from indirect indices, dissatisfaction with all aspects of life in the society was gradually growing, manifesting itself most obviously in the 1990s and giving rise to a great number of conflicts.

On the whole, satisfaction with life in the 1990s was extremely low and on the decline (see table 1). In Moscow in 1988, 73% were satisfied with their work; 42%, with salaries; 32%, with everyday cultural conditions, 24%, with medical conditions; 12%, with distribution of goods; 45%, with cultural institutions; and 47%, with transport ([249] 1992). According to VCIOM data, the proportion of people, who, according to their own estimates, lived more or less decently, dropped from 53% to 46% in from 1989 to 1990. In 1991, dissatisfaction with life as a whole reached 55%; dissatisfaction with medical service was 66%; 55–60% of those polled did not trust the ruling authorities; 80% of respondents saw themselves as ill equipped to solve their own problems ([190c]). In 1992, asked how their living conditions had changed in the previous several months, about 60% of the respondents answered that the situation was taking a turn for the worse ([190d]). On the whole, half of respondents considered conditions under which the majority live to be tolerable; the other half considered them intolerable ([154g]).

Aspirations and hopes raised by perestroika had not been fulfilled among a substantial portion of the population; 15% of those polled in 1992 fully agreed with the statement that it would have been better to leave everything as it was in 1985, without any economic, political, or ideological reforms; 36% agreed partly with this statement ([154n]).

Dissatisfaction with salaries/wages and work, the lack of opportunity to realize one's creative potential, and low demand for skilled workers and specialists led to a situation in which many people, the highly educated, became anxious to leave the country (see tables 2, 3).

Table 1

Responses to the question, "Is your life improving?" (%)

	Saratov 1974	Moscow 1988
Yes	74	48
No	9	21

Source: [249], p. 438.

Table 2

Responses to the question, "Would you like to work abroad?" Moscow (%)

	1991	1992	1993
Yes, definitely	27.8	23.7	12.1
Yes, under good conditions	18.3	16.4	23.1
Yes, but I do not know how to do it	6.5	7.1	7.4
No	47.1	48.4	53.5
Do not know	2.3	4.4	4.9

Source: [1621].

Table 3

Responses to the question, "Would you like to leave this country forever?" Moscow (%)

	1991	1992	1993
Yes, certainly	4.5	7.2	4.3
Yes, under good conditions	5.4	3.7	3.7
Yes, but I do not know how to do it	1.5	4.2	1.8
No	83.4	78.5	87.7
Do not know	5.2	6.4	3.5

Source: [1621].

From the 1970s to the 1990s, the number of those dissatisfied with the content of their work grew. When a person was tied to the workplace by a great number of social links, explicit demands for labour rights were rare and decisively suppressed. The reaction was that many workers lowered their production output, produced low-quality work, violated discipline, and changed jobs or workplace.

The trend toward equalization of wages gave rise to dissatisfaction due to the lack of opportunity for self-fulfilment at work. Formerly, many people were satisfied with any work offered to them, but in the 1980s, their expectations rose sharply, whereas the opportunities remained unchanged (see tables 4, 5). This situation gave rise to dissatisfaction with the content of and compensation for work.

Table 4
Satisfaction with possibilities of fulfilling one's potential in production activity, 1986–89 (%)

	1986	1989
Not fulfilling my potential completely	40.0	42.2
Could work much better	57.0	41.9

Source: [270], p. 75.

Table 5
Respondents' opinion on correlation of their earnings to their work contribution, 1988–91 (%)

	1988	1990	1991
Generally they correlate	47.9	29.1	21.2
I deserve higher remuneration	46.9	61.2	72.8
I don't always work for my pay	2.5	4.8	2.4
Other answers	0.5	0.3	0.0
Difficulty answering	2.3	4.8	3.7

Sources: [288], p. 54.

In the 1980s and, especially, the 1990s the number of those dissatisfied with their material situation grew rapidly (see tables 6, 7, and 8). Wages and salaries constituted approximately 70% of all income from the 1960s to the 1980s. The gap between desired and real wages grew from 1.5 times in 1986 to 2.5 times in 1991. This growth in the gap was the same for all groups. In assessing what average monthly income per capita would enable them fully to satisfy current family needs, respondents in 1990 cited sums that exceeded their own incomes by an average factor of 2.8. These aspirations were, to a certain degree, the result of the impossibility of maintaining the former standard of living with actual incomes, reflecting the gap between the inflation rate and wages ([155]).

The level of satisfaction with social institutions fell. From the 1960s to the 1980s, pre-school institutions were always overcrowded because of a lack of buildings; in 1989, 503,000 more children were placed in kindergartens than were allowed by health standards; the proportion of schoolchildren attending schools in the afternoon and evening increased from 19.3% in 1985 to 22.3% in 1989; over 60,000 children were being educated in a late-evening shift ([175]).

The ever-increasing growth in demand for consumer goods and services remained unsatisfied in the 1990s (see table 9). Every year, people had been queueing up to buy home appliances, cars, and furniture and to receive accommodations, and so on; stoppages and interruptions in delivery of tobacco items, hard liquor, and

Table 6
Responses to the question, "Are you satisfied with your income?" 1988–91 (%)

	1988	1990	1991
Generally, yes	40.3	19.6	12.0
Generally, no	58.3	77.5	87.4
Difficulty answering	1.3	2.8	0.6

Sources: [288], p. 55.

Table 7
Respondents' estimation of their family incomes, 1981–91 (%)

	1981[a]	1986[b]	1991[c]
We can hardly make ends meet, we often have to borrow money to buy necessities, saving money is out of the question	10	13	21
We have enough money for everyday expenditures, but purchasing clothes is difficult: we have to save or borrow money	24	34	46
Generally, we have enough money, we can even save some, but we have to borrow to purchase expensive durable goods or buy on credit	40	37	23
We can afford to purchase most durable goods, but we cannot afford to buy a car or costly accommodations for summer vacation	16	13	8
At present, we can afford some costly purchases, if we wished, we might get money to buy a car, expensive furniture, to pay for expensive, foreign accommodations, summer house – in short, we can afford to buy anything	7	3	1

Source: [323], pp. 44–52.
[a] 10,150 respondents.
[b] 10,150 respondents, USSR.
[c] 1,175 respondents, Russia.

Table 8
Response by workers to question about what they perceive would be a fair salary for them, taking into account their skills and experience, 1986, 1991

	1986			1991	
Real salary (roubles)	Desired salary (roubles)	Difference (%)		Desired salary (roubles)	Difference (%)
Less than 120 roubles	180–200	+45		–	–
120–200	250–380	+50		663	320
201–300	280–360	+40		734	285
301–400		+60%		946	275
401–500				1,167	
501–800				1,573	
over 800				2,391	

Sources: [302], p. 82; [345], pp. 44–52.

Table 9
Proportion of respondents who felt that the situation in some branches of socio-cultural sphere had deteriorated, 1989 (%)*

Provision of food stuffs	77.5
Provision of manufactured goods	83.4
Provision of medicines	67.5
Public food service	41.5
Public transportation	27.2

Source: [176], pp. 212–13.
* Multiple answers allowed.

school copybooks had become more frequent, and a rationing system was introduced in a number of cities after the mid-1970s. This system ended in the mid-1990s, when most of the goods and services were more readily available to the most prosperous segment of the population, thus increasing the level of social tension.

Satisfaction with personal health declined sharply. In 1986–87, an all-Union poll showed that 25.9% of men and 11.2% of women considered their health to be excellent; 40.5% and 33.5%, respectively, considered their health to be good; 20.7% and 28.8%, respectively, found their health satisfactory; 7.3% and 16.5%, respectively, felt that their health was not very good; and 1.4% and 3.4%, respectively, reported that they were in poor health; 4.2% and 6.6%, respectively, did not answer ([75]). In 1990, only 2.5% of Muscovites considered themselves to be in excellent health, while 56.7% believed that their state of health was not very good or quite poor. The poll also showed that 77.8% of Muscovites had health problems; 15.4% suffered from serious diseases; 27.8% were chronically sick, suffering from two or three diseases; and 34.8% had one or two health disorders ([150]).

Satisfaction with organization of cultural life in one's neighbourhood decreased (see table 10). Satisfaction was higher in villages, which could be explained by the fact that rural dwellers had less interest in frequenting cultural institutions (theatres, concert halls, libraries, cultural centres, and so on) ([283]).

Dissatisfaction with housing conditions was very high after some improvement in the 1960s and early 1970s (see table 11). To a certain extent, this was associated with dissatisfaction with marriage and with high levels of divorces, alcoholism, and criminality.

In the 1990s, the main dissatisfaction was with income. Money was seen as a solution to most problems that had been accumulating for years.

Table 10
Satisfaction with organization of cultural life, urban residents, 1982, 1985 (%)

	1982	*1985*
Satisfied	4.0	2.0
Dissatisfied	76.0	79.0
No answer	20.0	19.0

Source: [283], p. 57.

Table 11
Improvement of housing conditions of families and single persons, 1986–91

	1986	*1987*	*1988*	*1989*	*1990*	*1991*
Number of families and single persons who improved their living conditions (000)	1,214	1,382	1,346	1,264	1,296	1,100
Average time families and single persons spend waiting to improve their living conditions	15	17	15	14	13	11
Share of families on a waiting list among all families	23	25	25	25	20	20

Sources: [171], p. 227; [176], p. 231.

I.A. Boutenko

17.2 Perception of Social Problems

Until 1990, housing was the most acute social problem; in the 1970s, shortages of consumer goods and services were worsening; later, these concerns were replaced by rising prices and dropping incomes. In the 1980s, concern shifted from foreign to domestic affairs. The image of "the enemy" was changing and being diffused.

A high degree of politicization of everyday life was observed throughout the entire period of the Soviet power. Officially, from 1960 to the 1980s, interest in international politics predominated. Moreover, such a focus permitted criticism and, to some extent, pluralism. The point of greatest interest in and politicization of domestic affairs was reached in the late 1980s (see table 1), followed by a sharp decline. In the late 1980s and early 1990s, political events, such as withdrawal of troops from Afghanistan, the political demands of striking miners (1989), the election of B. Yeltsin as chairman of the Supreme Soviet of Russia (1990), and the putsch (1991) were of paramount importance in the mind of the public; by 1992, however, economics was the prevailing concern ([162a]).

In the 1970s and 1980s, enemy number one, according to the official propaganda, was world imperialism. By the beginning of the 1990s, the picture had changed. In 1992, over 55% of Muscovites polled believed that they did not have any enemies, whereas the other 45% considered representatives of the new economy, the Mafia, and communists to be enemies; one quarter of the respondents sensed danger or felt hostility manifested toward them on the part of individuals, groups, or abstract forces. The prevalence of such feelings was higher among men (33%) than among women (24%); apprehension was greatest among those with a higher education. Jewish respondents were much more sceptical about their safety than were other Muscovites ([154k]).

As a result of a dramatic deterioration in the economic situation and crises of various kinds, the level of conflicts experienced in interpersonal relations rose: over two-thirds of the Russians polled noted a high degree of irritability, ill will, and hostile attitudes toward others ([154r]).

In the 1990s, public opinion turned from discussing the threat of world imperialism and of a new war to more day-to-day human problems. In 1985, the threat of nuclear war worried 97% of Soviet schoolchildren, whereas only 72% of American children had this concern ([224]).

Table 1
Perception of social problems according to surveys, 1963–94

1963 [a]	1982 [b]	1990 [c]	1992 [d]	1993 [e]	1994 [f]
Housing	International relations	Lack of food products and of consumer goods	High prices	Rise in prices	High prices
Slow salary growth	Family, moral problems	High prices and low wages	Low incomes	Criminality	Criminality
Slow growth of school networks	Slow increase in well-being	Criminality	Social and household problems	Threat of unemployment	Low incomes
Low production of food	Art and literature problems	Intra-ethnic conflict	Lack of housing, poor housing conditions	Lack of state authority	Uncertain future
Slow increase in manufacturing consumer goods	Sports problems	Pollution	Shortage of consumer goods	Ecology	Social injustice
Reduction in work hours		Breaking laws, official graft	Morals, cultural problems	Disintegration of the USSR	Corruption

Sources: [79], p. 176; [154l]; [154p]; [162a]; [162e]; [226], p. 143.
Questions asked:
[a] In your opinion what problem is of primary importance? (All-Union survey)
[b] What topics (see list below) covered in newspapers, on TV, on the radio, in journals, etc., are you most interested in? (Polling of Muscovites)
[c] Which problem out of those listed below do you find most serious in society? (All Union survey)
[d] Which problems, in your opinion, evoke the highest dissatisfaction and indignation in people to date? (Polling of Russians)
[e] Which domestic problems of our society are you most worried about? (Polling of Russians)
[f] same as (e).

In 1992, 42% of Muscovites polled felt that environmental pollution was the most acute problem, presenting the greatest threat for the planet's inhabitants; 19% named interethnic conflicts; 16%, poverty among large numbers of the population; 13%, depletion of natural resources; 6%, the threat of world war. There was a correspondence between assessment of the situation prevailing in one's country and of the most acute problems on a global level ([154r]).

Recognition in the 1990s of the need to solve economic problems, as compared to ecological ones, was independent of age, education, sphere of business, and size of municipality ([154l]).

Personal-safety problems, formerly thought of as a social scourge for the citizens of the industrialized countries of Europe and America, had not worried Russians, but in the late 1980s these problems became urgent. When asked whether they worried about their safety in the street at night, 67.4% of males and 86.3% of females answered in the affirmative in 1989 ([176]). In 1992, 90% of Russians were worried about the cruelty and violence that prevailed in the country. Over 50% of those polled believed that danger lay in wait for them and that they themselves could be victims of a severe crime. Crime and violence upset twice as many urban dwellers as rural dwellers. In the year preceding the poll, urban inhabitants reported that they or their relatives had fallen victim to crime twice as often as did people living in rural localities (31% versus 16%); every third person living in the Moscow and 40% of those in western Siberia reported that they had witnessed or experienced a criminal offence (190c]).

From the 1960s to the 1980s, egalitarian values predominated over those connected with quality of labour output. Social justice was very often identified with equality, a reflection of an ideological postulate of socialism concerning "new historical integrity," or a homogeneous Soviet people. The idea that there would be less wealth but that it would be more equally distributed prevailed ([97]). In the late 1980s, this ideology led, for example, to the notion that the ruling authorities should be deprived of their privileges, irrespective of the scope and effectiveness of their work contribution. By the beginning of the 1990s, the situation had changed: in 1992, 42% felt that the gap in the level of personal incomes should be reduced, while 13% gave no answer ([154i]). Values such as the creativeness of work, ownership of one's means of production, possibilities of entrepreneurial activity, and economic freedom and the consequent risks were not very widespread but became current in the mid-1990s.

Over 50% of Rusians polled, irrespective of sex or profession, believed that circumstances and living conditions were the primary cause of poverty ([288]).

In the 1970s a certain particularism started to emerge and spread rooted in the fragmented nature of the planning of objectives that went back to the 1930s. Furthmore, tolerance toward petty larceny, awe of large-scale fraud schemes, and a condescending attitude toward rudeness, alcoholism, slackness, lack of discipline, and the misleading of foreigners emerged and became more prevalent.

Social and economic "infantilism" prevailed until the 1990s. This was reflected in confidence in the unlimited availability of material and the state's financial resources, which allegedly could satisfy the needs of citizens, irrespective of how much they worked.

In 1990, 42% of Russians intended to compensate for shortfalls in income through additional earning activities. Each fifth respondent intended to live on credit, while every tenth was ready to protest ([154p]). Personal attitudes toward individual security and the need to reject government paternalism were slowly changing. People were beginning to get used to the idea that they should take care of themselves and stop depending on the government (see tables 2, 3). In 1991, 70% of Russians polled were of the opinion that the government should cease making efforts to distribute all material wealth equally, but they believed that it should create the opportunities necessary to allow each person to earn as much as he or she could ([198a]).

Up to 1990, unemployment did not present a threat for most of the population. In the mid-1980s, respondents to the all-Union survey believed that they would be able to find a similar job after taking a retraining course; one third felt that those who lost their jobs would have to take a job of a lower qualification, which would lead to lower earnings, or they would have to leave the public sector; 58% of those polled felt that unemployment in the USSR was impossible and inadmissible by the authorities; 17% thought that unemployment might arise as a temporary and limited phenomenon ([97]). In 1993, however, only four years later, four fifths of the Russian population believed that people were very much afraid of losing their jobs. In 1995, unemployment ranked fourth among the problems worrying Muscovites (see table 4).

Among social problems that had accumulated during the Soviet regime, the housing problem remained predominant. Nevertheless, in the 1970s and 1980s, it was somewhat overtaken by the problem of the shortage of consumer goods and services; in 1989 the most burning problem was that of prices and incomes. Many social problems preoccupied Russians. In 1989, 87% of respondents to the all-Union survey were concerned with ecological issues; 82%, with the shortage and poor quality of food products; 79%, with the housing shortage; 74%, with the low quality, shortage, and poor choice of manufactured goods; 73%, with unfair distribution of material wealth; and 67%, with prices ([97]).

By the 1990s, a widespread transition from public values to private values had begun. When asked what bothered people most of all, 43% of Muscovites named personal affairs; 12%, concerns at work; 38%, the current situation in the country ([162a]; see also table 5).

Table 2

Responses to the question, "Who is responsible for social protection?" 1990–91 (%)*

	1990	1991
Social protection should be expanded, the state should assume greater responsibility	36.1	34.0
The state should provide citizens with minimal level of social protection	17.3	11.4
The state should provide only for incapacitated citizens, disabled persons, orphans	25.3	27.3
The state should provide only under extreme circumstances	5.4	2.6
Social protection of workers/employees should be assumed by the enterprise where they work	30.5	43.4
People should provide for themselves, not depend on the state	15.1	28.0
No answer	6.0	3.0

Source: [288], p. 55.

* Multiple responses possible.

Table 3

Responses to the question, "Must government directly set limits on growth of personal incomes? If yes, within what limits?" 1990–93 (%)

	1990	1992	1993
The state should not set a limit on growth of incomes, payment for work contribution	39	48	43
The state must set a limit on growth of incomes only to a certain extent, so that there are no millionaires	18	15	11
The state anthority must set a limit on growth of incomes, so that the difference between lowest and highest incomes is no more than 3–4 times	29	15	18
No answer	14	22	29

Source: [342c], p. 7.

Table 4
Responses to the question "What worries you most?" by Muscovites and those in Moscow suburbs, 1995 (%)*

	Men	Women	Total
Inflation	41	57	49
Crime	46	47	46
The environment	31	49	41
Unemployment	21	28	25
Anarchy	21	19	20
Disintegration of Russia	16	16	16
Health care	11	19	16
Corruption	15	16	15
Decline of science	16	10	13
Nationalism	9	7	8
Poverty	4	8	6

Source: [111p].
* Multiple answers possible.

Table 5
Distribution of answers to the question, "What do you wish for your relatives for 1995?" (%)*

Health	84
Order and stability	36
Money	36
Good attitude toward others	30
Success	21
Other answer	1
Don't know	4

Source: [162f].
* More than one response possible.

I.A. Boutenko

17.3 Attitudes Toward the Future

The ideology of "communism as the radiant future for the whole of mankind" dominated for a long period of time, and many things were assessed from this point of view. In the 1960s and 1970s, general feelings among the population were fairly optimistic; perestroika, from 1985 to 1989, evoked different attitudes toward the events that were occurring. In the early 1990s, there was a period of profound pessimism, which was replaced by a gradual improvement.

The actual onset of a "radiant future" was continually pushed off to an ever more distant future by the official ideology. In the 1960s, a prevailing concept was imposed upon people to the effect that the present generation would attain the "radiant future" under communism. Later, this epoch gave way to a period of "developed socialism," and then to "socialism with human face," according to the terminology used by the official ideology. In the public mind, "radiant communist" ideals, so vividly described in folklore, receded even further over the horizon. However, from 1987 to 1990, perestroika gave rise to some promises and hopes.

From 1979 to 1981, most Russians felt that their life was improving over time. However, by 1988, the number of optimists had dropped (see tables 1–5). In 1989, only a very small proportion (3% to 5% in various groups) expected an improvement in the supply of goods and services and the health-care system in the succeeding two to three years. One half of all citizens polled, and 37% of rural dwellers, did not expect any improvement. Only one fifth of the population held out hope for a slight improvement ([175]).

According to 1989 VCIOM data, 90% of the population were worried about their future and as few as 4% felt confident about their future. In 1990, 49% of the respondents believed that their economic condition would worsen with the transition to the market economy; 20% believed that the situation would first worsen and then would improve; 4% were of the opinion that it would get better; and 7% felt that it would remain unchanged ([189]). In the same year, another survey found that 46% of respondents thought that their material situation would worsen in the next five years; 22% hoped for improvement; and 17% thought that it would remain unchanged ([154g]). Nevertheless, nearly one half of adult Russians still believed that others aspired to a better life ([154j]).

By 1992, 41% of respondents believed that their lives might change for the better by the end of the year; 17% thought that everything would remain unchanged; and

Table 1
Responses to the question, "How optimistic are you?" (%)

	1990	1992
Fully	4	3
For the most part	49	44
Not much	31	32
Not at all	11	15

Source: [154l].

Table 2
Responses to the question, "Do you expect any changes for the better in your life?" 1989–93 (%)

	1989	1990	1991	1992	1993
Yes, in the next year or two	10	3	10	12	17
Yes, within 5 years	15	10	12	14	11
Yes, by the year 2000	13	16	17	13	12
Yes, but it will take a long time	31	41	35	26	25
No, I won't live that long	14	21	23	27	28
No answer	17	9	10	11	8

Source: [247], p. 38.

Table 3
Assessment of prospects of changes in material well-being of respondents' own families, 1989–93 (%)

	1989	1990	1992	1993
It will improve	25	22	5	5
It will not change	41	46	24	34
It will worsen	17	22	58	44
No answer	17	10	13	17

Source: [342d], p. 37.

40% thought that things would definitely change for the worse. The percentages were distributed equally among all groups of respondents (education, profession, ec.) with substantial discrepancies in terms of increased pessimism being attributed only to age ([154h]).

Hence, by 1990, a relatively homogeneous generally optimistic group had been replaced by a large number of groups with different attitudes. The intensive process of differentiation began in 1990. Among those who were generally optimistic were a large number of executives, managers, women, employees. Those under 24 years of age more often saw their future as vague and uncertain ([185]).

Table 4

Responses to the question, "What changes in income will take place for the majority of people in the next 2 to 3 years?" three top answers, 1989–93 (%)

	1989	1990	1992	1993
Those who are prosperous will get wealthier	45	49	37	45
The rich will get richer, while the poor will get poorer	42	47	57	61
Those who manage to find a good job will earn more	40	29	30	35
Those who work honestly and efficiently will earn more	24	26	13	13
Those who earn more money now will receive still higher pay in the future	20	23	–	–
Only self-employed people with their own business will have large incomes	–	23	15	13
No answer	5	8	6	8

Source: [342e], p. 7.

Table 5

Responses to the question "In how many years do you think queues will disappear?" 1988 (%)

	Women	Men
Before 2000	10.5	12.9
In the 21st century	14.4	21.8
In a long time	29.6	28.8
Never	38.0	9.3
No answer	8.7	8.3

Source: [247], p. 8.

Changes associated with perestroika did not make most people any more optimistic. A rise and subsequent decline in optimism with regard to the political situation took place in the second half of the 1980s, with a trend toward pessimistic expectations for immediate changes for the better ([246]).

Nor did privatization arouse any enthusiasm, though the authors of perestroika had made many efforts to mobilize popular expectations. Asked whether privatization of housing would improve their life, 25% of respondents felt that it would, while 40% felt that it would not ([154h]); nor did people expect queues to disappear (see table 5). Scepticism prevailed as regards to eventual remuneration according to work contribution. When asked how they thought income would be re-distributed in the coming two to three years, the responses, in descending order of importance were: 1) only people who make money dishonestly will become richer; 2) rich people will get richer, while the poor will get poorer; 3) only those who can find a good position will receive more money; 4) those who work well will get more ([288]).

Conditioned from childhoood to do so, people continued to believe in the possibilities of science. Thus, 92% of Soviet children, compared to 61% of American children, thought that the most important problems of life could be solved by science ([224]). In 1992, 44% of Russians polled were of the opinion that modern science and technology undoubtedly could solve the problem of depletion of natural resources ([154i]).

Most people were not worried about the threat of a new world war, despite opposition of the two systems that prevailed in the 1960s and especially in the 1980s. This problem ranked fifth among the most burning problems in a 1992 survey of Muscovites, obtaining less than 15% of responses ([154j]).

In a 1987 poll, 71% of Soviet children, compared to 50% of American children, said that their children would have a better life. The proportions of those who thought the contrary were 1% and 11%, respectively ([224]). In 1992, 38% of adult Russians felt that giving birth to children at the present time, was irresponsible, despite the fact that in a survey on satisfaction with life, as a whole, as few as 14% of the Russian reported their lives as poor or very poor, while 56% of those polled assessed their life as satisfactory; 23%, as fairly good; and 4%, as excellent ([154i]).

I.A. Boutenko

17.4 Values

In the 1980s, the former so-called integrity of the values of the population ("moral and political unity of all Soviet people") was undergoing a crisis. Pluralism began to be revealed as an obvious phenomenon, developing against the background of the emergence of a general humanistic value orientation, as opposed to class only. A trend toward an encapsulation of private life became evident, as did a current of neoconservatism. Values pertaining to personal well-being and consumption regained importance.

Though the value of human life has increased compared to the situation prevailing in the epoch of totalitarism, it remains on a very low level compared to that in industrialized countries (see table 1). The increase in criminal violence and contracted assassinations is a manifestation of the low esteem in which human life is still held by many.

Table 1
Indicators of value of life*

	USSR/Russia	France	Japan	US
1900	0.67	1.12	0.92	1.01
1930	6.92	1.54	1.34	2.78
1960	3.48	2.92	4.71	6.36
1990	3.32	11.55	21.64	21.20
2020	6.33	30.22	86.40	43.45

Source: [71].

* This indicator includes aggregate national income, national aggregate income spent for military needs, population numbers, expenditures on nourishment in the family budget, coefficient of mortality rate, and average life expectancy.

Human values have gradually taken over from class values in the 1990s. When the major value of socialism – collectively inspired labour – was displaced, a wide range of subsidiary values ceased to be effective on the policy level. Social dependence was eroded and the population came to realize that they had to assume personal responsibility. Nevertheless, dependence on the relationship with the workplace, an affiliation that had been the major, and sometimes the only, source of substistence, continued into the early 1990s.

The interest in politics that had materialized in the late 1980s dissipated for the majority of the population by 1993 (see table 2). The reference to societal aspirations was imploding, while the reference to purely individual values was exploding. All of this was associated with the new prevalence of notion of the individual as a free agent.

Intolerance and ruthlessness toward opponents and adversaries have been replaced by "an everyman's humanism" that appears as a universal value frame integrating behaviour of people in all strata of society, despite the fact that overall tolerance remained low ([281]).

Enthusiasm for labour, an attitude characteristic of the 1940s and 1950s, gradually vanished. In the early 1960s, because of equalizing of remuneration and the growth of shortages, the desire for a good income and material well-being partially lost its significance, whereas the desire to get an interesting job took some precedence. In the 1970s, the social, psychological, economic, and health conditions of work became more important, along with a simultaneous strengthening trend toward equalization of wages. Values pertaining to the content of work suffering in favour of values connected with material well-being, and the significance of consumerism was rising. In the 1980s, the proportion of persons oriented on consuming, as the major value, increased (see table 3); the increase occurred especially among young people.

Table 2
Interest in political campaigns, 1990–92 (%)

1990	1991	1992
70	20	12

Source: [141], p. 47.

Table 3
Share of respondents for whom consumerism
is the primary objective, 1988–93 (%)

1988	1993
10	37

Source: [141], p. 47.

The majority of those polled in 1991 did not value their professional skills acquired through training and were prepared to take a job not related to their specialty, should they happen to lose their job (67%); moreover, 58% reported that they were willing to master a new skill (58%) ([154a]). Money was acquiring a new status, connected with the emergence of a market economy. Pragmatism was on the rise. According to evaluations by young people (1992), the most important thing now was to be fairly well off, then came the family, an interesting job, an education, entertainment, and public involvement ([154m]). Among other age groups, many also showed a preference for consumer values.

Instead of "socialist internationalism," which was, in fact, very similar to both patriotism and great-power chauvinism, there emerged in the 1980s a recognition of individuals' right to live in the country of their choice. Over 51% of respondents agreed with this idea ([141]). At the same time, in 1990, in the country where so many ethnic groups, who were the products of different historical epochs and cultures, lived together, various forms of previously concealed ethnic conflicts were becoming evident and a revival of nationalistic chauvinism started to manifest itself.

In the mid-1990s, education, previously held in high esteem, was losing its attractiveness. In the 1960s, young workers in Leningrad assigned the most importance, in terms of attitudes and life plans, to the values of education and family, while the value of work was ranked lowest. In the 1970s, a survey of schoolchildren and students conducted in six regions showed that values for the future were as follows: satisfaction of spiritual needs, authority, creative work. Later, personality-oriented values gradually rose to top rank. In the 1990s, the primary values were professional efficiency, material well-being, and public approval, whereas the value of creativity was insignificant ([141]). In the mid-1990s, education regained its value.

The notion of authority as an object of contestation is traditional for Russians. Authority is depicted as an alternative to enjoyment of a clear conscience. In 1982, 30% of respondents assessed the relative importance of the moral characteristics of leading authorities as significant, whie 70% of respondents saw the professional characteristics of leading authorities as significant; in 1988, respondents were split evenly, 50%–50%, on the significance of these characteristics; in 1992, opinions had reversed, and 70% felt moral characteristics were most significant, versus 30% who felt that professional characteristics were most significant ([87]).

The notion of prosperity (well-being) in life was expressed in 1988 in the following terms: happy family life, 66%; availability of compatible, devoted friends, 53%; good housing conditions, 47%; absence of material difficulties, 46%; interesting, creative work, 25%; ([302]). In the 1990s, having a clear conscience acquired a special value, linked to kindness, beauty and truth, good relations with friends, interesting work, and freedom. A number of other values began to be comprehended from this standpoint. Thus, modesty as an important element of dignity was replaced, in the 1990s, by a burgeoning desire to join the elite members of one's social group in order to distinguish oneself ("careerism"). In place of social justice, as mode for redistribution of material wealth, the denial of imposed equality of remuneration became a value in itself. Indeed, while enterprising nonconformism came gradually to be accepted, power-loving ambitious egoism was rejected ([87]).

At the end of 1980s, the public increasingly connected success with hard work, but by 1992 the values of skilled labour, talent, and abilities came to be seen as secondary to having good connections. The significance of having rich parents became more important (see table 4).

By the late 1980s, there was a sharp decline in respect for the law and a resurgence of a desire for power. Crimes and everyday conflicts became more and more brutal.

In place of an anthropocentric attitude toward nature and a desire to master it, people came to appreciate the necessity of more careful treatment of the environment.

Individuals' health came to be perceived as a private matter as the market economy began to develop, at which time there appeared a clear preference for healthy and attractive employees in private enterprises, where remuneration was two to ten times higher than in state enterprises. At the former, people were often paid "under the table" supplements to compensate them for extra time on the job; coincidentally, they had no insurance and, hence, no motivation to be absent.

Table 4
Responses to the question, "What is needed to achieve success in life?" 1988, 1992 (%)*

	1988	1992
Work hard, with a clear purpose	45	32
Know one's job	35	30
Be capable	26	30
Be resourceful	19	31
Be well connected	17	31
Encounter real, worthwhile people	14	8
Have well-off parents	10	14
Have relatives who hold high positions	8	9
Be a social activist (on a large scale)	6	1
Have a good personal and professional record	4	1
Have intelligent parents	2	1
Be born a man (a woman)	2	4

Source: [342e].
* Multiple answers possible.

Nevertheless, there was competition at state industrial enterprises in the 1990s by elderly women attempting to take on risky jobs because the earnings and privileges associated with these jobs were higher ([350]).

I.A.Boutenko

17.5 National Identification

The role of nationality was always very important in the life of Soviet citizens during the entire period of Soviet power. Only in the 1990s did its significance fade. With the disintegration of the USSR, the chauvinism associated with being a citizen of a great power disappeared. In the mid-1980s, self-identification of the population as "the Soviet people" changed, among some groups, to that of "democrat" or "communist" and, in the 1990s, to that of certain ethnic groups, which experienced a rebirth of national self-consciousness.

In a state that officially proclaimed equality of all nationalities, the nationality of an individual was nevertheless always mentioned on all documents – for instance, when entering school, taking a job, joining the Communist Party, becoming a member of a public library, and so on. Children took the nationality of either of their parents.

According to the 1989 population census, Russians comprised 81.5% of the total population of the Russian Federation. This does not make Russia a particularly multinational state in comparison with some other countries of the world ([108]). Official ideology constantly emphasized the multinational character of the USSR (120 nationalities) and the equality of all the nations. This ideology strove for the creation of a new historical community, the "Soviet people," but in practice it was a process of Russification of the population. Most non-Russians mentioned their respective ethnic group's language as their mother tongue (see table 1). From 1979 to 1989, however, the proportion of such mentions decreased in all national republics except Bashkirs ([175]).

Jews, who had been nicknamed "invalids of the fifth paragraph" (that is the fifth point about one's nationality in standard questionnaires) were discriminated against when applying to higher-education institutions and for prestige jobs, especially in the military-industrial complex, as well as in everyday life.

The demonstration of any national specificity in art (except by some officially sponsored music groups and writers) and in daily life was not encouraged and even persecuted as nationalism and "carry-overs from the past."

Throughout the period of Soviet power, superpower chauvinism was cultivated under the slogan "Soviet means excellent." In the 1960s and 1970s, the majority of citizens of the USSR, including those who lived in Russia, called themselves Soviet, but as the USSR disintegrated and lost territories, a concomitant process of disintegration of superpower consciousness intensified. Before the 1990s, according to VCIOM polls, a superpower-type of national self-identification was characteristic of 52–55% of the population; conservative-ideological identification, 10–13% (including Slavophile, 7–8%); national-democratic, 9–10%; democratic, 6–7% (see table 2). Russians and those who live in Russia and consider themselves Russian citizens more often identify with state power – with Russian military might and huge territory, but their number is diminishing ([89]; see table 2).

Xenophobia, actively used by the official ideology to unite people against a common enemy ("world imperialism"), began to change its objective just before the 1990s. In the 1940s and 1950s, Soviet xenophobia was directed mainly and officially against "imperialists" and Jews. During the 1970s, some loyal citizens found it appropriate to demonstrate hostility toward dissidents. In the late 1980s and early 1990s, certain groups began to embody an image of ethnic or social "otherness," in relation to whom much of the population could affirm themselves as Russian: these other groups were Caucasians, Chechens, Asians, Mafia, foreigners,

Table 1
Proportion of those of a given nationality who consider their national language or the Russian language as their mother tongue (peoples more than 800,000 in number), 1989

	Language of their nationality	Russian	Other language
The whole population	94.6	5.1	0.3
Russians	99.9	–	0.05
Tatars	85.6	14.2	0.2
Ukrainians	42.9	57.9	0.1
Chauvashes	77.5	22.3	0.2
Bashkirs	72.8	10.1	17.1
Belorussians	36.2	63.5	0.3
Mordvans	64.0	30.9	0.1
Chechns	98.8	1.1	0.1
Germans	41.8	58.0	0.2

Source: [175], p. 74.

Table 2
Russians living in Russia who consider themselves Soviets or Russians, 1991, 1993 (%)

	1991	1993
Soviets	63	26
Russians	25	41

Source: [342e], p. 12.

democrats, and promoters of privatization ([190l]). Consequently, there was a noticeable growth in xenophobia: in 1990, 8% of respondents were xenophobic; in 1992, this description applied to 12% ([342c]).

Beginning in the 1970s, feelings of national pride of the Russian (Soviet) people were often accompanied by a certain sense of humiliation (see table 3). After 1990, most people lost their belief that they could achieve the living standards of the developed countries in the near future; euphoria had disappeared (see table 4).Though Russians officially had "their own" national state in the USSR, the real status of this group in the political and cultural arenas has been and still is dominant. The Russian culture and language are the referent culture and language for the entire federation. Public-opinion polls showed that, in spite of the superpower consciousness, kindred feelings toward people of their own nationality are characteristic of 85% of Russians. Two thirds not only recognize but also can define certain features common to their compatriots. For example, the replies to such questions as "What

Table 3
Negative responses to the question, "To whom and in what
respect could your country give a good example?" (%)

	1988	1989	1990
To nobody and in nothing	6	34	50

Source: [342e], p. 12.

Table 4
Responses to the question, "What country's achievements are most important to your country?"
1988–92 (%)

	1988	1989	1990	1991	1992
US	13	28	32	25	13
Japan	26	35	32	28	12
Germany (East Germany)	3	5	17	15	7
Sweden	2	8	4	7	3
China	4	4	3	6	5

Source: [342a], p. 14.

unites you with your nation?" are divided equally among such features as language, culture (life style, customs, rituals), and character (temperament, behaviour, etc.). Replies such as historical fate were less frequently mentioned ([14]).

Russians' predominant orientation toward their own national culture shows that both synchronic and diachronic cultural ties of the members of this nation are concentrated mainly inside their ethnic community. This fact is regarded as a sign of ethnocultural stability, as a certain cultural self-sufficiency of the Russian nation ([249]).

At the end of the 1980s national self-awareness of different nations in Russian Federation grew dramatically, leading in the 1990s to ejections of other ethnic populations, especially Russians, from the territories of the former national autonomous regions, deprivation of citizenship and ethnic preferences in electoral procedures, and other acts.

VCIOM polls show that young people are more nationalistic than is the population in general. This was connected, in particular, with the fact that the consciousness of young people was for many years being influenced by the denigration of official internationalism. In regions where ethnic tension existed openly, nationalistic tendencies were more explicitly expressed among young people. They understood the problem of national consciousness not as one of national renaissance, but as a possible mode of self-affirmation.

In the 1990s, the growth of national consciousness led in some cases to the formation of "national states." The USSR disintegrated under the determining influence of the doctrine of ethnic nationalism and the slogan of national self-definition. Before 1993, 21 nations within Russia had raised their status to that of "national state." Simultaneously, the majority of respondents from these different nations often expressed a fairly optimistic view concerning the future of Russia as a federative state ([108]). Nevertheless, an active search for new identities was taking place in the newly formed states.

As a result of various social problems, the moral and political disorientation of Russians, and the fact that all the misfortunes and injustices of Russia were credited to them by other ethnic groups, the trend toward Russian ethnic nationalism increased. According to some forecasts, by the next population census, in 1999, the number of ethnic Russians in Russia will have decreased from 82% to 70%, and not only because of a low birth rate; millions of Russians of mixed origin, who previously called themselves ethnic Russians, will prefer to change their ethnic identification under the pressure of social, political, and cultural conditions ([292]).

Ethnic problems had a very slight impact on demography, although there was a certain deceleration in the proportion of mixed families (see table 5).

Table 5
The proportion of families in which husband and wife are of different nationality, among all families, 1959–79 (%)

1959	1970	1979
8.3	10.7	12.0

Source: [342a], p. 153.

I.A. Boutenko

REFERENCES

1. Алексеев В.А. *Иллюзии и догмы* (Alekseev V.A. *Illusions and Dogmas*). Москва: Политиздат, 1991.

2. Алексеенко С.Р. Аренда: препятствия на взлете / *Социол. исслед.* (Alekseenko, S.P. "Rent: Obstacles at "Taking-off"." *Sociological Studies*), 1990, № 1.

3. Альтернативные профсоюзы: возможность и реальность ("Круглый стол" редакции) / *Социол. исслед.* ("Alternative Trade Unions. A Round Table Discussion." *Sociological Studies*), 1990, № 2.

4. Аналитический доклад по результатам мониторинга социально-трудовой сферы (Ministry of Kabour and Employment *Analythical Report on Social and Labour Sphere Monitoring*). Москва: Мин. Труда и занятости России, 1994.

5. Андреева И.Н., Новикова Л.Г. Молодежная субкультура / *Социол. исслед.* (Andreyeva, I.N. and L.G.Novikova "Youth Sub-culture." *Sociological Studies*), 1989, № 4.

6. Андреенкова Н.В., Воронкова Г.А. Развитие трудовых конфликтов в период перехода к рыночной экономике / *Социол. исслед.* (Andreenkova, N.V., and G.A.Voronkova "Development of Labour conflicts in the cousse of transfer to market economy." *Sociological Studies*), 1993, № 8.

7. Аникеева Л.В. *Социально-экономические проблемы пенсионного обеспечения в условиях перехода к рыночным отношениям.* Научный доклад. (Anykeeva, L.V. *Social and Economic Problems of Pension Supply Under the Transition to Market*). Москва: НИИ Труда, 1994.

8. Аничкин А. Семья и рождаемость. — В кн.: *Население России. Ежегодный демографический обзор* (Anichkin, A. "Family and Birth-Rate". In: *Population of Russia. A Year Demographical Review*). Москва: Финансы и статистика, 1993.

9. Антонян Ю.М., Перцова Л.В., Саблина Л.С. Опасные девицы / *Социол. исслед.* (Antonian, Iu.M., L.V.Perzova, and L.S.Sablina. "Dangerous Girls." *Sociological Studies*), 1991, № 7.

10. Анурин В.Ф. Тайна вклада / *Социол. исслед.* (Anurin, V.F. "Bank Secrecy." *Sociological Studies*), 1988, № 2.

11. Анурин В.Ф. Справедливость и общественные фонды потребления / *Социол. исслед.* (Anurin, V.F. "Justice and Social Funds of Consumption." *Sociological Studies*), 1990, № 12.

12a. Аргументы и факты (*Arguments and Facts*), 1991, № 4.

12b Аргументы и факты (*Arguments and Facts*), 1992, № 41.

12c. Аргументы и факты (*Arguments and Facts*), 1993, № 3.

12d. Аргументы и факты (*Arguments and Facts*), 1993, № 14.

12e. Аргументы и факты (*Arguments and Facts*), 1992, № 10.

When a work was published in a small town, publisher is not mentioned because there was only one state publisher: the state.

12f. Аргументы и факты (*Arguments and Facts*), 1993, № 17.

12g. Аргументы и факты (*Arguments and Facts*), 1994, № 4.

12h. Аргументы и факты (*Arguments and Facts*), 1994, № 12.

12i. Аргументы и факты (*Arguments and Facts*), 1994, № 14.

12j. Аргументы и факты (*Arguments and Facts*), 1994, № 32.

12k. Аргументы и факты (*Arguments and Facts*), 1994, № 46.

12l. Аргументы и факты (*Arguments and Facts*), 1995, № 15.

13. Артемов В.А. Исследование бюджета времени работающего населения г. Рубцовска в 1972 и 1980 г.г. — В кн.: *Рабочее и свободное время*, отв. ред. Т.М.Караханова (Artemov, V.A. "The Research of Time Budget of the Working Population in the City of Rubzovsk in 1972 and 1980s." In T.M.Karahanova, ed., *Work and Free Time*). Москва: ИСИ АН СССР, 1987, кн. 1.

14. Артемов В.А. Динамика образа жизни сельского населения / *Социол. исслед.* (Artemov, V.A. "Dynamics of Life Style of the Rural Population." *Sociological Studies*), 1990, № 4.

15. Арутюнян М. *Особенности семейного взаимодействия в семьях с различным распределением бытовых ролей* (Aroutiunian, M. *Peculiarities of Family Interaction in Families with Different Distribution of Everyday Dutes*). Автореф. канд. дис. — Москва: ИСИ АН СССР, 1984.

16. Арутюнян М., Здравомыслова О. Молодежь: импровизации на тему прошлого / Культура и жизнь (Aroutiunian, M. and O. Zdravomyslova "Youth: Looking at the Past." *Culture and Life*), 1994, № 10.

17. Арутюнян Ю.В. О развитии и сближении культуры советских народов / *Социол. исслед.* (Aroutiunian, Yu.V. "On the development and Rapprochement of Soviet Nations' Culture" *Sociological Studies*), 1974, № 2.

18. Арутюнян Ю.В. Социально-культурное развитие и национальное самосознание / *Социол. исслед.* (Aroutiunian,Yu.V. "Social and Cultural Development and National Self-Conciousness." *Sociological Studies*), 1990, № 7.

19. Арутюнян Ю.В. Испытание устойчивости нового политического сознания русских / *Этнограф. обозр.* (Arutiunian, Yu.V. "Testing Stability of New Political Consciousness of the Russians". *Ethnographic Review*), 1994, № 3.

20. Балыкова Н.А. *Пути сокращения домашнего труда* (Balykova, N.A. *The ways of Housekeeping Work Reduction*). Москва: ИСИ АН СССР, 1978.

21. Барбаров Ф.П., Гусева А.С. Кабинетная этика / *Социол. исслед.* (Barbarov, F.P. and Guseva, A.S. "The Office Ethics." *Sociological Studies*), 1989, № 5.

22. Баскакова М.Е. Квалификационный уровень работниц в промышленности. — В кн.: *Проблемы охраны труда и здоровья женщин на современном этапе и пути их решения*, отв. ред. Г.В.Морозов (Baskakova, M.E. "Qualification Level of the Working Women in Industry. In *Morosov, G.V. Problems of Women's Labour and Health Protection at the Present Stage and Means of their Solution*). Иваново, 1988.

23. Безгребельная И., Кузьминова М. Социальные контуры рынка труда / *Человек и труд* (Bezgrebelnaya, I. and M.Kuzminova "Social contours of the Labour Market." *Man and Labour*), 1993, № 12.

24. *Безработица в России: между прошлым и будущим*. Информационный бюллетень (*Unemployment in Russia: Between the Past and the Future*. Information Bulletin). Москва: Федеральная служба занятости России, 1993.

25. Белова В. Повторные браки и рождаемость — В кн.: *Социально— демографические исследования брака, семьи, рождаемости и репродуктивных установок*, отв. ред. П.Л.Рыбаковский (Belova, V. "Second Marriages and childbearing." In P.L.Rybakovsky, ed., *Social and Demographic Investigations of Marriage, Family, Childbearing and Perpoduction Attitudes*). Москва: ИСИ АН СССР, 1983.

26. Белова Н.Ф., Дмитриев И.И. *Семейный бюджет. Статистический аспект* (Belova, N.P., and I.I.Dmitriev *Family Budget. Statistical Aspect*). Москва: Финансы и статистика, 1990.

27. Беляева И.Ф. Материальное стимулирование в новом хозяйственном механизме / *Социол. ислед.* (Belyaeva, I.F. "Money Stimulas in the New Economic System." *Sociological Studies*), 1989, № 3.

28. Березин И. Социальная дифференциация в переходный период / *Вопр. экономики* (Berezin, I. "The Social Differentiation During the Transitional Period." *Problems of Economy*), 1993, № 12.

29. Берзин Б.Ю., Коган Л.Н. Профессиональная культура партийного работника / *Социол. исслед.* (Berzin, B.Yu. and L.N.Kogan "Professional Culture of a Party Worker." *Sociological Studies*), 1989, № 3.

30. Бетанели Н.И,. Лапаева В.В. Социологическая служба 1 Съезда народных депутатов СССР: первый опыт / *Социол. исслед.* (Betaneli, N.I. and V.V.Lapayeva "The Sociological Service of the 1st Congress of the People's Deputies of the USSR: The First Experience." *Sociological Studies*), 1990, № 4.

31. *Биржевые ведомости* (*The News of the Burse*), 1994, № 27.

32. Богачев В. *Совершенствование системы управления кадрами* (Bogachev, V. Improvement of the Management Personnel Regulation). Москва: Экономика, 1975.

33. Богданова Т.В., Журавлева И.В. Активный отдых и тенденции его развития у трудящихся промышленности — В кн.: *Тенденции изменения бюджета времени трудящихся*. отв. ред. В.Д.Патрушев (Bogdanova, T.V., and I.V.Zhuravleva. Active Leisure and the Trends of Its Development Among the Industrial Workers." In V.D.Patroushev, ed., *Tendencies of Workers' Time Budget Changes*). Москва: ИСИ АН СССР, 1979.

34. Богомолов Ю., Балацкий Э. Профессиональный аспект высвобождения кадров / *Экономист* (Bogomolov, V., and E.Balatsky "The Professional Aspect of Personnel Lay-off." *Economist*), 1994, № 7.

35. Божков О.Б., Голофаст В.Б. Разделение труда в городской семье / *Социол. исслед.* (Bozhkov, O.B., and V.B.Golofast "Distribution of Duties in Urban Family." *Sociological Studies*), 1986, № 4.

36. Борзенко В.И. Религия в посткоммунистической России / *Экономические и социальные перемены: мониторинг общественного мнения* (Borsenko, V.I. "Religion in Postcommunist Russia." *Economic and Social Changes: A Public Opinion Monitoring*), 1993, № 4.

37. Борзикова Л.В., Докторова Л.Д., Лебедев П.Н. На вершине управленческой пирамиды / *Социол. исслед.* (Borzikova, K.V., L.D.Doctorova, and P.N.Lebedev "On the Top Management Level." *Sociological Studies*), 1990, № 1.

38. Борисов С.Б. Эротические тексты как источник сексуального самообразования / *Социол. исслед.* (Borissov, S.B. "Erotic Texts as a Source for Sexual Self-Education." *Sociological Studies*), 1989, № 1.

39. Бочарова О. Сексуальная свобода: слова и дела / *Человек* (Bocharova, O. "Sexual Freedom: Words and Actions." *Man*), 1994, № 5.

40. Бутенко И.А. Кумиры читающей публики (беглый взгляд на массовое чтение времен оттепели и перестройки) / *Вестник АН СССР* (Boutenko, I.A. "The Idols of the Reading Public." *Herald of the Academy of Sciences of the USSR*), 1990, № 11.

41. Бутенко И.А. "Изящная словесность" девочек-подростков / *Советская педагогика* (Boutenko, I.A. "Writings of Teenaged Girls." *Soviet Pedagogics*), 1991, № 10.

42. Бутенко И.А. Особенности женского чтения / *Советское библиотековедение* (Boutenko, I.A. "The Peculiarities of Women's Reading." *Soviet Library Science*), 1991, № 10.

43. Бутенко И.А. Социодинамика читательских интересов. — В кн.: *Книга. Исследования и материалы*, отв. ред. А.П.Толстиков (Boutenko, I.A. Social Dynamics of Readers' Interests." In A.P.Tolstikov, ed., *The Book: Research and Documentation*). Москва: Всероссийская книжная палата, 1992, т. 64.

44. Бутенко И.А. Из истории черного юмора / *Социол. исслед.* (Boutenko,I.A. "On the history of Black humour." *Sociological Studies*), 1994, № 11.

45. Бутенко И.А. Информационные и культурные потребности жителей региона. — В кн.: *Региональные проблемы деятельности библиотек, отв.* ред. И.В.Даньшина (Boutenko,I.A. "Information and Cultural Needs of the Population of the Region" In I.Danshina, ed., *Regional Problems in the Libraries' Functionning*). Москва: РГБ, 1995.

46. Бутенко И.А., Плотников С.Н. *Отчет Ассоциации "Молодежь и культура" Фонду культуры СССР по исследованию "Культура, нравственность и молодежь"* (Boutenko,I.A., and S.N.Plotnikov, eds., *Culture, Morality and Youth. Report of the "Youth and Culture" Association*). Москва: Сов. Фонд Культуры, 1991.

47. Быкова С.Н., Любвиц В.П. Бедность по-русски и по-итальянски / *Социол. исслед.* (Bykova, S.N., and V.P.Lubvitz "Poverty in Russian and in Italian." *Sociological Studies*), 1993, № 2.

48. Бытко Ю.И., Ландо А.С. Девиантное поведение подростков / *Социол. ис-след.* (Bytko, Yu.I., and A.S.Lando "Deviant Behaviour of Teenagers." *Sociological Studies*), 1988, № 4.

49. Быховская И.М. *Человеческая телесность в социокультурном изменении: традиции и современность* (Bychovskaya, I.M. *Human Body in Social and Cultural Changes: Tradition and Modernity*). Москва: Рос. Гос. Академия Физической культуры, 1993.

50. *Бюллетень Центра социологических исследований МГУ (Bulletin of the Center for Sociological Researches of Moscow State University)*, 1994, № 1.

51. *Ваш выбор (Your Choice)*, 1994, № 1.

52. Веселов С. Телевизионная реклама: счет пошел на миллиарды / *Московские новости* (Veesslov, S. TV Advertising: Couting Billions." *Moskovskiye Novosty*), 1993, № 8.

53a. *Вестник статистики (Statistical Gerald)*, 1990, № 5.

53b. ibid, 1991, № 11.

54. Вишневский А.Г. На полпути к городскому обществу / *Человек* (Vishnevsky, A.G. "On the Half-way to Urban Society." *Man*), 1992, № 1.

55. Войнова В.Д., Ушкалов И.Г. Современные эмиграционные процессы в России / *Социол. исслед.* (Voinova, V.D., and I.G.Ushkalov "Modern Emigration Processes in Russia." *Sociological Studies*), 1994, № 1.

56. Волков А.Г. *Семья — объект демографии* (Volkov, A. *Family as an Object of Demography*). Іосква: Мысль, 1986.

57. Воронина О.А. Женщина в "Мужском обществе" / *Социол. исслед.* (Voronina, O. "Female in "Male" Society." *Sociological Studies*), 1988, № 2.

58. Вохменцева Г.М., Камаева О.П., Ильин А.Л. Авторитет общественных организаций / *Социол. исслед.* (Vokhmenceva G.N., O.P.Kamaeva, and A.Iliyn "Public Associations' Authority." *Sociological Studies*), 1989, № 5.

59. *Время и его использование*, отв. ред.В.Д.Патрушев (V.D. Patroushev, ed., *Time and Its Use*). Москва: ИСИ АН СССР, 1988.

60. *Время населения: динамика его использования*, отв. ред. Т.М.Караханова (T.M.Karahanova, ed., *Time of Population: Dynamics of Its Use*). Москва: ИС РАН, 1992.

61. Габиани А.А. *На краю пропасти: наркомания и наркоманы* (Gabiany, A.A. *On the Verge of Disaster. Narcotism and Drug Addicts*). Москва: Мысль, 1990.

62. Гаспаришвили А.Т., Туманов В.С. На опросных фронтах / *Социол. исслед.* (Gasparishvili, A.T., and V.S.Toumanov "At the Public Opinion Polls' Fronts." *Sociological Studies*), 1993, № 6.

63. Гамс Э.С., Петров В.И.. Глас народа — глас "избранных"? / *Социол. исслед.* (Gams, E.S. and V.J.Petrov "The people's voice — the voice of the "elected?" *Sociological Studies*), 1990, № 8.

64. Гилинский Я.И. Смолинский Л.Г. Социодинамика самоубийств / *Социол. исслед.* (Guilinskyi,Ia.I., and L.G.Smolinskyi "Social Dymnamics of Suicides." *Sociological Studies*), 1988, № 5.

65. Гимпельсон В.Е., Могун В.С. В ожидании перемен / *Социол. исслед.* (Gimpelson, V.E. and V.S.Mogun "Expecting changes.*" Sociological Studies*), 1990, № 1.

66. Головин С.Д. О классификации явлений теневой экономики / *Вестник Моск. ун-та. Сер. экономика* (Golovin, S.D. "On the Shady Economy Phemonena Classification." *Herald of Moscow University. Economics)*, 1992, № 1.

67. Голод С.И. *Стабильность семьи: социологический и демографический аспекты* (Golod, S.I. *Family Stability: Social And Demographic Aspects*). — Ленинград: Наука, 1984.

68. Голод С.И. Изучение половой морали в 20-е г.г. / *Социол. исслед.* (Golod, S.I. "The Studies of the Sexual Morals of the 20s." *Sociological Studies)*, 1986, № 2.

69. Голод С.И. Проституция в контексте изменений половой морали / *Социол. исслед.* (Golod S.I. "Prostitution under the Context of the Changes of Sex' Morality." *Sociological Studies)*, 1988, № 2.

70. Гольденберг И.А. Классовая сущность "симбиоза". Теневая экономика в административно-командной системе / *Социол. исслед.* (Goldenberg, I.A. Class Essence of the "Symbiosis". Shady Economy in Command Economy." *Sociological Studies)*, 1991, № 1.

71. Гольц Г. Почему мы такие, какие мы есть? / *Известия* (Goltz, G. "Why Are We What We Are?" *Izvestia)*, 16.10.1993.

72. Гордон Л.А., Клопов Э.В. *Человек после работы. Социальные проблемы быта и внерабочего времени* (Gordon, L.A., and E.V.Klopov *Man After Work. Social Problems of Everyday Life and the Out-of Work Time)*. Москва: Наука, 1972.

73. *Городские поселения РСФСР: По данным Всесоюзной переписи населения 1989 г.* (State Statistic Committee *Urban Settlements of Russia According to All-Union Census in 1989)*. Москва: Респ. инф.-издат. центр, 1991.

74. Горяновский А. Украсть можно все (результаты включенного наблюдения) / *Социол. исслед.* (Goryanovsky, A. "Everything Can Be Stolen." *Sociological Studies)*, 1990, № 2.

75. Госкомстат сообщает / *Социол. исслед.* ("State Statistic Commettee Informs." *Sociological Studies)*, 1989, № 2.

76. Градницын А.А. Общественное мнение о возрождении донского казачества / *Социол. исслед.* (Gradnistin, A.A. "Public Opinion on the Revival of Don's Cossacks." *Sociological Studies)*, 1991, № 12.

77. Грицевич Н.Г. Проблемы энергосбережения в условиях перехода к рынку / *Экономист* (Gritzevich, N. G. "Problems of Energy Saving Under the Transition to the Market." *Economist)*, 1993, № 2.

78. Гришко А.Я. О наркомании среди подростков / *Социол. исслед.* (Grishko, A.Ia. "On narcotism Among Teenagers." *Sociological Studies)*, 1990, № 2.

79. Грушин Б.А. *Мир мнений и мнение о мире* (Groushin, V.A. *The World Of Opinions and the Opinion on the World)*. Москва: Политиздат, 1967.

80. Гульдан В.В. и др. Представления школьников о наркомании и токсикомании / *Социол. исслед.* (Guldan, V.V. et al. "Schoolchildren's Views of the Narcotism and Toxicism." *Sociological Studies),* 1989, № 3.

81. Демидов А.М. Секреты избирателей / *Социол. исслед.* (Demidov, A.M. "Voters' Secrets." *Sociological Studies),* 1989, № 5.

83. Демидов А.М. Москвичи о выборах / *Социол. исслед.* (Demidov, A.M. "Muscovites on Elections." *Sociological Studies),* 1990, № 10.

83. *Демографические перспективы России,* отв. ред. Е.М.Андреев (Andreev, E.M. ed., *Demographic Prospects of Russia*). Москва: Респ. инф.-издат. центр, 1993.

84. *Демографический ежегодник СССР* (State Statistic Committee *Demography Yearbook of the USSR*). Москва: Финансы и статистика, Госкомстат СССР, 1990.

85. Денисова Г.С. Социальное расслоение как фактор напряженности в городе / *Социол. исслед.* (Denisova, G.S. "Social Stratification as a Reason for Social Tension." *Sociological Studies),* 1992, № 9.

86. *Детские и юношеские организации России. Справочник,* ред. И.В.Титов (I.V.Titov, ed., *Children's and Youth Organizations of Russia: Guidebook*). Москва: Ред.-издат. база Фонда "Молодежь выбирает будущее", 1994.

87. Дмитриев А.В. О социальной дезинтеграции и конфликте / *Социол. исслед.* (Dmitriev, A.V. "On Social Desintegration And Conflict." *Sociological Studies),* 1992, № 10.

88. *Доклад по результатам эпидемиологического исследования Государственного научного центра наркологии* (State Scientific Centre for Narcology. *A Report on Results of Epidemiology Survey*). Москва: Гос. научный центр наркологии, 1992.

89. *Есть мнение: Итоги социологического опроса,* ред. Ю.А.Левада (Yu.A.Levada, ed., *There Is an Opninon*). Москва: Прогресс, 1990.

90. *Женщина в меняющемся мире,* ред. Н.М.Римашевская (N.M.Pimashevskaya, ed., *Woman in a Changing World*). Москва: Наука, 1992.

91. *Женщины в обществе: реалии, проблемы, прогнозы,* ред. Н.М.Римашевская (N.M.Rimashevskaya, ed., *Women in the Society. Reality, Problems, Forecasts*). Москва: Наука, 1991.

92. *Женщины и социальная политика (гендерный аспект),* ред. З.А.Хоткина (Z.A.Hotkina, ed., *Women and Social Policy. Gender Aspects*). Москва: Ин-т социально-экономических проблем народонаселения РАН, 1992.

93. *Жизнь и кошелек* (*Life and Money*), 1994, № 9.

94. Заикина Г., Фатеева Е. Общественное мнение о семье / *Моск. новости* (Zaikina, G. and E.Fateeva "Public Opinion on Family." Moscowskie Novosty), 1988, № 35.

95. Залкинд А.Б. *Половой вопрос в условиях советской общественности* (Zalkind, A.B. *Sexual Problem in the Soviet Society*). — Ленинград., 1926.

96. *Занятость и безработица в России. Экспресс-информация* (*Employment and Unemployment in Russia. Current Information*), 1994, № 11.

97. Заславская   Т.И. Подлинный оптимизм основывается на реализме / Социол. исслед. (Zaslavskaya, T.I. "True Optimism Is Based On Realism." *Sociological Studies*), 1989, № 6.

98. Захарова О. Перспективы рождаемости и воспроизводство населения России. — В кн: *Население СССР в 80-е г.*, ред. Г.П.Киселева (Zakharova, O. Perspectives of Fertility and Reproduction of Population in Russia. In G.P.Kyceleva, ed., *Population of the USSR at the 80-ies*). Москва: ИС АН СССР, 1991.

99. Здоровье нации / *Экон. новости России и содружества* ("Nation's Health." *Economic News from Russia and Commonwealth*), 1994, № 14.

100. Здравомыслов А.Г., Матвеева С.Я. *Межнациональные конфликты в России и постсоветском пространстве* (Zdravomyslov, A.G., and S.Ia.Matveeva *National Conflicts in Russia and Post-Soviet Area*). Москва: Росс. незав. ин-т социальных и национальных проблем, 1995.

101. Здравомыслова Е.О. Социологический подход к анализу общественных движений / *Социол. исслед.* (Zdravomyslova, E.O. "Sociological Approach to the Social Movements' Analysis." *Sociological Studies*), 1990, № 7.

102. *Здравоохранение в СССР. Сборник статистических материалов* (State Statistic Committee *Health Care in the USSR. Collection of Statistics*). Москва: Минздрав СССР, 1988.

103. *Здравоохранение Российской Федерации* (State Statistic Committee *Health Care of the Russian Federation*). Москва: Медицина, 1991.

104. Зотова А.Ю. Кому нужен секс-телефон? / *Социол. исслед.* (Zotova, A.Iu. "Who Needs a Sex-Telephone?" *Sociological Studies*), 1994, № 1.

105. Зубаткин В. Вторая экономика / *Вопр. экономики* (Zubatkin, V. "The Second Economy." *Problems of Economy*), 1994, № 11.

106. Зюзин Д. И. Влияние фондов социального развития на отношение к труду / *Социол. исслед.* (Zyuzin, D.I. "The Influence of The Social Development Funds on Attitude to Labour." *Sociological Studies*), 1989, № 3.

107. Ибрагимова С.Г. Очередь в надомники / *Социол. исслед.* (Ibragimova, S.Y. "Queueing Those Who Work at Home." *Sociological Studies*), 1990, № 9.

108. Иванов В.Н. Межнациональные отношения в России / *Социол. исслед.* (Ivanov, V.N. "Inter-ethnic Relations in Russia." *Sociological Studies*), 1994, № 6.

109. Иванова А.Е. Прогноз здоровья взрослого населения России / *Социол. исслед.* (Ivanova, A.E. A Forecast of the Adult Population's Health." *Sociological Studies*), 1992, № 9.

110. *Изменения в уровне жизни и социальные проблемы адаптации населения к рынку*, ред. Н.М.Римашевская (N.M.Rymashevskaya, ed., *Changes in the Level of Life and Social Problems of Population's Adaptation to Market Relations*). Москва: Наука, 1994.

111a. *Известия* (*Izvestia*), 11.05.1991.

111b. *Известия* (*Izvestia*), 23.03.1993.

111c. *Известия* (*Izvestia*), 28.12.1993.

111d. *Известия* (*Izvestia*), 31.12.1993.

111e. *Известия* (*Izvestia*), 14.04.1994.

111f. *Известия* (*Izvestia*), 22.06.1994.

111g. *Известия* (*Izvestia*), 27.06.1994.

111h. *Известия* (*Izvestia*), 29.06.1994.

111i. *Известия* (*Izvestia*), 16.09.1994.

111j. *Известия* (*Izvestia*), 24.10.1994.

111k. *Известия* (*Izvestia*), 26.10.1994.

111l. *Известия* (*Izvestia*), 23.12.1994.

111m. Известия (*Izvestia*), 04.04.1995.

111n. *Известия* (*Izvestia*), 16.04.1995.

111o. *Известия* (*Izvestia*), 27.04.1995.

111p. *Известия* (*Izvestia*), 11.05.1995.

112. Илларионов Л., Лейард Р., Оршаг П. Как живут россияне? / *Экон. прил. к газете "Российские вести"* (Illarionov, L., R.Leilard, and R.Orshag "How Do Russian People Live?" *Economy Supplement to "Rossiyskie Vesty"*), 1992, № 5.

113. *Информационный бюллетень Отдела внешних церковных сношений Русской Православной церкви* (*Information Bulletin of the Department of Exterior Relations of the Russian Orthodox Church*), 1993, № 24.

114. *Итоги всесоюзной переписи 1989 г.* (State Statistic Committee *Results of the All-Union census 1989*). Москва: Финансы и статистика, 1990.

115. *Итоги единовременного учета численности рабочих по профессиям, тарифным разрядам, формам и системам оплаты труда в промышленности в 1972, 1975, 1979* (State Statistic Committee *Results of Simultaneous Estimation of the Numbers of Workers by Professions, Types and Systems of Payments in Industry in 1972, 1975, 1979*). Москва: Госкомстат СССР, 1980.

116. *К здоровой России. Политика укрепления здоровья и профилактики заболеваний. Доклад Гос. Центра профилактической медицины (*State Scientific Center for Preventive Medicine *Towards the Healthy Russia. State Report*). Москва: АО "Водолей", 1994.

117. Климова С.Г. Контроль отклоняющегося поведения со стороны государства и общества / *Социол. исслед.* (Klimova, S.G. "State and Society's Control of Deviant Behaviour." *Sociological Studies*), 1990, № 10.

118. Климова С.Г. Изменения в алкогольном поведении молодежи (по данным сравнительных исследований в Московской области в 1984, 1988 и 1991 годах) / *Социол. исслед.* (Klimova, S.G. "Changes in Alcohol Consumption of the Young (After the Data of Comparative Researches in Moscow Region in Years 1984, 1988 and 1991." *Sociological Studies*), 1992, № 8.

119. Клопов Э.В. *Рабочий класс СССР* (Klopov, E.V. *Working Class of the USSR*). Москва: Мысль, 1985.

120. Книга в нашем доме: социологическая информация / *Экслибрис. Науч.-информ. бюлл.* ("Book in our Home: Sociological Information." *Exlibris. Scientific and Information Bulletin)*, 1989, № 1.

121. Кобецкий В.Д. *Социологическое изучение религиозности и атеизма* (Kobetzkiy, V.D. *Sociological Study of Religiosity and Atheism)*. — Ленинград: ЛГУ, 1978.

122. Ковалева А.И. Кризис системы образования / *Социол. исслед.* (Kovaleva, A.I. "The Crisis of the Education System." *Sociological Studies)*, 1994. № 3.

123. Когай Л. Рынок товаров народного потребления: тенденции и меры по улучшению состояния / *Плановое хозяйство* (Kogai, L. "The Consumer Market: Trends and Means for Its Optimisation.", *Planned Economy)*, 1990, № 11.

124. Коган Л.Н. *Человек и его судьба* (Kogan, L.N. *Man and Fate)*. Москва: Мысль, 1988.

125. Козлов В.Д. Почему рабочие ограничивают выработку? / *Социол. исслед.* (Kozlov, V.D. "Why do Workers Limit Their Output?" *Sociological Studies)*, 1990, № 2.

126. Комаровский В.С. Типология избирателей / *Социол. исслед.* (Komarovsky, V.S. "Typology of Voters." *Sociological Studies)*, 1990, № 1.

127. Комозин А.Н. Самоуправление в трудовом коллективе / *Социол. исслед.* (Komosin, A.N. Self-Government in a Working People Collective." *Sociological Studies)*, 1989, № 4.

128. Комозин А.Н. Как изучать коллективный подряд / *Социол. исслед.* (Komosin, A.N. "Studying Collective Contract System." *Sociological Studies)*, 1990, № 9.

129. Комозин А.Н., Кравченко А.И. *Популярная социология. В помощь профактиву* (Komosin A.N., and A.I.Kravchenko *Popular Sociology. A guide Book for a Trade-Union Militant)*. Москва: Профиздат, 1991.

130a. *Комсомольская правда (Komsomolskaya Pravda)*, 07.02. 1992.

130b. *Комсомольская правда (Komsomolskaya Pravda)*, 07.07.1992.

131. Кон И.С. *Психология ранней юности*: книга для учителя (Kon, I.S. *Psychology of Early Youth. A Teacher's Book)*. Москва: Просвещение, 1989.

132. Кон И.С. *Введение в сексологию* (Kon, I.S. *Introduction to Sexology)*. Москва: Медицина, 1989.

133. Корягина Т.И. Теневая экономика в СССР. Аанализ, оценки, прогнозы/ *Вопр. экономики* (Koriaguina, T.I. "Shady Ecomony in the USSR. Analysis, Estemes, Forecasts." *Problems of Ecomony)*, 1990, № 3.

134. Косова Л.Б. Удовлетворенность жизнью и интенсивность реформ / *Социол. исслед.* (Kossova, L.B. "Satisfaction With Life and the Intensity of Reforms." *Sociological Studies)*, 1994, № 10.

135. Кулешова Л.М. *Использование труда на режимах неполного рабочего времени* (Kouleshova, L.M. *Labour Forse Use in Part Time Work)*. Москва: Экономика, 1987.

136. *Культурная деятельность и культурная политика*, отв. ред. Т.В.Томко (T.V.Tomko, ed., *Cultural Activity and Cultural Policy*). Москва: НИИ Культуры, 1991.

137. *Культурно-досуговая деятельность рабочих областных центров РСФСР*, отв. ред. О.М.Егоров (O.M.Egorov, ed., *Cultural and Leisure Activity of Workers in the Region Centres of the RSFSR*). Москва: НИИ Культуры, 1990.

138. Купцов О.В., Пахомов Н.Н., Соколова Л.И. *Разнообразие сферы образования*. Аналитический обзор (Kouptzov, O.V., N.N.Pahomov, and L.I.Sokolova *Differentiation in the Educational Spheres*). Москва: Всероссийское обество "Знание", 1989.

139. Курганов С.И. Мотивы действий несовершеннолетних правонарушителей / *Социол. исслед.* (Kourganov, S.I. "The Motives of Action of the Criminals Ander Age." *Sociological Studies*), 1989, № 5.

140. Лапин Н.И. Тяжкие годы России / *Мир России* (Lapin, N.I. "Hard Years for Russia." *The World of Russia*), 1992, № 1.

141. Лапин Н.И. Социальные ценности и реформы в кризисной России / *Социол. исслед.* (Lapin, N.I. "Social Values and Reforms in the Russia under Crisis." *Sociological Studies*), 1993, № 9.

142. Лебедев А.А. *Конкретные исследования в атеистической работе* (Lebedev, A.A. *Applied Researches in Atheists Activities*). Москва: Политиздат, 1976.

143. Лебедева Е.А. И потекут сокровища мои... / *Моск. новости* (Lebedeva, E.A. "And My Treasures Will Flow..." *Moskovskie Novosty*), 1994, № 13.

144. Левада Ю.А. Динамика общественно-политической ситуации / *Экономические и социальные перемены. Мониторинг общественного мнения* (Levada, Yu.A. "Dynamics of the Social and Political Situation." *Economic and Social Changes: Monitoring of Public Opinion*), 1993, № 6.

145. Лелеко В.Д. Очарование социальной роли возлюбленной / *Социол. исслед.* (Leleko, V.D. "The Charm of the Social Role of a Loved One." *Sociological Studies*), 1992, № 9.

146. *Лидер (Leader)*, 1994, № 3.

147. *Литературное обозрение (Literature Review)*, 1991, № 11.

148. Лукачер Г.Я., Макшанцева Н.В., Чудиновский В.А. Одурманивающие средства в подростковой среде / *Социол. исслед.* (Loukacher, G.Ia, N.V.Makshantzeva, and B.A.Choudinovskiy "Dope and Drugs among Teenagers." *Sociological Studies*), 1990, № 4.

149. Магун В., Литвинцева А. *Жизненные притязания ранней юности и стратегии их реализации: 80-е и 90-е г.г.* (Magun, V. and A.Litvintseva *Aspirations of Early Youth and Strategies of Their Realization: the 80-s and the 90-s*). Москва: ИС РАН, 1993.

150. МакКихан М., Кэмпбелл Р., Туманов С.В. Образ жизни, привычки, влияющие на здоровье москвичей и на закон о медицинском страховании 1991-1993 г.г. / *Социол. исслед.* (McKihan,M., R.Campbell, and S.V.Toumanov "Life

Style, Habits, Influencing the Muscovites' Health and the Legislation on Medical Insurance." *Sociological Studies*), 1993, № 3.

151. Максимов А.Л. *Рабочее и свободное время в условиях развитого социализма* (Maksimov, A.L. *Work and Free Time Under the Developed Socialism*). Москва: Наука, 1981.

152. *Материалы делегату XIX съезда профсоюзов СССР* (*Materials for the Delegate of the XIXth Congress of the USSR Trade Unions*). Москва: ВЦСПС, 1990.

153. Мацковский М. Интервью / *Аргументы и факты* (Matzkovsky, M. "An Interview." *Arguments and Facts*), 1991, № 27.

154a. *Мир мнений. Бюлл. Службы изучения общественного мнения Vox Populi* (*The World of Opinions: Bulletin of the Service for Public Opinion Polls "Vox Populi"*), 1991, № 2.

154b. *Мир мнений. Бюлл. Службы изучения общественного мнения Vox Populi* (*The World of Opinions: Bulletin of the Service for Public Opinion Polls "Vox Populi"*, 1991, № 5.

154c. *Мир мнений. Бюлл. Службы изучения общественного мнения Vox Populi* (*The World of Opinions: Bulletin of the Service for Public Opinion Polls "Vox Populi"*, 1991, № 7.

154d. *Мир мнений. Бюлл. Службы изучения общественного мнения Vox Populi* (*The World of Opinions: Bulletin of the Service for Public Opinion Polls "Vox Populi"*, 1991, № 9.

154e. *Мир мнений. Бюлл. Службы изучения общественного мнения Vox Populi* (*The World of Opinions: Bulletin of the Service for Public Opinion Polls "Vox Populi"*, 1991, № 10.

154f. *Мир мнений. Бюлл. Службы изучения общественного мнения Vox Populi* (*The World of Opinions: Bulletin of the Service for Public Opinion Polls "Vox Populi"*, 1991, № 12.

154g. *Мир мнений. Бюлл. Службы изучения общественного мнения Vox Populi* (*The World of Opinions: Bulletin of the Service for Public Opinion Polls "Vox Populi"*, 1992, № 1.

154h. *Мир мнений. Бюлл. Службы изучения общественного мнения Vox Populi* (*The World of Opinions: Bulletin of the Service for Public Opinion Polls "Vox Populi"*, 1992, № 2.

154i. *Мир мнений. Бюлл. Службы изучения общественного мнения Vox Populi* (*The World of Opinions: Bulletin of the Service for Public Opinion Polls "Vox Populi"*, 1992, № 3.

154j. *Мир мнений. Бюлл. Службы изучения общественного мнения Vox Populi* (*The World of Opinions: Bulletin of the Service for Public Opinion Polls "Vox Populi"*, 1992, № 4.

154k. *Мир мнений. Бюлл. Службы изучения общественного мнения Vox Populi* (*The World of Opinions: Bulletin of the Service for Public Opinion Polls "Vox Populi"*, 1992, № 5.

154l. *Мир мнений. Бюлл. Службы изучения общественного мнения Vox Populi* (*The World of Opinions: Bulletin of the Service for Public Opinion Polls "Vox Populi"*, 1992, № 6.

154m. *Мир мнений. Бюлл. Службы изучения общественного мнения Vox Populi* (*The World of Opinions: Bulletin of the Service for Public Opinion Polls "Vox Populi"*, 1992, № 7.

154n. *Мир мнений. Бюлл. Службы изучения общественного мнения Vox Populi* (*The World of Opinions: Bulletin of the Service for Public Opinion Polls "Vox Populi"*, 1992, № 8.

154o. *Мир мнений. Бюлл. Службы изучения общественного мнения Vox Populi* (*The World of Opinions: Bulletin of the Service for Public Opinion Polls "Vox Populi"*, 1992, № 9.

154p. *Мир мнений. Бюлл. Службы изучения общественного мнения Vox Populi* (*The World of Opinions: Bulletin of the Service for Public Opinion Polls "Vox Populi"*, 1992, № 10.

154г. *Мир мнений. Бюлл. Службы изучения общественного мнения Vox Populi* (*The World of Opinions: Bulletin of the Service for Public Opinion Polls "Vox Populi"*, 1992, № 11.

154s. *Мир мнений. Бюлл. Службы изучения общественного мнения Vox Populi* (*The World of Opinions: Bulletin of the Service for Public Opinion Polls "Vox Populi"*, 1992, № 12.

155. Миронов А.Н. От зарплаты до зарплаты / *Социол. исслед.* (Mironov, A.N. "Since Payment Time Till Payment Time." *Sociological Studies*), 1991, № 7.

156. Мичурин М. Слушая Патриарха / *Сегодня* (Michourin, M. Listening to the Patriarch." *Segodnya*), 03.12.1994.

157. *Молодежь России: положение, тенденции, перспективы,.* ред. И.М.Ильинского (Ilinski, I.M., ed., *Youth of Russia: Status, Tendencies, Perspectives.*). — Iосква: Молодая гвардия, 1993.

158. *Молодежь СССР. Стат. сборник* (State Statistic Committee *The Youth of the USSR*). Iосква: Финансы и статистика, 1990.

159. Морозова Г.Ф. Современные миграционные явления: беженцы и эмигранты / *Социол. исслед.* (Morozova G.F. "Modern Migration Phenomena: Migrants and Refugees." *Sociological Studies*), 1992, № 3.

160. *Московская правда* (*Moskovskaya Pravda),* 10.09.1993.

161a. *Московские новости* (*Moscovskiye Novosty*), 1993, N1.

161b. ibid, 1993, № 15.

162a. *Московский комсомолец* (*Moskovsky Komsomolets*), 20.02.1993.

162b. *Московский комсомолец* (*Moskovsky Komsomolets*), 22.09.1993.

163c. *Московский комсомолец* (*Moskovsky Komsomolets*), 10.02.1994.

162d. *Московский комсомолец* (*Moskovsky Komsomolets*), 02.11.1994.

162e. *Московский комсомолец* (*Moskovsky Komsomolets*), 11.11.1994.

162f. *Московский комсомолец* (*Moskovsky Komsomolets*), 31.12.1994.

162g. *Московский комсомолец (Moskovsky Komsomolets)*, 11.04.1995.

163. Мчедлов М.П. и др. Религия в зеркале общественного мнения / *Социол. исслед.* (Mchedlov, M.P et al. "Religion in the Mirror of Public Opinion." *Sociological Studies*), 1994, № 5.

164. Народ и политика. Круглый стол / *Полит. исслед.* ("People and Policy. A Round Table Discussion." *Political Studies*), 1994, № 4.

165. *Народное благосостояние. Методология и методика исследований*, ред. Н.М. Римашевская, Л.А. Оникова (Rimashevskaya, N.M., and L.A.Onikov, eds., *People's Wealth. Methodology and Methods of Research*). Москва: Наука, 1991.

166. *Народное образование и культура в РСФСР*. Госкомстат РСФСР (State Statistic Committee *People's Education and Culture*). Москва: Респ. инф.-издат. центр, 1991.

167. *Народное образование и культура в СССР*. Госкомстат СССР (State Statistic Committee *People's Education and Culture in the USSR*). Москва: Статистика, 1977.

168. *Народное образование и культура в СССР*. Госкомстат СССР (State Statistic Committee *People's Education and Culture in the USSR*). Москва: Финансы и статистика, 1989.

169. *Народное образование в СССР. 1917-1967*. Статистический сборник *(People's Education in the USSRю 1917-1967*. A Collection of Statistics*)*. Москва: Финансы и статистика, 1989.

170. *Народное образование в СССР*. Сборник нормативных актов *(People's Education in the USSR. A Collection of Legislative Papers)*. Москва: Юридическая литература, 1987.

171. *Народное хозяйство Российской Федерации. 1992.* (State Statistic Committee *National Economy of the Russian Federation. 1992*). Москва: Респ. инф.-издат. центр, 1992.

172. *Народное хозяйство РСФСР в 1970 г.* Статистический ежегодник (State Statistic Committee *National Economy of the RSFSR in 1970*). Москва: Финансы и статистика, 1971.

173. *Народное хозяйство РСФСР в 1972 г.* (State Statistic Committee *National Economy of the RSFSR in the 1972*). Москва: Финансы и статистика, 1973.

174. *Народное хозяйство РСФСР в 1985 г.* (State Statistic Committee *National Economy of the RSFSR in the 1985*). Москва: Финансы и статистика, 1986.

175. *Народное хозяйство РСФСР в 1989 г.* (State Statistic Committee *National Economy of the RSFSR in the 1989*). Москва: Финансы и статистика, 1990.

176. *Народное хозяйство РСФСР в 1990 г.* (State Statistic Committee *National Economy of the RSFSR in the 1990*). Москва: Респ. инф.-издат. центр, 1991.

177. *Народное хозяйство РСФСР за 70 лет.* (State Statistic Committee *National Economy of the RSFSR over 70 years*). Москва: Финансы и статистика, 1988.

178. *Народное хозяйство СССР в 1975 г.* (State Statistic Committee *National Economy of the USSR in the 1975*). Москва: Финансы и статистика, 1976.

179. *Народное хозяйство СССР в 1982 г.* (State Statistic Committee *National Economy of the USSR in the 1982*). Москва: Финансы и статистика, 1983.

180. *Народное хозяйство СССР в 1989.* (State Statistic Committee *National Economy of the USSR in the 1989*). Москва: Финансы и статистика, 1990.

181. *Население и трудовые ресурсы.* Справочник, сост. А.Г. Новицкий. (A.G.Novitsky, ed., *Population and the Labour Sources*). Москва: Мысль, 1990.

182. *Население Москвы. Прошлое. Настоящее. Будущее,* отв. ред. В.Н.Моисеенко (V.N.Moiceenko, ed., *Population of Moscow. Past. Present. Future*). Москва: МГУ, 1992.

183. *Население России.* (State Statistic Committee. *The Population of Russia. An annual demographic report*). Москва: Респ. инф.-издат. центр, 1993.

184. *Население СССР за 70 лет,* отв. ред. П.Л.Рыбаковский (P.L.Rybakovsky, ed., *Population of the USSR over 70 years*). Москва: Наука, 1988.

185. Наумова Н.Ф. Человек в переходный период / *Коммунист* (Naumova, N.F. "Man in a transitional Period." *Communist*), 1991, № 7.

186. *Научно-технический прогресс в СССР,* отв. ред. В.В.Великий (V.V.Veliky, ed., *Scientific and Technical Progress in the Russian Federation*).Москва: Финансы и статистика, 1990.

187. Немировский Д.Э. Мотивы противоправных действий молодежи / *Социол. исслед.* (Nemirovsky D.E. The Motives of criminal's actions of the Youth, *Sociological Studies*), 1992, № 3.

188. Немцов А. Стали ли мы меньше пить? / *Известия* (Nemtzov, A. "Do We Drink Less?" *Izvestia*), 04.09.1993.

189. Нешитой А.С. и др. *Экономика и планирование кооперативной торговли* (Neshitoy, A.S. et al. *Economics and Cooperative Trade Planning*). Москва: Экономика, 1989.

190. *О положении дел в области социальной защиты и занятости населения и перспективы на второе полугодие 1994 года.* (Ministry of Labour and Employment of Russia *On the state of Art in Welfare and Employment in the Second Half of 1994*). Москва: Мин. Труда и занятости России, 1994.

191. *Оплата труда. Нормативные документы и разъяснения* (Ministry of Labour and Employment of Russia *On the salaries. Regulations and Comments*). Москва: Мин-во труда и занятости России, 1995, вып. 2.

192. *О работе Службы разрешения коллективных трудовых конфликтов при Министерстве труда России.* Информ. отчет (Ministry of Labour and Employment of Russia *On the Activity of the Service for Labour Conflicts Settlement. Information Report*). Москва: Мин-во труда и занятости России, 1994.

193. *О развитии экономических реформ в Российской Федерации / Январь-март 1993 г.* Статистический сборник (State Statistic Comittee *On the Development of Economic Reforms in Russia.* January-March 1993). Москва: Респ. инф.-издат. центр, 1993.

194. О состоянии здоровья населения Российской Федерации. Государственный доклад (Ministry of Health *Health of the Population of the Russian Federation. The State of the Art*). Москва: Мин-во здравоохранения, 1992.

195. О положении семей в Российской Федерации. (Ministry of Social Protection *On Social Position of the family in Russia. Analytical Report*). Москва: Юридическая литература, 1994.

196. *Образование в России.* Справочник (Institute of High Education *Education in Russia. A Guidebook*). Москва: НИИ Высшего образования, 1993.

197. *Образование в Российской Федерации* (Ministry of High Education *Education in the Russian Federation* in 1992). Москва: Госкомстат, 1995.

198a. *Общественное мнение в цифрах. Бюллетень ВЦИОМ (Public Opinion in Figures. VCIOM Bulletin)*, 1991, № 8.

198b. *Общественное мнение в цифрах. Бюллетень ВЦИОМ (Public Opinion in Figures. VCIOM Bulletin)*, 1991, № 9.

198c. *Общественное мнение в цифрах. Бюллетень ВЦИОМ (Public Opinion in Figures. VCIOM Bulletin)*, 1991, № 10.

198d. *Общественное мнение в цифрах. Бюллетень ВЦИОМ (Public Opinion in Figures. VCIOM Bulletin)*, 1992, № 2.

198e. *Общественное мнение в цифрах. Бюллетень ВЦИОМ (Public Opinion in Figures. VCIOM Bulletin)*, 1992, № 3.

198f. *Общественное мнение в цифрах. Бюллетень ВЦИОМ (Public Opinion in Figures. VCIOM Bulletin)*, 1993. № 7.

199. Озимитин В.Д. Раскрестьянивание и окрестьянивание по-российски / *Социол. исслед.* (Ozimitin, V.D. "Peasans In and Out Russian Style." *Sociological Studies*), 1994, № 3.

200. Ольховиков А.В., Уварова А.А. Типология телевизионной аудитории / *Социол. исслед.* (Olhovikov, A.V., and A.A. Uvarova "Typology of the TV Audience." *Sociological Studies*), 1992, № 7.

201. Орлов Г.П. *Свободное время — условие развития человека и мера общественного богатства* (Orlov, G.P. *Free Time as a Condition for Personal Development and a Measure of Social Treasure*). — Свердловск: УрГУ, 1989.

202. Осипов А.М. Мотивы переселения из деревни в город / *Социол. исслед.* (Ossipov, A.M. "The Causes of Migration From the Country to the Cities." *Sociological Studies*), 1988, № 2.

203. *Основные сводные данные по физкультуре и спорту* (State Committee for Physical Training and Tourism *Main Gleaned Data on Physical Training and Sports*). Москва: Госкомитет по физкультуре и туризму, 1993.

204. *Откуда исходит угроза миру* (Ministry of Defence *Where the Threat to Peace Comes From*). Москва: Воениздат, 1987.

205. Отношение военнослужащих к комплектованию на новой основе / *Обозреватель. Спец. выпуск* ("Militarymen's Attitudes Toward New Mode of Recruiting." *Observer. Special Issue*). 1994, № 21-24.

206. *Официальная хроника.* Журнал Московской Патриархии (Moskow Patriarchy *Official Cronicle*), 1993, № 1.

207. Панкратова М.Г., Янкова З.А. Советская женщина. Социальный портрет / *Социол. исслед.* (Pankratova M.G., and Z.A.Yankova "Soviet Woman. Social Portrait." *Sociological Studies*), 1978, № 1.

208. *Партийный активист (Party Militant),* 1990, № 2.

209. Патрушев В.Д. Как и с кем проводят свободное время горожане? / *Социол. исслед.* (Patroushev, V.D. "How and With Whom Do the Towndwellers Spend Their Free Time?" *Sociological Studies*), 1986, № 4.

210. *Патрушев В.Д. Как и с кем проводим мы свободное время?* (Patroushev, V.D. *How and with Whom Are We Spending Free Time?*). Москва: ИСИ АН СССР, 1987.

211. Патрушев В.Д. Региональные различия в использовании бюджета времени городским населением СССР / *Социол. исслед.* (Patroushev, V.D. "Regional Differences in Using Free Time Budget Among the Urban Population of the USSR. *"Sociological Studies*), 1990, № 2.

212. Патрушев В.Д. Изменения в использовании свободного времени городского населения за двадцать лет (1965-1986) / *Социол. исслед.* (Patroushev, V.D. "Changes in Free Time Usage of Urban Population over 20 Years (1965-1986)." *Sociological Studies*), 1991, № 3.

213. Патрушев В.Д., Караханова Т.М., Кушнарева О.Н. Свободное время жителей Москвы и Московской области / *Социол. исслед.* (Patroushev, V.D., T.M.Karahanova, and O.N.Koushnareva "Free Time of the Population of Moscow and Moscow Region." *Sociological Studies*), 1992, № 6.

214. Переведенцев В. Насколько правдива правда о разводах / *Семья* (Perevedentzev, V. "Is the Truth About Devorces True?" *Family*), 1989, № 14.

215. *Печать Российской Федерации в 1993 г. Статистический сборник* (Russian Book Chamber. *Printed Media in Russia. A Collection of Statistics).* Москва: Росс. книжная палата, 1994.

216. Пиво: специальный тематический выпуск / *Коммерсант* ("Beer: A Special Theme Issue." *Kommersant*), 10.10.1994.

217. Писарчук В.И., Скляр Л.И. Социально-демографические факторы, влияющие на выбор профессии / *Социол. исслед.* (Pissarchuk, V.I., and L.I.Sklyar "Socio-demographic Factors Influencing the Choice of Profession." *Sociological Studies*), 1992, № 10.

218. Позднякова М.Е., Рыбакова Л.Н. Преступная страсть / *Социол. исслед.* (Pozdniakova, M.E., and L.N.Rybakova "A Criminal Passion." *Sociological Studies*), 1989, № 4.

219a. *Поиск (Poisk),* 1993, № 23.

219b. *Поиск (Poisk),* 1994, № 16.

220. *Показатели деятельности библиотек за 1992-1993 г.г.* (Ministry of Culture *Indicators of the Libraries Activities*). Москва: ГИВЦ Минкультуры, 1994.

221. *Показатели деятельности культурно-просветительных учреждений за 1992-1993 г.г.* (Ministry of Culture *Indicators of the Activities of the Cultural and Educational Institutions*). Москва: ГИВЦ Минкультуры, 1994.

222. Покровская М.В. Социальная справедливость в потреблении и ее стереотипы / *Социол. исслед.* (Pokrovskaya, M.V. "Social Justice in Consumption and Related Stereotypes." *Sociological Studies*), 1990, № 3.

223. *Политика укрепления здоровья и профилактики заболеваний.* Государственный доклад (Ministry of Health *Policy of Health Strengthening and Disease Prevention. A State Report*). Москва: Мин-во здравоохранения РФ, 1993.

224. Попова Н.П. и др. Школьники СССР и США о войне и мире / *Социол. исслед.* (Popova, N.P. et al. "Schoolchildren in the USSR and in the USA on War and Peace." *Sociological Studies*), 1988, № 3.

225. Прессман А.М. Пришельцы из "застоя" / *Социол. исслед.* (Pressman, A.M. The Ghosts From "Stagnation". *Sociological Studies*), 1989, № 5.

226. *Проблемы сбора первичных данных в социологии средств массовой информации,* отв. ред. В.И.Петров (Petrov, V.I, ed., *The Problems of Primary Data Collection in the Sociology of Mass Media*). Москва: ИСИ АН СССР, 1984.

227. Прокофьев В.В. Свободное время промышленных рабочих / *Социол. исслед.* (Prokofiev, V.V. "Free Time of Industrial Workers." *Sociological Studies*), 1989, № 1.

228. Пронина Л.И. *Повышение эффективности социального обеспечения* (Pronina, L.I. *The Raise of Efficiency of the Social Welfare*). Москва: Экономика, 1990.

229. *Пятьдесят лет Вооруженных Сил СССР. 1918-1968* (Ministry of Defense *Fifty Years of The Armed Forses. 1918-1968*). Москва: Воениздат, 1968.

230. *Рабочая трибуна* (*Rabochaya Tribuna*), 21.01.1992.

231. *Разработка концепции социального обслуживания пожилых людей и инвалидов в условиях рыночной экономики.* Отчет. (Institute of Labour of the Ministry of Labour and Employment *Elaboration of the Concept of the Social Services for the Elder and Handicaped Persons Under the Market Economy*). Москва: И-т труда Минтруда и занятости России, 1994.

232. Ракетные войска стратегического назначения / *Военно-историч. журнал* ("Strategic Rocket Troups." *Military History Review*), 1992, № 4.

233. Раковская О. Переход к рынку и молодежь. — В кн: *Молодежь России на рубеже 90-х г.г.,* отв. ред. Н. Малышева (Rakovskaya, O. Transition to Market and the Youth, In N.Malysheva, ed., *Young People of Russia on the Eve of the 90-ies*). Москва: ИС РАН, 1992.

234. *Регистр Министерства юстиции Российской Федерации* (*Register of the Ministry of Justice of the Russian Federation*). Москва: Мин-во юстиции, 1994.

235. Религиозность — демократичность — авторитарность. Круглый стол / *Полит. исслед.* ("Religiousity — Democracy — Autocracy. A Round Table Discussion." *Political Studies*), 1993, № 3.

236. *Реформирование России: мифы и реальность*, сост. Г.В.Осипов и др. (Ossipov, G.V., et al., eds., *Reforming Russia: Myths and Reality*). Москва: Academia, 1994.

237. Ржаницына Л. Работа не всегда хороша, но необходима / *Человек и труд* (Rzanitzyna, L. "Work Is Not Always Pleasant, But It Is Necessary." *Man and Labour*), 1993, № 5-6.

238. Ромашов О.Д. Социальная защита трудящихся: проблемы, пути решения / *Социол. исслед.* (Romashov, O.D. "Social Defense of Working People: Problems, Ways of Their Solution." *Sociological Studies*), 1993, № 1.

239. *Российская газета* (*Rossyiskaya Gazeta*), 24.10.1991.

240. *Российская Федерация в цифрах, 1991 г.* Госкомстат (State Statistic Committee *Russian Federation in Figures in 1991*). Москва: Респ. инф.-издат. центр, 1992.

241. *Российская Федерация в цифрах, 1992 г.* (State Statistic Committee *Russian Federation in Figures in 1992*). Москва: Респ. инф.-издат. центр, 1993.

242. *Российская Федерация в цифрах, 1993 г.* (State Statistic Committee *Russian Federation in Figures in 1993*), Москва: Респ. инф.-издат. центр, 1994.

243. *Россия в 1993 году: социально-демографическая ситуация* (State Statistic Committee *Russia in 1993: Social and Demographical Situation*). Москва: Респ. инф.-издат. центр, 1994.

244. *Российский статистический ежегодник. Январь 1995* (State Statistic Committee *Russian Statistic Yearbook. January 1995*). Москва: Экономика, 1995.

245. Рукавишников В.О. Очередь / *Социол. исслед.* (Roukavishnikov, V.O. "The Queue." *Sociological Studies*), 1989, № 4.

246. Рукавишников В.О. Пик напряженности под знаком белого коня / *Социол. исслед.* (Roukavishnikov, V.O. "Peak of the Social Tension Guided by the "White Horse"." *Sociological Studies*), 1990, № 10.

247. Рукавишников В.О. Социальная динамика и политический конфликт в России: весна 1993 — адаптация к кризису / *Социол. исслед.* (Roukavishnikov, V.O. "Social Dynamics and Political Conflict in Russia: Spring of 1993 as aPeriod of Adaptation to the Crisis." *Sociological Studies*), 1993, № 9.

248. Рукавишников В.О. и др. Социальная напряженность: диагноз и прогноз / *Социол. исслед.* (Roukavishnikov, V.O., et al. "Social Tension: Analysis and Prognosis." *Sociological Studies*), 1992, № 3.

249. *Русские. Этно-социологические очерки*, отв. ред. Ю.В.Арутюнян (Yu.V.Arutyunyan, ed., *Russians. Ethno-sociological Essays*). Москва: Наука, 1992.

250. Руткевич М.Н. Социальная ориентация выпускников средней школы / *Социол. исслед.* (Routkevich, M. "Social Orienting Points of the Basic School Graduates." *Sociological Studies*), 1994, № 12.

251. Рыбаков А.А. Ценностно-нормативные представления о потреблении алкоголя / *Социол. исслед.* (Rybakov, A.A. "Value and Normative Notions of Alcohol Consumption." *Sociological Studies*), 1988, № 2.

252. Рыбаковский Л.Л., Тарасова Н.В. Миграционные процессы в СССР: новые явления / *Социол. исслед.* (Rybakovskiy, L.L., and N.V.Tarasova "Migration in the USSR: New Phenomena." *Sociological Studies*), 1990, № 7.

253. Рывкина Р.В. Управленческие кадры агропромышленного комплекса /
Социол. исслед. (Ryvkina, R.V. "Managerial Personnel of the Agrarian Complex." *Sociological Studies*), 1988, № 6.

254. Салдбаев Т.С. *Ислам и общество* (Saldbaev, T.S. *Islam and Society*). Таш-
кент, 1978.

255. Семейное предпринимательство / *Малый бизнес: рынок и общество* ("Family Enterprise." *Small Business: Market and Society*), 1993, № 1-4.

256. *Семья* (*Semya*), 1988, № 3.

257. *Семья и народное благосостояние*, отв. ред. Н.М.Римашевская (N.M.Ry-
mashevskaya, ed., *Family and People's Wealth*). Москва: ИСИ АН СССР,
1985.

258. Сергеева Г.П. *Профессиональная занятость женщин: проблемы и перспективы* (Sergeyeva, G.P. *Professional Employment of Women: Problems and Prospects*). Москва: ИСИ АН СССР, 1987.

259. Сидоров В.В., Смирнов Г.Г. Товарный дефицит и его криминогенные
последствия / *Социол. исслед.* (Sidorov, V.V., and G.G.Smirnov "Shortage of
Goods and Its Criminal Consequences." *Sociological Studies*), 1990, № 7.

260. Силласте Г.Г. Новая наркоситуация в России. Результаты исследования /
Социол. исслед. (Sillaste, G.G. "New Narcosituation in Russia. Research Results." *Sociological Studies*), 1994, № 4.

261. Симонова Н.Н., Чубрикова Л.Н. Социально-демографические аспекты
здоровья пожилых людей — В кн: *Социальные проблемы здоровья и продол-
жительности жизни*, ред. И.В.Журавлева (Simonova, N.N. and Chubrikova,
L.N. "Social and Demographical Aspects of Health of Elderly People." In I.V.Ju-
ravleva, ed., *Social Problems of Health and Life Span Expectancy*). Москва: ИСИ
АН СССР, 1989.

262. Слесарев Г.А., Янкова З.А. Женщина на промышленном предприятии и в
семье. — В кн.: *Социальные проблемы труда и производства*. Советско-польские сравнительные исследования, ред. Г.В.Осипов (Slesarev G.A., and
Z.A.Yankova "Women in the Enterprises and in Family." In G.V.Osypov, ed.,
Social Problems of Labour and Production). Москва: Мысль, 1969.

263. Смидович С.Г. Самоубийства в зеркале статистики / *Социол. исслед.*
(Smidovitch, S.G. "Suicides Reflected in Statistics." *Sociological Studies*),
1990, № 4.

264. Смольков В.Г. Предпринимательство как особый вид деятельности / *Социол. исслед.* (Smolkov, V.G. "Enterprenership as a Special Kind of Activity."
Sociological Studies), 1994, № 2.

265. Советская социология, отв. ред. Г.В.Осипов (G.V.Osypov, ed., *Soviet Sociology*). Москва: Наука, 1975, т.1.

266. Советская социология, отв. ред. Г.В.Осипов (G.V.Osypov, ed., *Soviet Sociology*). Москва: Наука, 1982.

267. *Советский город: социальная структура*, ред. Н.А.Аитов (N.A.Aitov, ed., *Soviet Town: the Social Structure*). Москва: Мысль, 1988.

268. Советский простой человек. Опыт социального портрета на рубеже 90-х годов, ред. Ю.А.Левада (Yu.A.Levada, ed., *Soviet Ordinary Person: An Attempt of a Social Portrait on the Eve of the 1990s*). Москва: Мировой океан, 1993.

269. *Советское здравоохранение (The Soviet Health Care)*, 1983, № 9.

270. Соколова Н.Г. Стали ли мы жить лучше? / *Социол. исслед.* (Sokolova, N.G. "Are We Living Better?" *Sociological Studies*), 1992, № 2.

271. Солдатова Г.У. Этничность и конфликты на Северном Кавказе. — В кн.: *Конфликтная этничность и этнические конфликты*, отв. ред. Л.М.Дробижева (Soldatova, G.U. "Ethnicity and conflicts in the North Caucasus." In Drobigeva, L.M., *Conflicting Ethnicity and Ethnic Conflicts*). Москва: ИЭиА, 1994.

272. *Солидарность (Socidarity)*, 16 окт. 1994 г.

273. Солодовников В.В. Накануне развода / *Социол. ислед.* (Solodovnikov, V.V. "On the Eve of a Divorce." *Sociological Studies*), 1988, № 1.

274. Социальная структура советского общества и социалистический образ жизни, ред. Т.В.Рябушкин (T.V.Riaboushkin, ed., *Social Structure of the Soviet Society and the Socialist Lifestyle*). Москва: ИСИ АН СССР, 1978.

275. *Социально-культурный облик советских наций. Этно-социологические исследования*, ред. Ю.В.Арутюнян (Yu.V.Aroutunian, ed., *Social and Cultural Aspect of Soviet Nations. Ethno-Sociological Surveys*). Москва: Наука, 1986.

276. *Социально-педагогические проблемы общего образования взрослых* ред. С.Г.Вершловский (S.G.Vershlovskiy, ed., *Social and Pedagogical Problems of the Basic Education of the Adults*). Москва: АПН СССР, 1983.

277. Социально-экономическое положение и развитие экономических реформ в Российской Федерации в 1992 году / *Экономика и жизнь* ("Social and Economic Situation and the Progress of Economic Reforms in Russian Federation in 1992." *Economics and Life*), 1993, № 4.

278. Социально-экономическое положение России в 1993 г. / *Общество и экономика* ("Social-economic situation in Russia in 1993." *Society and Economics*), 1993, № 11-12.

279. *Социальное развитие Российской Федерации в 1992 г. (*State Statistic Committee *Social Development of the Russian Federation in 1992*). Москва: Респ. инф.-издат. центр, 1993.

280. *Социальное развитие и уровень жизни населения СССР. Статистич. сборник* (State Statistic Committee, *Social Development and the Population's Level of Life*). Москва: Инф.-изд. центр, 1989.

281. *Социальные ориентиры обновления: человек и общество*, ред. Т.И.Заславская (Zaslavskaya, T.I., ed., *Social References for Renovation: Man and Society*). Москва: Политиздат, 1990.

282. *Социальные отклонения*, ред. В.Н.Кудрявцев (Koudriavtzev, V.N., ed., *Social Deliquencies*). Москва: Юридическая литература, 1989.

283. *Сравнительный анализ организации культурной жизни в различных типах поселений*, ред. Л.Б.Волынская (L.B.Volinskaia, ed., *Comparative Analysis of the Cultural Life Organising in Settlements of Different Kinds*). Москва: Нии культуры, 1990.

284. *Срочные проблемы совершенствования организации труда*, (Ministry of Labor and Employment. *Urgent Problems of Perfecting of Labour Resources Organisation*). Москва: Мин. Труда и занятости, 1993.

285a. *Статистический пресс-бюллетень* (*Statistic Press-bulletin*), 1994, № 6.

285b. *Статистический пресс-бюллетень* (*Statistic Press-bulletin*), 1995, № 11.

286. *Статистическое обозрение (Statistic Review)*, 1995, № 1.

287. Сундиев И.Ю. Неформальные молодежные объединения: опыт экспозиции / *Социол. исслед.* (Sundiev, I.Yu." Unofficial Associations of Youth. Attempt at Presentation" *Sociological Studies*), 1987, № 5.

288. Сычева В.С. Переходный период по оценкам населения. Обзор социологических исследований / *Социол. исслед.* (Sycheva, V.S. "Transition Period by the Population's Estemates. A review of Sociological Surveys." *Sociological Studies*), 1993, № 3.

289. *Тенденции изменения бюджета времени трудящихся*, ред. В.Д.Патрушев (V.D.Patroushev, ed., *Trends in the Time Budget of Working People*). Москва: ИСИ АН СССР, 1979.

290. *Теневая экономика*, сост. Б.А.Дружинин (B.A.Druzhinin, ed., *Shady Economy*). Москва: Экономика, 1991.

291. Тепляков М.К. Победа атеизма в различных социальных слоях советского общества / *Вопр. научн. атеизма.* (Tepliakov, M.K. "The Victory of Atheism in Different Social Stratas of the Soviet Society." *Problems of Scientific Atheism*), 1967, № 4.

292. Тишков В.А. Этничность, национализм и государство / *Вопр. социологии* (Tishkov, V.A. "Ethnicity, Nationalism and the State." *Problems of Sociology*), 1993, № 1/2.

293. Тольц М. Характеристика некоторых компонентов рождаемости в большом городе — В кн.: *Демографический анализ рождаемости*, отв. ред. Д.И.Валентей (Toltz, M. Some components of Childbearing in a City. In D.I.Valentey, ed., *Demographic Analysis of Childbearing*).Москва: Статистика, 1974.

294. Тольц М.С., Оберг Л.Я., Шишко О.А. Начальные этапы реализации репродуктивной функции женщин / *Здравоохранение Российской Федерации* (Toltz, M.S., L.Ia.Oberg and O.A.Shishko "Initial Stages of the Women's Reproductive Function." *Healthcare of the Russian Federation*), 1984, № 7.

295. Топилин А.В. Влияние миграции на этнонациональную структуру / *Социол. исслед.* (Topilin, A.V. "The Migration Influence upon Ethnic Structure." *Sociological Studies*), 1992, № 2.

296. Тощенко Ж.Т. Русские беженцы: трагедия или издержки имперского сознания? / *Социол. исслед.* (Toshchenko, Zh.T. "Russian Refugees: A Tragedy or Expences of Imperial Consciousness?" *Sociological Studies*), 1992, № 2.

297. Тощенко Ж.Т. и др. Экономическое сознание: ориентиры и предубеждения / *Социол. исслед.* (Toshchenko, Zh.T., et al. "Economy Consciousness: Reference Points and Prejudices." *Sociological Studies*), 1988, № 3.

298. Трубина Л.В., Нещадин А.А., Кашин В.К. Синусоиды общественного мнения / *Социол. исслед.* (Trubina, L.V., A.A.Neshchadin, and V.K.Kashin "Sinusoids of Public Opinion." *Sociological Studies*), 1993, № 7.

299. Труд в РСФСР. Статистич. сборник (State Statistic Committee, *Labour in the RSFSR. A Collection of Statistics*). Москва: Финансы и статистика, 1988.

300. Труд в СССР. Статистич. сборник, Госкомстат СССР (State Statistic Committee, *Labour in the USSR. A Collection of Statistics*). Москва: Финансы и статистика, 1983.

301. Трудовое законодательство: новые тенденции и направления / *Экономика и жизнь* ("Labor Legislation: New Trends and Directions." *Economics and Life*), 1994, № 6.

302. *Трудовой коллектив: воспитательный потенциал перестройки*, ред. В.Червяков (V.Chervyakov ed., *A Collective of Working People: The Educative Potential of Perestroika*). Москва: Профиздат, 1988.

303. Турунцев Е.В. *Тенденции развития организационных форм труда и их влияние на изменение содержания труда*. Автореф. канд. дисс. (Turuntsev, E.V. *Tendencies in the Work Organisation and Their Influence on the Changes of the Labour Content*). Москва: Ин-т экономики АН СССР, 1990.

304. *Урбанизация и рабочий класс в условиях научно-технической революции*, ред. О.Яницкий (O.Yanitsciy, ed., *Urbanisation and the Working Class Under the Scientific and Technological Revolution*). Москва: Сов. фонд мира, 1970.

305. *Уровень жизни населения Российской Федерации* (State Statistic Committee *Level of life of the Population in the Russian Federation*). Москва: Госкомстат России, 1995.

306. *Условия труда и быта женщин. Статистич. сборник* (State Statistic Committee *Conditions of Women's Labour and Everyday Life*). Москва: Респ. инф.-издат. центр, 1992.

307. Фальцман В. Промышленная стратегия России в период кризиса / *Вопр. экономики* (Faltzman, V. "Industrial Strategy of Russia in the Period of Crisis." *Problems of Economics*), 1993, № 3.

308. Фетисов Э.Н., Яковлев И.Г. Предпринимательству — государственную поддержку / *Социол. исслед.* (Fetisov, E.N. and I.G.Yakovlev "State Support to Business." *Sociological Studies*), 1994, № 2.

309. *Физическая культура и образ жизни*, ред. М.Титма (Titma, M., ed., *Physical Training and Lifestyle*), Москва: ИСИ АН СССР, 1983.

310. *Физическая культура и спорт в СССР.* Цифры и факты (State Statistic Committee *Physical Training and Lifestyle. Figures and Facts*). Москва: Финансы и статистика, 1986.

311. Филатов С.Б., Воронцова Л.М. Как проходит религиозное возрождение в России / *Наука и религия* (Filatov, S.B., and L.M.Vorontzova "How Does the Religion Renaissance Proceede in Russia." *Sociological Studies*), 1993, № 6.

312. Филатов С.Б., Фурман Д.Е. Религия и политика в массовом сознании / *Социол. исслед.* (Filatov S.B., and D.E.Furman "Religion and Policy in the Mass Conciousness." *Sociological Studies*), 1992, № 7.

313a. *Финансовые известия* (*Finansovye Izvestia*), 1994, № 2.

313b. *Финансовые известия* (*Finansovye Izvestia*), 1995, № 1.

313c. *Финансовые известия* (*Finansovye Izvestia*), 1995, № 5.

314. *Финансы и хозрасчет в НИИ и КБ,* ред. В.М.Логачев (V.M.Logachev, ed., *Finances and self Suppport Activity*). Москва: Финансы и статистика, 1987.

315. Фролькис В. Наступление на старость / *Литер. газета* (Frolkis, V. "Advancement in the Old Age." *Literaturnaya gazeta*), 06.09.1983.

316. Харчев А.Г. *Брак и семья в СССР* (Kharshev, A. *Marriage and Family in the USSR*). Москва: Мысль, 1979.

317. Харчев А.Г., Голод С.И. Производственная работа женщин и семья. — В кн.: *Социальные проблемы труда и производства,* Советско-польские сравнительные исследования, отв. ред. Г.В.Осипов и Я.Щепаньский (Kharchev, A.G., and S.I.Golod "Women's Employment In Production and the Family." In Osipov, G.V., and Shepanscy J., eds., *Social Problems of Labour and Production*). Москва: Мысль, 1969.

318. Хворостов А.В. Информатика в московских школах: обыденность новизны / *Социол. исслед.* (Khvorostov, A.B. "Information Science in Moscow Schools: Everyday of Novelty." *Sociological Studies*), 1993, № 9.

319. Хвощев В.Е. Интервальное исследование пьянства и алкоголизма / *Социол. исслед.* (Knvoshchev, V.E. "The Longitude Survey of Hard Drinking and Alcoholism." *Sociological Studies*), 1988, № 4.

320. *Ценности и символы национального сомосознания в условиях меняющегося общества,* ред. Л.М.Дробижева и др. (Drobigeva, L.M., et al., eds., *Values and Symbols of National Self-Consciousness in the Changing Society*). Москва: ИЭиА, 1994.

321. *Центр-Плюс* (*Centre-Plus*), 1994, № 7.

322. Цыпин В. *История русской православной церкви. 1917-1990 г.г.* (Tzypin, V. *The History of the Russian Orthodox Church.* 1917-1990). Москва: Патриархия, 1994.

323. Червяков В.В., Чередниченко А.Ф., Шапиро В.Д. Россияне о предпринимательстве и предпринимателях / *Социол. исслед.* (Cherviakov, V.V., A.F.Cherednichenko, and V.D.Shapiro "Russians on Enterhrenership and Enterpreners." *Sociological Studies*), 1992, № 10.

324. Чередниченко Г.А., Шубкин В.А. *Молодежь вступает в жизнь* (Cherednichenko, G.A. and V.A.Shubkin *Youth Enters Life*). Москва: Мысль, 1985.

325. Чередниченко Г.А., Шубкин В.А. *От поколения к поколению* (Cherednichenko, G.A. and V.A.Shubkin *From Generation to Generation*). Москва: Мысль, 1989.

326. Чернина Н.В. Бедность как социальный феномен российского общества / *Социол. исслед.* (Chernina, N.V. "Poverty as Social Phenomenon in Russian Society." *Sociological Studies*), 1994, № 3.

327. Черных А.Н. Социальная сфера предприятия / *Социол. исслед.* (Chernykh, A.N. "The Social Sphere of an Enterprise." *Sociological Studies*), 1990, № 5.

328. Черныш М.Ф. Социальная мобильность и массовое сознание / *Социол. исслед.* (Chernysh, M.F. "Social Mobility and Mass Mentality." *Sociological Studies*), 1995, № 1.

329. *Численность, естественное движение и миграция населения в 1990. Статистич. бюллетень* (State Statistic Committee *Numbers, Natural Movement and Migration of the Population in the Russian Federation in 1990. A Statistic bulletin*). Москва: Инф.-издат. центр, 1991.

330. Численность и состав населения СССР (State Statistic Committee *Numbers and Composition of the USSR Population*). Москва: Финансы и статистика, 1984.

331. Чистякова Т. Социально-психологическое самочувствие незамужних женщин в СССР (Chistiakova, T. *Social and Psychological Feelings of Unmarried Women in the USSR. A Report*). Москва: ИСИ АН СССР, 1990.

332. Шаленко В.Н. Производственные забастовки как объект социологического анализа / *Социол. исслед.* (Shalenko, V.N. "Industrial Strikes as an Object to Sociological Analysis, *Sociological Studies*), 1990, № 7.

333. Шаленко В.Н. *Конфликты в трудовых коллективах* (Shalenko, V.N. *Conflicts in the Collectives of Working People*). Москва: МГУ, 1992.

334. Шереги Ф.Э. Стуктура читательских предпочтений / *Социол. исслед.* (Sheregi, F.Z. "The Structure of Readers' Preferences." *Sociological Studies*), 1986, № 3.

335. Шихирев П.Н. *Жить без алкоголя? Социально-психологические проблемы пьянства и алкоголизма* (Shikhirev, P.N. *To Be wihtout Alcohol? Social and Psychological Problems of Hard Drinking and Alcoholism*). Москва: Наука, 1988.

336. Шляпентох В.Э. *Социология для всех* (Shlyapentokh, V.E. *Sociology for Everyone*). Москва: Советская Россия, 1970.

337. Шмаров А.И. *Труд и свободное время* (Shmarov, A.I. *Labour and Free Time*). Москва: Экономика, 1987.

338. Шохин А.Н. *Потребительский рынок* (Shohin, A.I. *Consumer Market*). Москва: Знание, 1989.

339. Шохин А.Н. Теневая экономика: мифы и реальность / *Экономика и жизнь* (Shohin, A.I. "Shady Economy: Myths and Reality." *Economics and Life*), 1990, № 33.

340. Шубкин В.Н. *Социологические опыты* (Shubkin, V.N. *Sociological Exercises*). Москва: Мысль, 1970.

341. *Эволюция семьи и семейная политика в СССР*, ред. А.Г.Вишневский (A.G.Vishevskiy, ed., *Evolution of a Family and Family Policy in Russia*). Москва: Наука, 1992.

342a. *Экономические и социальные перемены: мониторинг общественного мнения.* Информ. бюлл. ВЦИОМ (*Economic and Social Changes: Monitoring of Public Opinion.* Information Bulletin of VCIOM), 1993, № 1.

342b. *Экономические и социальные перемены: мониторинг общественного мнения.* Информ. бюлл. ВЦИОМ (*Economic and Social Changes: Monitoring of Public Opinion.* Information Bulletin of VCIOM), 1993, № 3

342c. *Экономические и социальные перемены: мониторинг общественного мнения.* Информ. бюлл. ВЦИОМ (*Economic and Social Changes: Monitoring of Public Opinion.* Information Bulletin of VCIOM), 1993, № 4.

342d. *Экономические и социальные перемены: мониторинг общественного мнения.* Информ. бюлл. ВЦИОМ (*Economic and Social Changes: Monitoring of Public Opinion.* Information Bulletin of VCIOM), 1993, № 6.

342e. *Экономические и социальные перемены: мониторинг общественного мнения.* Информ. бюлл. ВЦИОМ (*Economic and Social Changes: Monitoring of Public Opinion.* Information Bulletin of VCIOM), 1993, № 7.

342f. *Экономические и социальные перемены: мониторинг общественного мнения.* Информ. бюлл. ВЦИОМ (*Economic and Social Changes: Monitoring of Public Opinion.* Information Bulletin of VCIOM), 1994, № 1.

342g. *Экономические и социальные перемены: мониторинг общественного мнения.* Информ. бюлл. ВЦИОМ (*Economic and Social Changes: Monitoring of Public Opinion.* Information Bulletin of VCIOM), 1994, № 5.

342h *Экономические и социальные перемены: мониторинг общественного мнения.* Информ. бюлл. ВЦИОМ (*Economic and Social Changes: Monitoring of Public Opinion.* Information Bulletin of VCIOM), 1994, № 11.

343a. *Экономические новости России и стран содружества* (*Economic News from Russia and Commonwealth*), 1994, № 13.

343b. ibid, 1994, № 14.

344. *Экономические обзоры Российской Федерации. Август 1993* (*Economy Reviews of Russian Federation. August 1993*). Москва: Респ. инф.-издат. центр, 1993.

345. *Экономические показатели деятельности театров и концертных организаций РСФСР за 1988-1989 гг.* (Ministry of Culture *Economy Indicators of the Activities of Theatres and Concert Organisations in Russian Federation in 1988-1989*). Москва: ГИВЦ МК РСФСР, 1990.

346. *Показатели деятельности культпросветучреждений* (Ministry of Culture *Economy Indicators of the Activities of Culture Institutions*). Москва: ГИВЦ МК РСФСР, 1991.

347a. *Экономика и жизнь* (*Economics and Life*), 1990, № 47.

347b. *Экономика и жизнь* (*Economics and Life*), 1991, № 12.

347c. *Экономика и жизнь* (*Economics and Life*), 1994, № 6.

348. Юркевич Н.Г. *Советская семья* (Yurkevich N.G. *Soviet Family*). Минск, 1970.

349. Ямпольская С.М. Динамика досугового общения / *Социол. исслед.* (Yampolskaya, S.M. "Dynamics of Leisure Communication." *Sociological Studies*), 1989, № 6.

350. Яницкий О.Н. Индустриализм и энвайроментализм: Россия на рубеже культур / *Социол. исслед.* (Janitskiy, O.N. "Industrialism and Environmentalism: Russia in Between Cultures." *Sociological Studies*), 1994, № 3.

351. Янкова З.А. *Советская женщина*. Социальный проект (Iankova, Z. *Soviet Woman. A Social Portrait*). Москва: Политиздат, 1978.